# Quantitative Portfolio Optimization

Founded in 1807, John Wiley & Sons is the oldest independent publishing company in the United States. With offices in North America, Europe, Australia and Asia, Wiley is globally committed to developing and marketing print and electronic products and services for our customers' professional and personal knowledge and understanding.

The Wiley Finance series contains books written specifically for finance and investment professionals as well as sophisticated individual investors and their financial advisors. Book topics range from portfolio management to e-commerce, risk management, financial engineering, valuation and financial instrument analysis, as well as much more.

For a list of available titles, visit our website at www.WileyFinance.com.

# Quantitative Portfolio Optimization

*Advanced Techniques and Applications*


MIQUEL NOGUER ALONSO
JULIÁN ANTOLÍN CAMARENA
ALBERTO BUENO GUERRERO


WILEY

Published by John Wiley & Sons, Inc., Hoboken, New Jersey.
Published simultaneously in Canada.



***Library of Congress Cataloging-in-Publication Data:***
Names: Noguer Alonso, Miquel, author. | Camarena, Julián Antolín, author. | Bueno Guerrero, Alberto, author.
Title: Quantitative portfolio optimization: Advanced techniques and applications / Miquel Noguer Alonso, Julián Antolín Camarena, Alberto Bueno Guerrero.
Description: Hoboken, New Jersey: John Wiley and Sons, Inc, [2025] | Series: Wiley finance | Includes bibliographical references and index. | Summary: "*Quantitative Portfolio Optimization: Advanced Techniques and Applications* offers a comprehensive exploration of portfolio optimization, tracing its evolution from Harry Markowitz's Modern Portfolio Theory to contemporary techniques. The book combines foundational models like CAPM and Black-Litterman with advanced methods including Bayesian statistics, machine learning, and quantum computing. It bridges theory and practice through detailed explanations, real-world data applications, and case studies. Aimed at finance professionals, researchers, and students, the book provides tools and insights to address future financial challenges and contributes to the field's ongoing development"– Provided by publisher.
Identifiers: LCCN 2024041151 (print) | LCCN 2024041152 (ebook) | ISBN 9781394281312 (hardback) | ISBN 9781394281336 (pdf) | ISBN 9781394281329 (epub)
Subjects: LCSH: Portfolio management–Mathematical models. | Asset allocation–Mathematical models. | Finance–Mathematical models.
Classification: LCC HG4529.5.N537 2025 (print) | LCC HG4529.5 (ebook) | DDC 332.6–dcundefined
LC record available at https://lccn.loc.gov/2024041151
LC ebook record available at https://lccn.loc.gov/2024041152

Cover image(s): Seamless moroccan pattern. Square vintage tile. Blue and white watercolor ornament painted with paint on paper. Handmade. Print for textiles. Seth grunge texture. © Flovie/Shutterstock
Cover design by Wiley

Set in 10/12 pt Sabon LT Std by Lumina Datamatics

SKY10093334_120924

# Contents

# Preface

Quantitative portfolio optimization is a cornerstone of modern financial management, providing a rigorous framework for balancing risk and return in investment portfolios. This book, *Quantitative Portfolio Optimization: Advanced Techniques and Applications*, aims to serve as both a comprehensive introduction for those new to the field and a deep dive into the latest advancements for experienced practitioners and researchers.

The genesis of portfolio optimization can be traced back to Harry Markowitz's Modern Portfolio Theory (MPT) in the 1950s, which introduced the now-fundamental concepts of diversification and mean-variance optimization. Since then, the field has evolved significantly, integrating a wide array of quantitative methods, including Bayesian statistics, machine learning algorithms, and advanced optimization techniques. These methods have transformed portfolio management from a discipline grounded in basic statistical principles to one that leverages innovative computational techniques to solve increasingly complex problems.

This book is structured to reflect this evolution, beginning with foundational theories before progressing to advanced applications. We explore not only traditional models such as the Capital Asset Pricing Model (CAPM) and the Black-Litterman model but also the latest developments in areas such as reinforcement learning, deep learning, and graph-based portfolio construction. Additionally, we cover emerging topics like quantum computing's role in portfolio optimization and the integration of partial differential equations (PDEs) for modeling portfolio dynamics.

Each chapter is meticulously designed to bridge theory with practice, offering detailed explanations of the mathematical underpinnings of each technique, followed by practical applications using real-world data. The mathematical rigor is complemented by code implementations and case studies that demonstrate the practical utility of the methods discussed.

Whether you are a professional, researcher, or student in the field of finance, we hope this book enhances your understanding of quantitative portfolio optimization and equips you with the knowledge to apply these techniques effectively. As the financial markets continue to evolve, so must the methods we use to manage them. We believe that the approaches detailed in this book will be instrumental in addressing the challenges and opportunities of tomorrow's financial world.

Finally, we extend our deepest gratitude to our colleagues, students, and family members, whose support and encouragement have been invaluable throughout the creation of this book. It is our sincere hope that this work contributes meaningfully to the ongoing development of the field of quantitative portfolio optimization.

# Acknowledgements

**Miquel** I would like to express my gratitude to all those who have contributed to the development and success of this book, especially my co-authors and Alejandro Rodriguez Dominguez. Special thanks to my colleagues in the Quant Community. My mother Maria del Carmen, my sons Jordi and Arnau, and my brother Jordi who always supported me. A lot of people in finance, mathematics, and computer science have inspired me to author this book, to do my best. To Emmanuel, Garud, Peter, Petter, Matthew, Igor, and Gordon. To my dad Jordi, I love you.

**Julián** I am deeply indebted to my wife, Esther; my parents, Antonio and Cecilia; my brother, Omar; and all of my friends who always support me in whatever I may choose to do. I thank and love you all. And of course, my much beloved pug, Nibbler, who always puts a smile on my face. I love you, kiddo.

I also thank my friends and co-authors Miquel and Alberto, with whom I have had engrossing and fun conversations, and without whom I would not have been a part of this book.

**Alberto** My first thanks go to my wife Elena, for her continued support and encouragement in everything I do. Also, to my children, Iván, Leo, Elena, and Hugo, for their help, respect, and affection. I could not forget my mother, María del Carmen, who brought me into this world and has always believed in me; and my father, Francisco, who is no longer with us, and who instilled in me his love of knowledge. Special thanks also go to my brother, Francisco José, who has always been an example for me.

# About the Authors

**Miquel Noguer Alonso** is a seasoned financial professional and academic with over 30 years of experience in the industry. He is the Founder of the Artificial Intelligence Finance Institute and Head of Development at Global AI. His career includes roles such as Executive Director at UBS AG and CIO for Andbank. He has served on the European Investment Committee UBS for a decade. He is on the advisory board of FDP Institute and CFA NY.

Mr. Noguer is also an academic, teaching AI, Big Data, and Fintech at institutions like NYU Courant Institute, NYU Tandon, Columbia University, and ESADE. He pioneered the first Fintech and Big Data course at the London Business School in 2017. He is the author of 10 papers on Artificial Intelligence.

He holds an MBA and a Degree in business administration from ESADE, a PhD in quantitative finance from UNED, and other prestigious certifications. His research interests span asset allocation, machine learning, algorithmic trading, and Fintech.

**Julián Antolín Camarena** holds a bachelor's, master's and a PhD in physics. For his master's, he worked on the foundations of quantum mechanics examining alternative quantization schemes and their application to exotic atoms to discover new physics. His PhD dissertation work was on computational and theoretical optics, electromagnetic scattering from random surfaces, and nonlinear optimization. He then went on to a postdoctoral stint with the US Army Research Laboratory working on inverse reinforcement learning for human-autonomy teaming. He then worked as an Applied AI Researcher at Point72 Asset Management where his research was to develop algorithms for time series analysis using machine learning algorithms and developing deep learning architectures. Currently, works in applying AI to quantitative bioimaging and biophysics at Arizona State University.

**Alberto Bueno Guerrero** has two bachelor's degrees in physics and economics, and a PhD in banking and finance. Since he received his doctorate, he has dedicated himself to research in mathematical finance. His work has been presented at various international conferences and published in journals such as *Quantitative Finance; Journal of Derivatives, Mathematics; and Chaos, Solitons and Fractals.*

Among the topics addressed in his research are the term structure of interest rates, the valuation and hedging of derivatives, the immunization of bond portfolios, and a quantum-mechanical model for interest rate derivatives. His article "Bond Market Completeness Under Stochastic Strings with Distribution-Valued Strategies" has been considered a feature article in *Quantitative Finance*.

In 2020, he was interviewed for the article "Interviews with Researchers Who Started Their Career in Physics but Moved to Finance," for the special issue of the *Journal of Derivatives* titled "Physics and Financial Derivatives."

He has also functioned as anonymous reviewer for various journals, and regularly reviews articles for Mathematical Reviews of the American Mathematical Society.

# CHAPTER 1
# Introduction

## 1.1 EVOLUTION OF PORTFOLIO OPTIMIZATION

Portfolio optimization has undergone significant transformation since its inception. Initially, the focus was on maximizing returns without much regard for risk. This changed with the introduction of Modern Portfolio Theory (MPT) by Harry Markowitz in the 1950s, which introduced the concept of balancing risk and return. Markowitz's mean-variance optimization laid the groundwork for the systematic assessment of portfolio risk and diversification.

Over the years, portfolio optimization has evolved to incorporate various advanced techniques and models. These include the Capital Asset Pricing Model (CAPM), Arbitrage Pricing Theory (APT), and more sophisticated approaches like the Black-Litterman model, risk parity, and hierarchical risk parity. Recently, machine learning methods have also been integrated into portfolio optimization, providing new ways to manage complex data and uncover hidden patterns in financial markets. Moreover, the integration of reinforcement learning, and graph-based methods has opened new avenues for dynamic and complex portfolio strategies. Sensitivity-based portfolios, which focus on the sensitivity of portfolio returns to changes in underlying factors, have also become an important aspect of modern portfolio management.

## 1.2 ROLE OF QUANTITATIVE TECHNIQUES

Quantitative techniques play a crucial role in modern portfolio optimization. These techniques allow for the systematic analysis and management of risk, the development of models to predict asset returns, and the optimization of portfolios to achieve desired outcomes. Key quantitative methods used in portfolio optimization include:

- **Mean-Variance Optimization:** This foundational technique balances expected return against risk, measured as the variance of returns. It involves calculating the expected returns and covariances of all assets, then solving for the weights that minimize portfolio variance subject to a desired return. The efficient frontier is derived from this process, representing the set of optimal portfolios.
- **Factor Models:** These models, such as the CAPM and multifactor models, explain asset returns based on various macroeconomic factors or firm-specific factors. The CAPM, for example, relates an asset's return to the return of the market portfolio, adjusted for the asset's sensitivity to market movements.
- **Bayesian Methods:** Bayesian techniques incorporate prior beliefs and observed data to update the estimation of expected returns and risks. The Black-Litterman model is a popular application in portfolio optimization, combining market equilibrium with investor views to produce more stable and diversified portfolios. Bayesian methods are particularly useful for handling parameter uncertainty and incorporating subjective views.
- **Machine Learning:** Machine learning algorithms are used to identify patterns in large datasets, making them valuable for predictive modeling in portfolio optimization. Techniques like neural networks, decision trees, and generative models can uncover complex relationships between asset returns and various predictors. These methods can enhance the forecasting of returns and risks as well as optimize trading strategies.
  - **Neural Networks:** These are used to model nonlinear relationships between inputs and outputs. In portfolio optimization, they can predict asset returns based on historical data and other variables.
  - **Decision Trees:** These algorithms split the data into subsets based on feature values, creating a tree-like model of decisions. They are useful for capturing the nonlinear relationships in financial data and can be used to identify important variables influencing asset returns.
  - **Generative Models:** These models, such as Generative Adversarial Networks (GANs) and Variational Autoencoders (VAEs), are used to generate new data samples that are like the training data. In portfolio optimization, generative models can be used to simulate realistic market scenarios and generate synthetic data for stress testing and risk management.

- **Reinforcement Learning (RL):** RL involves training algorithms to make sequences of decisions by rewarding desirable actions and penalizing undesirable ones. In portfolio optimization, RL can dynamically adjust the asset allocation based on market conditions and investment goals. An RL agent learns a policy that maximizes cumulative rewards, which can correspond to returns in a portfolio context. Techniques like Q-learning and policy gradients are commonly used in RL for portfolio management.
  - **Q-learning:** This algorithm learns the value of actions in different states and aims to maximize the expected reward over time. It updates its estimates using the Bellman equation.
  - **Policy Gradients:** These methods optimize the policy directly by computing gradients of the expected reward with respect to the policy parameters.
- **Graph-based Methods:** These methods use graph theory to represent and analyze the relationships between assets. Graphs can model the dependencies and correlations among assets, aiding in the construction of diversified and robust portfolios.
  - **Graph Theory:** This involves studying graphs, which are mathematical structures used to model pairwise relations between objects. In portfolio optimization, nodes can represent assets, and edges can represent the correlations or co-movements between them.
  - **Hierarchical Risk Parity (HRP):** This approach uses clustering and tree structures to construct portfolios. It aims to distribute risk more evenly across different clusters of assets, improving diversification.
- **Sensitivity-based Portfolios:** These portfolios focus on the sensitivity of portfolio returns to changes in underlying factors, such as economic variables or market indices. By analyzing how small changes in these factors impact on the portfolio, managers can better understand and manage risk.
  - **Sensitivity Analysis:** This involves examining how the variation in the output of a model can be attributed to different variations in the inputs. In portfolio optimization, sensitivity analysis helps in understanding the impact of changes in asset returns and other factors on the portfolio performance.
  - **Partial Differential Equations (PDEs):** PDEs can be used to model the dynamics of portfolio values over time, considering factors like interest rates and asset prices. Solving these equations provides insights into the optimal portfolio allocation under different market conditions.
- **Risk Measures and Management:** Techniques like Value-at-Risk (VaR) and Conditional Value-at-Risk (CVaR) are used to quantify the risk

of loss in a portfolio. These measures are essential for understanding potential downside risks and making informed decisions about risk mitigation strategies. Advanced risk measures also consider tail risks and the distribution of returns.

- **Optimization Algorithms:** Several optimization algorithms are employed to solve portfolio optimization problems. These include:
  - **Quadratic Programming:** Used in mean-variance optimization to find the optimal asset weights that minimize portfolio variance for a given return.
  - **Monte Carlo Simulation:** Used to model the probability of different outcomes in a process that cannot easily be predicted due to the intervention of random variables. In portfolio optimization, it is used to simulate the performance of different portfolio strategies under various market conditions.
  - **Genetic Algorithms:** These algorithms mimic natural selection processes to generate high-quality solutions for optimization problems. They are particularly useful in finding optimal portfolios in large, complex investment universes.
  - **Dynamic Programming:** Applied in multi-period portfolio optimization to make decisions that consider the evolution of the portfolio over time.

## 1.3 ORGANIZATION OF THE BOOK

This book is structured to provide a comprehensive understanding of quantitative portfolio optimization techniques, from foundational theories to advanced applications. The chapters are organized as the list describes:

- **Chapter 2: History of Portfolio Optimization:** A review of the key developments in portfolio optimization, from early theories to modern advancements.
- **Chapter 3: Modern Portfolio Theory:** A detailed study of mean-variance analysis, the CAPM, and APT, including their applications and limitations. We introduce a new framework Mean Variance with CVAR constraints.
- **Chapter 4: Bayesian Methods in Portfolio Optimization:** An exploration of Bayesian techniques and their application to portfolio optimization.
- **Chapter 5: Risk Models and Measures:** A discussion on various risk measures, including Value-at-Risk (VaR) and Conditional Value-at-Risk (CVaR), and their estimation methods.

- **Chapter 6: Factor Models and Factor Investing:** Examination of single and multifactor models, factor risk, and performance attribution.
- **Chapter 7: Market Impact, Transaction Costs, and Liquidity:** Insights into market impact, transaction costs, and liquidity considerations in portfolio optimization.
- **Chapter 8: Optimal Control:** Coverage of dynamic programming, optimal control, and their applications in portfolio optimization.
- **Chapter 9: Markov Decision Processes:** Discussion on fully observed and partially observed MDPs, infinite and finite horizon problems, and the Bellman equation.
- **Chapter 10: Reinforcement Learning:** Examination of reinforcement learning techniques and their applications in portfolio optimization.
- **Chapter 11: Deep Learning in Portfolio Management:** Introduction to deep learning methods and their integration into portfolio management.
- **Chapter 12: Graph-based Portfolios:** Exploration of graph theory-based portfolios and their applications.
- **Chapter 13: Sensitivity-based Portfolios:** Insights into modeling portfolio dynamics with partial differential equations and sensitivity analysis.
- **Chapter 14: Backtesting in Portfolio Management:** Discussion on backtesting methods, trading rules, and transaction costs.
- **Chapter 15: Scenario Generation:** Techniques for generating scenarios and their application in portfolio optimization.

This structure ensures a logical progression from basic concepts to advanced techniques, providing readers with the tools and knowledge necessary to optimize portfolios effectively in today's complex financial markets.

CHAPTER 2

# History of Portfolio Optimization

This chapter is dedicated to a non-exhaustive review of the main contributions to portfolio optimization, from Markowitz's precursors to the modern machine learning methods, including Markowitz's mean-variance approach, the Black-Litterman model, Risk Parity, and Hierarchical Risk Parity. Only the Black-Litterman model and the Risk Parity approach will be addressed in depth. An alternative derivation of the Black-Litterman model, based on Bayesian methods, will be presented in Chapter 4. A more detailed treatment of the Markowitz model, the Hierarchical Risk Parity algorithm and some machine learning methods will be postponed to subsequent chapters.

## 2.1 EARLY BEGINNINGS

Harry Markowitz is unanimously recognized as the father of Modern Portfolio Theory (MPT). His seminal works, Markowitz (1952, 1959), settled the foundations of the mean-variance analysis upon which other aspects of MPT were built.

The groundbreaking nature of Markowitz (1952) can be inferred from its scarce set of references: Uspensky (1937), Williams (1938) and Hicks (1939). The first one is a text on Mathematical Probability, to which the reader was referred. Of the two remaining references, only Williams (1938) played a role in the development of the 1952 paper, as we will see soon. Therefore, it is not surprising that Mark Rubinstein stated the following: "What has always impressed me most about Markowitz's 1952 paper is that it seemed to come out of nowhere" (Rubinstein, 2002). Nevertheless, the key ideas of mean-variance analysis (i.e., diversification, mean returns, and a risk measure as variables) were present in previous literature. The rest of the section will be dedicated to analyzing some of these early contributions.

According to Markowitz (1999), written references to the concept of diversification can be traced back to Shakespeare's *The Merchant of Venice*, in which the following passage can be found (Act I, Scene I):

*My ventures are not in one bottom trusted,*
*Nor to one place; nor is my whole state*
*Upon the fortune of this present year*
*Therefore my merchandise makes me no sad.*

In the academic field, Daniel Bernouilli, in his 1738 paper on the Saint Petersburg paradox (Bernouilli, 1954), offered this diversification advice for risk-averse investors: "... it is advisable to divide goods which are exposed to some small danger into several portions rather than to risk them all together." In the twentieth century, the first reference related to Portfolio Theory appears in *The Nature of Capital and Income* (Fisher, 1906), in which variance is suggested as a measure of economic risk. Hicks, in his treatise *Theory of Money* (Hicks, 1935), introduces a qualitative analysis regarding the probabilities associated with the risk of an investment, concluding that they can be represented by a mean value and an appropriate measure of risk (although he does not mention any specific measure).

Marschak (1938) takes a step forward specifying the nature of the parameter measuring risk: "It is sufficiently realistic, however, to confine ourselves, for each yield, to two parameters only: the mathematical expectation ('lucrativity') and the coefficient of variation ('risk')." Although Marschak was the advisor of Markowitz's thesis, we cannot state (as Markowitz himself acknowledges) that Marschak had an influence on Markowitz's work. In fact, Marschak did not inform to Markowitz of the existence of Marschak (1938).

The only previous work that had a clear impact on Markowitz is Williams (1938). According to Markowitz (1991): "The basic principles of portfolio theory came to me one day while I was reading John Burr Williams *The Theory of Investment Value*. Williams was remarkably prescient. He provided the first derivation of the 'Gordon growth formula,' the Modigliani-Miller Capital Structure Irrelevancy Theorem, and strongly advocated the dividend discount model. But Williams had very little to say about the effects of risk on valuation (pp. 67–70), because he believed that all risk could be diversified away." In the opinion of Mark Rubinstein: "Markowitz had the brilliant insight that, while diversification would reduce risk, it would not generally eliminate it" (Rubinstein, 2002).

We cannot conclude this section dedicated to the predecessors of MPT without considering Roy (1952), of which Markowitz wrote the following: "On the basis of Markowitz (1952), I am often called the father of modern portfolio theory (MPT), but Roy can claim an equal share of this honor" (Markowitz, 1999). In fact, Roy (1952) presents an analysis very similar to that of Markowitz (1952). Specifically, Roy includes correlations between asset prices in the analysis and, like Markowitz, realizes that "the principle of maximising expected return does not explain the well-known phenomenon of the diversification of resources among a wide range of assets." Moreover, Roy also considers the expected value of returns, $m$; and the standard deviation of returns, $\sigma$, as the only parameters on which investment decisions are based. However, instead of minimizing the standard deviation, as Markowitz did, Roy maximizes $(m - d)/\sigma$, where $d$ is a level of returns that can be considered a disaster. This maximization procedure leads Roy to obtain the efficient frontier as a hyperbola in the $(\sigma, m)$ space. According to Markowitz (1999), the main differences between Roy's paper and his 1952 paper are that Markowitz (1952) worked only with long positions and allowed the investors to select one portfolio from the efficient frontier, whereas Roy (1952) worked also with short positions and recommended one specific portfolio.

Given that Roy arrived at the same results as Markowitz independently and using similar methods, it is reasonable to wonder why Roy did not also receive the Nobel Prize. Markowitz thought the reason was his greater visibility: Roy's paper was his last (and only) publication in finance, whereas Markowitz wrote two books and a collection of papers related to this subject (Markowitz, 1999).

## 2.2 HARRY MARKOWITZ'S MODERN PORTFOLIO THEORY (1952)

Before delving into the analysis of Markowitz's paper, we introduce some of the definitions and the notation that we will use. We consider portfolios composed of $n$ risky assets, with returns $r_1, \ldots, r_n$; which are random variables with expectations $R_i = \mathbb{E}\left[r_i\right]$ and covariances $\sigma_{ij} = cov\left(r_i, r_j\right)$, $i, j = 1, \ldots, n$. We will usually work in matrix form, with the vector of expected returns $\mathbf{R} = \left(R_1, \ldots, R_n\right)^T$ and the covariance matrix $\boldsymbol{\Sigma}$ with $(\boldsymbol{\Sigma})_{ij} = \sigma_{ij}$. The variances of asset returns are given by the diagonal elements of $\boldsymbol{\Sigma}$, $\sigma_i^2 = \sigma_{ii}$. As the assets in the portfolio are risky assets, we have $\sigma_i^2 > 0$, $i = 1, \ldots, n$, and then, $\boldsymbol{\Sigma}$ is a positive definite matrix, that is, $\mathbf{x}^T \boldsymbol{\Sigma} x > 0$ for any nonzero $n$-vector $\mathbf{x}$. In addition, we will assume that $\boldsymbol{\Sigma}$ is nonsingular, $|\boldsymbol{\Sigma}| \neq 0$, meaning that none of the asset returns is perfectly correlated with the return of the portfolio composed of the remaining assets.

Each portfolio is determined by a vector $\mathbf{w} = \left(w_1, \ldots, w_n\right)^T$ in which $w_i$ is the proportion of investor's wealth allocated to the $i$-th asset. By this definition we have $\sum_{i=1}^{n} w_i = 1$, or in matrix notation, $\mathbf{w}^T\mathbf{1} = 1$, where $\mathbf{1}$ is the $n$-vector given by $\mathbf{1} = (1, \ldots, 1)^T$. The expected return of the portfolio is given by $R_p = \mathbf{w}^T\mathbf{R}$, and the variance of its return is $\sigma_p^2 = \mathbf{w}^T\boldsymbol{\Sigma}\mathbf{w}$.

In his 1952 paper, Markowitz begins by rejecting the maximization of expected returns as a guiding principle for investment behavior. This decision is rooted in the often-understated principle of diversification, a key aspect of Markowitz's work. In his own words: "[...] a rule of behavior which does not imply the superiority of diversification must be rejected both as a hypothesis and as a maxim."

Diversification, as a rule leading to the reduction of the risk of a portfolio, measured by the variance of its return, finds support in theoretical arguments. As the following simple result shows, under certain assumptions, perfectly diversified portfolios become asymptotically risk-free. In other words, the variance of the portfolio return diminishes as the number of component assets increases.

**Proposition 2.1** *Consider an equally weighted portfolio whose asset returns are independent random variables with the same variance $\sigma^2$. Then, the variance of the portfolio return, $\sigma_p^2$, satisfies*

$$\lim_{n\to\infty} \sigma_p^2 = 0,$$

*Proof.* As the portfolio is equally weighted, we have $\mathbf{w} = \frac{1}{n}\mathbf{1}$, and by the independence assumption, $\boldsymbol{\Sigma} = \sigma^2\mathbf{I}$, where $\mathbf{I}$ is the identity matrix. Then, the portfolio variance is

$$\sigma_p^2 = \mathbf{w}^T\boldsymbol{\Sigma}\mathbf{w} = \frac{1}{n^2}\sigma^2\mathbf{1}^T\mathbf{I}\mathbf{1} = \frac{\sigma^2}{n},$$

from where we obtain the desired result. ■

While the previous result is intellectually appealing, its assumptions are hardly satisfied in actual markets. First, there is empirical evidence suggesting that returns follow stable Paretian distributions, characterized by infinite variances (Mandelbrot, 1963; Fama, 1965a).[1] Second, it is difficult, if not impossible, to find a substantial number of assets with totally independent returns and equal variance. Therefore, as Markowitz himself pointed out: "The returns from securities are too intercorrelated. Diversification cannot eliminate all variance."

[1]According to Fama (1965b), in the context of stable Paretian distributions, there is a range of conditions under which diversification is a meaningful economic activity.

Once the diversification principle is accepted, Markowitz turns his attention to the maximization of expected returns, for the case of no short sales allowed. We will formalize Markowitz's reasoning in the following result, which also includes short sales.

**Proposition 2.2** *If all the available assets have different expected returns, the portfolio with maximum expected return consists of only one asset with the highest expected return. This result holds true whether short sales are allowed or not.*

*Proof.* Consider first the case of short sales allowed. The optimization problem can be stated as

$$\begin{aligned} \max \quad & R_p = \mathbf{w}^T\mathbf{R} \\ s.t. \quad & \mathbf{w}^T\mathbf{1} = 1 \end{aligned}$$

with variable $\mathbf{w} \in \mathbb{R}^n$. The corresponding Lagrangian is

$$L(\mathbf{w}, \lambda) = \mathbf{w}^T\mathbf{R} - \lambda\left(\mathbf{w}^T\mathbf{1} - 1\right),$$

and the first-order conditions are

$$\frac{\partial L}{\partial \mathbf{w}} = \mathbf{R} - \lambda\mathbf{1} = 0 \tag{2.1}$$

$$\frac{\partial L}{\partial \lambda} = \mathbf{w}^T\mathbf{1} - 1 = 0.$$

From equation (2.1) we obtain $R_1 = \cdots = R_n = \lambda$, and all the assets in the portfolio must have the same expected return $\lambda$. As by hypothesis all the expected returns are different, the portfolio must be composed of only one asset, with the highest expected return.

If short sales are not allowed, we must include the additional constraint $\mathbf{w} \geq 0$, i.e., $w_i \geq 0$, $i = 1, \ldots, n$. The Karush-Kuhn-Tucker first-order conditions for the problem are

$$\mathbf{R} + \lambda - \nu\mathbf{1} = 0 \tag{2.2}$$

$$\mathbf{w}^T\mathbf{1} = 1$$

$$\mathbf{w} \geq 0$$

$$\lambda \geq 0$$

$$\lambda \circ \mathbf{w} = 0, \tag{2.3}$$

where $\nu$ is a Lagrange multiplier, $\lambda = (\lambda_1, \ldots, \lambda_n)^T$ is a vector of Lagrange multipliers, and "$\circ$" stands for the Hadamard (component-wise) product. If the $k$-th asset is included in the optimal portfolio, then $w_k > 0$, and by (2.3), $\lambda_k = 0$. Replacing this value in equation (2.1), we obtain $R_k = \nu$, and thus, all the assets in the portfolio must have the same expected return. Therefore, the optimal portfolio is composed only of the asset with the highest return. ■

**Remark 2.1** *In the unlikely case in which there are several assets with the same expected return, an optimal portfolio would be composed of all these assets in any proportion.*

Considering the previous result, and diversification as a first principle, Markowitz rejects the maximization of portfolio return as a maxim. The next step involves considering the expected return-variance of return rule, which leads to the so-called mean-variance (MV) analysis.

The assumptions of this approach, not explicitly stated by Markowitz, are the following (Constantinides and Malliaris, 1995).

i) **The investor considers only the mean and the variance of returns to form her optimal portfolios.** As pointed out in Meucci (2005), considering only the first two moments of the distribution of returns can be considered as an approximation to the broader problem of dealing with all the moments. This approximation is exact if portfolio returns follow a normal distribution, although this is not an assumption of the MV analysis.
ii) **Given the expected return of the portfolio, the investor will choose the portfolio with the lowest variance of returns.** Markowitz (1952) assumes that the knowledge of expected returns is available to the investor, without addressing the problem of its estimation. On the other hand, he considers variance as a measure of portfolio risk, and then, the investor wants to reduce its value, while maintaining expected returns as high as possible. In his words, the investor "considers expected return a desirable thing and variance of returns an undesirable thing."
iii) **The investment horizon is one period.** This is a restrictive assumption of the model, which will be relaxed in subsequent chapters of this book, where we consider the dynamic nature of portfolio management. Nevertheless, as pointed out in Kolm et al. (2014b), practitioners typically use one-period models to rebalance portfolios from one period to another.

iv) **The investor's individual decisions do not affect market prices.** This assumption is equivalent to excluding market impact (i.e., changes in prices caused by the trade itself) from the analysis. As market impact depends on the ratio of the trade size to the average trade volume, Markowitz is assuming, implicitly, that the investor rebalances her portfolio by trading in relatively tiny amounts.

v) **Fractional shares may be purchased.** This is a mathematical requirement not satisfied in actual markets, although it does not impose a severe restriction because portfolios are defined by their weights in each asset, and not by absolute amounts.

vi) **Transaction costs and taxes do not exist.** This assumption separates the model from the actual functioning of markets. We will see in subsequent chapters how to include transaction costs in the study.

vii) **Investors can sell assets short.** In fact, Markowitz (1952) does not allow short sales to simplify the analysis. We will present the MV approach with short sales allowed and refer to the situation in which they are forbidden.

Once stated the MV optimization problem, Markowitz (1952) intentionally avoids the mathematical formulation and instead presents a geometrical analysis for the case of only three assets. We avoid here these geometrical considerations and refer the reader to the original paper.

With the preceding considerations, we can now state the optimization program associated with the MV analysis as

$$\begin{aligned} \min \quad & \sigma_p^2 = \mathbf{w}^T \boldsymbol{\Sigma} \mathbf{w} \\ \text{s.t.} \quad & \mathbf{w}^T \mathbf{1} = 1 \\ & \mathbf{w}^T \mathbf{R} = R_p \end{aligned} \tag{2.4}$$

with variable $\mathbf{w} \in \mathbb{R}^n$.

The problem in equation (2.4) is a convex problem with strictly convex objective function, and then the optimal set contains at most one point. We will find this optimal solution in Chapter 3.

## 2.3 BLACK-LITTERMAN MODEL (1990s)

In 1989, while at Goldman Sachs, Fisher Black and Robert Litterman were assigned the task of developing an asset allocation model with the objective of diversifying their clients' global bond portfolios. The result of their work is known today as the Black-Litterman model and was published in the *Journal of Fixed Income* (Black and Litterman, 1991a).

The authors begin the presentation of their model by considering a portfolio manager who maximizes total return for any given level of risk, namely, who follows the MV approach. Nevertheless, they propose a model that goes beyond the standard framework, to address the main problem that portfolio managers face when applying the Markowitz model: the weights in optimal portfolios are very sensitive to small changes in expected returns, giving rise to extremely unbalanced portfolios (Green and Hollifield, 1992). Furthermore, this problem involves considering the degree of uncertainty about the expected returns, which has no place in MV analysis.

Black and Litterman rule out some of the solutions provided to these problems, such as restricting the weights in the portfolio or including transaction costs. Instead, they propose incorporating two key ingredients into the analysis. On the one hand, taking the values of expected returns, which are inputs to the Markowitz model (see Chapter 3), from an equilibrium model, specifically, the International CAPM (ICAPM).[2] According to the authors themselves, the use of these equilibrium values "significantly ameliorates the usual tendency of mean-variance models to map seemingly reasonable views into what appears to be extremely unbalanced portfolios."

On the other hand, allowing portfolio managers to modify the equilibrium values according to their own views, specifying relative strengths for each view. In the words of Black and Litterman: "The simple idea that expected returns ought to be consistent with market equilibrium, except to the extent that the investor explicitly states otherwise, turns out to be of critical importance in making practical use of the model."

The assumptions of the Black-Litterman model can be stated as follows:

i) **The expected return of each asset is consistent with the equilibrium, with a given confidence level determined by the portfolio manager.** In this assumption, the term "consistent" means that the difference between equilibrium expected returns and "true" expected returns is a random variable with zero mean. The confidence level of the equilibrium expected returns is included as a parameter in the covariance matrix of the random variable (see equation [2.7]).
ii) **The portfolio manager includes her views on each asset, with a given confidence level about each view.** These views can be expressed in absolute or relative terms with respect to the equilibrium values of expected returns.

[2]Regarding the ICAPM, the authors cite the references Solnik (1974), Adler and Dumas (1983), and Black (1989).

iii) **The errors corresponding to the equilibrium values and to the manager views follow a zero-mean Gaussian distribution and are independent.** This is a simplifying assumption that will allow us to obtain the distribution of the estimator of expected returns.

In order to formalize the previous assumptions, we will consider, as usual, that the equilibrium model that generates the expected returns is the CAPM of Sharpe (1964), Lintner (1965) and Mossin (1966) (see Chapter 3). Therefore, the equilibrium expected return of the $i$-th asset, $R_i$, is given by (see equation [2.5])

$$R_i = R_0 + \beta_i^M \left(R_{p,M} - R_0\right), \tag{2.5}$$

where $R_0$ is the return of the riskless asset, $\beta_i^M$ is the beta of the $i$-th asset, $\beta_i^M = \frac{cov(r_i, r_{P,M})}{\sigma_{p,M}^2}$, and $\sigma_{p,M}^2$, $R_{p,M}$ are, respectively, the variance and the expected return of the market portfolio.[3]

From equation (2.5) we have

$$\begin{aligned} E_i \equiv R_i - R_0 &= \frac{cov\,(r_i, r_{P,M})}{\sigma_{p,M}^2}\left(R_{p,M} - R_0\right) \\ &= \frac{R_{p,M} - R_0}{\sigma_{p,M}^2} \sum_{j=1}^{n} cov\,(r_i, r_j) w_{j,M}, \end{aligned}$$

where $E_i$ is the equilibrium expected excess return of the $i$-th asset, and $w_{j,M}$ is the weight of the $j$-th asset in the market portfolio. This expression can be written in matrix form as

$$\mathbf{E} = \delta \mathbf{\Sigma} \mathbf{w}_M \tag{2.6}$$

where $\delta = \frac{R_{p,M} - R_0}{\sigma_{p,M}^2}$, and $\mathbf{w}_M = \left(w_{1,M}, \ldots, w_{n,M}\right)^T$ is the market portfolio.

According to assumptions i) and iii), we can write

$$\mathbf{E} = \boldsymbol{\mu} + \varepsilon_E, \quad \varepsilon_E \sim N(0, \tau\mathbf{\Sigma}), \tag{2.7}$$

where $\boldsymbol{\mu}$ is the vector of true expected excess returns, and $\tau > 0$ is the parameter expressing the confidence on the equilibrium estimates. Values of $\tau$ close to zero would imply a high confidence in the estimates.

[3]The market portfolio is the portfolio of risky assets that has the same weights as the entire market (see Chapter 3).

On the other hand, assumptions ii) and iii) lead to

$$\mathbf{q} = \mathbf{P}\mu + \varepsilon_q, \quad \varepsilon_q \sim N(0, \mathbf{\Phi}), \tag{2.8}$$

where $\mathbf{q}$ is a $k$-vector representing the manager views, $\mathbf{P}$ is a $k \times n$ matrix expressing the modifications of equilibrium values, and $\mathbf{\Phi}$ a $k \times k$ invertible matrix accounting for the manager's confidence in her own views on the assets. The matrix $\mathbf{\Phi}$ is usually taken as a diagonal matrix whose elements represent the variances of the errors in the views for each asset. Values close to zero would correspond to high confidence in the views.

For example, in a portfolio with three assets ($n = 3$), if the manager has two views (one absolute and the other relative):

- The first asset will have a return of 1.2%,
- The second asset will outperform the third one by 3%,

and she assigns a standard deviation of 0.5% to the first view and a 1.7% to the second view, we will have

$$\mathbf{q} = \begin{bmatrix} 1.2 \\ 3 \end{bmatrix}, \mathbf{P} = \begin{bmatrix} 1 & 0 & 0 \\ 0 & 1 & -1 \end{bmatrix}, \mathbf{\Phi} = \begin{bmatrix} 0.5^2 & 0 \\ 0 & 1.7^2 \end{bmatrix}.$$

The main result of the model is an estimator of the true expected excess return, and it is presented in the following theorem.

**Theorem 2.1** *The best linear unbiased estimator (BLUE) of the expected excess return in the Black-Litterman model is given by*

$$\widehat{\mu}_{BL} = \left[(\tau\mathbf{\Sigma})^{-1} + \mathbf{P}^T\mathbf{\Phi}^{-1}\mathbf{P}\right]^{-1}\left[(\tau\mathbf{\Sigma})^{-1}\mathbf{E} + \mathbf{P}^T\mathbf{\Phi}^{-1}\mathbf{q}\right] \tag{2.9}$$

*and satisfies*

$$\widehat{\mu}_{BL} \sim N\left(\mu, \left[(\tau\mathbf{\Sigma})^{-1} + \mathbf{P}^T\mathbf{\Phi}^{-1}\mathbf{P}\right]^{-1}\right). \tag{2.10}$$

*Proof.* Stacking equations (2.7) and (2.8), we have the linear model

$$\mathbf{y} = \mathbf{X}\mu + \varepsilon, \quad \varepsilon \sim N(0, \mathbf{\Delta}) \tag{2.11}$$

where $\mathbf{y} = \begin{bmatrix} \mathbf{E} \\ \mathbf{q} \end{bmatrix}$, $\mathbf{X} = \begin{bmatrix} \mathbf{I} \\ \mathbf{P} \end{bmatrix}$ and $\mathbf{\Delta} = \begin{bmatrix} \tau\mathbf{\Sigma} & 0 \\ 0 & \mathbf{\Phi} \end{bmatrix}$, with $\mathbf{I}$ the $n \times n$ identity matrix. Equation (2.11) is a general linear regression model. As $\mathbf{\Delta}$ is known, by the Gauss-Markov Theorem (Kariya and Kurata, 2004; Theorem 2.1), the estimator

$$\widehat{\boldsymbol{\mu}}_{BL} = \left(\mathbf{X}^T\boldsymbol{\Delta}^{-1}\mathbf{X}\right)^{-1}\mathbf{X}^T\boldsymbol{\Delta}^{-1}\mathbf{y} \tag{2.12}$$

is the BLUE estimator of $\boldsymbol{\mu}$, with

$$\begin{aligned} \mathbb{E}\left(\widehat{\boldsymbol{\mu}}_{BL}\right) &= \boldsymbol{\mu} \\ cov\left(\widehat{\boldsymbol{\mu}}_{BL}\right) &= \left(\mathbf{X}^T\boldsymbol{\Delta}^{-1}\mathbf{X}\right)^{-1}. \end{aligned} \tag{2.13}$$

Replacing the expressions of $\mathbf{X}$, $\boldsymbol{\Delta}$ and $\mathbf{y}$ in (2.12) and (2.13), we have

$$\begin{aligned} \widehat{\boldsymbol{\mu}}_{BL} &= \left[\begin{bmatrix}\mathbf{I} & \mathbf{P}^T\end{bmatrix}\begin{bmatrix}(\tau\boldsymbol{\Sigma})^{-1} & 0 \\ 0 & \boldsymbol{\Phi}^{-1}\end{bmatrix}\begin{bmatrix}\mathbf{I} \\ \mathbf{P}\end{bmatrix}\right]^{-1}\begin{bmatrix}\mathbf{I} & \mathbf{P}^T\end{bmatrix}\begin{bmatrix}(\tau\boldsymbol{\Sigma})^{-1} & 0 \\ 0 & \boldsymbol{\Phi}^{-1}\end{bmatrix}\begin{bmatrix}\mathbf{E} \\ \mathbf{q}\end{bmatrix} \\ &= \left[\begin{bmatrix}\mathbf{I} & \mathbf{P}^T\end{bmatrix}\begin{bmatrix}(\tau\boldsymbol{\Sigma})^{-1} \\ \boldsymbol{\Phi}^{-1}\mathbf{P}\end{bmatrix}\right]^{-1}\begin{bmatrix}\mathbf{I} & \mathbf{P}^T\end{bmatrix}\begin{bmatrix}(\tau\boldsymbol{\Sigma})^{-1}\mathbf{E} \\ \boldsymbol{\Phi}^{-1}\mathbf{q}\end{bmatrix} \\ &= \left[(\tau\boldsymbol{\Sigma})^{-1} + \mathbf{P}^T\boldsymbol{\Phi}^{-1}\mathbf{P}\right]^{-1}\left[(\tau\boldsymbol{\Sigma})^{-1}\mathbf{E} + \mathbf{P}^T\boldsymbol{\Phi}^{-1}\mathbf{q}\right] \end{aligned}$$

and

$$cov\left(\widehat{\boldsymbol{\mu}}_{BL}\right) = \left[(\tau\boldsymbol{\Sigma})^{-1} + \mathbf{P}^T\boldsymbol{\Phi}^{-1}\mathbf{P}\right]^{-1}.$$

Finally, by assumption iii), $\widehat{\boldsymbol{\mu}}_{BL}$ has a Gaussian distribution, and (2.10) holds. ■

Once the theorem is stated and proved, some remarks are worth making.

**Remark 2.2** *The existence of the Black-Litterman estimator $\widehat{\boldsymbol{\mu}}_{BL}$ of equation (2.9) is guaranteed by the Gauss-Markov Theorem, as long as the matrix $\mathbf{X}$ has full rank. Moreover, this theorem does not require any distributional assumption, thus equation (2.9) is valid even in the non-Gaussian case.*

**Remark 2.3** *Theorem 2.1 is not valid for the case in which $\tau = 0$, i.e., when the manager is* 100% *confident in the equilibrium values. In this case, from equation (2.7) we have $\boldsymbol{\varepsilon}_E = 0$, $\boldsymbol{\mu} = \mathbf{E}$, and the Black-Litterman approach is not relevant. Another situation in which Theorem 2.1 does not hold is when the manager has views different from the equilibrium estimates ($\mathbf{P} \neq 0$) with* *a 100% confidence ($\mathbf{\Phi} = 0$). Then, $\mathbf{\Phi}^{-1}$ does not exist and we cannot apply equation (2.9).*

The following result proves the consistency of Theorem 2.1 with the CAPM when the manager does not incorporate any views.

**Corollary 2.1** *If the manager has no views modifying equilibrium estimates ($\mathbf{P} = 0$), then $\widehat{\boldsymbol{\mu}}_{BL} = \mathbf{E}$, and she will end up holding the market portfolio.*

*Proof.* The equality $\widehat{\boldsymbol{\mu}}_{BL} = \mathbf{E}$ is immediate from equation (2.9). On the other hand, the minimum variance portfolio is given by (see equation [3.18]) $\mathbf{w} = \lambda\mathbf{\Sigma}^{-1}\mathbf{E}$, with $\lambda$ a Lagrange multiplier. Replacing equation (2.6) in this expression, we get

$$\mathbf{w} = \lambda\mathbf{\Sigma}^{-1}\delta\mathbf{\Sigma}\mathbf{w}_M = \lambda\delta\mathbf{w}_M.$$

As $\mathbf{w}$ and $\mathbf{w}_M$ are portfolios, we have

$$1 = \mathbf{w}^T\mathbf{1} = \lambda\delta\mathbf{w}_M\mathbf{1} = \lambda\delta,$$

and then, $\mathbf{w} = \mathbf{w}_M$. ■

**Corollary 2.2** *The Black-Litterman estimator of equation (2.9) can be written as*

$$\widehat{\boldsymbol{\mu}}_{BL} = \mathbf{w}_E\mathbf{E} + \mathbf{w}_{\widetilde{\mu}}\widetilde{\boldsymbol{\mu}},$$

*where $\widetilde{\boldsymbol{\mu}} = \left(\mathbf{P}^T\mathbf{P}\right)^{-1}\mathbf{P}^T\mathbf{q}$, and the weights $\mathbf{w}_E$ and $\mathbf{w}_{\widetilde{\mu}}$ are matrices given by*

$$\mathbf{w}_E = \left[(\tau\mathbf{\Sigma})^{-1} + \mathbf{P}^T\mathbf{\Phi}^{-1}\mathbf{P}\right]^{-1}(\tau\mathbf{\Sigma})^{-1}$$
$$\mathbf{w}_{\widetilde{\mu}} = \left[(\tau\mathbf{\Sigma})^{-1} + \mathbf{P}^T\mathbf{\Phi}^{-1}\mathbf{P}\right]^{-1}\mathbf{P}^T\mathbf{\Phi}^{-1}\mathbf{P}$$

*that satisfy $\mathbf{w}_E + \mathbf{w}_{\widetilde{\mu}} = \mathbf{I}$, where $\mathbf{I}$ is the identity matrix of order $n$.*

*Proof.* It suffices to consider that $\mathbf{P}\left(\mathbf{P}^T\mathbf{P}\right)^{-1}\mathbf{P}^T = \mathbf{I}$ and replace $\mathbf{P}^T\mathbf{\Phi}^{-1}\mathbf{q}$ by $\mathbf{P}^T\mathbf{\Phi}^{-1}\mathbf{P}\widetilde{\boldsymbol{\mu}}$ in equation (2.9). ■

When the manager is 100% confident in her views, $\mathbf{\Phi} = 0$, and from equation (2.8) we have $\mathbf{q} = \mathbf{P}\boldsymbol{\mu}$ and $\boldsymbol{\mu} = \left(\mathbf{P}^T\mathbf{P}\right)^{-1}\mathbf{P}^T\mathbf{q} = \widetilde{\boldsymbol{\mu}}$. Then, $\widetilde{\boldsymbol{\mu}}$ is the estimate of the expected returns in that case. Therefore, Corollary 2.2 has the interpretation that the Black-Litterman estimator is a weighted linear combination of equilibrium and investor estimates.

According to Fabozzi et al. (2007), the most important contribution of the Black-Litterman model is that it adjusts the entire vector of equilibrium expected excess returns with the manager's views. Due to the correlation between returns, views on only a few assets imply changes in the expected excess returns of all assets. Mathematically, the contribution of the manager's views to the estimator in equation (2.9) is determined by the term $\mathbf{P}^T\boldsymbol{\Phi}^{-1}\mathbf{q}$. Since $\mathbf{P}^T\boldsymbol{\Phi}^{-1}$ is a $n \times k$ matrix and $\mathbf{q}$ is a $k$-vector, the effect of the $k$ views will end up propagating to the $n$ components of the estimator, even when $k << n$. Intuitively, estimation errors spread to all assets, making $\hat{\boldsymbol{\mu}}_{BL}$ less sensitive to errors in asset-specific views, mitigating the problem initially exposed by Black and Litterman.

## 2.4 ALTERNATIVE METHODS: RISK PARITY, HIERARCHICAL RISK PARITY AND MACHINE LEARNING

### 2.4.1 Risk Parity

The risk parity approach was born in 1996 with the launch of the *All Weather Fund* by Bridgewater Associates, but the concept of Risk Parity Portfolios first appeared in Qian (2005), where they are defined as "a family of efficient beta portfolios that allocate market risk equally across asset classes, including stocks, bonds and commodities."

The reasoning behind the risk parity approach is to realize that the traditional practice of diversification based on balancing a portfolio in terms of capital allocation can lead to a high concentration of risk in certain types of assets. To illustrate this effect, Qian (2005) presents as an example, a 60/40 portfolio with 60% stocks and 40% bonds, apparently balanced, in which stocks contribute 93% of risk, while bonds only account for the remaining 7%.

Based on these considerations, if we want to limit the impact of large losses coming from one of the components of the portfolio, we need the expected contribution to risk being (approximately) the same for all asset types in the portfolio, which leads to the risk parity approach.

To formalize these ideas, we define the *risk contribution* of the $i$-th asset in the portfolio, $RC_i$, as

$$RC_i(\mathbf{w}) = w_i \frac{\partial \sigma_p}{\partial w_i} = \frac{w_i \sum_{j=1}^{n} w_j \sigma_{ij}}{\sigma_p}, \tag{2.14}$$

where $\sigma_p(\mathbf{w}) = \sqrt{\mathbf{w}^T\boldsymbol{\Sigma}\mathbf{w}}$ is the volatility of the portfolio, used as a measure of its risk. The following result states that the risk contribution is well-defined.

**Proposition 2.3** *The risk of the portfolio is equal to the sum of the risk contributions of its components:*

$$\sigma_p(\mathbf{w}) = \sum_{i=1}^{n} RC_i(\mathbf{w}). \tag{2.15}$$

*Proof.* It is not difficult to show that $\sigma_p(\lambda\mathbf{w}) = \lambda\sigma_p(\mathbf{w})$ for any $\lambda > 0$, and then $\sigma_p$ is a homogeneous function of degree one. By Euler's Theorem, we obtain

$$\sigma_p(\mathbf{w}) = \sum_{i=1}^{n} w_i \frac{\partial \sigma_p}{\partial w_i} = \sum_{i=1}^{n} RC_i(\mathbf{w}).$$

■

As we have seen, the original risk parity approach considered the equalization of the risk contributions of all assets. As this concept has evolved to include different extensions, we will give the portfolios obtained under this approach the name of *Equal Risk Contributions* (ERC) portfolios. Thus, following Maillard et al. (2010), we define an ERC portfolio as the portfolio $\mathbf{w}^*$ that satisfies

$$\begin{gathered} \mathbf{w}^* \succ 0 \\ RC_i(\mathbf{w}^*) = RC_j(\mathbf{w}^*),\ i,j = 1,\ldots,n. \end{gathered} \tag{2.16}$$

As the following result states, it is possible to find expressions for the weights, $w_i^*$, of ERC portfolios in some specific cases.

**Proposition 2.4** *a) If the correlations between assets are equal, then*

$$w_i^* = \frac{\sigma_i^{-1}}{\sum_{j=1}^{n} \sigma_j^{-1}}. \tag{2.17}$$

*b) If the volatilities of all assets are equal, then*

$$w_i^* = \frac{\left(\sum_{k=1}^{n} w_k \rho_{ik}\right)^{-1}}{\sum_{j=1}^{n} \left(\sum_{k=1}^{n} w_k \rho_{ik}\right)^{-1}}. \tag{2.18}$$

*c) In the general case of unrestricted volatilities and correlations*

$$w_i^* = \frac{\beta_i^{-1}}{\sum_{j=1}^n \beta_j^{-1}} = \frac{\beta_i^{-1}}{n}, \tag{2.19}$$

*where* $\beta_i = \frac{cov(r_i, r_p)}{\sigma_p^2}$ *is the beta of the i-th asset (see Chapter 3).*

*Proof.* a) Using equation (2.14) and that $\rho_{ij} = \rho$ for $i \neq j$, we have

$$RC_i = \frac{w_i\sigma_i\left[\rho \sum_{k=1}^n w_k\sigma_k + (1-\rho)\, w_i\sigma_i\right]}{\sigma_p},$$

and therefore, the condition $RC_i(\mathbf{w}^*) = RC_j(\mathbf{w}^*)$ for ERC portfolios is satisfied if $w_i^*\sigma_i = w_j^*\sigma_j$. From this expression we get

$$1 = \sum_{j=1}^n w_j^* = w_i^*\sigma_i \sum_{j=1}^n \sigma_j^{-1}$$

from where we obtain equation (2.17).

b) Following a reasoning similar to that of the case a), we have

$$RC_i = \frac{w_i\sigma_i^2 \sum_{k=1}^n w_k\rho_{ik}}{\sigma_p},$$

and then, $RC_i(\mathbf{w}^*) = RC_j(\mathbf{w}^*)$ implies

$$w_j^* = \frac{w_i^* \sum_{k=1}^n w_k^*\rho_{ik}}{\sum_{k=1}^n w_k^*\rho_{jk}},$$

Imposing the condition $\sum_{j=1}^n w_j^* = 1$, we find equation (2.18).

c) Considering that $r_p = \sum_{j=1}^n w_j r_j$, we have $cov(r_i, r_p) = \sum_{j=1}^n w_j\sigma_{ij}$. Replacing this result in equation (2.14), we get $RC_i(\mathbf{w}^*) = w_i\beta_i\sigma_p$. Following a procedure analogous to the one used previously, we obtain

$$w_i^* = \frac{\beta_i^{-1}}{\sum_{j=1}^n \beta_j^{-1}}.$$

Applying that for ERC portfolios $RC_i = \frac{\sigma_p}{n}$, $i = 1, \ldots, n$, we find that $\beta_j^{-1} = nw_j$, from where the last equality in (2.19) follows. ■

It is important to note that of the three expression that appear in Proposition 2.4, only equation (2.17) can be considered as an explicit solution for the weights. Expressions in equations (2.18) and (2.19) provide an intuitive interpretation of the solution, but do not allow it to be obtained explicitly, since the right-hand side also depends on the weights. Thus, in the general case without restrictions on correlations and volatilities, it is necessary to resort to numerical algorithms.

Maillard et al. (2010) present three algorithms for ERC portfolios. The first one is the sequential quadratic programming (SQP) algorithm given by

$$\begin{aligned} \mathbf{w}^* &= \arg\min \sum_{i,j=1}^{n} \left[RC_i(\mathbf{w}) - RC_j(\mathbf{w})\right]^2 \\ s.t. \quad & \mathbf{1}^T\mathbf{w} = 1 \\ & 0 \preceq \mathbf{w} \preceq \mathbf{1}. \end{aligned}$$

This first algorithm is the one preferred by the authors, since it is the easiest to solve as it does not incorporate nonlinear inequality constraints. Nevertheless, they are cases in which numerical optimization is tricky (see Maillard et al. [2010] for details and solutions).

The second algorithm is

$$\begin{aligned} \mathbf{y}^* &= \arg\min \sqrt{\mathbf{y}^T \boldsymbol{\Sigma} \mathbf{y}} \\ s.t. \quad & \sum_{i=1}^{n} \ln y_i \geq c \\ & \mathbf{y} \succeq 0 \end{aligned} \tag{2.20}$$

with $c$ an arbitrary constant, and the ERC portfolio is given by $w_i^* = \frac{y_i^*}{\sum_{j=1}^{n} y_j^*}$. This formulation has the advantage of having a unique solution for any value of $c$, with $\sum_{i=1}^{n} \ln y_i^* = c$ (Maillard et al., 2010; Appendix A.2).

The third algorithm is a modification of the second one, given by

$$\begin{aligned} \mathbf{w}^* &= \arg\min \sqrt{\mathbf{w}^T \boldsymbol{\Sigma} \mathbf{w}} \\ s.t. \quad & \sum_{i=1}^{n} \ln w_i \geq d \\ & \mathbf{1}^T\mathbf{w} = 1 \\ & \mathbf{w} \succeq 0. \end{aligned} \tag{2.21}$$

As the constant $c$ in the second algorithm, the constant $d$ can be interpreted as the minimum level of diversification in order to obtain an ERC portfolio. It is not difficult to verify that an ERC portfolio $\mathbf{w}^*$ obtained solving equation (2.20) with a value $c$ can be obtained from equation (2.21) with the value

$$d = c - n \ln\left(\sum_{j=1}^{n} y_j^*\right). \tag{2.22}$$

In the extreme case with $d \to -\infty$, the first constraint disappears and the solution is the global minimum variance (GMV) portfolio, that is, the portfolio with the smallest possible variance for any given expected return (see Chapter 3). Another extreme case appears when $d = -n \ln n$, which corresponds to the equally weighted (EW) portfolio.[4] This last algorithm allows us to show that the risk of ERC portfolios is placed between that of GMV and EW portfolios.

**Proposition 2.5** *The volatility, $\sigma_{ERC}$, of an ERC portfolio satisfies*

$$\sigma_{GMV} \le \sigma_{ERC} \le \sigma_{EW},$$

*where $\sigma_{GMV}$ and $\sigma_{EQ}$ are, respectively, the volatilities of the GMV and the EW portfolios.*

*Proof.* Taking logarithms in the arithmetic mean-geometric mean inequality

$$\sqrt[n]{\prod_{i=1}^{n} w_i} \le \frac{\sum_{i=1}^{n} w_i}{n}, \quad w_i \ge 0$$

we have

$$\frac{1}{n}\sum_{i=1}^{n} \ln w_i \le \ln\left(\sum_{i=1}^{n} w_i\right) - \ln n,$$

and using $\sum_{i=1}^{n} w_i = 1$, we obtain

$$\sum_{i=1}^{n} \ln w_i \le -n \ln n. \tag{2.23}$$

[4]To see this, it suffices to write the first constraint as $w_1 \ldots w_n \ge n^{-1} \overset{n)}{\cdots} n^{-1}$, and use that the maximum of the product of positive numbers with constant sum is reached when all the numbers are equal.

Thus, the maximum value of $d$ in the program in equation (2.21) is $d = -n \ln n$, and therefore, $d \in (-\infty, -n \ln n]$.

On the other hand, $d_1 \leq d_2 \Rightarrow \sigma(\mathbf{w}^*(d_1)) \leq \sigma(\mathbf{w}^*(d_2))$, since the first constraint in equation (2.21) is less restrictive with $c_1$ than with $c_2$. Therefore, the solution $\mathbf{w}^*$ satisfies

$$\sigma_{GMV} = \sigma(\mathbf{w}^*(-\infty)) \leq \sigma(\mathbf{w}^*(d)) \leq \sigma(\mathbf{w}^*(-n \ln n)) = \sigma_{EW} \qquad (2.24)$$

for every $d \in (-\infty, -n \ln n]$. We know that for any value of $c$, the solution $\mathbf{y}^*$ of program (2.20) determines an ERC portfolio with $w_i^* = \frac{y_i^*}{\sum_{j=1}^n y_j^*}$. Replacing this value in the inequality (2.23) we obtain

$$-n \ln n \left( \sum_{j=1}^n y_j^* \right) \leq -n \ln n - \sum_{j=1}^n \ln y_j^* = -n \ln n - c, \qquad (2.25)$$

where in the last equality we have used that the solution $y_i^*$ of (2.20) satisfies $\sum_{i=1}^n \ln y_i^* = c$. Using equation (2.25) in (2.22), we have that $d \leq -n \ln n$, and then $d \in (-\infty, -n \ln n]$. Thus, we can write (2.24) as

$$\sigma_{GMV} \leq \sigma_{ERC} \leq \sigma_{EW},$$

which concludes the proof. ■

The following result states that ERC portfolios are MV efficient if the Sharpe ratios of the assets are equal and the correlations between them also coincide.

**Theorem 2.2** *Consider the expected excess return of the i-th asset,* $E_i = R_i - R_0$, *where* $R_0$ *is the return of the riskless asset, and assume that* $S_i \equiv \frac{E_i}{\sigma_i} = s$ *for* $i = 1, \ldots, n$ *and* $\rho_{ij} = \rho$ *for* $i, j = 1, \ldots, n$, *with* $i \neq j$. *Then, the ERC portfolio is a MV-efficient portfolio.*

*Proof.* MV-efficient portfolios are given by (see Chapter 3, equations [3.14]–[3.15])

$$\mathbf{w} = \frac{\sigma_p^2}{E_p} \mathbf{\Sigma}^{-1} \mathbf{E},$$

where $\mathbf{E} = (E_1, \ldots, E_n)^T$ and $E_p^\bullet = \mathbf{w}^T \mathbf{E}$. Premultiplying by $\mathbf{\Sigma}$ we obtain

$$\mathbf{\Sigma w} = \frac{\sigma_p^2}{E_p} \mathbf{E}. \qquad (2.26)$$

On the other hand, by equation (2.14), we can write the vector of risk contributions, RC, as

$$\mathbf{RC} = \frac{\mathbf{W\Sigma w}}{\sigma_p}, \tag{2.27}$$

where $\mathbf{W}$ is the $n \times n$ matrix with $diag(\mathbf{W}) = (w_1, \ldots, w_n)$ and $(\mathbf{W})_{ij} = 0$ for $i \neq j$. Replacing equations (2.26) in (2.27), we get

$$\mathbf{RC} = \frac{\sigma_p}{E_p}\mathbf{WE}$$

and thus, the individual risk contribution of a MV-efficient portfolio is $RC_i = \frac{\sigma_p}{E_p} w_i E_i$. Applying the ERC condition $RC_i = RC_j$, we obtain $w_i E_i = w_j E_j$. By assumption, we have $E_i = s\sigma_i$, $i = 1, \ldots, n$, and then $w_i \sigma_i = w_j \sigma_j$. Using $\sum_{i=1}^{n} w_i = 1$ we arrive at

$$w_i = \frac{\sigma_i^{-1}}{\sum_{j=1}^{n} \sigma_j^{-1}}. \tag{2.28}$$

By a) of Proposition 2.4, we know that, with equal pairwise correlations, expression in equation (2.28) is an ERC portfolio, and the proof is complete. ■

Kaya and Lee (2012) have empirically studied whether the conditions for optimality of ERC portfolios are met, with negative results, at least for short horizons. However, for longer-term allocations, the portfolios are close to optimal.

Among the **virtues** of the risk parity approach mentioned in the literature, we can highlight the following:

- **Risk Parity Portfolios provide better downside protection** (Qian, 2005, 2006). This is because expected percentage contributions to loss bear close relationship to the percentage contributions to risk.
- **It is not necessary to formulate expected return assumptions** (Chaves et al., 2011). The only input is the covariance matrix, which can be estimated more accurately than expected returns (Merton, 1980).
- **Risk Parity Portfolios show a higher Sharpe ratio than competing approaches such as GMV or MV** (Chaves et al., 2011). Moreover, the Sharpe ratios of Risk Parity Portfolios are less volatile over time.

Like any other approach, risk parity also has **deficiencies**, among them we can point out the following:

- **The expected returns of Risk Parity Portfolios may be too low to meet an investor's desired return (Hurst et al., 2010; Qian, 2011).** To avoid this problem, managers usually resort to leverage to raise the expected returns.
- **Risk Parity Portfolios are sensitive to the inclusion decision for assets (Chaves et al., 2011).** The methodology does not provide information about how many asset classes and what asset classes to include.
- **Risk Parity Portfolios do not consistently outperform a simple EW portfolio or even a 60/40 equity/bond portfolio (Chaves et al., 2011).** This drawback can be mitigated by using leverage (Qian, 2011).

### 2.4.2 Hierarchical Risk Parity

Hierarchical Risk Parity (HRP) is a portfolio allocation algorithm presented in López de Prado (2016b) and designed to address some of the issues related to Markowitz's mean-variance modeling.[5] Specifically, the paper refers to the problems of instability, concentration, and underperformance, already discussed in Section 2.3.

According to López de Prado, these problems are due to the numerical errors introduced when inverting the covariance matrix. These errors increase with the size of the matrix, giving rise to the so-called *Markowitz's curse*: "The most correlated the investments, the greater the need for diversification, and yet the more likely we will receive unstable solutions. The benefits of diversification often are more than offset by estimation errors" (López de Prado, 2016b).

This author argues that the problem behind the instability of MV methods is the consideration of all correlations between assets, which in terms of graphs would result in a fully connected graph. For a portfolio of $n$ assets, this would give rise to $\frac{1}{2}n(n+1)$ edges (i.e., correlations), the number of which grows rapidly with $n$, magnifying small estimation errors, and leading to incorrect solutions. Instead, he proposes using machine learning methods, specifically *hierarchical clustering*, to replace the complete graph with a tree with only $n - 1$ edges. This procedure allows us to include in portfolio allocation the concept of *hierarchy*, that is, the notion that in a portfolio not all assets are equally replaceable with each other.

[5]Actually, López de Prado (2016b) refers to problems related to the Critical Line Algorithm (CLA) of Markowitz et al. (1993), but these problems are shared with the standard MV approach.

The HRP algorithm can be divided into three successive stages: tree clustering, quasi-diagonalization and recursive bisection.

- **Tree Clustering.** An agglomerative clustering algorithm is performed. Each data point is placed initially in its own cluster and at each step, the two most similar clusters are joined into a larger cluster. The algorithm continues until all clusters are members of a single large cluster.
- **Quasi-Diagonalization.** The rows and columns of the covariance matrix are rearranged so that the largest values appear near the diagonal. As a result of this rearrangement, similar assets are placed together, and dissimilar assets appear far apart.
- **Recursive Bisection.** It starts from the list of assets ordered according to the quasi-diagonalization stage, with all their weights equal to 1. This list is divided into clusters with (approximately) the same number of elements, sequentially, until reaching clusters with a single asset. At each stage, the weights are reassigned according to a distribution proportional to the inverse of the variance of the cluster. The result is the distribution of weights in the portfolio resulting from the algorithm.

In Chapter 12, a more detailed explanation of the stages of the HRP algorithm is performed.

### 2.4.3 Machine Learning

Machine learning (ML) is a branch of artificial intelligence (AI) dedicated to the development of algorithms and models capable of learning from data and generalizing what is learned to unseen data. The application of ML techniques in finance dates to the 1980s, when some banks began to offer their clients solutions based on AI, such as the Personal Financial Planning System from Chase Lincoln First Bank in 1987. Since then, it has been applied to areas such as credit scoring or financial fraud detection, although its application to portfolio management has been more recent.

Today, ML is closely related to big data, that is, the use of a high number of observations, a high number of variables, or both. In general, many observations improve the precision of ML techniques, like what happens with classical econometric techniques, but when it comes to handling a large number of variables, ML outperforms these econometric methods. There are two main categories of ML: *supervised learning* and *unsupervised learning*.[6] In what follows we will briefly describe these two categories, the corresponding methods of ML, and give examples of their application in portfolio management.

[6]There are other less-used categories of ML, but important in some financial applications, such as reinforcement learning, to which we will dedicate Chapter 10.

**Supervised Learning** In a typical supervised learning scenario, we aim to predict an outcome measurement based on a set of features. To do that, we have a set of data (the *training* set), in which we observe the features and the outcome for a set of objects. Using this data, we develop a prediction model (the *learner*), which will predict the outcome for new unseen objects.

There are several supervised learning methods, with various levels of complexity. In general, more complex methods provide higher prediction performance but less interpretability than simple methods.

The main supervised learning methods are *linear regression with ordinary least squares (OLS) estimator, regularized linear methods, tree-based methods,* and *neural networks.*

- **Linear regression with OLS estimator.** OLS provides an excellent interpretability, but a weak out-of-sample prediction performance. Fama and French (1993) proposed a linear regression for explaining excess returns with an overall market factor, firm size, and book-to-market equity as predictor variables. The Fama-French three factor model will be analyzed in greater depth in Chapter 6.
- **Regularized linear methods.** These methods introduce bias to improve OLS prediction performance. This is achieved by adding a penalty term in the optimization function to penalize large variable coefficients with little informational content. The *least absolute shrinkage and selection operator (LASSO)* method penalizes the $l_1$-norm of the coefficients, driving irrelevant coefficients to zero. In *ridge regression*, the penalty term is the $l_2$-norm, which does not drive coefficients to zero, and thus is less interpretable. *Elastic net regression* uses a penalty term, which is a linear combination of the penalty terms of LASSO and ridge regression. Regularized linear methods have been applied to portfolio selection, in the form of LASSO, within the classical MV framework in Brodie et al. (2009).
- **Tree-based methods.** These methods split the feature space into a set of rectangles and perform a simple fit (usually a constant) in each one. Tree-based methods have been applied to stock selection in Sorensen et al. (2000), which uses a *classification and regression tree (CART)*, and in Tan et al. (2019), which implements a random forest.[7]
- **Neural networks.** A neural network is made up of simple units called *neurons*, which are arranged in *layers*, and *links* between neurons in one layer and the next layer. The *input layer* receives the predictor variables, and the information flows to the next layers (the

[7]A random forest combines the output of a multitude of decision trees to obtain an output that is the class selected by most trees (Breiman, 2001).

*hidden layers*), where it is processed until reaching the *output layer*, which provides the value of the prediction. Typically, each neuron performs a weighted average of its inputs, and after applying a nonlinear function (the *activation function*), the result is sent to the neurons of the next layer to which it is connected.[8] Fernández and Gómez (2007) apply neural networks to the portfolio selection problem in a generalization of the standard Markowitz MV problem.

**Unsupervised Learning** In an unsupervised learning problem, we observe only the features and have no measurements of the outcome. The aim of unsupervised learning is data structure inference.

Among the methods of unsupervised learning, we can highlight *clustering* and *dimensionality reduction.*

- **Clustering.** In this method, observations are grouped into clusters, so that there is high similarity within clusters and low similarity between clusters. *Centroid-based methods* form clusters around multiple central points called *centroids*. One of the most used centroid methods is *K-means*. *Density-based methods* group observations based on the density of points in the observation space. *Distribution-based methods* group data based on the likelihood that they belong to the same probability distribution in the data. *Hierarchical methods* construct clusters with a hierarchical structure that can be represented as a dendrogram. The tree clustering stage of HRP is a hierarchical clustering method. Clustering algorithms have been used to select portfolios in Tola et al. (2008).
- **Dimensionality reduction.** This technique has the objective of decreasing the dimensionality of the dataset while retaining as much information as possible. *Principal Component Analysis (PCA)* consists of achieving linear combinations of the original variables, called *principal components*, so that a few of them explain most of the variance in the data. *Methods based on neural networks* use certain special architectures such as *autoencoders* (Goodfellow et al., 2016). Avellaneda (2020) applies a variant of PCA known as Hierarchical PCA to portfolio management and Heaton et al. (2017) uses autoencoders in portfolio construction.

The number of finance-relevant publications related to ML techniques has increased dramatically in recent years, tripled in 2018, quintupling in

[8]Chapter 11 will be dedicated to a study of neural networks and their applications to portfolio optimization.

2019, and increasing seven- and eleven-fold in 2020 and 2021, respectively. It is expected that this trend will continue in the future, but this will require these techniques to overcome their main limitations, which are low interpretability, the need for large datasets and high computational costs Hoang and Wiegratz (2023). To conclude this chapter dedicated to the history of portfolio optimization, we present in Figure 2.1 a timeline with different portfolio allocation methods.

```
Decade Model
|
1950s-|
|     |-- Modern Portfolio Theory (MPT) [1952]
|     |
1960s-|
|     |-- Capital Asset Pricing Model (CAPM) [1964-1966]
|     |
1970s-|
|     |-- Arbitrage Pricing Theory (APT) [1976]
|     |
1980s-|
|     |
1990s-|-- Black-Litterman Model [1990]
|     |-- Fama-French Three-Factor Model [1992]
|     |-- Conditional Value at Risk (CVaR) [Late 1990s]
|     |
2000s-|-- Risk Parity [Early 2000s]
|     |-- Factor Investing Models
|     |
2010s-|-- Goal-Based Investing Models
|     |-- Fama-French Five-Factor Model [2015]
|     |-- Hierarchical Risk Parity [2016]
|     |-- Early ML applications (e.g., Random Forests, SVMs)
|     |   [Late 2010s]
2020s-|-- Advanced Machine Learning Models
|     |   |-- Deep Neural Networks for asset allocation
|     |   |-- Natural Language Processing for sentiment analysis
|     |   |-- Ensemble Methods for robust predictions
|     |
|     |-- Reinforcement Learning Models
|     |   |-- Deep Q-Networks for trading strategies
|     |   |-- Policy Gradient methods for portfolio optimization
|     |   |-- Multi-Agent RL for market simulation
|
```

**FIGURE 2.1** Timeline of portfolio allocation models.

## 2.5 NOTES

The main references used in Section 2.1 have been Rubinstein (2002) and some works by the father of portfolio theory himself: Markowitz (1952, 1991, 1999). The content of Section 2.2 is based primarily on the original work Markowitz (1952). The mathematical formalism, not included in Markowitz's paper, is inspired by Constantinides and Malliaris (1995).

The first written reference to the Black-Litterman model appeared as a Goldman Sachs report in Black and Litterman (1990). This first work, dedicated to fixed-income securities, was continued by Black and Litterman (1991b), which incorporated equities as well as bonds and currencies. Related papers are He and Litterman (1999) and Black and Litterman (1992a).

The exposition of the Black-Litterman model used here is taken mainly from Black and Litterman (1991a) and Fabozzi et al. (2007) and is known in the literature as mixed estimation method (see also Wey [2023]). An alternative approach, based on Bayesian methods, can be found in Satchell and Scowcroft (2000). Another derivation based on sampling theoretical methods can be found in Mankert and Seiler (2011).

A step-by-step guide to implementing the Black and Litterman model appears in Idzorek (2004). An overview of the model including its derivation, different extensions, advantages and disadvantages, and practical considerations can be found in Kolm et al. (2014a). Different extensions of the original Black and Litterman model have appeared, among which we can mention Meucci (2008), Meucci (2010) and Chen et al. (2015).

In Meucci (2008) an extension of the Black and Litterman model is proposed, known as Entropy Pooling, which allows the inclusion of nonlinear views and non-normal markets. It is a Bayesian model in which the prior is the joint distribution of the risk factors. Managers incorporate their views as functions of the factors, which will be nonlinear. The posterior market distribution is the one that minimizes the relative entropy between the prior factor distribution and the distribution of the manager's views. Furthermore, Meucci introduces a pooling parameter that allows the manager's level of confidence in his views to be adjusted.

The main references for risk parity have been Qian (2005) and Maillard et al. (2010). The analysis carried out with volatility as a risk measure can be extended to VaR (Qian, (2006) and other measures Stefanovits (2010). Alternative algorithms to those presented here for obtaining ERC portfolios can be found in Chaves et al. (2012).

Various extensions to the initial ERC portfolio model have been developed, among which we can mention Kaya and Lee (2012), based on utility maximization; Fisher et al. (2015), where the study of Risk Parity Portfolios is addressed from the point of view of Game Theory; Roncalli and Weisang (2016), which includes risk factors in the analysis; and Haugh et al. (2014), which presents the so-called Generalized Risk Budgeting approach. Another interesting line of research, derived from risk parity analysis, is what is known as *Diversified Risk Parity*, which began with Meucci (2009) and has been continued by Lohre et al. (2012) and Lohre et al. (2014). It is based on Principal component analysis and computes the allocations so that the contribution to risk of each principal component is the same.

The exposition of HRP is based mainly on López de Prado (2016b, 2018). Other references used have been Raffinot (2018a) and Kaae and Karppinen (2022). See the Notes of Chapter 12 for more references related to HRP.

The presentation of Machine Learning methods is inspired by Hoang and Wiegratz (2023) and Hastie et al. (2009). Some interesting studies with extensive literature reviews can be found in Cavalcante et al. (2016), Nazareth and Ramana Reddy (2023) and Sutiene et al. (2024).

# PART One

# Foundations of Portfolio Theory

CHAPTER 3

# Modern Portfolio Theory

Building on the foundational work of Markowitz, this chapter is dedicated to a detailed study of the three branches of what is currently known as Modern Portfolio Theory: Mean-Variance (MV) Analysis, Capital Asset Pricing Model (CAPM), and Arbitrage Pricing Theory (APT).

These related approaches are decades old, and their advantages and disadvantages are well known. However, since they provide the conceptual and terminological basis for all modern developments in Portfolio Management, they deserve a chapter in this book. Furthermore, most expositions of Modern Portfolio Theory address specific parts of the theory and lack detailed proofs and explanations of the main concepts.

We develop an in-depth study of the main aspects of the theory, with rigorous statements and proofs of the results, in a concise and self-contained way. Additional references, extensions and practical issues are deferred to the Notes section at the end of the chapter.

## 3.1 EFFICIENT FRONTIER AND CAPITAL MARKET LINE

We introduced in Section 2.2 the MV problem and presented the associated optimization program in equation (2.4). In this section, we first solve this program as it was previously stated, and then we consider an extension including the presence of a riskless asset in the portfolios.

### 3.1.1 Case Without Riskless Asset

We recall here the MV optimization program in equation (2.4) in the slightly different form

$$\begin{aligned} \min \quad & \frac{1}{2}\mathbf{w}^T\boldsymbol{\Sigma}\mathbf{w} \\ \text{s.t.} \quad & \begin{bmatrix}\mathbf{1} & \mathbf{R}\end{bmatrix}^T \mathbf{w} = \begin{bmatrix}1 \\ R_p\end{bmatrix}, \end{aligned} \tag{3.1}$$

where we have taken transpose in the restrictions of equation (2.4), and we have expressed them in a more compact form. The factor $\frac{1}{2}$ does not alter the result and has been included for convenience. The explicit solution of the MV optimization problem in equation (3.1) was not presented in Markowitz's 1952 paper, and was Merton who obtained it analytically (Merton, 1972). We present the solution of the MV problem in the following result.

**Theorem 3.1** *If not all components of* **R** *are equal, the minimum variance portfolio, solution of equation (3.1), is given by*

$$\mathbf{w} = \boldsymbol{\Sigma}^{-1} \begin{bmatrix} \mathbf{1} & \mathbf{R} \end{bmatrix} \boldsymbol{\Pi}^{-1} \begin{bmatrix} 1 \\ R_p \end{bmatrix}, \tag{3.2}$$

*where the matrix* $\boldsymbol{\Pi}$ *is the invertible square matrix defined by*

$$\boldsymbol{\Pi} = \begin{bmatrix} \mathbf{1} & \mathbf{R} \end{bmatrix}^T \boldsymbol{\Sigma}^{-1} \begin{bmatrix} \mathbf{1} & \mathbf{R} \end{bmatrix}. \tag{3.3}$$

*The variance of this portfolio,* $\sigma_p^2$, *can be written as*

$$\sigma_p^2 = \frac{aR_p^2 - 2bR_p + c}{d}, \tag{3.4}$$

*where* $a = \mathbf{1}^T\boldsymbol{\Sigma}^{-1}\mathbf{1} > 0$, $b = \mathbf{1}^T\boldsymbol{\Sigma}^{-1}\mathbf{R}$, $c = \mathbf{R}^T\boldsymbol{\Sigma}^{-1}\mathbf{R}$ *and* $d = ac - b^2$.

*Proof.* The Lagrangian corresponding to the program in equation (3.1) is

$$L(\mathbf{w}, \lambda) = \frac{1}{2}\mathbf{w}^T\boldsymbol{\Sigma}\mathbf{w} - \lambda^T \left( \begin{bmatrix} \mathbf{1} & \mathbf{R} \end{bmatrix}^T \mathbf{w} - \begin{bmatrix} 1 \\ R_p \end{bmatrix} \right),$$

and the first-order conditions can be written as

$$\frac{\partial L}{\partial \mathbf{w}} = \boldsymbol{\Sigma}\mathbf{w} - \begin{bmatrix} \mathbf{1} & \mathbf{R} \end{bmatrix} \lambda = 0 \tag{3.5}$$

$$\frac{\partial L}{\partial \lambda} = \begin{bmatrix} \mathbf{1} & \mathbf{R} \end{bmatrix}^T \mathbf{w} - \begin{bmatrix} 1 \\ R_p \end{bmatrix} = 0. \tag{3.6}$$

As $\boldsymbol{\Sigma}$ is assumed to be invertible, we obtain from equation (3.5)

$$\mathbf{w} = \boldsymbol{\Sigma}^{-1} \begin{bmatrix} \mathbf{1} & \mathbf{R} \end{bmatrix} \lambda. \tag{3.7}$$

Replacing this expression in (3.6), we get

$$\begin{bmatrix} 1 & \mathbf{R} \end{bmatrix}^T \boldsymbol{\Sigma}^{-1} \begin{bmatrix} 1 & \mathbf{R} \end{bmatrix} \lambda = \begin{bmatrix} 1 \\ R_p \end{bmatrix},$$

which can be rewritten as

$$\boldsymbol{\Pi}\lambda = \begin{bmatrix} 1 \\ R_p \end{bmatrix}, \tag{3.8}$$

where the square $2 \times 2$ matrix $\boldsymbol{\Pi}$ is given by equation (3.3)

$$\boldsymbol{\Pi} = \begin{bmatrix} 1 & \mathbf{R} \end{bmatrix}^T \boldsymbol{\Sigma}^{-1} \begin{bmatrix} 1 & \mathbf{R} \end{bmatrix} = \begin{bmatrix} \mathbf{1}^T\boldsymbol{\Sigma}^{-1}\mathbf{1} & \mathbf{1}^T\boldsymbol{\Sigma}^{-1}\mathbf{R} \\ \mathbf{R}^T\boldsymbol{\Sigma}^{-1}\mathbf{1} & \mathbf{R}^T\boldsymbol{\Sigma}^{-1}\mathbf{R} \end{bmatrix} = \begin{bmatrix} a & b \\ b & c \end{bmatrix}.$$

In the last step we have used that $\boldsymbol{\Sigma}$ is a symmetric matrix, whereby $\boldsymbol{\Sigma}^{-1}$ is also symmetric, and then $\mathbf{R}^T\boldsymbol{\Sigma}^{-1}\mathbf{1} = \mathbf{1}^T\boldsymbol{\Sigma}^{-1}\mathbf{R} = b$.

Under the assumptions of the theorem, the matrix $\boldsymbol{\Pi}$ is positive definite. To prove this, consider any $\begin{bmatrix} x_1 \\ x_2 \end{bmatrix} \neq \begin{bmatrix} 0 \\ 0 \end{bmatrix}$. We can write

$$\begin{aligned} \begin{bmatrix} x_1, & x_2 \end{bmatrix} \boldsymbol{\Pi} \begin{bmatrix} x_1 \\ x_2 \end{bmatrix} &= \begin{bmatrix} x_1, & x_2 \end{bmatrix} \begin{bmatrix} 1 & \mathbf{R} \end{bmatrix}^T \boldsymbol{\Sigma}^{-1} \begin{bmatrix} 1 & \mathbf{R} \end{bmatrix} \begin{bmatrix} x_1 \\ x_2 \end{bmatrix} \\ &= (x_1\mathbf{1} + x_2\mathbf{R})^T \boldsymbol{\Sigma}^{-1} (x_1\mathbf{1} + x_2\mathbf{R}) > 0 \end{aligned}$$

since $(x_1\mathbf{1} + x_2\mathbf{R}) \neq 0$, because not all $R_j$ are equal. Thus, $\boldsymbol{\Pi}$ is non-singular, and we can solve the system (3.8) obtaining

$$\lambda = \boldsymbol{\Pi}^{-1} \begin{bmatrix} 1 \\ R_p \end{bmatrix}.$$

Replacing this expression in equation (3.7) we arrive at equation (3.2). The portfolio variance is obtained replacing $\mathbf{w}$ from equation (3.2) in $\sigma_p^2 = \mathbf{w}^T \boldsymbol{\Sigma} \mathbf{w}$:

$$\sigma_p^2 = \begin{bmatrix} 1, & R_p \end{bmatrix} \left(\boldsymbol{\Pi}^{-1}\right)^T \begin{bmatrix} \mathbf{1} & \mathbf{R} \end{bmatrix}^T \left(\boldsymbol{\Sigma}^{-1}\right)^T \boldsymbol{\Sigma}\boldsymbol{\Sigma}^{-1} \begin{bmatrix} \mathbf{1} & \mathbf{R} \end{bmatrix} \boldsymbol{\Pi}^{-1} \begin{bmatrix} 1 \\ R_p \end{bmatrix}$$

$$= \begin{bmatrix} 1, & R_p \end{bmatrix} \left(\boldsymbol{\Pi}^{-1}\right)^T \boldsymbol{\Pi}\boldsymbol{\Pi}^{-1} \begin{bmatrix} 1 \\ R_p \end{bmatrix} = \begin{bmatrix} 1, & R_p \end{bmatrix} \boldsymbol{\Pi}^{-1} \begin{bmatrix} 1 \\ R_p \end{bmatrix}, \tag{3.9}$$

where we have used the symmetry of $\boldsymbol{\Sigma}$ and $\boldsymbol{\Pi}$. Replacing

$$\boldsymbol{\Pi}^{-1} = \frac{1}{d} \begin{bmatrix} c & -b \\ -b & a \end{bmatrix} \tag{3.10}$$

in equation (3.9), we obtain the expression in equation (3.4). Finally, $a > 0$ since $\boldsymbol{\Sigma}^{-1}$ is positive definite as $\boldsymbol{\Sigma}$. ■

Equation (3.4) expresses the minimum portfolio variance we can achieve for a given expected portfolio return $R_p$, and determines a parabola in the space expected return-variance, called *minimum variance portfolio frontier*. Note that, for $(R_p, \sigma_p^2)$ be a minimum, it must be the case that $\frac{a}{d} > 0$ and, given that $a > 0$, we have that $d > 0$.

The portfolio with the smallest possible variance for any given expected portfolio return is called *global minimum variance portfolio*, and its characteristics are presented in the following result.

**Proposition 3.1** *The expected return,* $R_G$, *variance,* $\sigma_G^2$, *and weights vector,* $\mathbf{w}_G$, *of the global minimum variance portfolio, are given by*

$$\begin{aligned} R_G &= \frac{b}{a} \\ \sigma_G^2 &= \frac{1}{a} \\ \mathbf{w}_G &= \frac{1}{a} \boldsymbol{\Sigma}^{-1} \mathbf{1}. \end{aligned} \tag{3.11}$$

*Proof.* Applying the well-known expression for the vertex of a parabola, we find the first equation. Replacing this result in equation (3.4) and using that $d = ac - b^2$, we obtain $\sigma_G^2$. For the third equation, using equations (3.2), (3.10), and the value of $R_G$, we have

$$\mathbf{w}_G = \mathbf{\Sigma}^{-1}\begin{bmatrix}\mathbf{1} & \mathbf{R}\end{bmatrix}\frac{1}{d}\begin{bmatrix} c & -b \\ -b & a \end{bmatrix}\begin{bmatrix} 1 \\ b/a \end{bmatrix} = \mathbf{\Sigma}^{-1}\begin{bmatrix}\mathbf{1} & \mathbf{R}\end{bmatrix}\frac{1}{d}\begin{bmatrix} c - b^2/a \\ 0 \end{bmatrix},$$
$$= \frac{c - b^2/a}{d}\mathbf{\Sigma}^{-1}\mathbf{1} = \frac{1}{a}\mathbf{\Sigma}^{-1}\mathbf{1}$$

which concludes the proof. ■

As the minimum variance frontier has two symmetric parts, divided by $R_G = \frac{b}{a}$, for each value of the variance $\sigma_p^2 \neq \sigma_G^2$, we have two portfolios with different expected returns. The part with $R_p > \frac{b}{a}$ contains the portfolios with the highest return for a given variance, and it is called *mean-variance efficient frontier*.

If we represent the minimum variance portfolio frontier in the space expected return-standard deviation, we obtain a hyperbola, given by

$$\sigma_p = \sqrt{\frac{aR_p^2 - 2bR_p + c}{d}}. \tag{3.12}$$

The usual representation of the mean-variance portfolio frontier depicts $\sigma_p$ in the horizontal axis and $R_p$ in the vertical axis as in Figure 3.1.

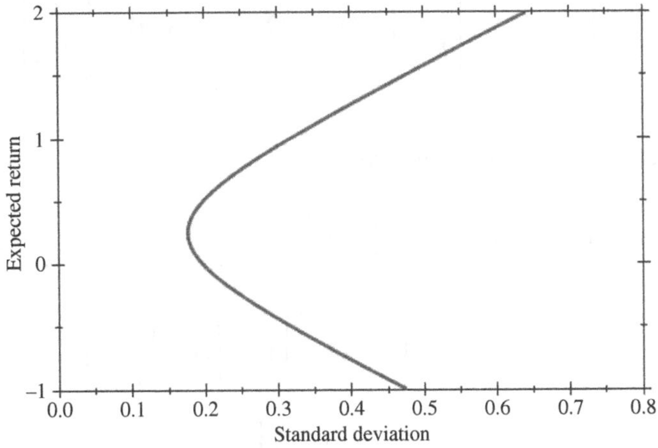


**FIGURE 3.1** Minimum variance frontier.

The following result states an important property of minimum variance portfolios known as *two-fund separation*: The entire minimum variance portfolio frontier can be generated by specific linear combinations of any two different minimum variance portfolios. Moreover, any convex combination of two different minimum variance efficient portfolios is also a minimum variance efficient portfolio.

**Theorem 3.2** *(Two-fund separation) Consider two minimum variance portfolios, $\mathbf{w}_a$ and $\mathbf{w}_b$, with expected returns $R_{p,a}$ and $R_{p,b}$, respectively, and such that $R_{p,a} \neq R_{p,b}$. Then:*

*a) $\mathbf{w}$ is a minimum variance portfolio, if and only if $\mathbf{w} = \alpha \mathbf{w}_a + (1-\alpha)\mathbf{w}_b$, with $\alpha \in \mathbb{R}$.*

*b) If $\mathbf{w}_a$ and $\mathbf{w}_b$ are minimum variance efficient portfolios, then $\alpha \mathbf{w}_a + (1-\alpha)\mathbf{w}_b$ is a minimum variance efficient portfolio for any $\alpha$ with $0 \le \alpha \le 1$.*

*Proof.* a) For the necessary condition, let $R_p$ be the expected return of the portfolio $\mathbf{w}$, and choose $\alpha = \frac{R_p - R_{p,b}}{R_{p,a} - R_{p,b}}$. As $\mathbf{w}$ is a minimum variance portfolio, by (3.2) we obtain

$$\mathbf{w} = \boldsymbol{\Sigma}^{-1}\begin{bmatrix}\mathbf{1} & \mathbf{R}\end{bmatrix}\boldsymbol{\Pi}^{-1}\begin{bmatrix}1\\ R_p\end{bmatrix} = \boldsymbol{\Sigma}^{-1}\begin{bmatrix}\mathbf{1} & \mathbf{R}\end{bmatrix}\boldsymbol{\Pi}^{-1}\begin{bmatrix}\alpha + (1-\alpha)\\ \alpha R_{p,a} + (1-\alpha)R_{p,b}\end{bmatrix}$$

$$= \alpha\boldsymbol{\Sigma}^{-1}\begin{bmatrix}\mathbf{1} & \mathbf{R}\end{bmatrix}\boldsymbol{\Pi}^{-1}\begin{bmatrix}1\\ R_{p,a}\end{bmatrix} + (1-\alpha)\boldsymbol{\Sigma}^{-1}\begin{bmatrix}\mathbf{1} & \mathbf{R}\end{bmatrix}\boldsymbol{\Pi}^{-1}\begin{bmatrix}1\\ R_{p,b}\end{bmatrix}.$$

$$= \alpha\mathbf{w}_a + (1-\alpha)\mathbf{w}_b$$

The sufficient condition follows from

$$\alpha\mathbf{w}_a + (1-\alpha)\mathbf{w}_b = \alpha\boldsymbol{\Sigma}^{-1}\begin{bmatrix}\mathbf{1} & \mathbf{R}\end{bmatrix}\boldsymbol{\Pi}^{-1}\begin{bmatrix}1\\ R_{p,a}\end{bmatrix}$$

$$+ (1-\alpha)\boldsymbol{\Sigma}^{-1}\begin{bmatrix}\mathbf{1} & \mathbf{R}\end{bmatrix}\boldsymbol{\Pi}^{-1}\begin{bmatrix}1\\ R_{p,b}\end{bmatrix}$$

$$= \boldsymbol{\Sigma}^{-1}\begin{bmatrix}\mathbf{1} & \mathbf{R}\end{bmatrix}\boldsymbol{\Pi}^{-1}\begin{bmatrix}1\\ \alpha R_{p,a} + (1-\alpha)R_{p,b}\end{bmatrix}.$$

b) By a), we know that $\alpha\mathbf{w}_a + (1-\alpha)\mathbf{w}_b$ is a minimum variance portfolio, and thus we only need to prove that $R > R_G$, where $R_G$ is the expected return of the global minimum variance portfolio. As $\mathbf{w}_a$ and $\mathbf{w}_b$ are minimum variance efficient portfolios, we have that $R_{p,a}, R_{p,b} > R_G$. Suppose without losing generality, that $R_{p,a} < R_{p,b}$. Since $0 \leq \alpha \leq 1$, and $R = \alpha R_{p,a} + (1-\alpha) R_{p,b}$, we have $R_{p,a} \leq R_p \leq R_{p,b}$, and then, $R > R_G$. ■

Part b) of Theorem 3.2 has an interesting economic implication. An investor who wants to invest in a specific minimum variance efficient portfolio does not need to select the appropriate weights in the $n$ assets. Instead, she can just divide her wealth between two mutual funds if they are minimum variance portfolios.

### 3.1.2 Case with a Riskless Asset

Now we incorporate a riskless asset in our portfolios, with constant return $R_0$, and weight $w_0$. We maintain the notation $\mathbf{w}$ for the portfolio of risky assets, which now must satisfy the new restriction $w_0 + \mathbf{w}^T\mathbf{1} = 1$. Instead of working with the vector of expected returns of risky assets, now we will work with the vector of *expected excess returns*, $\mathbf{E} = (E_1, \dots, E_n)^T$, with $E_i = R_i - R_0$, $i = 1, \dots, n$.

The expected excess return of a portfolio composed of risky assets and the riskless asset, $E_p$, is given by

$$E_p = \left(\mathbf{w}^T\mathbf{R} + w_0 R_0\right) - R_0 = \mathbf{w}^T\mathbf{R} + \left(1 - \mathbf{w}^T\mathbf{1}\right) R_0 - R_0 = \mathbf{w}^T\mathbf{E}$$

and its variance is $\sigma_p^2 = \mathbf{w}^T\boldsymbol{\Sigma}\mathbf{w}$, since the riskless asset has zero variance.

The MV optimization program in this case is

$$\begin{aligned} \min \quad & \frac{1}{2}\mathbf{w}^T\boldsymbol{\Sigma}\mathbf{w} \\ \text{s.t.} \quad & \mathbf{w}^T\mathbf{E} = E_p \end{aligned} \tag{3.13}$$

and its solution is given in the following result, analogous to Theorem 3.1.

**Theorem 3.3** *The minimum variance portfolio, solution of (3.13), is given by*

$$\mathbf{w} = \frac{E_p}{\mathbf{E}^T\boldsymbol{\Sigma}^{-1}\mathbf{E}}\boldsymbol{\Sigma}^{-1}\mathbf{E}. \tag{3.14}$$

*The variance of this portfolio, $\sigma_p^2$, can be written as*

$$\sigma_p^2 = \frac{1}{\mathbf{E}^T\boldsymbol{\Sigma}^{-1}\mathbf{E}}E_p^2. \tag{3.15}$$

*Proof.* The Lagrangian of the problem is

$$L(\mathbf{w}, \lambda) = \frac{1}{2}\mathbf{w}^T\mathbf{\Sigma}\mathbf{w} - \lambda\left(\mathbf{w}^T\mathbf{E} - E_p\right)$$

and its first-order conditions are

$$\frac{\partial L}{\partial \mathbf{w}} = \mathbf{\Sigma}\mathbf{w} - \lambda\mathbf{E} = 0 \tag{3.16}$$

$$\frac{\partial L}{\partial \lambda} = \mathbf{w}^T\mathbf{E} - E_p = 0. \tag{3.17}$$

Recalling that $\mathbf{\Sigma}$ is invertible, from (3.16) we have

$$\mathbf{w} = \lambda\mathbf{\Sigma}^{-1}\mathbf{E}. \tag{3.18}$$

Replacing this result in equation (3.17) and using $\left(\mathbf{\Sigma}^{-1}\right)^T = \mathbf{\Sigma}^{-1}$, we obtain the Lagrange multiplier as

$$\lambda = \frac{E_p}{\mathbf{E}^T\mathbf{\Sigma}^{-1}\mathbf{E}},$$

which substituted in equation (3.18) gives equation (3.14). Equation (3.15) is immediate from the expression of $\sigma_p^2$ and (3.14). ■

In order to represent equation (3.15) in the space expected return-standard deviation, taking square root and using that $E_p = R_p - R_0$, we obtain

$$R_p = R_0 \pm \sqrt{\mathbf{E}^T\mathbf{\Sigma}^{-1}\mathbf{E}}\sigma_p \tag{3.19}$$

that are the equations of two rays emanating from the point $\left(\sigma_p, R_p\right) = (0, R_0)$ and with slopes $\pm\sqrt{\mathbf{E}^T\mathbf{\Sigma}^{-1}\mathbf{E}}$, which constitute the MV frontier when a riskless asset is present.

Now, it is reasonable to ask if there is some relation between the hyperbola of the case with only risky assets and the cone corresponding to the case with a riskless asset. Assuming that the expected return of the MV portfolio is greater than the return of the riskless asset, which is an economically meaningful assumption, the following result affirms that there is a unique point in which the rays of equation (3.19) are tangent to the hyperbola of equation (3.12).

**Theorem 3.4** ***(Tangency portfolio)*** *If* $\mathbf{E} \neq 0$ *and* $R_0 < R_G$*, then there is a unique portfolio,* $\mathbf{w}_T$*, that belongs to the efficient frontiers with and without risk-free asset, and it is given by*

$$\mathbf{w}_T = \frac{1}{\mathbf{1}^T\boldsymbol{\Sigma}^{-1}\mathbf{E}}\boldsymbol{\Sigma}^{-1}\mathbf{E} \tag{3.20}$$

*This portfolio corresponds to the point of tangency between both efficient frontiers, and its coordinates* $\left(\sigma_{p,T}, R_{p,T}\right)$ *are*

$$\sigma_{p,T} = \frac{\sqrt{aR_0^2 - 2bR_0 + c}}{b - aR_0} \tag{3.21}$$

$$R_{p,T} = \frac{c - bR_0}{b - aR_0}, \tag{3.22}$$

*Proof.* As $\mathbf{w}_T$ belongs to the efficient frontier without riskless asset, we have $w_0 = 0$, and then, using equation (3.14), we can write

$$1 = \mathbf{w}^T\mathbf{1} = \mathbf{1}^T\mathbf{w} = \frac{E_p}{\mathbf{E}^T\boldsymbol{\Sigma}^{-1}\mathbf{E}}\mathbf{1}^T\boldsymbol{\Sigma}^{-1}\mathbf{E},$$

from where we obtain

$$E_{p,T} = \frac{\mathbf{E}^T\boldsymbol{\Sigma}^{-1}\mathbf{E}}{\mathbf{1}^T\boldsymbol{\Sigma}^{-1}\mathbf{E}}, \tag{3.23}$$

where $E_{p,T}$ is the expected excess return of the portfolio $\mathbf{w}_T$. Replacing equation (3.23) in (3.14), we obtain expression in equation (3.20).

As $\mathbf{E} \neq 0$, the positive definiteness of $\boldsymbol{\Sigma}^{-1}$ implies $\mathbf{E}^T\boldsymbol{\Sigma}^{-1}\mathbf{E} > 0$. On the other hand:

$$\mathbf{1}^T\boldsymbol{\Sigma}^{-1}\mathbf{E} = \mathbf{1}^T\boldsymbol{\Sigma}^{-1}\mathbf{R} - R_0\mathbf{1}^T\boldsymbol{\Sigma}^{-1}\mathbf{1} = b - R_0 a > 0 \tag{3.24}$$

where we have used that $R_0 < R_G = \frac{b}{a}$. These two last inequalities lead to $E_{p,T} > 0$. From equation (3.19), we have $E_p = \pm\sqrt{\mathbf{E}^T\boldsymbol{\Sigma}^{-1}\mathbf{E}}\sigma_p$. As $\sigma_p > 0$ and $E_{p,T} > 0$, we have that

$$E_{p,T} = \sqrt{\mathbf{E}^T\boldsymbol{\Sigma}^{-1}\mathbf{E}}\sigma_{p,T} \tag{3.25}$$

and then, the portfolio given by equation (3.20) belongs to the ray with positive slope, that is, the efficient frontier.

The coordinates $(\sigma_{p,T}, R_{p,T})$ of the portfolio $\mathbf{w}_T$ can be obtained as follows:

$$\sigma_{p,T}^2 = \mathbf{w}_T^T \boldsymbol{\Sigma} \mathbf{w}^T = \frac{1}{\left(1^T\boldsymbol{\Sigma}^{-1}\mathbf{E}\right)^2}\mathbf{E}^T\boldsymbol{\Sigma}^{-1}\boldsymbol{\Sigma}\boldsymbol{\Sigma}^{-1}\mathbf{E} = \frac{1}{\left(1^T\boldsymbol{\Sigma}^{-1}\mathbf{E}\right)^2}\mathbf{E}^T\boldsymbol{\Sigma}^{-1}\mathbf{E}$$

$$= \frac{(\mathbf{R} - R_0\mathbf{1})^T\boldsymbol{\Sigma}^{-1}(\mathbf{R} - R_0\mathbf{1})}{\left(1^T\boldsymbol{\Sigma}^{-1}\mathbf{E}\right)^2} = \frac{aR_0^2 - 2bR_0 + c}{(b - aR_0)^2}$$

$$R_{p,T} = R_0 + E_{p,T} = R_0 + \frac{\mathbf{E}^T\boldsymbol{\Sigma}^{-1}\mathbf{E}}{1^T\boldsymbol{\Sigma}^{-1}\mathbf{E}} = R_0 + \frac{aR_0^2 - 2bR_0 + c}{b - aR_0} = \frac{c - bR_0}{b - aR_0},$$

where in the last expression we have used in equation (3.24).

To see that $(\sigma_{p,T}, R_{p,T})$ is a tangency point between the two efficient frontiers, we only must check the equality of the slopes at that point. Taking partial derivative on (3.4) we have

$$\frac{\partial \sigma_p}{\partial R_p}(R_p) = \frac{aR_p - b}{d\sigma_p},$$

from where we obtain the slope of the hyperbola at the point $(\sigma_{p,T}, R_{p,T})$ as

$$\frac{\partial \sigma_p}{\partial R_p}(R_{p,T}) = \frac{a\left(\frac{c-bR_0}{b-aR_0}\right) - b}{d\frac{\sqrt{aR_0^2-2bR_0+c}}{b-aR_0}} = \frac{1}{\sqrt{aR_0^2 - 2bR_0 + c}}. \tag{3.26}$$

On the other hand, we can obtain from equation (3.19) the slope of the efficient line as

$$\frac{\partial \sigma_p}{\partial R_p}(R_p) = \frac{1}{\sqrt{\mathbf{E}^T\boldsymbol{\Sigma}^{-1}\mathbf{E}}} = \frac{1}{\sqrt{aR_0^2 - 2bR_0 + c}}. \tag{3.27}$$

As the slopes of equations (3.26) and (3.27) coincides, the point $(\sigma_{p,T}, R_{p,T})$ is a point of tangency. ■

The portfolio $\mathbf{w}_T$ of equation (3.20) is known as *tangency portfolio* in the literature, and the efficient frontier when a riskless asset is considered (the ray with positive slope) is called the *capital market line* (CML, see Figure 3.2).

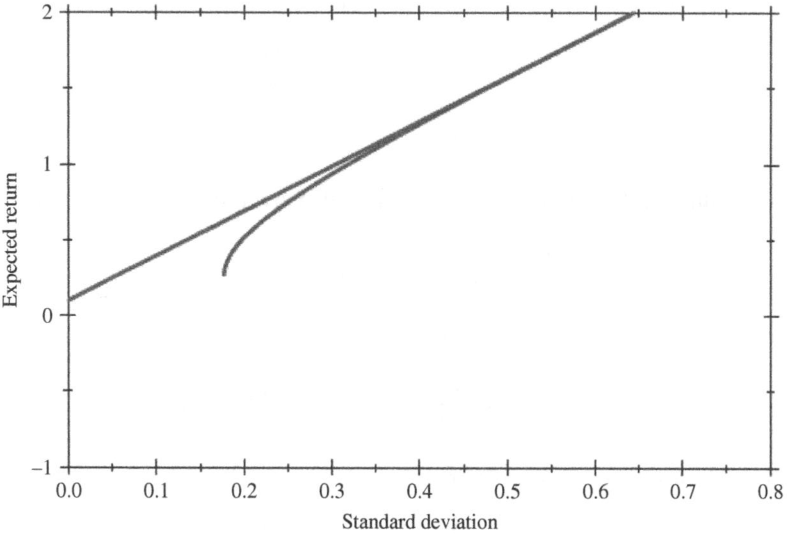


**FIGURE 3.2** Mean-variance efficient frontier and capital market line.

Following what was made in Theorem 3.2, it is not difficult to show that a two-fund separation theorem also holds when we include a riskless asset. For each minimum variance portfolio $\mathbf{w}$ satisfying equation (3.14) we have that $\mathbf{w} = \alpha \mathbf{w}_T$, with $\alpha = \frac{\mathbf{1}^T \Sigma^{-1} \mathbf{E}}{\mathbf{E}^T \Sigma^{-1} \mathbf{E}} E_p \in \mathbb{R}$. Thus, in the case with a riskless asset, we have the advantage that we can obtain any efficient portfolio as a linear combination of the riskless asset and the tangency portfolio, that is, we can choose the two mutual funds to be the riskless asset and a portfolio with only risky assets.

Another interesting property of the tangency portfolio is related to a concept used to measure the performance of a portfolio, namely, the *Sharpe ratio*, $S_p$, defined as the quotient between the expected excess return of the portfolio and the standard deviation of its return

$$S_p = \frac{R_p - R_0}{\sigma_p} = \frac{E_p}{\sigma_p}.$$

**Proposition 3.2** *The tangency portfolio is the portfolio with the highest Sharpe ratio among all the portfolios without riskless asset.*

*Proof.* We just have to prove that the optimization problem

$$\begin{aligned} \max \quad & S_p = \frac{R_p - R_0}{\sigma_p} = \frac{\mathbf{R}^T\mathbf{w} - R_0}{\sqrt{\mathbf{w}^T\boldsymbol{\Sigma}\mathbf{w}}} \\ \text{s.t.} \quad & \mathbf{w}^T\mathbf{1} = 1 \end{aligned}$$

has as solution the portfolio with Sharpe ratio given by (see equation [3.25])

$$\frac{E_{p,T}}{\sigma_{p,T}} = \sqrt{\mathbf{E}^T\boldsymbol{\Sigma}^{-1}\mathbf{E}}.$$

The Lagrangian of the problem is

$$L(\mathbf{w}, \lambda) = \frac{\mathbf{R}^T\mathbf{w} - R_0}{\sqrt{\mathbf{w}^T\boldsymbol{\Sigma}\mathbf{w}}} - \lambda\left(\mathbf{w}^T\mathbf{1} - 1\right),$$

and the first-order conditions are

$$\frac{\partial L}{\partial \mathbf{w}} = \frac{\left(\mathbf{w}^T\boldsymbol{\Sigma}\mathbf{w}\right)\mathbf{R} - \left(\mathbf{R}^T\mathbf{w} - R_0\right)\boldsymbol{\Sigma}\mathbf{w}}{\mathbf{w}^T\boldsymbol{\Sigma}\mathbf{w}\sqrt{\mathbf{w}^T\boldsymbol{\Sigma}\mathbf{w}}} - \lambda\mathbf{1} = 0 \tag{3.28}$$

$$\frac{\partial L}{\partial \lambda} = 1 - \mathbf{w}^T\mathbf{1} = 0. \tag{3.29}$$

From equation (3.28), we have

$$\frac{\mathbf{R}}{\sqrt{\mathbf{w}^T\boldsymbol{\Sigma}\mathbf{w}}} - \frac{\left(\mathbf{R}^T\mathbf{w} - R_0\right)}{\mathbf{w}^T\boldsymbol{\Sigma}\mathbf{w}\sqrt{\mathbf{w}^T\boldsymbol{\Sigma}\mathbf{w}}} - \lambda\mathbf{1} = 0. \tag{3.30}$$

Premultiplying by $\mathbf{w}^T$ and applying equation (3.29), we obtain the Lagrange multiplier $\lambda = \frac{R_0}{\sqrt{\mathbf{w}^T\boldsymbol{\Sigma}\mathbf{w}}}$. Replacing this value in equation (3.30) and using the equalities $\mathbf{R} - R_0\mathbf{1} = \mathbf{E}$, and $\frac{\mathbf{R}^T\mathbf{w} - R_0}{\sqrt{\mathbf{w}^T\boldsymbol{\Sigma}\mathbf{w}}} = S_p$, we arrive at

$$\mathbf{E} = \frac{S_p}{\sqrt{\mathbf{w}^T\boldsymbol{\Sigma}\mathbf{w}}}\boldsymbol{\Sigma}\mathbf{w},$$

from where we can write

$$\mathbf{E}^T\boldsymbol{\Sigma}^{-1}\mathbf{E} = \frac{S_p^2}{\mathbf{w}^T\boldsymbol{\Sigma}\mathbf{w}}\mathbf{w}^T\boldsymbol{\Sigma}^T\boldsymbol{\Sigma}^{-1}\boldsymbol{\Sigma}\mathbf{w} = S_p^2,$$

and then $S_p = \pm\sqrt{\mathbf{E}^T\boldsymbol{\Sigma}^{-1}\mathbf{E}}$. The minus sign corresponds to the minimum Sharpe ratio, and $S_p = \sqrt{\mathbf{E}^T\boldsymbol{\Sigma}^{-1}\mathbf{E}}$ is the maximum Sharpe ratio. ■

We conclude this section with two properties related to the capital market line. The first one states that, for a given level of volatility, an investor will always prefer a portfolio with a riskless asset, except in the case of the tangency portfolio. The second one describes the characteristics of portfolios in the CML on both sides of the tangency portfolio.

**Proposition 3.3** *Under the conditions of Theorem 3.4, for any fixed value of $\sigma_p \geq \sigma_G$, the return of the efficient portfolio of the CML is greater than the return of the efficient portfolio without risky asset, except when $\sigma_p = \sigma_{p,T}$, in which case the returns are equal.*

*Proof.* The case with $\sigma_p = \sigma_{p,T}$ is immediate from the definition of the tangency portfolio. For the case in which $\sigma_p \neq \sigma_{p,T}$, as we know that there is only one point in common between both efficient frontiers, we just need to find one value of $\sigma_p$ for which the return in the CML is the highest. Consider the point $\sigma_p = \sigma_G$. The corresponding value of the portfolio return on the CML can be obtained from equation (3.19) as

$$R_p = R_0 + \sqrt{\mathbf{E}^T\mathbf{\Sigma}^{-1}\mathbf{E}}\sigma_p = R_0 + \sqrt{aR_0^2 - 2bR_0 + c}\frac{1}{\sqrt{a}}$$

$$= R_0 + \sqrt{R_G^2 - 2R_GR_0 + \frac{c}{a}} = R_0 + \sqrt{(R_G - R_0)^2 + \frac{d}{a^2}},$$

where we have used that $\mathbf{E}^T\mathbf{\Sigma}^{-1}\mathbf{E} = aR_0^2 - 2bR_0 + c$ (see proof of Theorem 3.4), $\sigma_p = \sigma_G = \frac{1}{\sqrt{a}}$ and $d = ca - b^2$. As $d > 0$, we have $R_p > R_G$. Then, at the point $\sigma_p = \sigma_G$, the CML is above the hyperbola, which concludes the proof. ∎

**Proposition 3.4** *Under the conditions of Theorem 3.4, points on the CML with $\sigma_p > \sigma_{p,T}$ ($\sigma_p < \sigma_{p,T}$) correspond to portfolios with a short (long) position in the riskless asset.*

*Proof.* Premultiplying equation (3.14) by $\mathbf{1}^T$ and taking into account equation (3.23), we obtain

$$\mathbf{1}^T\mathbf{w} = \frac{E_p}{\mathbf{E}^T\mathbf{\Sigma}^{-1}\mathbf{E}}\mathbf{1}^T\mathbf{\Sigma}^{-1}\mathbf{E} = \frac{E_p}{E_{p,T}},$$

which is valid for any MV portfolio with a riskless asset. As the efficient frontier in this case is the CML, given by $E_p = \sqrt{\mathbf{E}^T\mathbf{\Sigma}^{-1}\mathbf{E}}\sigma_p$, we have that

$E_p$ is increasing with $\sigma_p$. Then, $\sigma_p > \sigma_{p,T}$ implies $E_p > E_{p,T}$, and $\mathbf{1}^T\mathbf{w} > 1$. Using the portfolio restriction $w_0 + \mathbf{w}^T\mathbf{1} = 1$, we find $w_0 < 0$. The case with $\sigma_p < \sigma_{p,T}$ can be proven analogously. ■

## 3.2 CAPITAL ASSET PRICING MODEL

In this section, we will obtain the Capital Asset Pricing Model (CAPM) in two different but related versions, corresponding to the two cases of the previous section, namely, absence or existence of a riskless asset. In the first situation, we will find the so-called zero beta CAPM of Black (1972). The second case, in which a riskless asset is present, is the standard CAPM of Sharpe (1964), Lintner (1965) and Mossin (1966). As the CAPM is based on the mean-variance analysis, we will consider the same assumptions of Section 2.2, to which we will add other ones, depending on the case.

### 3.2.1 Case Without Riskless Asset

Assume that we are working under the framework of Subsection 3.1.1 and consider two minimum variance portfolios $\mathbf{w}$ and $\mathbf{w}_\perp$. We say that the portfolios $\mathbf{w}$ and $\mathbf{w}_\perp$ are *orthogonal* if the covariance of their returns is zero:

$$\mathbf{w}_\perp^T \mathbf{\Sigma} \mathbf{w} = 0.$$

Given a minimum variance portfolio, different from the global minimum variance portfolio, there is a unique minimum variance portfolio such that both portfolios are orthogonal.

**Proposition 3.5** *Consider a minimum variance portfolio,* $\mathbf{w} \neq \mathbf{w}_G$, *with expression*

$$\mathbf{w} = \mathbf{\Sigma}^{-1} \begin{bmatrix} \mathbf{1} & \mathbf{R} \end{bmatrix} \mathbf{\Pi}^{-1} \begin{bmatrix} 1 \\ R_p \end{bmatrix}$$

*and define the portfolio* $\mathbf{w}_\perp$ *by*

$$\mathbf{w}_\perp = \mathbf{\Sigma}^{-1} \begin{bmatrix} \mathbf{1} & \mathbf{R} \end{bmatrix} \mathbf{\Pi}^{-1} \begin{bmatrix} 1 \\ R_{p,\perp} \end{bmatrix}$$

*with* $R_{p,\perp} = \frac{c-bR_p}{b-aR_p}$. *Then,* $\mathbf{w}$ *and* $\mathbf{w}_\perp$ *are orthogonal portfolios. Moreover, if* $\mathbf{w}$ *is on the efficient frontier, then* $\mathbf{w}_\perp$ *is not on the efficient frontier and vice versa.*

*Proof.* By their definitions, $\mathbf{w}$ and $\mathbf{w}_\perp$ are minimum variance portfolios. On the other hand:

$$\begin{aligned}
\mathbf{w}_\perp^T \boldsymbol{\Sigma} \mathbf{w} &= \begin{bmatrix} 1, & R_{p,\perp} \end{bmatrix} \boldsymbol{\Pi}^{-1} \begin{bmatrix} \mathbf{1} & \mathbf{R} \end{bmatrix}^T \boldsymbol{\Sigma}^{-1} \boldsymbol{\Sigma} \boldsymbol{\Sigma}^{-1} \begin{bmatrix} \mathbf{1} & \mathbf{R} \end{bmatrix} \boldsymbol{\Pi}^{-1} \begin{bmatrix} 1 \\ R_p \end{bmatrix} \\
&= \begin{bmatrix} 1, & R_{p,\perp} \end{bmatrix} \boldsymbol{\Pi}^{-1} \begin{bmatrix} \mathbf{1} & \mathbf{R} \end{bmatrix}^T \boldsymbol{\Sigma}^{-1} \begin{bmatrix} \mathbf{1} & \mathbf{R} \end{bmatrix} \boldsymbol{\Pi}^{-1} \begin{bmatrix} 1 \\ R_p \end{bmatrix} \\
&= \begin{bmatrix} 1, & R_{p,\perp} \end{bmatrix} \boldsymbol{\Pi}^{-1} \begin{bmatrix} 1 \\ R_p \end{bmatrix} = \begin{bmatrix} 1, & R_{p,\perp} \end{bmatrix} \frac{1}{d} \begin{bmatrix} c & -b \\ -b & a \end{bmatrix} \begin{bmatrix} 1 \\ R_p \end{bmatrix} \\
&= \frac{1}{d} \left( c - 2bR_{p,\perp} - aR_p R_{p,\perp} \right).
\end{aligned}$$

Equating the previous expression to zero, we obtain that $\mathbf{w}$ and $\mathbf{w}_\perp$ are orthogonal, if and only if $R_{p,\perp} = \frac{c-bR_p}{b-aR_p}$.

For the last part of the proposition, we must study the function $R_{p,\perp}(x) = \frac{c-bx}{b-ax}$. $R_{p,\perp}$ is continuous in its domain $\mathbb{R} - \{R_G\}$ and satisfies $\lim_{x \to R_G^+} R_{p,\perp}(x) = -\infty$, $\lim_{x \to +\infty} R_{p,\perp}(x) = R_G$. Moreover, $R'_{p,\perp}(x) = \frac{d}{(b-ax)^2} > 0 \; \forall x \neq R_G$, and then, $R_{p,\perp}$ is strictly increasing in $(R_G, +\infty)$. As a result, $R_p > R_G$ implies $R_{p,\perp}(R_p) < R_G$, and the claim is proved. ■

The existence of the orthogonal portfolio allows us to state the following result, which is close to the CAPM.

**Proposition 3.6** *If* $R_i$ *is the expected return of the i-th asset in a minimum variance portfolio,* $\mathbf{w} \neq \mathbf{w}_G$*, with return* $r_p$ *and expected return* $R_p$*, then it is satisfied that*

$$R_i = R_{p,\perp} + \beta_i \left( R_p - R_{p,\perp} \right), \tag{3.31}$$

*where* $\beta_i = \frac{cov(r_i, r_p)}{\sigma_p^2}$, $r_i$ *is the return of the i-th asset and* $R_{p,\perp}$ *is the expected return of the portfolio orthogonal to* $\mathbf{w}$.

*Proof.* Considering that $\mathbf{w}$ is a minimum variance portfolio, we can write

$$
\begin{aligned}
cov\left(r_i, r_p\right) &= \mathbf{e}_i^T \boldsymbol{\Sigma} \mathbf{w} = \mathbf{e}_i^T \boldsymbol{\Sigma} \boldsymbol{\Sigma}^{-1} \begin{bmatrix} \mathbf{1} & \mathbf{R} \end{bmatrix} \Pi^{-1} \begin{bmatrix} 1 \\ R_p \end{bmatrix} \\
&= \mathbf{e}_i^T \begin{bmatrix} \mathbf{1} & \mathbf{R} \end{bmatrix} \Pi^{-1} \begin{bmatrix} 1 \\ R_p \end{bmatrix} \\
&= \begin{bmatrix} 1, & R_i \end{bmatrix} \Pi^{-1} \begin{bmatrix} 1 \\ R_p \end{bmatrix},
\end{aligned}
$$

where $\mathbf{e}_i^T = \left(0, \ldots, \overset{i)}{1}, \ldots, 0\right)$.

On the other hand, the portfolio orthogonal to $\mathbf{w}$ satisfies

$$
0 = \mathbf{w}_{\perp}^T \boldsymbol{\Sigma} \mathbf{w} = \begin{bmatrix} 1, & R_{p,\perp} \end{bmatrix} \boldsymbol{\Pi}^{-1} \begin{bmatrix} 1 \\ R_p \end{bmatrix}.
$$

Subtracting the two last expressions we find

$$
\begin{aligned}
cov\left(r_i, r_p\right) &= \begin{bmatrix} 0, & R_i - R_{p,\perp} \end{bmatrix} \boldsymbol{\Pi}^{-1} \begin{bmatrix} 1 \\ R_p \end{bmatrix} \\
&= \begin{bmatrix} 0, & R_i - R_{p,\perp} \end{bmatrix} \frac{1}{d} \begin{bmatrix} c & -b \\ -b & a \end{bmatrix} \begin{bmatrix} 1 \\ R_p \end{bmatrix} \\
&= \frac{aR_p - b}{ac - b^2} \left(R_i - R_{p,\perp}\right) \equiv \gamma \left(R_i - R_{p,\perp}\right).
\end{aligned}
\tag{3.32}
$$

As this expression is valid for $i = 1, \ldots, n$, we can write

$$
\sigma_p^2 = cov\left(r_p, r_p\right) = \sum_{i=1}^{n} w_i cov\left(r_i, r_p\right) = \gamma \sum_{i=1}^{n} w_i \left(R_i - R_{p,\perp}\right) = \gamma \left(R_p - R_{p,\perp}\right)
$$

and obtain $\gamma = \frac{\sigma_p^2}{R_p - R_{p,\perp}}$. Replacing this value of $\gamma$ in (3.32) we finally obtain equation (3.31). ■

To state the fundamental result for the case without riskless asset, we need to introduce the concept of market portfolio, which is a key ingredient of the CAPM. The *market portfolio* is the portfolio of risky assets that has the same weights as the entire market. The weights of the market portfolio are, therefore, given by $\mathbf{w}^M = \frac{1}{W}\mathbf{W}$, where $\mathbf{W}$ is the vector with the total market value of each asset, and $W = \mathbf{1}^T\mathbf{W}$ is the total wealth invested in the market. In Section 2.2, we detailed the assumptions of the MV analysis. Specifically, assumptions i) and ii) lead to the conclusion that each individual investor chooses a minimum variance portfolio depending only on the mean and the variance of portfolio returns. To obtain the zero-beta CAPM, we only need the following additional assumption:

viii) **All the investors have homogeneous expectations.**

As an immediate consequence of this assumption, introduced by Sharpe (1964), investors agree on the means, variances and covariances of assets returns and, therefore, all of them choose portfolios on the same minimum variance efficient frontier.[1]

**Proposition 3.7** *The market portfolio is a minimum variance efficient portfolio.*

*Proof.* We proceed by induction on the number $m$ of investors. Consider $m = 1$. By our assumptions, the investor has a portfolio on the mean variance efficient frontier. Now assume that the portfolio formed by the aggregation of the portfolios of $m$ investors is a minimum variance efficient portfolio, with weights $\mathbf{w}_m$ and wealth $W_m$. Take the (minimum variance efficient) portfolio of another investor, with weights $\mathbf{w}_{m+1}$ and wealth $W_{m+1}$, and build the joint portfolio of the $m + 1$ investors. The resulting portfolio has wealth $W_m + W_{m+1}$ and weights $\alpha \mathbf{w}_m + (1 - \alpha)\mathbf{w}_{m+1}$, with $\alpha = \frac{W_m}{W_m + W_{m+1}}$. As $0 \leq \alpha \leq 1$, by the two-fund separation property b) of Theorem 3.2, the portfolio of $m + 1$ investors is a minimum variance efficient portfolio.

Thus, we have proved that the portfolio obtained aggregating any number of investors' portfolios is a minimum variance efficient portfolio. Considering all the investors in the market, we obtain the market portfolio, which is, therefore, a minimum variance efficient portfolio. ∎

**Theorem 3.5** *(Zero-beta CAPM) If $R_i$ is the expected return of any asset in the market, and $R_p^M$ is the expected return of the market portfolio*

[1]Sharpe attributes the term "homogeneity of investor expectations" to one of the referees.

*(assumed different from the global minimum variance portfolio), then*

$$R_i = R_{p,\perp}^M + \beta_i^M \left( R_p^M - R_{p,\perp}^M \right), \tag{3.33}$$

*where* $R_{p,\perp}^M$ *is the expected return of the portfolio orthogonal to the market portfolio, and* $\beta_i^M = \frac{cov\left(r_i, r_p^M\right)}{\left(\sigma_p^M\right)^2}$, *with* $r_p^M$ *and* $\left(\sigma_p^M\right)^2$, *the return and the variance of the market portfolio, respectively.*

*Proof.* By Proposition 3.7 the market portfolio is a minimum variance efficient portfolio. Then, we can make $R_p = R_p^M$, $\beta_i = \beta_i^M$, $R_{p,\perp} = R_{p,\perp}^M$ in Proposition 3.6, obtaining the desired result. ■

The expression in equation (3.33) is known as *zero-beta CAPM* because by the definition of orthogonality, the returns of the market portfolio, and its orthogonal portfolio have zero covariance. The coefficient $\beta_i^M$ is the *beta of the i-th asset* and represents the contribution of the *i*-th asset to the risk of the market portfolio measured by its variance.

### 3.2.2 Case with a Riskless Asset

In this case we will use a procedure like the one presented in the previous section, but without using orthogonal portfolios. The analogous result to Proposition 3.6 in this case is the following.

**Proposition 3.8** *If* $R_i$ *is the expected return of the i-th asset in the tangency portfolio with return* $r_{p,T}$ *and expected return* $R_{p,T}$, *then it is satisfied that*

$$R_i = R_0 + \beta_i^T \left( R_{p,T} - R_0 \right), \tag{3.34}$$

*where* $\beta_i^T = \frac{cov\left(r_i, r_{p,T}\right)}{\sigma_{p,T}^2}$, $r_i$ *is the return of the asset, and* $\sigma_{p,T}^2$ *is the variance of the tangency portfolio.*

*Proof.* The covariance of the returns of the *i*-th asset and the tangency portfolio is given by

$$cov\left(r_i, r_{p,T}\right) = \mathbf{e}_i^T \boldsymbol{\Sigma} \mathbf{w}_T = \mathbf{e}_i^T \boldsymbol{\Sigma} \frac{1}{\mathbf{1}^T \boldsymbol{\Sigma}^{-1} \mathbf{E}} \boldsymbol{\Sigma}^{-1} \mathbf{E} = \frac{1}{\mathbf{1}^T \boldsymbol{\Sigma}^{-1} \mathbf{E}} E_i,$$

where we have used the expression in equation (3.20) of the tangency portfolio, and $E_i = R_i - R_0$ is the expected excess return of the *i*-th asset.

Considering the last equality and expression in equation (3.21), we can write

$$\beta_i = \frac{cov\left(r_i, r_{p,T}\right)}{\sigma_{p,T}^2} = \frac{\frac{1}{\mathbf{1}^T\boldsymbol{\Sigma}^{-1}\mathbf{E}}E_i}{\frac{\mathbf{E}^T\boldsymbol{\Sigma}^{-1}\mathbf{E}}{\left(\mathbf{1}^T\boldsymbol{\Sigma}^{-1}\mathbf{E}\right)^2}} = \frac{\mathbf{1}^T\boldsymbol{\Sigma}^{-1}\mathbf{E}}{\mathbf{E}^T\boldsymbol{\Sigma}^{-1}\mathbf{E}}E_i = \frac{E_i}{E_{p,T}},$$

where $E_{p,T}$ is the expected excess return of the tangency portfolio (equation 3.23). Replacing in the previous expressions $E_i$ and $E_{p,T}$ by $R_i - R_0$ and $R_{p,T} - R_0$, respectively, we obtain equation (3.34). ■

To obtain the CAPM from equation (3.34), we just need to prove that the tangency portfolio is equal to the market portfolio. To achieve this result, we need one additional assumption.

**ix) The riskless asset is a financial security in zero net supply.**

**Proposition 3.9** *The tangency portfolio coincides with the market portfolio.*

*Proof.* We know that in the presence of a riskless asset, each investor holds a portfolio on the CML. By the homogeneity assumption viii), all investors share the same CML, and then, their portfolios consist of different proportions of riskless asset and the tangency portfolio. Aggregating all the portfolios, we are still on the CML, since any combination of efficient portfolios is an efficient portfolio. Finally, by assumption ix), the riskless asset part is zero, and the market portfolio is the tangency portfolio. ■

Now we can state the main theorem of this section.

**Theorem 3.6** *(CAPM) If $R_i$ is the expected return of any asset in the market and $R_0$ is the return of the riskless asset, then*

$$R_i = R_0 + \beta_i^M \left(R_{p,M} - R_0\right), \tag{3.35}$$

*where $\beta_i^M = \frac{cov\left(r_i, r_{p,M}\right)}{\sigma_{p,M}^2}$ is the beta of the i-th asset and $R_{p,M}$ is the expected return of the market portfolio.*

*Proof.* Immediate form propositions in equations (3.14) and (3.34). ■

The interpretation of the CAPM of equation (3.35) is that the expected excess return of an asset is proportional to the expected excess return of the market portfolio. Under this interpretation, the beta of the asset represents the sensitivity of the asset price to changes in the expected excess return of the market portfolio.

An alternative view of equation (3.35) is that the expected excess return of an asset is proportional to its beta. This interpretation allows us to see equation (3.35) as the equation of a straight line in the space $\left(\beta_i^M, R_i\right)$, called *security market line*.

An additional interpretation allows us to express equation (3.35) in the form

$$r_i = \alpha_i + \beta_i^M r_{p,M} + \varepsilon_i, \tag{3.36}$$

where $\alpha_i = R_0\left(1 - \beta_i^M\right)$, and $\varepsilon_i$ is a random variable. Taking into account equation (3.35) and the definition of $\beta_i^M$, it is not difficult to obtain that $\mathbb{E}\left(\varepsilon_i\right) = 0$ and $cov\left(\varepsilon_i, r_{p,M}\right) = 0$, and then, equation (3.36) can be used to obtain $\beta_i^M$ by linear regression. Moreover, by the last equality, we can write

$$\sigma_i^2 = \left(\beta_i^M\right)^2 \sigma_{p,M}^2 + \sigma_{\varepsilon_i}^2,$$

where $\sigma_\varepsilon^2 = var\left(\varepsilon_i\right)$. Thus, the variance of any asset can be decomposed in two parts: the term $\left(\beta_i^M\right)^2 \sigma_{p,M}^2$, known as *systematic risk*, and the term $\sigma_{\varepsilon_i}^2$, the *unsystematic, non-systematic* or *idiosyncratic* risk. To understand the reason for these names, we need to obtain the variance of the return of a portfolio, $\sigma_p^2$, under this setup. Using the general expression for $\sigma_p^2$, expression (3.36), and $cov\left(\varepsilon_i, r_{p,M}\right) = 0$, we obtain

$$\sigma_p^2 = \sum_{i=1}^{n}\sum_{j=1}^{n} w_i w_j cov\left(r_i, r_j\right) = \sum_{i=1}^{n}\sum_{j=1}^{n} w_i w_j \left\{\beta_i^M \beta_j^M \sigma_{p,M}^2 + cov\left(\varepsilon_i, \varepsilon_j\right)\right\}.$$

Therefore, the idiosyncratic risk, $\sigma_{\varepsilon_i}^2$, which is associated specifically to the $i$-th asset, can be reduced by forming a diversified portfolio, through the effect of the term $cov\left(\varepsilon_i, \varepsilon_j\right)$. Nevertheless, the systematic risk associated to the variance of the market portfolio, $\sigma_{p,M}^2$, cannot be eliminated through diversification.

## 3.3 MULTIFACTOR MODELS

The difficulty of empirically determining the market portfolio, and the restrictiveness of the assumptions of the CAPM, led to alternative proposals.[2] The most important of them was the Arbitrage Pricing Theory

[2]Regarding the initial criticisms of the CAPM see, for example, Jensen (1972), Blume and Friend (1973), and Roll (1977).

(APT) of Ross (1976). The main idea behind APT is to propose a new theory alternative to CAPM but retain some of its intuitive results. The APT imposes the no-arbitrage condition, which is one of the cornerstones of quantitative finance, to a framework determined by a multifactor model for asset returns.

In the previous section, we have seen that the CAPM is given by equation (3.35), according to which the return of any asset is obtained as the sum of a linear function of the excess return of the market portfolio and another idiosyncratic random variable with zero mean. Multifactor models extend this structure to consider different random variables (i.e., the factors) affecting asset returns in a linear way.

Specifically, a $k$-factor model is determined by the following equation in matrix form

$$\mathbf{e} = \mathbf{a} + \mathbf{B}\mathbf{f} + \boldsymbol{\varepsilon}, \tag{3.37}$$

where $\mathbf{e} = (e_1, \ldots, e_n)^T$ is the vector of excess asset returns, with $e_i = r_i - R_0$, $\mathbf{a} = (a_1, \ldots, a_n)^T$ is a vector of constants, $\mathbf{B} = (\beta_{ij})_{n\times k}$ is a matrix of constants known as *factor loadings* or *betas* of the assets, $\mathbf{f} = (f_1, \ldots, f_k)^T$ is a random vector of *factors*, and $\boldsymbol{\varepsilon} = (\varepsilon_1, \ldots, \varepsilon_n)^T$ is a random vector of *residuals* or *idiosyncratic risks*.

The factor model is completed with the following assumptions about the random variables:

i) $\mathbb{E}[\varepsilon_i] = 0, i = 1, \ldots, n,$
ii) $\mathbb{E}[f_j] = 0, j = 1, \ldots, k,$
iii) $cov(f_i, f_j) = \mathbb{E}[f_i f_j] = \delta_{ij}, i, j = 1, \ldots, k,$
iv) $cov(\varepsilon_i, f_j) = 0, i = 1, \ldots, n, j = 1, \ldots, k,$
v) $cov(\varepsilon_i, \varepsilon_l) = \mathbb{E}[\varepsilon_i \varepsilon_l] = \sigma^2_{\varepsilon_i}\delta_{il}$ with $\sigma^2_{\varepsilon_i} = var(\varepsilon_i), i, l = 1, \ldots, n,$ and
vi) $\exists S \in \mathbb{R} : \sigma^2_{\varepsilon_i} \leq S^2 \, \forall i \in \{1, \ldots, n\}.$

Assumptions i)-iv) are always possible through the appropriate choices of the factors and the parameters. Assumption v) is a simplifying assumption not guaranteed in general.[3] The last assumption is a boundedness

[3]It is possible to obtain similar results under factor models with correlated residuals, as in Chamberlain and Rothschild (1983) and Ingersoll (1984). To distinguish both kinds of models, the class with uncorrelated residuals is known as *strict factor models*, while models with correlated residuals are called *approximate factor models*. We will work, as Ross (1976), only with strict factor models, and refer the reader to the previous references for approximate factor models.

assumption for residual variances. Taking expectations in equation (3.37), and using assumptions i) and ii), we find that $\mathbf{a}$ is the vector of expected excess returns: $\mathbf{a} = \mathbb{E}[\mathbf{e}] = \mathbf{E} = \mathbf{R} - R_0\mathbf{1}$. Additional assumptions are $|a_i| \leq a < \infty$ and $|\beta_{ij}| \leq b < \infty$ for $i = 1, \ldots, n, j = 1, \ldots, k$, with $a, b \in \mathbb{R}^+$.

The second ingredient of APT is the absence of arbitrage opportunities. In this framework, we say that a *riskless arbitrage opportunity* exists with the portfolio $\mathbf{w}$ (Ingersoll, 1984), if the variance of its return is zero and it has positive expected return:

$$\sigma_p^2 = \mathbf{w}^T\mathbf{\Sigma}\mathbf{w} = 0$$

$$E_p = \mathbf{w}^T\mathbf{a} = \mathbf{w}^T\mathbf{E} > 0,$$

where

$$\mathbf{\Sigma}_{ij} = cov\left(r_i, r_j\right) = \sum_{l=1}^{k} \beta_{il}\beta_{jl} + \sigma_{\varepsilon_i}^2\delta_{ij}. \tag{3.38}$$

This last expression can be written in matrix form as $\mathbf{\Sigma} = \mathbf{B}\mathbf{B}^T + \mathbf{\Omega}$, with $\mathbf{\Omega}$ a diagonal matrix with diagonal elements $\left(\sigma_{\varepsilon_1}^2, \ldots, \sigma_{\varepsilon_n}^2\right)$. As $\mathbf{\Omega}$ is positive definite and $\mathbf{B}\mathbf{B}^T$ is positive semidefinite, then $\mathbf{\Sigma}$ is positive definite, and therefore, there are no riskless arbitrage opportunities. Nevertheless, APT was developed under the assumption of an infinite number of available assets, and in this case, asymptotic arbitrage opportunities might exist.

In order to deal with infinite assets, we follow Ingersoll (1984), and assume a fixed infinite economy with a sequence of assets in such a way that the $n$-th asset is added to the first $n - 1$ assets whose parameters do not change. We indicate the sequences with the subscript $n$ and their subsequences will be denoted with the subscript $\nu$. We will also assume that $\mathbf{B}$ has full column rank $k$ for all sufficiently large $n$.

A sequence $\mathbf{w}^n$ of portfolios generate an *asymptotic arbitrage opportunity* if a subsequence $\mathbf{w}^\nu$ exists, such that for all $\upsilon$

$$\lim_{\nu \to \infty} \sigma_{p,\nu}^2 = 0$$

$$E_{p,\nu} \geq \delta > 0,$$

where $E_{p,\nu}$ and $\sigma_{p,\nu}^2$ are, respectively, the expected excess return and the variance of the portfolio $\mathbf{w}^\nu$. The existence of an asymptotic arbitrage opportunity provides an opportunity for an investor to achieve unboundedly large wealth with probability 1 (Ingersoll, 1984, footnote 5).

**Theorem 3.7** *(APT) If the returns of the risky assets are generated by a k-factor model, and there are no asymptotic arbitrage opportunities, then there are constants $\lambda_1, \ldots, \lambda_k$ such that*

$$\lim_{n\to\infty} \frac{1}{n} \sum_{i=1}^{n} \left( R_i - R_0 - \sum_{j=1}^{k} \beta_{ik}\lambda_k \right)^2 = 0. \tag{3.39}$$

*Proof.* Consider the $i$-th asset and the linear regression of its expected excess return on the factor loadings, in the form

$$E_i = \sum_{j=1}^{k} \beta_{ij}\lambda_j + v_i,$$

where $v_i$ is the residual of the regression. The normal equations are

$$\sum_{i=1}^{n} v_i\beta_{ij} = 0, \; j = 1, \ldots, k, \tag{3.40}$$

which have a unique solution for $\lambda_1, \ldots, \lambda_k$ since the matrix $\mathbf{B}$ has full column rank.

Now define the portfolio $\mathbf{w}^n = \left( \|\mathbf{v}^n\| \sqrt{n} \right)^{-1} \mathbf{v}^n$, where $\mathbf{v}^n = \left( v_1, \ldots, v_n \right)^T$ and $\|\mathbf{v}^n\| = \sqrt{\sum_{i=1}^{n} v_i^2}$. The expected return of this portfolio is

$$E_{p,n} = (\mathbf{w}^n)^T \mathbf{E} = \frac{1}{\|\mathbf{v}^n\|\sqrt{n}} \left( \sum_{j=1}^{k} \lambda_j \sum_{i=1}^{n} v_i\beta_{ij} + \sum_{i=1}^{n} v_i^2 \right) = \frac{\|\mathbf{v}^n\|}{\sqrt{n}},$$

where we have used equation (3.40).

On the other hand, using expression in equation (3.38) and assumption vi), we can write the variance of the portfolio $\mathbf{w}^n$ as

$$\sigma_{p,n}^2 = (\mathbf{w}^n)^T \mathbf{\Sigma} \mathbf{w}^n = \sum_{i,j=1}^{n} w_i^n w_j^n cov\left( r_i, r_j \right) = \frac{1}{n\|\mathbf{v}^n\|^2} \sum_{i=1}^{n} v_i^2 \sigma_{\varepsilon_i}^2 \leq \frac{S^2}{n}. \tag{3.41}$$

Now, reasoning by contradiction, suppose that the theorem is false. Then

$$\lim_{n\to\infty} \frac{1}{n} \|\mathbf{v}^n\|^2 = \lim_{n\to\infty} E_{p,n}^2 \neq 0$$

and $\lim_{n\to\infty} E_{p,n} \neq 0$. As $R_{p,n}$ is a sequence of positive numbers, which does not converge to zero; it admits a subsequence, $E_{p,\nu}$, bounded from below by a positive number $\delta$, and therefore $E_{p,\nu} \geq \delta > 0$. From equation (3.41), the corresponding subsequence of variances, $\sigma^2_{p,\nu}$, satisfies $\sigma^2_{p,\nu} \leq \frac{S^2}{\nu}$, and $\lim_{\nu\to\infty} \sigma^2_{p,\nu} = 0$. Thus, the portfolio $\mathbf{w}^n$ generates an asymptotic arbitrage opportunity, which is a contradiction. ■

The expression in equation (3.39) tells us that the linear relationship between expected excess returns and factor loadings

$$\mathbf{E} = \mathbf{R} - R_0\mathbf{1} = B\lambda \tag{3.42}$$

holds only in mean and when the number of assets tends to infinity, that is, in mean square sense. In order to obtain relation in equation (3.42) as an exact result for a finite number of assets, we need to consider a more restricted version of the factor model in equation (3.37), with no residuals. In this case, we have the following result.

**Proposition 3.10** *If the vector* e *of excess returns of n assets is given by the following k-factor model without idiosyncratic risks*

$$\mathbf{e} = \mathbf{E} + \mathbf{Bf}, \tag{3.43}$$

*with $k < n$, and there are no riskless arbitrage opportunities, then there is a vector of constants $\lambda = (\lambda_1, \ldots, \lambda_n)^T$ such that*

$$\mathbf{R} = R_0\mathbf{1} + B\lambda.$$

*Proof.* Consider the matrix equality $\mathbf{w}^T\mathbf{B} = 0^T$ as a homogeneous linear system of equations with $k$ equations and $n$ unknowns, $w_1, \ldots, w_n$. As $B$ has range $k < n$, the system has an infinite number of solutions. Let $\mathbf{w}^* = \left(w_1^*, \ldots, w_n^*\right)^T$ be a non-trivial solution. The variance of the portfolio $\mathbf{w}^*$, $\left(\sigma_p^*\right)^2$, can be obtained as

$$\left(\sigma_p^*\right)^2 = var\left[\left(\mathbf{w}^*\right)^T r\right] = var\left[\left(\mathbf{w}^*\right)^T e\right] = var\left[\left(\mathbf{w}^*\right)^T (E + \mathbf{Bf})\right]$$
$$= var\left[\left(\mathbf{w}^*\right)^T \mathbf{Bf}\right] = 0.$$

Thus, the portfolio $\mathbf{w}^*$ is a riskless portfolio. As there are no riskless arbitrage opportunities, we have $E_p^* = (\mathbf{w}^*)^T \mathbf{E} = 0$. Since $\mathbf{w}^*$ is a solution of $\mathbf{w}^T\mathbf{B} = 0^T$, for it to also be a solution of $(\mathbf{w}^*)^T \mathbf{E} = 0$, the vector $\mathbf{E}$ must lie in the subspace generated by $\mathbf{B}$, and thus $\mathbf{E} = \mathbf{R} - R_0\mathbf{1} = B\lambda$, with $\lambda \in \mathbb{R}^k$. ■

Note that, under the assumptions of Proposition 3.10, $\mathbf{\Omega} = 0$ and $\mathbf{\Sigma} = \mathbf{BB}^T$, which is positive semidefinite, and then, the variance of the portfolio can be zero.

It is possible to obtain a generalization of the CAPM, from a one-factor model without idiosyncratic risk, just by choosing the appropriate factor, as is stated in the following result.

**Corollary 3.1** *Under the assumptions of Proposition 3.10 with a one-factor model ($k = 1$), consider the factor given by $f = r_{p,M} - R_{p,M}$, namely*

$$\mathbf{e} = \mathbf{E} + \mathbf{B}\left(r_{p,M} - R_{p,M}\right), \tag{3.44}$$

*where $r_{p,M}$ is the return of the market portfolio, $R_{p,M} = \mathbb{E}\left(r_{p,M}\right)$, and $\mathbf{B} = \left(\beta_1, \ldots, \beta_n\right)^T$. In these conditions, if there is an asset with a value of beta equal to one, $\beta_l = 1$, then it is satisfied that*

$$R_i = \alpha_i + R_0 + \beta_i^M\left(R_{p,M} - R_0\right), \tag{3.45}$$

*where $\alpha_i = \beta_i\left(r_l - r_{p,M}\right)$. In the case $r_l = r_{p,M}$, we reobtain the expression (3.35) of the CAPM.*

*Proof.* By Proposition 3.10 we have

$$R_i = R_0 + \beta_i\lambda. \tag{3.46}$$

As $\beta_l = 1$, from the previous expression we obtain $\lambda = R_l - R_0$. Replacing this value again in equation (3.46), we get

$$R_i = R_0 + \beta_i\left(R_l - R_0\right). \tag{3.47}$$

On the other hand, from equation (3.44) we obtain $R_l = r_l - r_{p,M} + R_{p,M}$, which replaced in equation (3.47) provides the desired result. ■

In this section, we have worked under the implicit assumption of the existence of a riskless asset with return $R_0$. Analogous results for an economy without a riskless asset can be obtained just by replacing **e** by **r**, **E** by **R**, and $R_0$ by another constant $\lambda_0$, which represents the return of any riskless portfolio constructed from risky assets (Ingersoll, 1987).

## 3.4 CHALLENGES OF MODERN PORTFOLIO THEORY

Portfolio allocation using Standard MPT faces several challenges. The two primary challenges in portfolio allocation are:

1. **Estimation Techniques:** Accurate estimation of key parameters such as covariance matrices, expected returns, and risk factors is crucial. These

estimations are inherently uncertain and subject to various biases. Techniques such as Jackknife estimation, shrinkage methods, and factor analysis are employed to improve the accuracy and reliability of these estimates.

2. **Non-Elliptical Nature of Returns:** Traditional portfolio theories often assume that asset returns follow an elliptical distribution, typically the multivariate normal distribution. However, empirical evidence suggests that asset returns exhibit skewness, kurtosis, and heavy tails, which are not captured by elliptical distributions. This non-elliptical nature of returns necessitates alternative risk measures and optimization techniques, such as Conditional Value-at-Risk (CVaR), to adequately capture and manage risks.

The following sections delve into these challenges in detail, discussing various estimation techniques and addressing the implications of non-elliptical return distributions on portfolio optimization.

### 3.4.1 Estimation Techniques in Portfolio Allocation

Accurate estimation is critical in financial engineering for modeling risks and returns. Various techniques are used to estimate parameters such as covariance, returns, and factors. Listed are detailed explanations of some commonly used estimation techniques:

1. **Jackknife Estimation:** The Jackknife is a resampling technique used to estimate the bias and variance of statistical estimators. It systematically leaves out one observation at a time from the sample set and calculates the estimate over $n$ different samples. Formally, for a sample of size $n$ and an estimator $\hat{\theta}$, the Jackknife estimate $\hat{\theta}_{(i)}$ is calculated as:

$$\hat{\theta}_{(i)} = \frac{1}{n-1} \sum_{j \neq i} \theta_j.$$

The Jackknife bias estimate is given by:

$$\text{Bias}_{\text{Jackknife}} = (n-1)\left(\bar{\theta} - \hat{\theta}\right),$$

where $\bar{\theta}$ is the average of the Jackknife estimates.

2. **Covariance Estimation:** Covariance estimation involves calculating the covariance matrix, which is essential for portfolio optimization. Several methods include:

(a) **Historical Covariance:** Uses historical return data to estimate the covariance matrix. The sample covariance matrix $\Sigma$ is given by:

$$\Sigma = \frac{1}{n-1}\sum_{i=1}^{n}\left(\mathbf{r}_i - \mu\right)\left(\mathbf{r}_i - \mu\right)^T,$$

where $\mathbf{r}_i$ is the return vector for the $i$-th period and $\mu$ is the mean return vector.

(b) **Shrinkage Estimators:** Combines sample covariance with a structured estimator to improve estimation accuracy. The Ledoit-Wolf shrinkage estimator is given by:

$$\hat{\Sigma} = \rho \mathrm{F} + (1-\rho)\, S,$$

where $\rho$ is the shrinkage parameter, $F$ is the structured estimator, and $S$ is the sample covariance matrix Ledoit and Wolf (2004).

3. **Returns Estimation:** Estimating expected returns is crucial for portfolio construction. Methods include:

(a) **Historical Average Returns:** The expected return $\mu$ can be estimated as:

$$\mu = \frac{1}{n}\sum_{i=1}^{n} r_i.$$

(b) **Black-Litterman Model:** Combines market equilibrium with investor views to provide a more robust estimate. The combined returns $\mu_{BL}$ are given by equation (2.9):

$$\mu_{BL} = \left[(\tau\Sigma)^{-1} + P^T\Omega^{-1}P\right]^{-1}\left[(\tau\Sigma)^{-1}\Pi + P^T\Omega^{-1}Q\right],$$

where $\Pi$ is the equilibrium excess returns, $P$ is the modification of equilibrium values, $Q$ represents the views, $\Omega$ is the uncertainty in views, and $\tau$ is a scalar (Black and Litterman [1992a]).

(c) **Factor Models:** Use economic factors to estimate expected returns. The return for asset $i$ is modeled as:

$$r_i = \alpha_i + \sum_{j=1}^{k} \beta_{ij} f_j + \epsilon_i,$$

where $\alpha_i$ is the intercept, $\beta_{ij}$ are the factor loadings, $f_j$ are the factor returns, and $\epsilon_i$ is the idiosyncratic error term. Chapter 6 is dedicated to the study of factor models and their application to factor investing.

4. **Cross-Validation:** Cross-validation is used to assess the performance of predictive models. It involves partitioning the data into $k$ subsets, training the model on $k - 1$ subsets, and validating it on the remaining subset. This process is repeated $k$ times (i.e., folds), and the average performance metric is computed. For example, in $k$-fold cross-validation, the data is divided into $k$ folds, and the model is trained $k$ times, each time leaving out one-fold for validation:

$$\text{CV}_k = \frac{1}{k} \sum_{i=1}^{k} \text{MSE}_i,$$

where $\text{MSE}_i$ is the mean squared error for the $i$-th fold (Arlot and Celisse [2010]).

5. **Bootstrapping:** Bootstrapping is a powerful statistical method that involves repeatedly sampling with replacement from the data set and recalculating the estimates. This technique allows for estimating the sampling distribution of an estimator and constructing confidence intervals. The bootstrap estimate of standard error is given by:

$$\widehat{\sigma}_{\text{boot}} = \sqrt{\frac{1}{B-1} \sum_{b=1}^{B} \left(\hat{\theta}^{*b} - \bar{\theta}^{*}\right)^2},$$

where $\hat{\theta}^{*b}$ is the estimate from the $b$-th bootstrap sample, $\bar{\theta}^{*}$ is the average of bootstrap estimates, and $B$ is the number of bootstrap samples (Efron and Tibshirani, 1994).

6. **Factor Analysis:** Factor analysis is used to identify underlying factors that explain the observed correlations among assets. Techniques include:
   (a) **Principal Component Analysis (PCA):** Reduces the dimensionality of data by transforming it into a set of uncorrelated components. The data matrix $X$ is decomposed as:

$$X = W \Lambda V^T,$$

   where $W$ are the principal components, $\Lambda$ is the diagonal matrix of singular values, and $V$ is the matrix of principal directions. See Section 6.1.1 for a more detailed discussion of PCA.

   (b) **Random Matrix Theory (RMT):** Differentiates between meaningful information and noise in the covariance matrix. The eigenvalues of the covariance matrix are analyzed, and the noise is filtered out based on theoretical predictions (Laloux et al., 1999).

7. **Shrinkage Techniques:** Shrinkage techniques improve the estimation of large covariance matrices by pulling the sample estimates toward a target. Methods include:
   (a) **Ledoit-Wolf Shrinkage:** A linear shrinkage method that adjusts the sample covariance matrix toward a more structured estimator. See 2.b above.
   (b) **Linear Regression and Characteristic Portfolios:** Uses regression techniques to shrink the estimates toward more stable values. The characteristic portfolio approach involves estimating the covariance matrix using the residuals from a factor model regression.
8. **Regularization Methods:** Regularization methods help prevent overfitting by adding a penalty to the estimation process. Common methods include:
   (a) **Least Absolute Shrinkage and Selection Operator (LASSO):** Adds an $L1$ penalty to the regression to promote sparsity. The Lasso regression solves the following optimization problem:

$$\min_{\beta}\left\{\frac{1}{2n}\sum_{i=1}^{n}(y_i - X_i\beta)^2 + \lambda\sum_{j=1}^{p}|\beta_j|\right\},$$

   where $\lambda$ is the regularization parameter.
   (b) **Ridge Regression:** Adds an $L2$ penalty to shrink the coefficients toward zero. The Ridge regression solves the following optimization problem:

$$\min_{\beta}\left\{\frac{1}{2n}\sum_{i=1}^{n}(y_i - X_i\beta)^2 + \lambda\sum_{j=1}^{p}\beta_j^2\right\},$$

   where $\lambda$ is the regularization parameter (Tibshirani, 1996).

### 3.4.2 Non-Elliptical Distributions and Conditional Value-at-Risk (CVaR)

1. **Non-Elliptical Distributions:** Non-elliptical distributions do not have elliptical contours and can exhibit skewness and kurtosis. These distributions are more flexible in modeling real-world financial returns, which often display asymmetrical and heavier tails than the normal distribution.

   Examples of non-elliptical distributions include:
   (a) **Skew-Normal Distribution:** Extends the normal distribution to allow for skewness.
   (b) **Skew-t Distribution:** Extends the t-distribution to allow for both skewness and heavy tails.

(c) **Pareto Distribution:** Models heavy-tailed behavior, often used in extreme value theory.

The use of variance as a risk measure in MPT is problematic for non-elliptical distributions because variance assumes symmetric distribution of returns and does not account for skewness and excess kurtosis. Artzner et al. (1999a) introduced the concept of coherent risk measures, which are designed to address these limitations. One such measure, Conditional Value-at-Risk (CVaR), proposed by Rockafellar and Uryasev (2000), provides a more comprehensive assessment of risk by focusing on tail losses.

2. **Conditional Value-at-Risk (CVaR):** Conditional Value-at-Risk (CVaR), also known as Expected Shortfall, is a risk measure that addresses some limitations of Value-at-Risk (VaR). While VaR provides the maximum loss not exceeded with a certain confidence level, it does not give any information about the magnitude of losses beyond this threshold. CVaR, on the other hand, considers the expected loss given that a loss exceeds the VaR threshold.

   Formally, CVaR at a confidence level $\alpha$ is defined as:

$$\text{CVaR}_\alpha = \mathbb{E}\left[L | L > \text{VaR}_\alpha\right],$$

   where $L$ is the loss and $\text{VaR}_\alpha$ is the Value-at-Risk at the confidence level $\alpha$.

   In mathematical optimization terms, CVaR can be formulated as:

$$\text{CVaR}_\alpha = \min_{\xi \in \mathbb{R}} \left\{ \xi + \frac{1}{1-\alpha} \mathbb{E}\left[ (L - \xi)^+ \right] \right\},$$

   where $(x)^+$ denotes the positive part of $x$.
   CVaR is particularly useful for risk management as it captures tail risk more effectively than variance, making it a more robust measure in the presence of heavy-tailed distributions, which are common in financial returns. See Section 5.2.2 for a more in-depth discussion of CVaR and other risk measures.

3. **Implications for Portfolio Optimization:** Using CVaR in portfolio optimization involves minimizing the expected shortfall rather than variance. This approach is more effective in capturing the risk of extreme losses, which is especially important for non-elliptical distributions with heavy tails.

   Empirical studies have shown that portfolios optimized using MPT can underperform when returns are non-elliptical. For instance, Kraus and Litzenberger (1976) found that investors have a preference for positive skewness, which is not captured by mean-variance optimization. Such preferences can lead to different portfolio choices and risk assessments.

While MPT remains a valuable framework, its limitations in dealing with non-elliptical distributions and its traditional reliance on variance as a risk measure are significant. Future research should focus on developing robust portfolio optimization techniques that can account for the complex characteristics of real-world asset returns, including skewness and heavy tails, and should consider using CVaR for a more comprehensive risk assessment.

## 3.5 QUANTUM ANNEALING IN PORTFOLIO MANAGEMENT

A quantum annealer consists of qubits, which are the basic units of quantum information. These qubits are coupled to form a quantum system that can represent complex optimization problems. The hardware architecture typically includes:

- **Qubits:** Superconducting qubits are commonly used, leveraging quantum superposition and entanglement.
- **Couplers:** Elements that link qubits, allowing them to interact and represent the problem's constraints.
- **Control Systems:** To manage the annealing schedule and control the quantum state.

A prominent example of a quantum annealer is the D-Wave system, which has been used extensively in research and commercial applications. The D-Wave quantum annealer uses a specific type of superconducting qubit called a "flux qubit," which operates at extremely low temperatures (close to absolute zero) to maintain quantum coherence. The couplers are designed to create an energy landscape that represents the optimization problem, and the control systems adjust the strength of the qubit interactions over time to guide the system toward the optimal solution.

The portfolio optimization problem can be formulated as a quadratic unconstrained binary optimization (QUBO) problem, suitable for quantum annealers. This involves defining an objective function that captures the trade-off between risk and return, subject to various constraints. The QUBO formulation typically involves encoding the decision variables (e.g., asset allocations) as binary variables and defining an objective function that represents the portfolio's risk and return characteristics. Constraints, such as budget limitations or investment restrictions, are incorporated into the objective function using penalty terms.

To implement quantum annealing for portfolio management, specialized software and programming frameworks are required. These tools allow users to encode the problem into a QUBO format and interface with the quantum hardware. Examples include the D-Wave Ocean SDK, a comprehensive suite for developing and running quantum applications on D-Wave systems, and QBsolv, an open-source solver that breaks down large QUBO problems into smaller parts suitable for quantum annealing.

These frameworks provide APIs and tools for defining the optimization problem, submitting it to the quantum annealer, and retrieving and interpreting the results. They also include utilities for problem decomposition, parameter tuning, and hybrid quantum-classical optimization.

The portfolio optimization problem involves selecting a combination of assets to maximize returns while minimizing risk. This can be mathematically expressed as:

$$\min\left(\sum_{i=1}^{n}\sum_{j=1}^{n} w_i w_j \sigma_{ij} - \lambda \sum_{i=1}^{n} \mu_i w_i\right), \tag{3.48}$$

where $w_i$ is the weight of the $i$-th asset in the portfolio, $\sigma_{ij}$ is the covariance between assets $i$ and $j$, $\mu_i$ is the expected return of the $i$-th asset, and $\lambda$ is a parameter that controls the trade-off between risk and return.

To solve the portfolio optimization problem using a quantum annealer, the problem must be encoded into a QUBO format:

$$H = \sum_{i=1}^{n} a_i q_i + \sum_{i=1}^{n} \sum_{j=i+1}^{n} b_{ij} q_i q_j, \tag{3.49}$$

where $q_i$ are binary variables representing the inclusion (1) or exclusion (0) of the $i$-th asset in the portfolio, and $a_i$ and $b_{ij}$ are coefficients derived from the risk and return parameters. The Hamiltonian $H$ is then minimized using quantum annealing, where quantum fluctuations allow the system to explore multiple configurations simultaneously and find the global minimum more efficiently.

The process involves encoding the portfolio optimization problem into a QUBO problem, programming the annealer using the D-Wave Ocean SDK or similar tools, running the quantum-annealing process to find the optimal portfolio, and interpreting the results from the quantum annealer's output.

Several studies have benchmarked the performance of quantum annealers against classical optimization algorithms. These comparisons often involve metrics, such as solution quality, computation time, and scalability. Results indicate that quantum annealers can outperform classical methods for certain problem instances, particularly as the problem size increases. In a study by Rosenberg et al. (2016), the authors used a D-Wave quantum annealer to solve the optimal trading trajectory problem, finding that the quantum annealer provided solutions that were competitive with classical methods, demonstrating its potential for real-world financial applications. Similarly, Venturelli et al. (2015) explored the application of quantum annealing to fully connected spin glasses, a problem closely related to portfolio optimization, and found that quantum annealers could handle large-scale problems more efficiently than traditional optimization techniques. Further insights into the applications and advancements of quantum annealing in financial optimization can be found in the work of Jacquier and Kondratyev (2022) and the comprehensive review by López de Prado (2016a).

## 3.6 MEAN-VARIANCE OPTIMIZATION WITH CVaR CONSTRAINT

Mean-Variance optimization seeks to maximize expected return for a given level of risk, where risk is quantified by variance. However, variance does not adequately capture extreme losses. To address this limitation, we incorporate a Conditional Value at Risk (CVaR) constraint into the optimization problem, following the methodology proposed by Rockafellar and Uryasev (2000). CVaR provides a coherent risk measure that accounts for tail risks.

### 3.6.1 Problem Formulation

The objective is to maximize expected return while minimizing risk, subject to a CVaR constraint. The problem can be simplified using `cvxpy`, allowing it to handle the auxiliary variable $z$. This results in the following formulations: To write the CVaR constraint in a way understood by convex solvers, we can reformulate it as an optimization problem.

#### CVaR Formula

$$\mathrm{CVaR}_\alpha = \mathrm{VaR}_\alpha + \frac{1}{(1-\alpha)m}\sum_{j=1}^{m} z_j, \tag{3.50}$$

where $z_j = \left(-w^\top R_j - \mathrm{VaR}_\alpha\right)_+ = \max\left(-w^\top R_j - \mathrm{VaR}_\alpha, 0\right)$, $\mathrm{VaR}_\alpha$ is the Value at Risk at confidence level $\alpha$, and $m$ is the number of scenarios.

**Minimization Problem** CVaR is also the solution of the following optimization problem

$$\mathrm{CVaR}_\alpha = \min_{\mathrm{VaR}_\alpha} \left( \mathrm{VaR}_\alpha + \frac{1}{(1-\alpha)m} \sum_{j=1}^{m} \left(-w^\top R_j - \mathrm{VaR}_\alpha\right)_+ \right). \tag{3.51}$$

### 3.6.2 Optimization Problem

The full optimization problem becomes:

$$\max_{w, \mathrm{VaR}_\alpha} \left(w^\top \mu - \lambda w^\top \Sigma w\right) \tag{3.52}$$

subject to:

$$\sum_{i=1}^{n} w_i = 1 \quad \text{(Fully invested portfolio)}, \tag{3.53}$$

$$w_i \geq 0,\ i = 1, \ldots, n \quad \text{(Non-negativity constraint)}, \tag{3.54}$$

$$\mathrm{VaR}_\alpha + \frac{1}{(1-\alpha)m} \sum_{j=1}^{m} z_j \leq \mathrm{CVaR}_{\mathrm{max}}, \tag{3.55}$$

$$z_j = \left(-w^\top R_j - \mathrm{VaR}_\alpha\right)_+,\ j = 1, \ldots, m. \tag{3.56}$$

Textbook formulations often include $z$ in the unknowns, and constrain it with inequalities. Since the "positive part" function is convex and recognized by `cvxpy`, this is not needed.

### 3.6.3 Clarification of Optimization Classes

The classes of optimization problems are listed from simplest to most general:

- **Quadratic Programming (QP)**: Suitable for problems with quadratic objectives and linear constraints (Boyd and Vandenberghe, 2004).
- **Second-Order Cone Programming (SOCP)**: Extends QP by allowing for conic constraints, making it suitable for certain types of risk measures like CVaR (Boyd and Vandenberghe, 2004).

- **Convex Programming:** A broader class that encompasses both QP and SOCP, handling general convex functions and constraints (Boyd and Vandenberghe, 2004).

### 3.6.4 Numerical Example

Consider a portfolio with three assets. The expected returns and covariance matrix are:

$$\mu = \begin{bmatrix} 0.10 \\ 0.12 \\ 0.15 \end{bmatrix}, \Sigma = \begin{bmatrix} 0.005 & 0.001 & 0.002 \\ 0.001 & 0.006 & 0.003 \\ 0.002 & 0.003 & 0.009 \end{bmatrix}.$$

We use the following historical return scenarios:

$$R_1 = \begin{bmatrix} 0.08 \\ 0.10 \\ 0.12 \end{bmatrix}, R_2 = \begin{bmatrix} 0.05 \\ 0.07 \\ 0.09 \end{bmatrix}, R_3 = \begin{bmatrix} 0.12 \\ 0.15 \\ 0.18 \end{bmatrix}, R_4 = \begin{bmatrix} 0.03 \\ 0.02 \\ 0.04 \end{bmatrix}, R_5 = \begin{bmatrix} 0.15 \\ 0.20 \\ 0.25 \end{bmatrix}$$

with parameters:

- Risk aversion coefficient: $\lambda = 5$.
- Confidence level: $\alpha = 0.95$.
- Maximum acceptable CVaR: $\text{CVaR}_{\text{max}} = 0.05$.

**Python Code** We can solve this problem with `cvxpy` as follows.

```
import cvxpy as cp
import numpy as np

# Define problem data
mu = np.array([0.1, 0.12, 0.15])
Sigma = np.array([[0.005, 0.001, 0.002],
                  [0.001, 0.006, 0.003],
                  [0.002, 0.003, 0.009]])
R = np.array([[0.08, 0.1, 0.12],
              [0.05, 0.07, 0.09],
              [0.12, 0.15, 0.18],
              [0.03, 0.02, 0.04],
              [0.15, 0.2, 0.25]])
```

```
# Define variables
w = cp.Variable(3)
VaR = cp.Variable()
z = cp.pos(-R @ w - VaR)

# Define constraints
constraints = [
    cp.sum(w) == 1,
    w >= 0,
    VaR + (1 / (0.05 * R.shape[0])) * cp.sum(z) <= 0.05
]

# Define objective function
objective = cp.Maximize(mu @ w - 5 * cp.quad_form(w, Sigma))

# Solve problem
problem = cp.Problem(objective, constraints)
problem.solve()
```

**Solution and Interpretation** Solving this problem yields the following:

- Optimal portfolio weights: $w^* = [0.05, 0.30, 0.65]^\top$.
- Optimal Value at Risk: $\text{VaR}_\alpha^* = 0$.
- Optimal conditional value at risk: $\text{CVaR}_\alpha^* = 0$.

The VaR and the CVaR are only equal because our example has too few scenarios.

The inclusion of the CVaR constraint in the Mean-Variance optimization framework allows for better management of tail risks, ensuring the portfolio is robust against extreme market movements. By treating $\text{VaR}_\alpha$ and $z_j$ as decision variables, the optimization process determines optimal risk levels that comply with the investor's risk tolerance. This approach provides a refined method for constructing portfolios less vulnerable to market crashes and sudden shifts in asset values.

## 3.7 NOTES

The general approach of the MV analysis and the related results are based on Constantinides and Malliaris (1995) and Merton (1972). Other interesting references are Meucci (2005), Fabozzi et al. (2007) and Back (2017). Alternative formulations of the optimization program in equation (3.1) can be found in Fabozzi et al. (2007). The MV problem with prohibited short selling has no analytic solution and must be solved by quadratic programming methods.

When applying the Markowitz model, it is usual to obtain $\mathbf{R}$ and $\mathbf{\Sigma}$ from their sample counterparts. Nevertheless, it has been shown that this method leads to portfolios that perform worse than equally weighted portfolios (Frankfurter and Seagle, 1976; Jobson and Korkię, 1980). Different approaches have emerged to address this problem, including the shrinkage estimator of Ledoit and Wolf (2003, 2004), the quasi-Bayesian method of Black and Litterman (1991a), the bootstrapping method of Michaud (1998), and the stochastic optimization approach of Lai et al. (2011).

Markowitz himself soon realized that variance "considers extremely high and extremely low returns equally undesirable", what led him to include semivariance, a downside risk measure, into the MV analysis (Markowitz, 1959). The resulting mean-semivariance portfolio optimization problem was embedded in his Critical Line Algorithm in (Markowitz et al., 1993). See also Ballestero (2005).

A large number of papers have been published extending Markowitz's initial framework to other risk measures, covering, among others, Value-at-Risk (Deng et al., 2013; Feng et al., 2015; Lwin et al., 2017), CVaR (Piri et al., 2014; Zhao et al., 2015; Krzemienowski and Szymczyk, 2016), or ERoD (Ding and Uryasev, 2022).

The CAPM presentation is inspired by Constantinides and Malliaris (1995). Another useful reference has been Luenberger (1997). Alternative derivations of the CAPM can be found in Ingersoll (1987), where a utility maximization method is used, and in Back (2017), where the CAPM is derived as a one-factor model.

The CAPM received criticism shortly after its appearance. In Jensen (1972) and Blume and Friend (1973), the inconsistencies of the model with the empirical data were exposed. On the other hand, Roll (1977) argued that assessing the CAPM is equivalent to testing the efficiency of the market portfolio and that, therefore, the CAPM is not testable. Ross objected to the conclusions of the latter article, responding that "if we take Roll's objections seriously, then no theory is testable" (Ross, 1977). The testability of the CAPM is supported by more recent studies (Guermat, 2014).

Although most of the papers related to the CAPM refer to empirical evidence of its validity, some extensions have also been developed, among which we can mention the international CAPM of Solnik (1974) and Ng (2004), and the intertemporal CAPM of Merton (1973).

The first rigorous presentation of APT, based on the author's earlier work, appeared in Ross (1976). We have followed a different approach based mainly on Ingersoll (1984, 1987) and Luenberger (1997). A more general version of Theorem 3.7, for approximate factor models, can be found in Ingersoll (1984). A completely general version, valid for arbitrary normed vector spaces, appears in Reisman (1988). The APT was initially presented as a testable alternative to the CAPM (Roll and Ross, 1980). However, Shanken (1982) questioned this statement with arguments similar to those used in Roll (1977) against the testability of the CAPM. Analogously to what happened with the CAPM, in a later article, Dybvig and Ross (1985) refuted Shanken's objection. Dybvig and Ross' article also contains a comprehensive list of theoretical and empirical papers related to APT. Continuing with the analogies with the CAPM, among the later developments of the APT, we can highlight the international APT of Solnik (1983) and the intertemporal APT of Reisman (1992).

CHAPTER 4

# Bayesian Methods in Portfolio Optimization

Bayesian methods have increasingly become integral in the field of finance (Rachev et al., 2008), and the domain of quantitative portfolio management is no exception. These methods provide a robust framework for making probabilistic inferences, allowing financial analysts and portfolio managers to make better-informed *decisions under uncertainty*. This uncertainty is not only modeled in the data but in the parameters that describe it as well.

Bayesian analysis is rooted in Bayes's Theorem, a fundamental theorem in probability theory (see Bernard and Smith [2000] for a standard reference on Bayesian analysis). The theorem is named after Presbyterian minister Thomas Bayes, an eighteenth-century mathematician and theologian. Mathematically, Bayes's Theorem is expressed as:

$$P(A|B) = \frac{P(B|A)\,P(A)}{P(B)}. \tag{4.1}$$

In this formula, $P(A|B)$ represents the posterior probability, or the probability of hypothesis $A$ given the data $B$. $P(B|A)$ is the likelihood, which is the probability of observing the data $B$ given that hypothesis $A$ is true. $P(A)$ is the prior probability, representing our initial belief about the hypothesis before observing the data, $B$. Finally, $P(B)$ is the marginal likelihood or evidence, which is the probability of observing the data under all possible hypotheses.

It is worth putting Bayes's Theorem in more intuitive notation:

$$\underbrace{p(\theta|x)}_{\text{posterior over parameters } \theta \text{ given data } x} = \frac{\overbrace{p(x|\theta)}^{\text{model likelihood}} \quad \overbrace{p(\theta)}^{\text{prior over parameters}}}{\underbrace{p(x)}_{\text{evidence of data}}}, \tag{4.2}$$

where $x$ is observed data, the *hypothesis*, $\theta$, is the set of parameters that are used in the available data model or likelihood function. The prior, as stated previously, is the expression of information, or belief of parameter values, before the experiment that yields data $x$ is performed.

In finance, Bayesian methods allow for the integration of both historical data and subjective beliefs in the assessment of risk and return in portfolio management. This approach contrasts with traditional or *frequentist* methods, which often rely solely on historical data. In contrast, Bayesian methods provide a more holistic view by combining prior knowledge with empirical data, which can be particularly valuable in financial decision-making where both historical data and market intuition play roles, like in the Black-Litterman model (see, *e.g.*, He and Litterman [1999] and Satchell and Scowcroft [2000]). Bayesian techniques are particularly powerful in dealing with complex models and in situations where data is scarce or noisy. Modeling the data noise is the role of the likelihood, as it provides a statistical model of the data for a given set of parameters. However, the Bayesian formalism also allows for the modeling of uncertainty in parameters, which is the role of the prior distribution, $p(\theta)$. And importantly, then, parameters in the Bayesian framework are *stochastic* (Bernard and Smith, 2000). Herein lies the main departure of the Bayesian and frequentist statistical camps. Also, note that the prior distribution, as already alluded to, describes *belief* about the system parameters. This is because the prior is invoked before any experiment is performed. Thus, the prior is also well-suited to incorporate know system structure and dynamics or the modeler's beliefs about them, at any rate.

For instance, in quantitative portfolio management, Bayesian methods can be used to update beliefs about the expected returns and risks of different assets as new data becomes available. This process involves continually updating the posterior distributions of the expected returns, allowing portfolio managers to adjust their strategies in a more dynamic and informed manner.

Another significant advantage of Bayesian methods is their ability to model uncertainty and incorporate it into the decision-making process. This is particularly useful in finance, where uncertainty is a constant factor. By quantifying uncertainty and incorporating it into models, Bayesian methods provide a more realistic framework for portfolio optimization and risk management.

Thus, to summarize this introductory discussion, Bayesian methods offer a powerful and flexible framework for decision-making in finance and portfolio management. These methods enable the integration of both objective data and subjective beliefs, providing a comprehensive approach to managing financial portfolios. As the financial world becomes increasingly complex and data-driven, the importance of Bayesian methods in finance is only likely to grow.

## 4.1 THE PRIOR

The prior as demarcated in (4.2) in Bayesian statistics is the Probability Density Function (PDF) associated with knowledge or belief of a system's workings. It is important to clarify why a belief might make its way into a quantitative analysis. This is the way we can express how a researcher might expect a system to behave before an experiment is conducted. For example, a portfolio comprised of $N$ stocks has dynamics that are unknown exactly, but the dynamics can be modeled roughly as a set of coupled geometric, fractional Brownian motions (gfBm) parameterized by $\boldsymbol{\theta} = (\mathbf{b}, \Sigma, \dots)$ that includes drift, $\mathbf{b}$, and covariance, $\Sigma$, among other possible parameters, for all stocks in the portfolio. Since the drift is a real number for each stock, it might be modeled by a normal distribution. However, this is not necessarily a desirable choice for the covariance matrix as it must be positive definite. To accommodate this, a choice is an inverse Wishart distribution.

**An Example: gfBm in Stock Prices** Let us dig into the example of the previous paragraph. See Rostek and Schöbel (2013) and Ibrahim et al. (2021) for detailed proofs of what is here given as fact. Note that gfBm has also been used in modeling option pricing (Misiran et al., 2012).

As stated, the example still requires some specification. First, note that gfBm is a generalization of a Brownian motion (Bm), and is a random walk (Angstmann et al., 2019). Ordinary Brownian motion is described by a Wiener process (see Schuss [2009] for a comprehensive treatment), $W_t$, characterized by:

1. $W_0 = 0$.
2. $W_t$ is continuous with probability 1.
3. $W_t$ has *independent increments*, meaning that for every finite sequence of times $0 < t_0 < t_1 < \cdots < t_N$, the random variables $W_{t_0}, W_{t_1} - W_{t_0}, W_{t_2} - W_{t_1}, \dots, W_{t_N} - W_{t_{N-1}}$ are all jointly independent.
4. $W_t - W_s \sim \mathcal{N}(0, t - s)$.

There are two parts to gfBm: the *geometric* part of Bm, and the *fractional* part of the Bm.

Let's first explain geometric Bm (gBm). The gBm for a stochastic process $S_t$ is defined by the stochastic differential equation (SDE, in one dimension):

$$dS_t = bS_t dt + S_t \sigma dW_t, \tag{4.3}$$

which, for a given initial condition $S_0$, admits a closed-form solution:

$$S_t = S_0 e^{\left(b - \frac{\sigma^2}{2}\right)t + \sigma W_t}. \tag{4.4}$$

Note that in a multivariate setting, the $i^{\text{th}}$ stock obeys the SDE:

$$dS_t^i = b^i S_t^i dt + S_t^i \sum_{j=1}^{N} \Sigma_{ij} dW_t^j. \tag{4.5}$$

Now, let us explore the fractional Bm (fBm), another generalization of the Wiener process, denoted by $W_t^H$, where $H$ is the so-called *Hurst exponent*. The exponent, $0 \leq H \leq 1$, determines the memory effect of the fBm:

1. $H = 1/2$ reduces fBm to regular Brownian motion.
2. $H > 1/2$ makes the increments positively correlated, defining a process with long-term memory. That is, increasing processes tend to keep increasing.
3. $H < 1/2$ makes the increments negatively correlated, defining a process with short-term memory. That is, the process at one time instance is negatively correlated with the process later instance, tending to lead to oscillatory behavior.

The fBm is a zero-mean *Gaussian process* defined by its covariance:

$$\Sigma^H(t,s) = \mathbb{E}\left[W_t^H W_s^H\right] = \frac{1}{2}\left(|t|^{2H} + |s|^{2H} - |t-s|^{2H}\right). \tag{4.6}$$

We will have much more to say about Gaussian processes in Section 4.6. An fBm path is given in terms of the regular Wiener process by:

$$\begin{aligned} W_t^H = W_0^H + \frac{1}{\Gamma(H+1/2)} \Bigg\{ & \int_{-\infty}^{0} \left[(t-s)^{H-1/2} - (-s)^{H-1/2}\right] dW_s \\ & + \int_0^t (t-s)^{H-1/2} dW_s \Bigg\}, \end{aligned} \tag{4.7}$$

where $\Gamma$ is the Gamma function. It can be shown that the path $W_t^H$ has stationary increments.

Finally, putting these facts together, the geometric, fractional Brownian motion in one dimension is expressed as an SDE:

$$dS_t = bS_t dt + S_t \sigma dW_t^H \tag{4.8}$$

whose solution is:

$$S_t = S_0 e^{bt - \frac{\sigma^2}{2} t^{2H} + \sigma W_t^H}. \tag{4.9}$$

Equipped with this knowledge, we can now dive into a problem in Bayesian estimation for gfBm.

Let us say that the problem of interest is to find the Hurst exponent. Thus, we place a distribution on $H$. Recalling that $0 \leq H \leq 1$, we choose the Beta distribution (see Figure 4.1), whose support is $[0, 1]$, with shape parameters $\alpha > 0$ and $\beta > 0$:

$$H \sim \text{Beta}\left(H|\alpha, \beta\right) = \frac{H^{\alpha-1}(H-1)^{\beta-1}}{\mathrm{B}\left(\alpha, \beta\right)}, \tag{4.10}$$

where the Beta function can be written in terms of the Gamma functions as

$$\mathrm{B}\left(\alpha, \beta\right) = \frac{\Gamma\left(\alpha\right)\Gamma\left(\beta\right)}{\Gamma\left(\alpha + \beta\right)}. \tag{4.11}$$

Recall that the mean of $\mathrm{B}\left(\alpha, \beta\right)$-distributed random variable is given by

$$\mathbb{E}\left[H\right] = \frac{\alpha}{\alpha + \beta}. \tag{4.12}$$

Considering the interpretation of the Hurst exponent given, we may expect that $\mathbb{E}\left[H\right]$ is roughly 1/2, which implies $\alpha = \beta$. This family of Beta distributions is symmetric about $H = 1/2$. Referring back to Figure 4.1, and considering the form of the Beta distribution in equation (4.10), $\alpha = \beta = 1$ is a uniform distribution, and $\alpha = \beta = 2$ yields an inverted parabola. Note that as $\alpha$ and $\beta$ increase, the Beta distribution becomes increasingly peaked, tending to a delta distribution centered at the mean of the Beta.

To continue our example, we may pick values around $\alpha = \beta = 100$ or so, since we expect the Hurst exponent to be close to 1/2. Some samples of this prior are shown in Figure 4.2. See Figure 4.3 for sample paths corresponding to different Hurst exponents. The next step is to choose a likelihood function, that is, the distribution of the data for a given set of parameters sampled for the prior, which is the topic of the upcoming section.

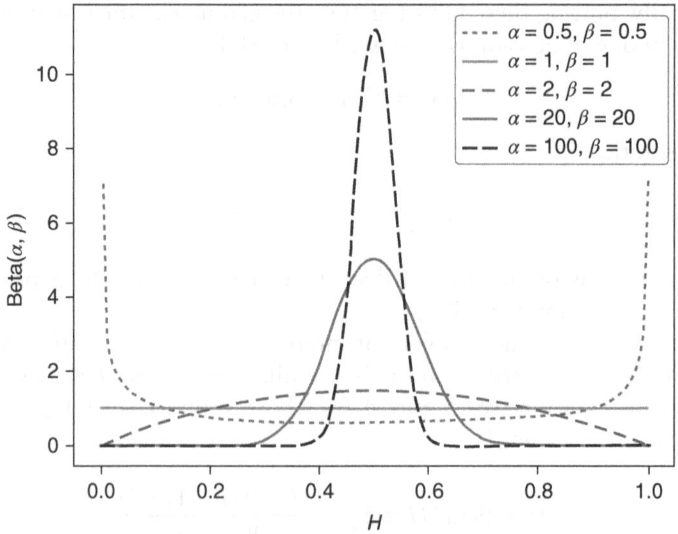


**FIGURE 4.1** Beta distribution as the PDF of the Hurst exponent, $H$.

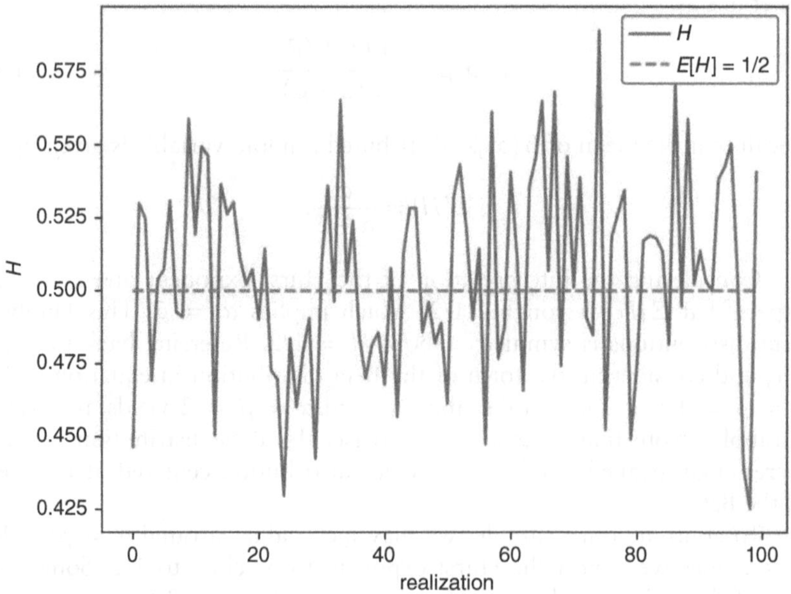


**FIGURE 4.2** Trace of samples of $H$ from the Beta(100,100) prior.

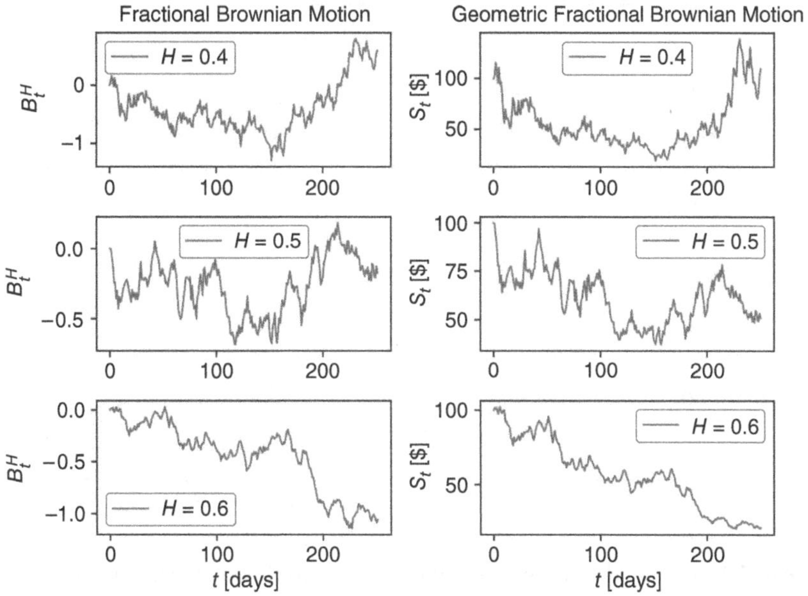


**FIGURE 4.3** Fractional and geometric fractional Brownian motions for different Hurst exponents to show the memory effect introduced by varying $H$: Lower $H$ results in anticorrelated increments, $H = 1/2$ is Brownian motion; higher $H$ results in correlated increments, showing a long-term memory effect.

## 4.2 THE LIKELIHOOD

So far we have discussed the selection of the prior that reflects what we might expect about a dataset's distribution parameters. What has not been discussed yet is how the data themselves are distributed, considering the parameters suggested by the prior. This is the *likelihood* function. The likelihood is a non-normalized distribution function conditional on the prior parameters. Importantly, the likelihood reflects our knowledge of the system's dynamics, $p(x|\theta)$ (see Bernard and Smith [2000]).

To continue with our example, we will present the normal distribution as it is often a viable choice because it models noise well (or exactly, in some scenarios). In the case of financial time series, Gaussian processes and noise are a common choice to price paths in the form of a stochastic differential equation, such as an Ornstein-Uhlenbeck process or a gfBm as we have chosen in our example. What we will assume about the data, besides being a gfBm, is that there is some added uncertainty in the process due to random market forces, and that this noise can be modeled as normal with meaning equal to the true price and constant variance set to 5. This value of the

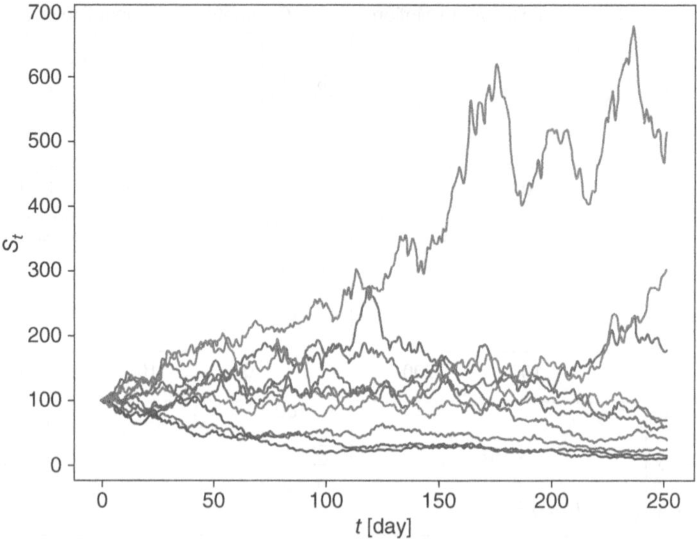


**FIGURE 4.4** Independent draws from the Gaussian likelihood in equation (4.13).

variance is chosen since the average starting price of the paths has been chosen to be 100, thus we may expect a 5% variation about the mean. Putting this all together, we have a likelihood for the data given by

$$s_t \sim \mathcal{N}\left(s_t|\mu_{s_t}, 5\right). \tag{4.13}$$

See Figure 4.4 for 10 independent draws from this likelihood function.

We close this section by mentioning the existence of *conjugate priors*. A prior is said to be *conjugate to a likelihood* if the resulting posterior is in the same distribution family as the prior. In our current example, the Beta distribution is conjugate to the Bernoulli, binomial, inverse binomial, and geometric distributions, which are not reasonable likelihoods for our price path data. In the next section, we discuss the posterior and approximate the Beta (100,100) by a sharp Gaussian to be able to get an analytical expression for the posterior.

## 4.3 THE POSTERIOR

We have reached the goal main of Bayesian statistics: a distribution over the parameters that is consistent with what we know about the system and the given data. This is the *posterior* distribution $p(\theta|x)$. Being able to compute statistics from this distribution allows for two important estimators for the parameters: the *maximum a posteriori* (MAP) estimate and the *minimum mean squared error* (MMSE). The former is the mode of the posterior whereas the latter is the mean (Bernard and Smith, 2000):

$$\text{MAP:} \quad \theta_{\text{MAP}} = \underset{\theta}{\operatorname{argmax}}\, p\left(\theta|x\right) \tag{4.14}$$

$$\text{MMSE:} \quad \theta_{\text{MMSE}} = \int \theta p(\theta|x). \tag{4.15}$$

Note that the MAP estimate is a maximum likelihood estimate of the parameters, which only depends on the likelihood and the prior but not on the evidence, hence it is often chosen as it does not require knowledge of the full posterior distribution. The same is clearly not true of the MMSE.

There are a few options to compute the posterior:

1. **Analytically:** For scenarios where the symbol manipulations lead to known distributions.
2. **Numerically:** This is generally the best option as the previous scenario is usually infeasible due to the complexity of real-world problems.
3. **Do not compute:** Depending on the problem, a MAP estimate may be sufficient. In this case, the maximum of the product of the likelihood and the prior may be computed without need for computing the full posterior.

**Algorithm 1:** Metropolis-Hastings Algorithm for estimation of $H$.

**Initialize:** Start with an initial parameter value $H^{(0)}$.
**Set:** Prior parameters $\alpha$ and $\beta$ for $H$.
**for** $i = 1$ **to** $N$ iterations **do**
  Propose $H' \sim q(H' \mid H^{(i-1)})$, where $q$ is the proposal distribution;
  Generate a sample path $s'$ using *gfBm*$(H')$;
  Calculate likelihood $L(D \mid H')$ using the proposed path;
  Calculate acceptance ratio:

$$A = \min\left(1, \frac{p(H')L(D \mid H')q(H^{(i-1)} \mid H')}{p(H^{(i-1)})L(D \mid H^{(i-1)})q(H' \mid H^{(i-1)})}\right)$$

  Accept or reject:
  **if** $u \sim \text{Uniform}(0, 1) < A$ **then**
    $H^{(i)} \leftarrow H'$;
  **else**
    $H^{(i)} \leftarrow H^{(i-1)}$;

To continue with our running example, we proceed to estimate $H$. This is done through a Markov Chain Monte Carlo (MCMC) sampling technique called the *Metropolis-Hastings* (MH) sampling algorithm (see Murphy [2023] for a modern exposition). Generally, speaking, MCMC is a broad family of stochastic sampling algorithms, within which MH is in the algorithm class called *accept-reject*. Its pseudo code for our example is provided in Algorithm 1. In broad terms, the algorithm works by initializing $H$, setting parameters for the distribution of $H$. We then proceed to propose a new value for the parameter $H$ and sample price paths under this proposal. Next, we compute the corresponding likelihood and the acceptance ratio. Whether the new parameter value is accepted or rejected depends on whether the newly sampled data is more or less likely than the previous sample. This process is continued for a predetermined number or iterations $N$. The results of this algorithm are shown in Figure 4.5, where the top panel shows the ground truth prior in black and the estimate in a gray histogram. The bottom panel shows the posterior estimate or the ground truth value of $H$.

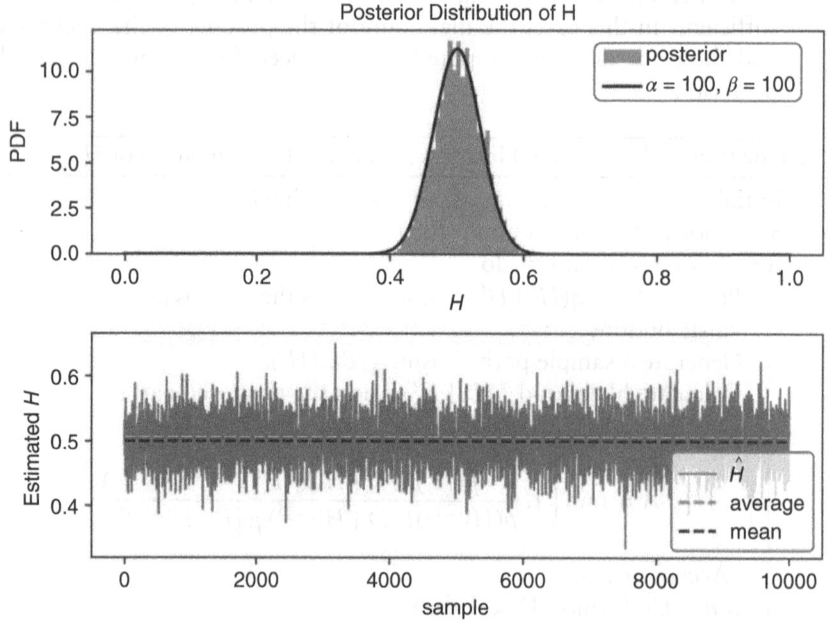


**FIGURE 4.5** **Top:** Estimated density of the MCMC sampled posterior in gray and the ground truth prior in black. **Bottom:** Samples of $H$ from MCMC sampling in gray, the sample average in dashed gray and the true mean in dashed black.

## 4.4 FILTERING

### The Kalman Filter

The Kalman filter, developed by Rudolf E. Kalman (1960a), is an algorithm that provides efficient computational means to estimate the state of a process in a way that minimizes the mean of the squared error. In this sense, it is the optimal estimator (Särkkä and Svensson, 2023). It is widely used in control systems (Lora-Millan et al., 2021), navigation systems (Kalita and Lyakhov, 2022), and for signal processing (Einicke, 2014).

The system state at time $k$ is represented as $\mathbf{x}_k$. The state space model is given by:

$$\mathbf{x}_k = \mathbf{A}_{k-1}\mathbf{x}_{k-1} + \mathbf{q}_{k-1} \tag{4.16}$$

$$\mathbf{y}_k = \mathbf{H}_k\mathbf{x}_k + \mathbf{r}_k, \tag{4.17}$$

where $\mathbf{x} \in \mathbb{R}^n$ is the state, $\mathbf{y} \in \mathbb{R}^m$ is the measurement, $\mathbf{A}_{k-1}$ is the state transition matrix, $\mathbf{H}_k$ is the measurement model matrix, $\mathbf{q}_{k-1} \sim \mathcal{N}(0, \mathbf{Q}_{k-1})$ is the process noise, and $\mathbf{r}_k \sim \mathcal{N}(0, \mathbf{R}_{k-1})$ is the measurement noise.

The Kalman filter typically is written as a probabilistic model, where sampling for the state is done by taking the product of the corresponding model matrix and the current value of the state, and samples with the corresponding variance covariance. Likewise, the measurement is updated after the underlying state is updated. The filter takes the form:

$$p(\mathbf{x}_k|\mathbf{x}_{k-1}) = \mathcal{N}(\mathbf{x}_k|\mathbf{A}_{k-1}\mathbf{x}_{k-1}, \mathbf{Q}_{k-1}) \tag{4.18}$$

$$p(\mathbf{y}_k|\mathbf{x}_k) = \mathcal{N}(\mathbf{y}_k|\mathbf{H}_k\mathbf{x}_k, \mathbf{R}_{k-1}). \tag{4.19}$$

It can be shown (Särkkä and Svensson, 2023) that the update equations can be solved in closed form, yielding the model:

$$p(\mathbf{x}_k|\mathbf{y}_{1:k-1}) = \mathcal{N}\left(\mathbf{x}_k|\mathbf{m}_k^-, \mathbf{P}_k^-\right) \tag{4.20}$$

$$p(\mathbf{x}_k|\mathbf{y}_{1:k}) = \mathcal{N}(\mathbf{x}_k|\mathbf{m}_k, \mathbf{P}_k) \tag{4.21}$$

$$p(\mathbf{y}_k|\mathbf{y}_{1:k-1}) = \mathcal{N}\left(\mathbf{y}_k|\mathbf{H}_k\mathbf{m}_k^-, \mathbf{S}_k\right). \tag{4.22}$$

The variables introduced in the model correspond to the prediction and update steps. The prediction step is

$$\mathbf{m}_k^- = \mathbf{A}_{k-1}\mathbf{m}_{k-1} \tag{4.23}$$

$$\mathbf{P}_k^- = \mathbf{A}_{k-1}\mathbf{P}_{k-1}\mathbf{A}_{k-1}^{\mathrm{T}} + \mathbf{Q}_{k-1}. \tag{4.24}$$

The update step is

$$\mathbf{v}_k = \mathbf{y}_k - \mathbf{H}_k \mathbf{m}_k^- \tag{4.25}$$

$$\mathbf{S}_k = \mathbf{H}_k \mathbf{P}_k^- \mathbf{H}_k^{\mathrm{T}} + \mathbf{R}_k \tag{4.26}$$

$$\mathbf{K}_k = \mathbf{P}_k^- \mathbf{H}_k^{\mathrm{T}} \mathbf{S}_k^{-1} \tag{4.27}$$

$$\mathbf{m}_k = \mathbf{m}_k^- + \mathbf{K}_k \mathbf{v}_k \tag{4.28}$$

$$\mathbf{P}_k = \mathbf{P}_k^- - \mathbf{K}_k \mathbf{S}_k \mathbf{K}_k^{\mathrm{T}}. \tag{4.29}$$

Implementing a Kalman filter requires recalculating the vectors and matrices at each iteration.

There are important applications of the Kalman filter, including:

In aerospace, the Kalman filter is used for trajectory estimation and navigation systems in aircraft and spacecraft.

Robotic systems use the Kalman filter for localization and mapping as well as for sensor fusion (i.e., merging of information from different sensors that provide disparate bits of information of the underlying state) to accurately understand the robot's environment.

In finance, the Kalman filter is applied in the context of time series analysis for predicting stock prices and for econometric modeling.

The Kalman filter remains a cornerstone in estimation theory with a wide range of applications. Its ability to provide optimal solutions under certain conditions makes it invaluable in many complex systems.

### The Extended Kalman Filter

The Kalman filter (KF) is optimal for linear systems with Gaussian noise. However, many real-world applications, including financial market modeling, involve nonlinear dynamics. The Extended Kalman filter (EKF) generalizes the KF to accommodate nonlinear state transitions and measurement models (Särkkä and Svensson, 2023).

In the EKF framework, the state space model is now described by:

$$\mathbf{x}_k = \mathbf{f}\left(\mathbf{x}_{k-1}, \mathbf{u}_{k-1}\right) + \mathbf{q}_{k-1} \tag{4.30}$$

$$\mathbf{y}_k = \mathbf{h}\left(\mathbf{x}_k\right) + \mathbf{r}_k, \tag{4.31}$$

where $\mathbf{f}$ and $\mathbf{h}$ are potentially nonlinear functions representing the state transition and measurement models, respectively. The other variables retain their meanings from the linear KF.

The probabilistic interpretation is similar to the linear KF:

$$p\left(\mathbf{x}_k|\mathbf{x}_{k-1}\right) = \mathcal{N}\left(\mathbf{x}_k|\mathbf{f}\left(\mathbf{x}_{k-1},\mathbf{u}_{k-1}\right),\mathbf{Q}_{k-1}\right) \tag{4.32}$$

$$p\left(\mathbf{y}_k|\mathbf{x}_k\right) = \mathcal{N}\left(\mathbf{y}_k|\mathbf{h}\left(\mathbf{x}_k\right),\mathbf{R}_{k-1}\right). \tag{4.33}$$

However, due to the nonlinearities, a closed-form solution is not available. The EKF addresses this by linearizing the functions **f** and **h** around the current state estimate using their Jacobian matrices:

$$\mathbf{F}_{k-1} = \left.\frac{\partial \mathbf{f}}{\partial \mathbf{x}}\right|_{\mathbf{x}=\mathbf{m}_{k-1}}, \quad \mathbf{H}_k = \left.\frac{\partial \mathbf{h}}{\partial \mathbf{x}}\right|_{\mathbf{x}=\mathbf{m}_k^-}. \tag{4.34}$$

With these linearizations, the EKF proceeds with the prediction and update steps, mirroring the structure of the linear KF:

**Prediction:**

$$\mathbf{m}_k^- = \mathbf{f}\left(\mathbf{m}_{k-1},\mathbf{u}_{k-1}\right) \tag{4.35}$$

$$\mathbf{P}_k^- = \mathbf{F}_{k-1}\mathbf{P}_{k-1}\mathbf{F}_{k-1}^{\mathrm{T}} + \mathbf{Q}_{k-1}. \tag{4.36}$$

**Update:**

$$\mathbf{v}_k = \mathbf{y}_k - \mathbf{h}\left(\mathbf{m}_k^-\right) \tag{4.37}$$

$$\mathbf{S}_k = \mathbf{H}_k\mathbf{P}_k^-\mathbf{H}_k^{\mathrm{T}} + \mathbf{R}_k \tag{4.38}$$

$$\mathbf{K}_k = \mathbf{P}_k^-\mathbf{H}_k^{\mathrm{T}}\mathbf{S}_k^{-1} \tag{4.39}$$

$$\mathbf{m}_k = \mathbf{m}_k^- + \mathbf{K}_k\mathbf{v}_k \tag{4.40}$$

$$\mathbf{P}_k = \mathbf{P}_k^- - \mathbf{K}_k\mathbf{S}_k\mathbf{K}_k^{\mathrm{T}}. \tag{4.41}$$

The EKF is not optimal like the KF for linear systems, as the linearization introduces approximations. However, it is a practical and widely used method for state estimation in nonlinear systems.

Note that careful initialization of the state estimate and covariance is essential for EKF convergence. The accuracy of the EKF depends on the validity of the linear approximations. Highly nonlinear systems may require more sophisticated filtering techniques. The EKF can be used in finance for tasks such as volatility estimation, portfolio optimization, and risk management, where models often incorporate nonlinear relationships. Likewise, the EKF can be used to estimate the hidden states of a financial model, such as the expected returns and volatilities of assets, which are then used as inputs to a portfolio optimization algorithm. The filter can adapt to changes in market conditions, providing real-time updates to the portfolio weights.

### Particle Filters

The Kalman filter (KF) and Extended Kalman filter (EKF) assume Gaussian distributions for the state and measurement noise (Särkkä and Svensson, 2023). However, financial markets often exhibit non-Gaussian behavior, such as fat tails and skewness. Particle filters (PFs) offer a flexible, non-parametric alternative for state estimation in such scenarios.

PFs, also known as Sequential Monte Carlo (SMC) methods, approximate the posterior distribution of the state $p\left(\mathbf{x}_k|\mathbf{y}_{1:k}\right)$ using a set of weighted particles:

$$p\left(\mathbf{x}_k|\mathbf{y}_{1:k}\right) \approx \sum_{i=1}^{N} w_k^{(i)} \delta\left(\mathbf{x}_k - \mathbf{x}_k^{(i)}\right). \tag{4.42}$$

$N$ is the number of particles, $\mathbf{x}_k^{(i)}$ is the $i$-th particle representing the state at time $k$, and $w_k^{(i)}$ is the weight associated with the $i$-th particle, representing its importance.

The PF algorithm iterates through two main steps: prediction and update.

**Prediction Step** Each particle is propagated according to the state transition model:

$$\mathbf{x}_k^{(i)} \sim p\left(\mathbf{x}_k|\mathbf{x}_{k-1}^{(i)}, \mathbf{u}_{k-1}\right). \tag{4.43}$$

**Update Step** The weights of the particles are updated based on the likelihood of the measurement:

$$w_k^{(i)} \propto w_{k-1}^{(i)} p\left(\mathbf{y}_k|\mathbf{x}_k^{(i)}\right), \tag{4.44}$$

and then normalized to sum to one.

To avoid degeneracy, where a few particles dominate the distribution, a resampling step is often performed. This involves discarding particles with low weights and duplicating those with high weights. PFs can be used to estimate the hidden states of complex financial models, such as stochastic volatility or regime-switching models. These estimates can then inform dynamic portfolio allocation strategies. For instance, the PF can track the evolution of asset volatilities, allowing for risk-sensitive adjustments to portfolio weights.

When applying PFs, it is important to consider the following:

1. **Particle Number:** The number of particles directly affects the accuracy of the approximation. A larger number of particles leads to better accuracy but also higher computational cost. Bayesian methods, such as the marginal likelihood or the deviance information criterion (DIC), can be employed to guide the selection of an appropriate particle number, balancing accuracy and computational efficiency.
2. **Resampling Strategy:** Different resampling strategies can be employed, each with their own trade-offs in terms of accuracy and computational efficiency. Some common strategies include:
   (a) **Multinomial Resampling:** This is the most basic strategy, where particles are resampled with probabilities proportional to their weights. It is simple to implement but can lead to sample impoverishment, where many particles become identical.
   (b) **Stratified Resampling:** This strategy divides the cumulative weight distribution into $N$ strata and samples one particle from each stratum. It helps to maintain particle diversity but can be computationally more expensive.
   (c) **Systematic Resampling:** Like stratified resampling, but particles are sampled at regular intervals along the cumulative weight distribution. It is computationally efficient but can introduce correlation between particles.
   (d) **Residual Resampling:** This strategy combines deterministic and probabilistic resampling. A fixed number of copies of each particle is first allocated based on their weights, and the remaining particles are sampled probabilistically. It can help to balance diversity and computational efficiency.

   The choice of resampling strategy depends on the specific application and the desired balance between accuracy, diversity, and computational cost.

PFs are a powerful tool for handling nonlinear and non-Gaussian dynamics in financial models, offering a flexible and robust approach to state estimation for quantitative portfolio management.

## 4.5 HIERARCHICAL BAYESIAN MODELS

Hierarchical Bayesian Models (HBMs) provide a powerful framework for modeling complex systems with multiple levels of uncertainty or various dependent stochastic variables that may be sampled sequentially

(Congdon, 2010). In quantitative portfolio management, HBMs offer several advantages over traditional methods, including the ability to incorporate prior knowledge, account for parameter uncertainty, and model dependencies between assets.

HBMs are characterized by a hierarchical structure, where parameters at one level are modeled as random variables with distributions that depend on parameters at higher levels. The joint posterior distribution of all parameters is then obtained using Bayes's Theorem:

$$p(\theta, \phi | \mathrm{y}) \propto p(\mathrm{y}|\theta) p(\theta|\phi) p(\phi), \tag{4.45}$$

where $\theta$ are the parameters of interest, such as asset returns or volatilities; $\phi$ are the hyperparameters that govern the distributions of $\theta$; and y are the observed data, such as historical asset prices or returns.

HBMs offer several advantages over traditional methods in quantitative portfolio management:

1. **Incorporation of Prior Knowledge:** HBMs allow for the incorporation of prior knowledge or beliefs about the parameters, which can help to improve the accuracy and stability of estimates, especially when data is limited (see Black and Litterman [1992b]).
2. **Accounting for Parameter Uncertainty:** HBMs explicitly model the uncertainty in parameter estimates, which can lead to more robust portfolio allocations (see Pástor and Stambaugh [2000]).
3. **Modeling Dependencies:** HBMs can capture dependencies between assets, such as correlations or common factors, which can improve portfolio diversification and risk management (see Engle [2002]).
4. **Shrinkage Estimation:** HBMs often induce shrinkage of parameter estimates toward a common mean, which can help to reduce estimation error and improve out-of-sample performance (see Jorion [1986]).
5. **Flexibility:** HBMs can accommodate a wide range of model specifications and prior distributions (see Gelman et al. [2013]), allowing for tailored solutions to specific portfolio management problems.

HBMs have been applied to various problems in quantitative portfolio management, including:

1. **Asset Allocation:** HBMs can be used to estimate expected returns, risks, and correlations for different asset classes, which are then used as inputs to a portfolio optimization algorithm (see Avramov and Zhou [2010]).
2. **Factor Modeling:** HBMs can be used to estimate the factor loadings and idiosyncratic volatilities in a multifactor model, which can help

to identify risk exposures and diversify portfolios (see Aguilar and West [2000]).
3. **Volatility Modeling:** HBMs can be used to estimate stochastic volatility models, which can capture the time-varying nature of volatility and improve risk forecasting (see Kim et al. [1998]).
4. **Portfolio Selection:** HBMs can be used to directly optimize portfolio weights, taking into account parameter uncertainty and prior beliefs (see Polson and Tew [2000]).

While HBMs offer many advantages, they also present some challenges. The specification of prior distributions can be subjective and may influence the results. MCMC methods can be computationally intensive, especially for large models and datasets. Model selection and validation can be challenging, as there are many model specifications and prior choices. Assessing the convergence of MCMC algorithms can be difficult, and there is a risk of obtaining inaccurate results if the algorithm has not converged.

Despite these challenges, the HBM remains a valuable tool for quantitative portfolio management, offering a flexible and powerful framework for modeling complex systems with multiple levels of uncertainty. With careful model specification, implementation, and validation, HBMs can lead to more robust and accurate portfolio allocations.

## 4.6 BAYESIAN OPTIMIZATION

Bayesian optimization is a powerful and efficient approach to solving complex optimization problems, particularly when the objective function is expensive to evaluate or lacks an explicit form (Frazier, 2018). This method combines principles from Bayesian statistics with Machine Learning to intelligently explore the parameter space and find optimal solutions with few function evaluations. At its core, Bayesian optimization uses a probabilistic model, typically a Gaussian process, to approximate the unknown objective function and guide the search process toward promising regions of the parameter space.

In the context of quantitative finance and portfolio management, Bayesian optimization has emerged as a valuable tool for tackling a wide range of challenges (see Dixon and Klabjan [2020], and Dixon et al. [2020] for a masterful exposition). From fine-tuning trading algorithms and optimizing portfolio allocations to calibrating complex financial models, this technique offers a robust and adaptable framework for decision-making under uncertainty. By leveraging prior knowledge and continuously updating beliefs based on new observations, Bayesian optimization provides a principled approach to balancing exploration and exploitation in the search for optimal solutions. This chapter will delve into the theoretical foundations of Bayesian optimization, explore its practical applications in finance, and discuss recent advancements that have further enhanced its effectiveness in navigating the complexities of modern financial markets.

### 4.6.1 Gaussian Processes in a Nutshell

Gaussian Processes (GPs) are powerful tools for modeling and understanding complex systems (see Rasmussen and Williams [2005] for a standard reference). They are a flexible, non-parametric approach to regression, classification, and other machine learning tasks. They offer a principled, practical, and probabilistic approach to learning in kernel machines.

A GP is a collection of random variables, any finite number of which have a joint Gaussian distribution. It is defined by a mean function $m(x)$ and a covariance function $k(x, x')$:

$$m(x) = \mathbb{E}[f(x)] \tag{4.46}$$

$$k(x, x') = \mathbb{E}[(f(x) - m(x))(f(x') - m(x'))]. \tag{4.47}$$

A GP can be written as:

$$f(x) \sim \mathcal{GP}(m(x), k(x, x')). \tag{4.48}$$

The function space view of GPs provides an intuitive understanding of how GPs define distributions over functions. Consider a set of input points $X = \{x_1, x_2, \ldots, x_n\}$. The corresponding function values $f(X) = \{f(x_1), f(x_2), \ldots, f(x_n)\}$ are jointly Gaussian:

$$f(X) \sim \mathcal{N}(m(X), K(X, X)), \tag{4.49}$$

where $m(X)$ is the mean vector, and $K(X, X)$ is the covariance matrix defined by the kernel function $k(x, x')$.

#### Covariance Functions

The choice of the covariance function $k(x, x')$ is crucial as it encodes our assumptions about the function we are modeling. Common choices include the squared exponential (or RBF) kernel, the Matérn kernel, and the periodic kernel. Each of these kernels incorporates different assumptions about the smoothness and periodicity of the underlying function.

**Squared Exponential Kernel** The squared exponential kernel is given by:

$$k(x, x') = \sigma^2 \exp\left(-\frac{\|x - x'\|^2}{2\ell^2}\right), \tag{4.50}$$

where $\sigma^2$ is the signal variance and $\ell$ is the length scale. This kernel assumes the function is infinitely differentiable, leading to smooth functions.

**Matérn Kernel** The Matérn kernel is parameterized by a smoothness parameter $\nu$:

$$k(x, x') = \sigma^2 \frac{2^{1-\nu}}{\Gamma(\nu)} \left(\frac{\sqrt{2\nu}\|x - x'\|}{\ell}\right)^{\nu} K_\nu\left(\frac{\sqrt{2\nu}\|x - x'\|}{\ell}\right), \tag{4.51}$$

where $K_\nu$ is a modified Bessel function. For $\nu = 3/2$ and $\nu = 5/2$, the Matérn kernel corresponds to less-smooth functions compared to the squared exponential kernel.

### Gaussian Process Regression

Gaussian Process Regression (GPR) provides a Bayesian approach to regression. Given training data $\mathcal{D} = \{(x_i, y_i) \mid i = 1, \ldots, n\}$, where $y_i = f(x_i) + \epsilon_i$ and $\epsilon_i \sim \mathcal{N}(0, \sigma_n^2)$ represents Gaussian noise, the goal is to predict the function value $f(x_*)$ at a new point $x_*$.

The joint distribution of the observed values $y$ and the function value at $x_*$ is:

$$\begin{bmatrix} y \\ f(x_*) \end{bmatrix} \sim \mathcal{N}\left(\begin{bmatrix} m(X) \\ m(x_*) \end{bmatrix}, \begin{bmatrix} K(X, X) + \sigma_n^2 I & k(X, x_*) \\ k(x_*, X) & k(x_*, x_*) \end{bmatrix}\right). \tag{4.52}$$

The predictive distribution for $f(x_*)$ given the data is Gaussian:

$$f(x_*) \mid X, y, x_* \sim \mathcal{N}(\mu_*, \sigma_*^2), \tag{4.53}$$

where

$$\mu_* = m(x_*) + k(x_*, X)\left[K(X, X) + \sigma_n^2 I\right]^{-1}(y - m(X)) \tag{4.54}$$

$$\sigma_*^2 = k(x_*, x_*) - k(x_*, X)\left[K(X, X) + \sigma_n^2 I\right]^{-1} k(X, x_*). \tag{4.55}$$

### Gaussian Process Classification

Gaussian Process Classification (GPC) extends GPs to classification tasks where the outputs are discrete class labels rather than continuous values.

The aim is to model the probability of class membership for a given input.

**Latent Function and Likelihood** In GPC, we introduce a latent function $f(x)$, which is mapped to the probability of class membership through a squashing function, such as the logistic sigmoid function for binary classification:

$$\sigma(f) = \frac{1}{1 + \exp(-f)}. \tag{4.56}$$

The likelihood of the observed class labels $y$ given the latent function values $f$ is then:

$$p(y_i|f_i) = \sigma(f_i)^{y_i}(1 - \sigma(f_i))^{1-y_i}, \tag{4.57}$$

where $y_i \in \{0, 1\}$.

**Posterior Distribution** The posterior distribution over the latent function values $f$ given the training data $(X, y)$ is obtained using Bayes' theorem:

$$p(f|X, y) = \frac{p(y|f)\,p(f|X)}{p(y|X)}, \tag{4.58}$$

where $p(f|X)$ is the prior distribution of the latent function values given by the GP:

$$f|X \sim \mathcal{N}(0, K(X, X)). \tag{4.59}$$

The likelihood $p(y|f)$ is the product of individual likelihoods for each training point.

Since the exact posterior distribution is analytically intractable, we resort to approximation methods such as Laplace approximation, Expectation Propagation (EP), or variational inference.

The Laplace approximation approximates the posterior with a Gaussian centered at the mode of the posterior. The steps are:

1. Find the mode $\hat{f}$ of the posterior by maximizing $\log p(f|X, y)$.
2. Approximate the posterior as a Gaussian around $\hat{f}$, using the Hessian of the negative log posterior.

$$p(f|X, y) \approx \mathcal{N}\left(\hat{f}, \left(K^{-1} + W\right)^{-1}\right), \tag{4.60}$$

where $W$ is a diagonal matrix with entries $W_{ii} = \sigma(f_i)(1 - \sigma(f_i))$.

Variational inference approximates the true posterior with a simpler distribution $q(f)$ by minimizing the Kullback-Leibler (KL) divergence between $q(f)$ and the true posterior:

$$KL(q(f) \| p(f|X,y)) = \int q(f) \log \frac{q(f)}{p(f|X,y)} df. \tag{4.61}$$

Given a new input $x_*$, the predictive distribution for the class label is obtained by integrating over the posterior distribution of the latent function:

$$p(y_* = 1|x_*, X, y) = \int \sigma(f_*) p(f_*|x_*, X, y)\, df_*. \tag{4.62}$$

For the Laplace approximation, this integral can be approximated using the Gaussian posterior of $f_*$.

**Multiclass Classification** For multiclass classification, where $y_i \in \{1, \ldots, K\}$, the latent function is extended to a vector $\mathrm{f}(x) = (f_1(x), \ldots, f_K(x))$. The softmax function is typically used to map the latent function to class probabilities:

$$p(y_i = k|\mathrm{f}(x_i)) = \frac{\exp(f_k(x_i))}{\sum_{j=1}^{K} \exp(f_j(x_i))}. \tag{4.63}$$

The posterior distribution and predictions are then managed in a comparable manner to the binary case, with appropriate modifications for the vector-valued latent function.

## Model Selection

Model selection in GPs involves choosing the kernel function and its hyperparameters. The kernel function encodes assumptions about the smoothness, periodicity, and other properties of the functions to be modeled. Common choices include the squared exponential (RBF) kernel, the Matérn kernel, and the periodic kernel.

Hyperparameters are typically learned by maximizing the marginal likelihood of the observed data:

$$\log p(y|X, \theta) = -\frac{1}{2} y^T K^{-1} y - \frac{1}{2} \log |K| - \frac{n}{2} \log 2\pi, \tag{4.64}$$

where $\theta$ represents the hyperparameters of the kernel function, and $K$ is the covariance matrix of the training inputs.

Gaussian Processes offer a powerful and flexible framework for probabilistic modeling. Their ability to capture uncertainties and their nonparametric nature make them suitable for a wide range of applications in machine learning. This essay has provided an overview of the key concepts and methods in Gaussian Processes, including their definition, regression, classification, and model selection.

### 4.6.2 Uncertainty Quantification and Bayesian Decision Theory

Uncertainty quantification (UQ) is a critical aspect of modern statistical and machine learning models (Soize, 2017; Sullivan, 2015). GPs provide a robust framework for modeling and managing uncertainties in complex systems. The core idea of a GP is to define a distribution over functions, allowing for predictions with quantified uncertainties.

In GPs, the typical setup for UQ is as follows. Given a set of observations $\mathcal{D} = \{(x_i, y_i) \mid i = 1, \ldots, n\}$, where $y_i = f(x_i) + \epsilon_i$ and $\epsilon_i \sim \mathcal{N}\left(0, \sigma_n^2\right)$, the goal is to make predictions at new input locations $\mathbf{x}_*$. Let $\mathbf{X} = \left[x_1, \ldots, x_n\right]^T$ and $\mathbf{y} = \left[y_1, \ldots, y_n\right]^T$. The joint distribution of the training outputs $\mathbf{y}$ and the test outputs $\mathbf{f}_*$ is:

$$\begin{bmatrix} \mathbf{y} \\ \mathbf{f}_* \end{bmatrix} \sim \mathcal{N}\left(0, \begin{bmatrix} K(\mathbf{X}, \mathbf{X}) + \sigma_n^2 I & K(\mathbf{X}, \mathbf{x}_*) \\ K(\mathbf{x}_*, \mathbf{X}) & K(\mathbf{x}_*, \mathbf{x}_*) \end{bmatrix}\right), \tag{4.65}$$

where $K(\mathbf{X}, \mathbf{X})$ is the covariance matrix evaluated at the training points, $K(\mathbf{X}, \mathbf{x}_*)$ is the covariance matrix between the training points and test points, and $K(\mathbf{x}_*, \mathbf{x}_*)$ is the covariance matrix at the test points.

The posterior distribution over the function values at the test points is given by:

$$\mathbf{f}_* \mid \mathbf{X}, \mathbf{y}, \mathbf{x}_* \sim \mathcal{N}\left(\bar{\mathbf{f}}_*, \operatorname{Cov}(\mathbf{f}_*)\right), \tag{4.66}$$

with

$$\bar{\mathbf{f}}_* = K(\mathbf{x}_*, \mathbf{X})\left[K(\mathbf{X}, \mathbf{X}) + \sigma_n^2 I\right]^{-1} \mathbf{y} \tag{4.67}$$

$$\operatorname{Cov}(\mathbf{f}_*) = K(\mathbf{x}_*, \mathbf{x}_*) - K(\mathbf{x}_*, \mathbf{X})\left[K(\mathbf{X}, \mathbf{X}) + \sigma_n^2 I\right]^{-1} K(\mathbf{X}, \mathbf{x}_*). \tag{4.68}$$

These equations provide both the mean prediction and the uncertainty (variance) of the predictions at new points $\mathbf{x}_*$.

Financial decision-making is typically done in scenarios of partial or noisy data adding a degree of uncertainty to any reached conclusions. Bayesian decision theory provides a framework for making optimal decisions under uncertainty.

Bayesian decision theory is built upon the following key elements Robert (2007):

1. **Parameter space $\Theta$:** The set of all states of nature.
2. **Action space $\mathcal{A}$:** The set of all actions available to the decision-maker.
3. **Loss function $L$: $\Theta \times \mathcal{A} \to \mathbb{R}$:** A function that quantifies the cost of taking an action given the true state of nature.
4. **Prior distribution $p(\theta)$:** The decision-maker's initial belief about the probability distribution of the parameters.
5. **Data $\mathcal{D}$:** Observations used to update the prior beliefs.
6. **Likelihood function $p(\mathcal{D}|\theta)$:** The probability of observing the data given the parameters.
7. **Posterior distribution $p(\theta|\mathcal{D})$:** The updated belief about the parameter distribution after observing the data.

**Decision Rules and Risk** A decision rule is a function $\delta : \mathcal{D} \to \mathcal{A}$ that maps observed data to actions. The quality of a decision rule is evaluated using the concept of risk.

**Definition 4.1 (Bayes Risk)** *The Bayes risk of a decision rule $\delta$ with respect to a prior distribution $p(\theta)$ is defined as:*

$$R(\delta, p) = \mathbb{E}_{\theta \sim p}\left[\mathbb{E}_{\mathcal{D}|\theta}\left[L(\theta, \delta(\mathcal{D}))\right]\right]. \tag{4.69}$$

**Optimal Decision Rules** The goal in Bayesian decision theory is to find the optimal decision rule that minimizes the Bayes risk.

**Theorem 4.1 (Bayes Decision Rule)** *The optimal decision rule $\delta^*$ that minimizes the Bayes risk is given by:*

$$\delta^*(\mathcal{D}) = \arg\min_{a \in \mathcal{A}} \mathbb{E}_{\theta|\mathcal{D}}[L(\theta, a)], \tag{4.70}$$

*where the expectation is taken with respect to the posterior distribution $p(\theta|\mathcal{D})$.*

Thus, Bayesian decision theory offers several advantages in quantitative portfolio optimization. For example, it provides a principled way to incorporate prior knowledge and uncertainty about market parameters. It naturally accounts for parameter uncertainty in the optimization process. It allows for continuous updating of beliefs as new market data becomes available. It can lead to more robust portfolio allocations compared to frequentist approaches, especially in the presence of estimation error. By leveraging Bayesian decision theory, quantitative portfolio managers can make more informed and potentially more robust investment decisions under uncertainty.

## 4.7 APPLICATIONS TO PORTFOLIO OPTIMIZATION

### 4.7.1 GP Regression for Asset Returns

Given a set of historical asset returns $\mathbf{y} = \{y_1, \ldots, y_n\}$ and corresponding input features $\mathbf{X} = \{\mathbf{x}_1, \ldots, \mathbf{x}_n\}$, we can use GP regression to predict future returns (Kocijan, 2009; Roberts et al., 2013). The predictive distribution for a new input $\mathbf{x}_*$ is Gaussian:

$$p\left(f_* | \mathbf{x}_*, \mathbf{X}, \mathbf{y}\right) = \mathcal{N}\left(f_* | \mu_*, \sigma_*^2\right), \tag{4.71}$$

where:

$$\mu_* = \mathbf{k}_*^T\left(\mathbf{K} + \sigma_n^2\mathbf{I}\right)^{-1}\mathbf{y} \tag{4.72}$$

$$\sigma_*^2 = k\left(\mathbf{x}_*, \mathbf{x}_*\right) - \mathbf{k}_*^T\left(\mathbf{K} + \sigma_n^2\mathbf{I}\right)^{-1}\mathbf{k}_*, \tag{4.73}$$

where $\mathbf{k}_*$ is the vector of covariances between $\mathbf{x}_*$ and the training inputs, $\mathbf{K}$ is the covariance matrix of the training inputs, and $\sigma_n^2$ is the noise variance.

GPs can be integrated into various portfolio optimization frameworks. One common approach is to use the predictive mean and variance from the GP to estimate expected returns and risks, and then substitute them into a mean-variance optimization or other utility maximization framework. This allows for the incorporation of model uncertainty into the optimization process, potentially leading to more robust portfolios.

### 4.7.2 Decision Theory in Portfolio Optimization

In quantitative portfolio optimization, Bayesian decision theory Robert (2007) may be applied as follows:

1. $\Theta$ represents the space of market states or parameter values (e.g., expected returns, covariances).
2. $\mathcal{A}$ is the set of portfolio allocations.
3. $L(\theta, a)$ could be the negative of the portfolio return or a more complex utility function.
4. $p(\theta)$ encapsulates prior beliefs about market parameters.

5. $\mathcal{D}$ consists of observed market data, such as historical returns.
6. The posterior $p(\theta|\mathcal{D})$ updates beliefs about market parameters based on observed data.
7. The optimal portfolio allocation $a^*$ is chosen to minimize the expected loss under the posterior distribution:

$$a^* = \arg\min_{a \in \mathcal{A}} \int_{\Theta} L(\theta, a)\, p(\theta|\mathcal{D})\, d\theta. \tag{4.74}$$

To illustrate the application of Bayesian decision theory in portfolio optimization, let us consider a simplified example involving two assets: a stock $S$ and a bond $B$. The problem setup is as follows:

1. **Parameter space $\Theta$:** Let $\theta = (\mu_S, \mu_B, \sigma_S, \sigma_B, \rho)$ represent the market parameters, where $\mu_S, \mu_B$ are expected returns, $\sigma_S, \sigma_B$ are volatilities, and $\rho$ is the correlation between S and B.
2. **Action space $\mathcal{A}$:** The set of portfolio weights $w = (w_S, w_B)$, where $w_S + w_B = 1$ and $0 \leq w_S, w_B \leq 1$.
3. **Loss function:** We will use the negative of the portfolio Sharpe ratio:

$$L(\theta, w) = -\frac{w_S\mu_S + w_B\mu_B - r_f}{\sqrt{w_S^2\sigma_S^2 + w_B^2\sigma_B^2 + 2w_S w_B \rho \sigma_S \sigma_B}}, \tag{4.75}$$

where $r_f$ is the risk-free rate.
4. **Prior distribution:** We will use independent normal priors for $\mu_S$ and $\mu_B$, and fixed values for the other parameters:

$$\mu_S \sim \mathcal{N}\left(0.08, 0.02^2\right) \tag{4.76}$$

$$\mu_B \sim \mathcal{N}\left(0.03, 0.01^2\right) \tag{4.77}$$

$$\sigma_S = 0.20 \tag{4.78}$$

$$\sigma_B = 0.05 \tag{4.79}$$

$$\rho = 0.1. \tag{4.80}$$

5. **Data:** Suppose we observe 1 year of daily returns, resulting in the following sample means:

$$\bar{r}_S = 0.10 \tag{4.81}$$

$$\bar{r}_B = 0.025. \tag{4.82}$$

6. **Likelihood function:** Assuming returns are normally distributed:

$$p\left(\bar{r}_S|\mu_S\right) \propto \exp\left(-\frac{n}{2\sigma_S^2}\left(\bar{r}_S-\mu_S\right)^2\right) \tag{4.83}$$

$$p\left(\bar{r}_B|\mu_B\right) \propto \exp\left(-\frac{n}{2\sigma_B^2}\left(\bar{r}_B-\mu_B\right)^2\right), \tag{4.84}$$

where $n = 252$ (trading days in a year).

We can now compute the posterior distributions for $\mu_S$ and $\mu_B$:

$$p\left(\mu_S|\bar{r}_S\right) \propto p\left(\bar{r}_S|\mu_S\right)p\left(\mu_S\right) \tag{4.85}$$

$$p\left(\mu_B|\bar{r}_B\right) \propto p\left(\bar{r}_B|\mu_B\right)p\left(\mu_B\right). \tag{4.86}$$

Given our normal priors and likelihoods, the posteriors are also normal distributions:

$$\mu_S|\bar{r}_S \sim \mathcal{N}\left(\mu_{S,post}, \sigma^2_{S,post}\right) \tag{4.87}$$

$$\mu_B|\bar{r}_B \sim \mathcal{N}\left(\mu_{B,post}, \sigma^2_{B,post}\right), \tag{4.88}$$

where:

$$\mu_{S,post} = \frac{\frac{0.08}{0.02^2}+\frac{252\cdot 0.10}{0.20^2}}{\frac{1}{0.02^2}+\frac{252}{0.20^2}} \approx 0.0991 \tag{4.89}$$

$$\sigma^2_{S,post} = \left(\frac{1}{0.02^2}+\frac{252}{0.20^2}\right)^{-1} \approx 0.000158 \tag{4.90}$$

$$\mu_{B,post} = \frac{\frac{0.03}{0.01^2}+\frac{252\cdot 0.025}{0.05^2}}{\frac{1}{0.01^2}+\frac{252}{0.05^2}} \approx 0.0253 \tag{4.91}$$

$$\sigma^2_{B,post} = \left(\frac{1}{0.01^2}+\frac{252}{0.05^2}\right)^{-1} \approx 0.0000099. \tag{4.92}$$

To find the optimal portfolio weights, we need to minimize the expected loss under the posterior distribution:

$$w^* = \arg\min_{w} \mathbb{E}_{\mu_S,\mu_B|\bar{r}_S,\bar{r}_B}\left[L\left(\left(\mu_S,\mu_B,\sigma_S,\sigma_B,\rho\right),w\right)\right]. \tag{4.93}$$

This expectation can be approximated using Monte Carlo simulation:

1. Generate $N$ samples from the posterior distributions of $\mu_S$ and $\mu_B$.
2. For each sample, compute the loss function for a grid of portfolio weights.
3. Average the loss function over all samples for each portfolio weight.
4. Select the portfolio weight that minimizes the average loss.

The Bayesian decision theory approach suggests allocating approximately 61% of the portfolio to the stock and 39% to the bond. This allocation balances the higher expected return of the stock with the lower volatility of the bond, considering the uncertainty in our estimates of the expected returns.

The expected Sharpe ratio of 0.3456 represents the risk-adjusted return we can anticipate from this optimal allocation, given our current beliefs about the market parameters.

This example illustrates several key advantages of using Bayesian decision theory in portfolio optimization:

1. **Incorporation of prior beliefs:** We started with prior distributions for the expected returns, which were then updated based on observed data.
2. **Handling of uncertainty:** The posterior distributions capture our uncertainty about the true expected returns, which is reflected in the final decision.
3. **Flexibility:** The framework can easily accommodate different prior beliefs, loss functions, or additional assets.
4. **Robustness:** By considering the full posterior distribution rather than point estimates, the resulting allocation is more robust to estimation error.

### 4.7.3 The Black-Litterman Model

The Black-Litterman model, introduced by Fischer Black and Robert Litterman in 1992 (Black and Litterman, 1992a), is a sophisticated approach to portfolio optimization that addresses some of the limitations of the traditional Mean-Variance Optimization (MVO) developed by Harry Markowitz. The Black-Litterman model combines prior market equilibrium returns with investor's views to generate a new set of expected returns, leading to more stable and intuitive portfolio weights.

In MVO, the goal is to construct a portfolio that minimizes the variance (risk) for a given level of expected return. Given $n$ assets, let $\mathbf{w}$ be the vector of portfolio weights, $\boldsymbol{\mu}$ be the vector of expected returns, and $\boldsymbol{\Sigma}$ be the covariance matrix of asset returns. The optimization problem can be formulated as:

$$\min_{\mathbf{w}} \mathbf{w}^T\mathbf{\Sigma}\mathbf{w}, \tag{4.94}$$

subject to the constraint:

$$\mathbf{w}^T\mathbf{1} = 1, \tag{4.95}$$

and

$$\mathbf{w}^T\boldsymbol{\mu} = \mu_p, \tag{4.96}$$

where $\mathbf{1}$ is a vector of ones and $\mu_p$ is the desired expected return of the portfolio.

The Black-Litterman model improves upon MVO by integrating market equilibrium returns (the prior) with subjective views from investors (the posterior). The equilibrium returns are derived from the Capital Asset Pricing Model (CAPM), which assumes that market portfolio weights $\mathbf{w}_m$ are known and that the market is in equilibrium. The equilibrium returns $\boldsymbol{\pi}$ are given by:

$$\boldsymbol{\pi} = \lambda\mathbf{\Sigma}\mathbf{w}_m, \tag{4.97}$$

where $\lambda$ is the risk aversion coefficient.

Investors may have views, in the form of expected returns, on certain assets or combinations of assets. These views can be expressed as:

$$\mathrm{Q} = \mathbf{P}\boldsymbol{\mu} + \epsilon, \tag{4.98}$$

where $\mathbf{P}$ is a matrix that identifies the assets involved in the views, Q is a vector of the views, and $\epsilon$ is the error term representing uncertainty in the views, with covariance matrix $\mathbf{\Omega}$.

The Black-Litterman model combines the prior distribution (market equilibrium) with the investor's views to obtain a posterior distribution of the expected returns. The combined expected returns $\boldsymbol{\mu}_{BL}$ are given by:

$$\boldsymbol{\mu}_{BL} = \left((\tau\mathbf{\Sigma})^{-1} + \mathbf{P}^T\mathbf{\Omega}^{-1}\mathbf{P}\right)^{-1}\left((\tau\mathbf{\Sigma})^{-1}\boldsymbol{\pi} + \mathbf{P}^T\mathbf{\Omega}^{-1}\mathrm{Q}\right), \tag{4.99}$$

where $\tau$ is a scalar representing the uncertainty in the prior estimate of the mean returns.

The updated covariance matrix $\mathbf{\Sigma}_{BL}$, incorporating the views, remains the same as the original covariance matrix $\mathbf{\Sigma}$ due to the model's assumption of independently distributed views and market returns.

To arrive at these results, note that the equilibrium returns $\boldsymbol{\pi}$ can be considered as the mean of a multivariate normal distribution with covariance $\tau\boldsymbol{\Sigma}$:

$$\boldsymbol{\pi} \sim \mathcal{N}(\boldsymbol{\mu}, \tau\boldsymbol{\Sigma}). \tag{4.100}$$

Similarly, the views Q are also normally distributed with mean $\mathbf{P}\boldsymbol{\mu}$ and covariance $\boldsymbol{\Omega}$:

$$\mathrm{Q} \sim \mathcal{N}(\mathbf{P}\boldsymbol{\mu}, \boldsymbol{\Omega}). \tag{4.101}$$

Using Bayesian inference, the posterior distribution of the returns $\boldsymbol{\mu}$ given the views Q is also normally distributed with the mean $\boldsymbol{\mu}_{BL}$ and covariance $\boldsymbol{\Sigma}_{BL}$:

$$\boldsymbol{\mu}|\mathrm{Q} \sim \mathcal{N}(\boldsymbol{\mu}_{BL}, \boldsymbol{\Sigma}_{BL}). \tag{4.102}$$

To combine the distributions, we need to use the formula for the posterior mean of a normal distribution. Given two normal distributions:

$$\mathrm{y}_1 \sim \mathcal{N}(\boldsymbol{\mu}_1, \boldsymbol{\Sigma}_1) \tag{4.103}$$

$$\mathrm{y}_2 \sim \mathcal{N}(\boldsymbol{\mu}_2, \boldsymbol{\Sigma}_2), \tag{4.104}$$

the posterior distribution y given both distributions is:

$$\mathrm{y} \sim \mathcal{N}\left(\left(\boldsymbol{\Sigma}_1^{-1} + \boldsymbol{\Sigma}_2^{-1}\right)^{-1}\left(\boldsymbol{\Sigma}_1^{-1}\boldsymbol{\mu}_1 + \boldsymbol{\Sigma}_2^{-1}\boldsymbol{\mu}_2\right), \left(\boldsymbol{\Sigma}_1^{-1} + \boldsymbol{\Sigma}_2^{-1}\right)^{-1}\right). \tag{4.105}$$

Applying this to the Black-Litterman model, we get:

$$\boldsymbol{\mu}_{BL} = \left(\tau\boldsymbol{\Sigma}^{-1} + \mathbf{P}^T\boldsymbol{\Omega}^{-1}\mathbf{P}\right)^{-1}\left(\tau\boldsymbol{\Sigma}^{-1}\boldsymbol{\pi} + \mathbf{P}^T\boldsymbol{\Omega}^{-1}\mathrm{Q}\right), \tag{4.106}$$

and the covariance matrix remains as:

$$\boldsymbol{\Sigma}_{BL} = \boldsymbol{\Sigma}. \tag{4.107}$$

1. **Determine Market Equilibrium Returns:** Calculate the equilibrium returns $\boldsymbol{\pi}$ using the market capitalization weights $\mathbf{w}_m$ and the covariance matrix $\boldsymbol{\Sigma}$.
2. **Specify Investor Views:** Define the matrix **P** and the vector Q that represent the investor's views, along with the uncertainty matrix $\boldsymbol{\Omega}$.
3. **Combine Prior and Views:** Calculate the combined expected returns $\boldsymbol{\mu}_{BL}$ using the formula derived.
4. **Optimize the Portfolio:** Use the combined expected returns $\boldsymbol{\mu}_{BL}$ and the covariance matrix $\boldsymbol{\Sigma}$ in the MVO framework to determine the optimal portfolio weights $\mathbf{w}_{BL}$.

### Example

Consider a simplified example with three assets. Suppose the equilibrium returns $\boldsymbol{\pi}$ are given, and an investor has a view on the first asset. The matrices P and Q might look like:

$$\mathrm{P} = \begin{pmatrix} 1 & 0 & 0 \\ 0 & 1 & -1 \end{pmatrix}, \quad \mathrm{Q} = \begin{pmatrix} 0.05 \\ 0.02 \end{pmatrix}.$$

Assuming $\tau = 0.05$ and $\boldsymbol{\Omega}$ is a diagonal matrix with small values representing low uncertainty or high variance, the combined expected returns $\boldsymbol{\mu}_{BL}$ can be calculated and used for optimization. To be sure, the uncertainty in the investor's views is represented by the covariance matrix $\boldsymbol{\Omega}$. This matrix indicates the confidence the investor has in their views. A smaller value in $\boldsymbol{\Omega}$ indicates higher confidence in that view, and a larger value indicates lower confidence.

As illustrated in the preceding, there are some advantages like:

1. **Stability:** By incorporating market equilibrium returns, the model generates more stable and realistic portfolio weights compared to traditional MVO.
2. **Flexibility:** Investors can express their views and the confidence in those views, which allows for a more customized approach.
3. **Intuitiveness:** The model produces results that are often more intuitive and aligned with investor expectations.

However, there are some drawbacks like:

1. **Complexity:** The model is mathematically complex and may be difficult to implement without a strong understanding of Bayesian statistics.
2. **Subjectivity:** The results depend on the accuracy of the investor's views and the uncertainty parameters, which can be subjective.
3. **Parameter Sensitivity:** The choice of $\tau$ and $\boldsymbol{\Omega}$ can significantly influence the results, requiring careful calibration.

The Black-Litterman model represents a significant advancement in portfolio optimization by integrating market equilibrium with investor views. Its Bayesian framework allows for a more stable and realistic estimation of expected returns, addressing some of the key limitations of the traditional Mean-Variance Optimization. Despite its complexity, the model's ability to incorporate subjective views and produce intuitive results makes it a valuable tool for advanced portfolio management.

## 4.8 NOTES

The foundation of Bayesian methods in statistics and probability theory can be traced back to Thomas Bayes and Pierre-Simon Laplace. For a comprehensive overview of Bayesian statistics, refer to Bernard and Smith (2000) and Gelman et al. (2013). Hierarchical Bayesian Models are extensively covered in Gelman and Hill (2006).

The application of geometric fractional Brownian motion (gfBm) to stock prices, as discussed in the prior section, is based on the work of Ibrahim et al. (2021). See Gatheral et al. (2018) for an application of gfBm in volatility.

For a detailed treatment of Bayesian filtering methods, including the Kalman filter, Extended Kalman filter, and Particle filters, see Särkkä and Svensson (2023). The Kalman Filter was originally introduced in Kalman (1960).

The section on Bayesian Optimization draws heavily from Garnett (2023) for general reference. The reader is encouraged to read Brochu et al. (2010) and Shahriari et al. (2016) for a more applied and condensed read including hierarchical reinforcement learning.

For a deeper understanding of Gaussian Processes, refer to the seminal work by Rasmussen and Williams (2005). The squared exponential kernel and Matérn kernel are well-discussed in Duvenaud (2014). For Gaussian Process Regression and Classification, Williams and Rasmussen (1996) provides a foundational treatment.

The connection between Bayesian decision theory and portfolio optimization is explored in the classic Bayesian analysis texts. See Robert (2007), Berger (1985), and Fabozzi et al. (2007) for a view of finance applications.

The Black-Litterman model, a key application of Bayesian methods in portfolio optimization, was introduced in Black and Litterman (1992a). For a comprehensive review and practical implementation guide, see Idzorek (2004).

Recent advancements in applying Gaussian Processes to financial time series and portfolio optimization can be found in Roberts et al. (2013) and Wu et al. (2019).

For a broader perspective on the integration of machine learning techniques, including Bayesian methods, in quantitative finance, refer to Dixon et al. (2020). This is a comprehensive text with a broad range of financial applications drawing from Bayesian methods, machine learning, and reinforcement learning.

PART

# Two

# Risk Management

CHAPTER 5

# Risk Models and Measures

Effective risk management is essential to protect portfolios from adverse market movements and ensure long-term investment success. That is why the search for an adequate measure of risk has been a concern of portfolio theory since its inception. An example of this is that Markowitz himself, shortly after presenting his mean-variance analysis, rejected the use of variance as a measure of risk, introducing semivariance in its place. Another example of the importance of this area of risk measurement has been the incorporation of this type of measures in the different regulations that affect the financial industry.

The search for an appropriate framework has stimulated research, giving rise to a considerable number of academic articles of high mathematical complexity, which propose different risk measures; as well as different properties that they should satisfy to be considered acceptable.

Despite this effort, quoting Fabozzi et al. (2007): "It is possible that we will never find a completely satisfactory answer to the question of which risk measure to use, and the choice, to some extent, remains an art."

The objective of this chapter is to offer a general overview of the current state of the measurement of risk, through the most common measures and estimation methods, in a rigorous manner, but maintaining the mathematical level within reasonable limits.

## 5.1 RISK MEASURES

We start by defining the mathematical concepts that we will need in the study of financial risk.

A *risk measure* is a map $\rho : \Gamma \to \mathbb{R}$, where $\Gamma$ is the set of all random variables defined for a given probability space $(\Omega, \mathcal{F}, \mathbb{P})$. Any random variable $X \in \Gamma$ is interpreted as the future net worth of a portfolio at a given horizon.

Negative values of a random variable represent losses of the corresponding position, whereas positive values are associated with profits.[1]

There are a considerable number of properties related to risk measures in the literature. We list those which will be needed in the sequel.

- **Translation invariance:** $\rho(X+m) = \rho(X) - m \quad \forall X \in \Gamma \quad \forall m \in \mathbb{R}$.
  Adding the quantity $m$ of cash to the position reduces the risk in the same amount. If a measure $\rho$ satisfies translation invariance, then $\rho\left(X + \rho\left(X\right)\right) = 0$ and thus, positive values of $\rho\left(X\right)$ should be interpreted as the minimum extra cash that must be added to this risky position $X$ to eliminate the risk.

- **Monotonicity:** $X \leq Y \Rightarrow \rho\left(X\right) \geq \rho\left(Y\right) \quad \forall X, Y \in \Gamma$.
  If the portfolio $Y$ has greater net worth than portfolio $X$ in almost every state of the nature, then the risk of $Y$ is lower than the risk of $X$.

A risk measure, which satisfies translation invariance and monotonicity, is called a *monetary risk measure*.

- **Subadditivity:** $\rho\left(X + X'\right) \leq \rho\left(X\right) + \rho\left(X'\right) \quad \forall X, X' \in \Gamma$.
  This property is the mathematical expression of the effect that diversification has on risk, or quoting Artzner et al. (1999b): "a merger does not create extra risk."

- **Positive homogeneity:** $\rho\left(\lambda X\right) = \lambda \rho\left(X\right) \quad \forall \lambda > 0, X \in \Gamma$.
  The interpretation of this property is that the risk of a position is proportional to its size.

- **Positivity:** $X \geq 0 \Rightarrow \rho\left(X\right) \leq 0 \quad \forall X \in \Gamma$.
  Positivity means that a position with profits has no risk.

- **Law invariance:** If $X, Y \in \Gamma$ and have the same distribution, then $\rho\left(X\right) = \rho\left(Y\right)$.
  This is a crucial property for a risk measure since it guarantees the consistency of its estimation from empirical observations.

- **Comonotonic additivity:** If $X, Y \in \Gamma$ are comonotonic random variables, then $\rho\left(X + Y\right) = \rho\left(X\right) + \rho\left(Y\right)$.

[1] We are working as in Artzner et al. (1999b) under the so called profit/loss (P/L) interpretation (Petters and Dong, 2016), namely, positive values related to profits and negative values corresponding to losses. The opposite approach (L/P) can also be found in the literature, and the definitions of the concepts may differ between the two. We will follow the interpretation (P/L) until otherwise stated.

Two random variables $X, Y$ are *comonotonic* if they are nondecreasing functions of the same random variable $Z$. Note that comonotonic additivity implies that diversification is inefficient for comonotonic risks.

A risk measure satisfying translation invariance, monotonicity, subadditivity, and positive homogeneity is called a *coherent risk measure.* It is not difficult to prove that an equivalent set of properties for coherence is obtained if we replace monotonicity with positivity.[2] Coherence is usually considered as a minimum requirement for a risk measure to be considered as such.

Neither the variance, nor the standard deviation are coherent risk measures. Variance does not satisfy positive homogeneity ($\sigma^2(\lambda X) = \lambda^2\sigma^2(X)$) and standard deviation fails translation invariance ($\sigma(X+m) = \sigma(X)$). Variance and standard deviations are examples of *dispersion measures,* which consider a positive deviation from the mean as risky as a negative deviation. As we already know, this drawback led to the consideration of *downside or safety measures,* which only consider a position as risky if the losses reach a certain level.[3] Semivariance (Markowitz, 1959) is a downside risk measure obtained as the variance, but considering only the negative deviations from the mean. Mathematically, the semivariance, $\sigma_-^2(X)$ is given by

$$\sigma_-^2(X) = \mathbb{E}\left\{\left[(X - \mathbb{E}(X))^-\right]^2\right\},$$

where $Y^- = Y\mathbf{1}_{Y<0}$. Semivariance is neither a coherent risk measure, since $\sigma_-^2(X+m) = \sigma_-^2(X)$, and it does not satisfy translation invariance.

To find (downside) coherent risk measures, we must introduce Value-at-Risk (VaR) and Conditional Value-at-Risk (CVaR).

## 5.2 VaR AND CVaR

VaR was introduced in the financial industry by JP Morgan in 1994 through the RiskMetrics™ software, and it was the first tool aimed to provide a quantitative assessment of capital requirements. The various problems

[2]To prove this it suffices to consider that, by subadditivity, $\rho(Y) \leq \rho(X) + \rho(Y - X)$, and if $X \leq Y$, then $\rho(Y - X) \leq 0$ by positivity.

[3]Among the dispersion measures we can also find other measures such as the mean-absolute deviation and the mean-absolute moment. Among the downside measures we can mention Roy's safety first, lower partial moments, Value-at-Risk and Conditional Value-at-Risk (Fabozzi et al., 2007). Due to their importance, we will dedicate a separate study to the last two measures.

related to VaR, which we will address later, led to the emergence of other risk measures, among which the most widespread is CVaR, introduced in Uryasev (2000) and Pflug (2000).

Before entering the formal study of VaR and CVaR, we need to define the concept of quantile function. Let $F_X$ be the cumulative distribution function associated to the position $X$, $F_X(x) = \mathbb{P}(X \leq x)$. A *quantile* of order $p \in (0,1)$ of $F_X$ is a value $x$ satisfying $F_X(x^-) \equiv \mathbb{P}(X < x) \leq p$ and $F_X(x) = \mathbb{P}(X \leq x) \geq p$. The *quantile function* of the distribution $F_X$ is the map $q_X : (0,1) \to \mathbb{R}$, given by

$$q_X(p) = \inf\{x \in \mathbb{R} : F_X(x) \geq p\}, \tag{5.1}$$

and it is well defined by the right continuity of cumulative distribution functions.[4]

The following result justifies the name of $q_X(p)$.

**Proposition 5.1** *$q_X(p)$ is a quantile of order $p$ of $F_X$.*

*Proof.* Fix $p \in (0,1)$ and define $y = q_X(p)$. By equation (5.1) and the right continuity of $F_X$, it is clear that $F_X(y) \geq p$. On the other hand, if $x < y$, then $F_X(x) < p$, and thus, $F_X(x^-) \leq p$. ■

### 5.2.1 VaR

The VaR of the position X at the level of probability $p \in (0,1)$ is formally defined as

$$VaR_p(X) = -q_X(p) = -\inf\{x \in \mathbb{R} : F_X(x) \geq p\}. \tag{5.2}$$

For continuous and strictly increasing $F_X$, the VaR is simply $VaR_p(X) = F_X^{-1}(p)$, where $F_X^{-1}$ is the inverse function of $F_X$. To gain more intuition about VaR, we need to express it under the L/P interpretation.

**Proposition 5.2** *Let $F_X$ be continuous and strictly increasing and define $Y = -X$. Then*

$$VaR_p(X) = -VaR_{1-p}(Y) = \inf\{y \in \mathbb{R} : F_Y(y) \geq 1-p\}. \tag{5.3}$$

[4]Actually, for general distributions, there are two possible definitions of quantile function, the *lower quantile*, $q_X^L(p) = q_x(p)$, and the *upper quantile*, $q_X^U(p) = \inf\{x \in \mathbb{R} : F_X(x) > p\}$ (see, for example, Acerbi and Tasche [2002a]), satisfying $q_X^L(p) \leq q_X^U(p)$. When $F_X$ is continuous and strictly increasing, the two quantile functions coincide, and the quantiles are unique. Throughout this chapter, we will work with the lower quantile function unless otherwise specified.

*Proof.* Under the assumptions, it is not difficult to show that $F_Y(x) = 1 - F_X(-x)$ and that the inverse functions $F_X^{-1}$ and $F_Y^{-1}$ exist. Thus, we can write $p = F_X\left[F_X^{-1}(p)\right] = 1 - F_Y\left[-F_X^{-1}(p)\right]$, from where we obtain $F_y\left[-F_X^{-1}(p)\right] = 1 - p$. Applying $F_Y^{-1}$ to both sides of the previous expression, we obtain $F_X^{-1}(p) = -F_Y^{-1}(1-p)$, which under our assumptions is equivalent to equation (5.3). ■

In the applications of VaR, it is usual to work under the L/P interpretation, namely, to take the random variable $Y$ representing losses, and making $p = 1 - \alpha$, where $\alpha$ is the *confidence level* of the VaR. In this case, we can write equation (5.3) in the form

$$VaR_\alpha(Y) = \inf\{y \in \mathbb{R} : F_Y(y) \geq \alpha\} = q_Y(\alpha) \tag{5.4}$$

and take it as the definition of VaR in the L/P interpretation. This definition allows us to say that $VaR_\alpha(Y)$ is the smallest value such that the probability of a loss being lower than this value is at least $\alpha$.[5]

Under certain assumptions on the distribution of losses, it is possible to obtain the VaR using closed-form expressions.

**Proposition 5.3** *a) If* $Y \sim N\left(\mu, \sigma^2\right)$, *then*

$$VaR_\alpha(Y) = \mu + \sigma\Phi^{-1}(\alpha), \tag{5.5}$$

*where* $\Phi$ *is the cumulative distribution function of a standard normal random variable.*

*b) If* $\frac{Y-\mu}{\sigma} \sim t_\nu$ *then*

$$VaR_\alpha(Y) = \mu + \sigma t_\nu^{-1}(\alpha), \tag{5.6}$$

*where* $t_\nu$ *is the cumulative distribution function of a Student's t random variable with* $\nu$ *degrees of freedom.*

*Proof.* As in both cases, $Y$ has a continuous and strictly increasing distribution function, we have that

$$VaR_\alpha(Y) = q_Y(\alpha) = F_Y^{-1}(\alpha),$$

[5] According to footnote 4, we can actually define two VaR values, the *lower VaR*, $VaR_\alpha^L(Y) = q_Y^L(\alpha) = VaR_\alpha(Y)$, and the *upper VaR*, $VaR_\alpha^U(Y) = q_Y^U(\alpha)$. Obviously, $VaR_\alpha^L(Y) \leq VaR_\alpha^U(Y)$.

or, equivalently

$$F_Y(VaR(Y)) = \alpha.$$

In the case a), we have

$$\begin{aligned} F_Y(VaR(Y)) &= \mathbb{P}(Y \leq VaR_\alpha(Y)) = \mathbb{P}\left(Y \leq \mu + \sigma\Phi^{-1}(\alpha)\right) \\ &= \mathbb{P}\left(Z \leq \Phi^{-1}(\alpha)\right) = \Phi\left(\Phi^{-1}(\alpha)\right) = \alpha, \end{aligned}$$

where $Z \to N(0,1)$. For the case b), the proof is analogous.

VaR satisfies the properties of translation invariance, monotonicity, and positive homogeneity, as can be proved directly from its definition, equation (5.2). Nevertheless, VaR fails to satisfy subadditivity (see Artzner et al. [1999b] for counterexamples).[6] This fact leads to the non-coherence of VaR, that we state as a proposition. ■

**Proposition 5.4** *VaR is not a coherent measure of risk.*

In addition to the lack of coherence of VaR, which disqualifies it as a *bona fide* measure, there is another important problem related to this measure: It does not consider the losses beyond the VaR value. In fact, VaR provides the same risk assessment to distributions with extremely different loss amounts beyond the VaR value, which is an undesirable feature for risk management.

These problems gave rise to different downside risk measures such as Conditional Value-at Risk (CVaR), that does not present these drawbacks.

### 5.2.2 CVaR

In the literature related to coherent risk measures, it is common to find diverse ways of naming CVaR, such as Expected Shortfall, Tail Conditional Expectation, or TailVaR. Other references differentiate these concepts but consider them equivalent to each other. Furthermore, it is possible to find works which affirm that these measures are not equivalent, in general, coinciding only in certain circumstances. To try to shed some light on this issue, following Acerbi and Tasche (2002b) and Acerbi and Tasche (2002a), we will define each of these concepts, state the assumptions under which they are equivalent, and determine which of them represent coherent risk measures.

[6]Although VaR is not, in general, subadditive, there are some exceptional cases in which this property holds (Artzner et al., 1999b).

In what follows, the random variable $X$ will represent profits (P/L interpretation), whereas $Y = -X$ will refer to losses (L/P interpretation).

The *Tail Conditional Expectation* (TCE) or *TailVaR* (TVaR) at the level of probability $p$, $TCE_p$, is defined as (Artzner et al., 1999b)

$$TCE_p = -\mathbb{E}\left[X \middle| X \leq -VaR_p(X)\right], \tag{5.7}$$

or, under the L/P interpretation of equation (5.4)

$$TCE_\alpha = \mathbb{E}\left[Y \middle| Y \geq VaR_\alpha(Y)\right], \tag{5.8}$$

where $\alpha = 1 - p$.

By expression in equation (5.8), we can interpret $TCE_\alpha$ as the expected amount of losses beyond the $VaR_\alpha$, and thus, TCE does not present the second problem of VaR mentioned previously. Nevertheless, TCE does not solve the main problem, since it is not a coherent risk measure (see Acerbi and Tasche [2002a], for a counterexample).

The *Conditional Value-at-Risk* (CVaR) at the level of probability $p$, $CVaR_p$, is given by (Uryasev, 2000; Pflug, 2000; Acerbi and Tasche, 2002a):

$$CVaR_p(X) = \inf\left\{p^{-1}\mathbb{E}\left[(X-s)^-\right] - s : s \in \mathbb{R}\right\}:$$

and in the L/P case by

$$CVaR_\alpha(Y) = \inf\left\{a + (1-\alpha)^{-1}\,\mathbb{E}\left[(Y-a)^+\right] : a \in \mathbb{R}\right\},$$

where $x^- = x\mathbf{1}_{x<0}$ and $x^+ = x\mathbf{1}_{x>0}$.

Rockafellar and Uryasev (2000) showed that, for smooth loss distributions, $CVaR_\alpha(Y) = TCE_\alpha(Y)$.[7]

*Expected Shortfall* (ES) was introduced in Acerbi and Tasche (2002a) and can be defined as (Acerbi and Tasche, 2002b):

$$ES_p(X) = -\frac{1}{p}\int_0^p q_X(u)\,du = \frac{1}{p}\int_0^p VaR_u(X)\,du, \tag{5.9}$$

or

$$ES_\alpha(Y) = \frac{1}{1-\alpha}\int_\alpha^1 VaR_u(Y)\,du, \tag{5.10}$$

and can be interpreted as the average of the $(\alpha \cdot 100)\,\%$ worst losses. Therefore, like TCE, ES is a coherent risk measure. Moreover, it also coincides with CVaR. We present these results in the following theorem, which corresponds to Proposition 3.1 and Corollary 4.3 of Acerbi and Tasche (2002a). We state the theorem without proof and refer the reader to the original reference.

[7]Actually, a less restrictive condition is sufficient for the equality to hold (see Acerbi and Tasche [2002a]).

**Theorem 5.1** *Assume $\mathbb{E}[X^-] < \infty$. Then, $ES_p(X) = CVaR_p(X)$ and both represent the same coherent risk measure.*

Summing up all the previous considerations, TCE is not, in general, a coherent measure. ES is coherent and is equal to CVaR. In the case of continuous distributions, the three measures coincide and are coherent.

As in the case of VaR, there are closed-form expressions for CVaR in some situations.

**Proposition 5.5** *a) If $Y \sim N(\mu, \sigma^2)$, then*

$$CVaR_\alpha(Y) = \mu + \frac{\sigma}{1-\alpha}\phi\left(\Phi^{-1}(\alpha)\right), \tag{5.11}$$

*where $\phi$ is the density function of a standard normal random variable.*

*b) If $\frac{Y-\mu}{\sigma} \sim t_\nu$ with $\nu > 1$, then*

$$CVaR_\alpha(Y) = \mu + \frac{\sigma}{1-\alpha}\left[\frac{\nu + \left(t_\nu^{-1}(\alpha)\right)^2}{\nu - 1}\right] g_\nu\left(t_\nu^{-1}(\alpha)\right),$$

*where $g_\nu$ is the density function of a Student's t random variable with $\nu$ degrees of freedom.*

*Proof.* a) Using equations (5.10) and (5.5), we have

$$CVaR_\alpha(Y) = \frac{1}{1-\alpha}\int_\alpha^1 \left(\mu + \sigma\Phi^{-1}(u)\right) du = \mu + \frac{\sigma}{1-\alpha}\int_\alpha^1 \Phi^{-1}(u)\, du$$

$$= \mu + \frac{\sigma}{1-\alpha}\int_{\Phi^{-1}(\alpha)}^{\infty} k\phi(k)\, dk = \mu + \frac{\sigma}{1-\alpha}\phi\left(\Phi^{-1}(\alpha)\right),$$

where in the last step, we have used that $\phi'(x) = -x\phi(x)$.

b) By an analogous procedure to that of a), we get

$$CVaR_\alpha(Y) = \frac{1}{1-\alpha}\int_\alpha^1 \left(\mu + \sigma t_\nu^{-1}(u)\right) du = \mu + \frac{\sigma}{1-\alpha}\int_\alpha^1 t_\nu^{-1}(u)\, du$$

$$= \mu + \frac{\sigma}{1-\alpha}\int_{t_\nu^{-1}(\alpha)}^{\infty} k g_\nu(k)\, dk$$

$$= \mu + \frac{\sigma}{1-\alpha}\left[\frac{\nu + \left(t_\nu^{-1}(\alpha)\right)^2}{\nu - 1}\right] g_\nu\left(t_\nu^{-1}(\alpha)\right),$$

where in the last step, we have used that $\frac{d}{dk}\left(\frac{k^2+\nu}{1-\nu}g_\nu(k)\right) = kg_\nu(k)$, and that for $\nu > 1$, $\lim_{k\to\infty} \frac{k^2+\nu}{1-\nu}g_\nu(k) = 0$. ■

The following proposition contains some properties of CVaR. The first one is a direct consequence of equation (5.8). The proofs of properties b), c), and d) can be found in Acerbi and Tasche (2002a).[8] The last property is stated and proven in Rockafellar and Uryasev (2002).

**Proposition 5.6** *a) For continuous distributions,* $CVaR_\alpha(Y) \geq VaR_\alpha(Y)$.
*b)* $CVaR_\alpha(Y)$ *is continuous with respect to* $\alpha$.
*c)* $CVaR_\alpha(Y) = \frac{1}{1-\alpha}\{\mathbb{E}\left[Y\mathbf{1}_{Y\geq VaR_\alpha(Y)}\right] - VaR_\alpha(Y)\left[\mathbb{P}(Y \geq VaR_\alpha(Y)) - (1-\alpha)\right]\}$.
*d)* $CVaR_\alpha(Y) = \lim_{n\to\infty} \frac{1}{\lfloor n(1-\alpha)\rfloor}\sum_{i=1}^{\lfloor n(1-\alpha)\rfloor} Y_{i:n}$ *with probability one, where* $Y_{1:n} \geq \cdots \geq Y_{n:n}$ *are the ordered statistics of* $Y_1, \ldots, Y_n$ *which is a sample drawn from independent copies of Y; and* $\lfloor x\rfloor = \max\{n \in \mathbb{Z} : n \leq x\}$ *is the integer part of x.*
*e)* $CVaR_\alpha(x) = min_\xi\left\{\xi + \frac{1}{1-\alpha}\mathbb{E}\left[(f(\mathbf{x},\mathbf{y}) - \xi)^+\right]\right\}$, *where* $\mathbf{x}$ *is a n-vector of portfolio holdings,* $\xi \in \mathbb{R}$, $\mathbf{y}$ *is a random n-vector describing the uncertain factors affecting the portfolio, and f is a function representing the loss associated to portfolio* $\mathbf{x}$ *(the loss function).*

Property a) of Proposition 5.6 tells us that CVaR is a more conservative risk measure than VaR, which is a consequence of considering losses beyond VaR. According to property b), CVaR does not present discontinuities with respect to $\alpha$, even if the distribution is not continuous. This is an advantage of CVaR over other tail risk measures such as VaR or TCE, which do not present this feature (see Acerbi and Tasche [2002a], Example 5.4). By property c), when $F_Y$ has no jumps at $VaR_\alpha(Y)$, i.e., $\alpha - \mathbb{P}(Y < VaR_\alpha(Y)) = \mathbb{P}(Y \geq VaR(Y)) - (1-\alpha) = 0$, then $CVaR_\alpha(Y) = \frac{1}{1-\alpha}\mathbb{E}\left[Y\mathbf{1}_{Y\geq VaR_\alpha(Y)}\right]$. If there is a jump at $VaR_\alpha(Y)$, we must subtract a term proportional to the length of the jump. As pointed out in Acerbi and Tasche (2002a), property d) is in accordance with the interpretation of ES (and therefore, of CVaR) as the average of the $(\alpha \cdot 100)\,\%$ worst losses. Property e) allows to obtain CVaR directly as the solution of an optimization problem, which has VaR as a byproduct. Moreover, in the case in which $f$ is linear in $\mathbf{x}$, it allows to minimize CVaR with respect to this variable with linear programming

[8]See also McNeill et al. (2005) and Prigent (2007) for the specific form of the properties presented here.

techniques (Rockafellar and Uryasev, 2000, 2002). Property e) can also be used in Mean-CVaR optimization (Krokhmal et al., 2001).[9]

## 5.3 ESTIMATION METHODS

Among the methods used to estimate VaR and CVaR, we can highlight the *variance-covariance* method, the *historical simulation* method and the *Monte Carlo simulation* method. Before describing each of these methods, we need to introduce some notation. The losses in the period $t+1$, $Y_{t+1}$ are described by $Y_{t+1} = l_t(\mathbf{f}_{t+1})$, where $l_t$ is the *loss operator*, and $\mathbf{f}_{t+1} \in \mathbb{R}^d$ are the risk factors changes at period $t+1$. Common choices of risk factors are logarithmic prices of financial assets, yields and logarithmic exchange rates.

### 5.3.1 Variance-Covariance Method

In this method, it is assumed that risk-factor changes have a multivariate normal distribution, $\mathbf{f}_{t+1} \sim N(\boldsymbol{\mu}, \boldsymbol{\Sigma})$. It is also assumed that losses are linear on the risk factors, namely

$$l_t(\mathbf{x}) = -\left(c_t + \mathbf{b}_t^T \mathbf{x}\right)$$

for some constant $c_t \in \mathbb{R}$ and $\mathbf{b}_t \in \mathbb{R}^d$, known at time $t$. Under these assumptions, we have that

$$Y_{t+1} = l_t(\mathbf{f}_{t+1}) \sim N\left(-c_t - \mathbf{b}_t^T \boldsymbol{\mu}, \mathbf{b}_t^T \boldsymbol{\Sigma} \mathbf{b}_t\right),$$

and then, we can obtain VaR and CVaR from equations (5.5) and (5.11).

The main advantage of this method relies on the use of analytical expressions to evaluate the risk, but it is achieved under two unrealistic assumptions: the linearity of losses with respect to factor changes and the normality of these changes.

### 5.3.2 Historical Simulation

Instead of assuming a certain parametric form for the distribution of losses, the historical simulation method estimates this distribution from a set of historical factor changes data, $\mathbf{f}_{t-n+1}, \ldots, \mathbf{f}_t$. Applying the loss operator to each of the historical observations, we obtain a set of historically simulated

[9]Under normally distributed loss functions, MV and Mean-CVaR generate the same efficient frontier (Rockafellar and Uryasev, 2000).

losses, $\overline{Y}_s = l_t(\mathbf{f}_s)$, $s = t-n+1,\ldots,t$, corresponding to losses that would happen to the current position if the risk factor changes $\mathbf{f}_s$ were to recur.

Assuming that the process of risk-factor changes is stationary, with distribution function $F_Y$, an appropriate form of the strong law of numbers for time series can be used to prove that

$$\lim_{n\to\infty}\frac{1}{n}\sum_{s=t-n+1}^{t} 1_{\overline{Y}_s \le l} = \mathbb{P}\left[l_t(\mathbf{f}) \le l\right] = F_Y(l),$$

where $\mathbf{f}$ is a generic vector of risk-factor changes with distribution $F_Y$ and $Y = l_t(\mathbf{f})$.

Once obtained the historically simulated distribution, the VaR can be calculated from the ordered statistics of $\overline{Y}_s$, $\overline{Y}_{1:n} \ge \cdots \ge \overline{Y}_{n:n}$, as $VaR_\alpha(Y) = \overline{Y}_{\lfloor n(1-\alpha)\rfloor:n}$. For example, if $n = 1000$ and $\alpha = 0.95$, we would estimate the VaR by taking the fiftieth largest value.[10] The computation of CVaR follows from d) of Proposition 5.6.

This method is easy to implement and no assumptions about distribution of losses or risk-factor changes are needed. However, the success of the method depends on the availability of a sufficient amount of synchronized data for all risk factors.

### 5.3.3 Monte Carlo Simulation

This method requires the simulation of a parametric model for risk-factor changes. Once the model is selected, it is calibrated to historical risk-factor changes data, $\mathbf{f}_{t-n+1},\ldots,\mathbf{f}_t$. Then, this calibrated model is used to generate $m$ independent realizations of risk-factor changes for the next period: $\tilde{\mathbf{f}}_{t+1}^{(1)},\ldots,\tilde{\mathbf{f}}_{t+1}^{(m)}$. Applying the loss operator to these simulated vectors, we obtain $m$ simulated realizations from the loss distribution, $\left\{\widetilde{Y}_{t+1}^{(i)}\right\}_{i=1}^{m}$, with $\widetilde{Y}_{t+1}^{(i)} = l_t\left(\tilde{\mathbf{f}}_{t+1}^{(i)}\right)$. Finally, VaR and CVaR are obtained from $\left\{\widetilde{Y}_{t+1}^{(i)}\right\}_{i=1}^{m}$ in the same way as was done in the historical simulation method.

This method has the disadvantage of being based on a parametric model, and it will be as good as the fit of the model to reality. Furthermore, for large portfolios, its computational cost can be high, because each simulation requires reevaluation of the portfolio.

[10]Nevertheless, as pointed out in Acerbi and Tasche (2002a), in the case of a non-unique quantile, $q_Y^L(\alpha) < q_Y^U(\alpha)$, $\overline{Y}_{\lfloor n(1-\alpha)\rfloor:n}$ does not converge to $VaR_\alpha(Y)$. This problem does not appear when obtaining CVaR from d) of Proposition 5.6.

## 5.4 ADVANCED RISK MEASURES: TAIL RISK AND SPECTRAL MEASURES

### 5.4.1 Tail Risk Measures

Until now we have studied VaR and CVaR as the two most important risk measures, due mainly to their inclusion in the regulatory frameworks for banking and insurance sectors (see, for example, Basel [2019]). Both measures can be considered as measures of "tail risk," that is, measures of the behavior of a risk beyond a certain quantile. However, there are reasons to deepen the study of tail risk measures beyond VaR and CVaR (Liu and Wang, 2021).

First, a general theory of tail risk measures for regulating purposes is needed, since the main concern of regulators is the tail part of a risk, which represents the possibility of large and unexpected losses. Second, VaR and CVaR represent simple statistics of the tail risk, but do not inform about its variability or shape. Third, the study of tail risk measures other than VaR and CVaR would provide additional valuable information that would help the regulator to better understand tail risk.

We begin the study by formalizing the concept of tail risk. Our exposition is based on Liu and Wang (2021). We refer the reader to this paper for proofs of the results.

Let $Y$ be a random variable representing the losses of a position. The *tail risk* of $Y$ beyond its $\alpha$ quantile, $Y_\alpha$, is the random variable defined as $Y_\alpha = q_Y(\alpha + (1-\alpha) U_Y)$, where $U_Y$ is a uniform random variable on $[0,1]$ such that $q_Y(U_Y) = Y$.[11] The following result provides the cumulative distribution function of $Y_\alpha$.

**Proposition 5.7** $F_{Y_\alpha}(y) = (1-\alpha)^{-1}[F_Y(y) - \alpha]^+$.

With this preliminaries, now we can define an *$\alpha$-tail risk measure* as a risk measure, $\rho$, that satisfies $\rho(Y) = \rho(Y')$ whenever $Y'_\alpha$ and $Y'_\alpha$ have the same distribution. In other words, the value of an $\alpha$-tail risk measure is determined only by the distribution of the risk beyond the $\alpha$-quantile.

From the definition of $\alpha$-tail risk measure, we can obtain immediately the following result.

**Corollary 5.1** *a) For $0 < \alpha' < \alpha < 1$, an $\alpha$-tail risk measure is also an $\alpha'$-tail risk measure.*

[11]The existence of this random variable is proven in (Föllmer and Schied [2016], Lemma A.32).

*b) For $0 < \alpha' < \alpha < 1$, $VaR^U_\alpha$ and $ES_\alpha$ ($CVaR_\alpha$) are $\alpha$-tail risk measures, and $VaR^L_\alpha$ is an $\alpha'$-tail risk measure.*[12]
*c) Any tail risk measure is law invariant.*

It is possible to define an $\alpha$-tail risk measure $\rho$ associated to any law-invariant measure, $\rho^*$, via

$$\rho(Y) = \rho^*(Y_\alpha). \tag{5.12}$$

If $\rho$ is defined this way, we call $\rho$ the *$\alpha$-tail risk measure generated by $\rho^*$*, and $\rho^*$ an *$\alpha$-generator of $\rho$*.

The following result states that any tail risk measure can be obtained by this generation procedure from law-invariant measures.

**Proposition 5.8** *$\rho$ is a tail risk measure if and only if it is generated by another (law-invariant) measure $\rho^*$.*[13]

Some properties of tail risk measures, such as translation invariance, positive homogeneity, and comonotonic additivity, are inherited from their generators; while others, such as subadditivity, are not. However, belonging to the class of coherent measures is a characteristic shared by a tail risk measure and its generator.

**Theorem 5.2** *$\rho$ is a coherent risk measure if and only if so is $\rho^*$.*

The previous theorem provides a procedure for obtaining coherent tail risk measures. It suffices to choose a (law-invariant) coherent measure and apply equation (5.12).

We conclude the study of tail risk measures by presenting an example of one such measure (Liu and Wang, 2021).

**Example 5.1** ***(Gini Shortfall)*** *The measure given for any $\beta > 0$ by*

$$\rho(Y) = ES_\alpha(Y) + \beta\mathbb{E}\left[|Y'_\alpha - Y''_\alpha|\right],$$

*where $Y'_\alpha$ and $Y''_\alpha$ are i.i.d. copies of $Y_\alpha$, is called Gini Shortfall (Furman et al., 2017), and is comonotonically additive, and coherent if $\beta \leq \frac{1}{2}$. The Gini Shortfall is generated by*

$$\rho^*(Y) = \mathbb{E}[Y] + \beta\mathbb{E}\left[|Y' - Y''|\right],$$

*where $Y'$ and $Y''$ are i.i.d. copies of $Y$.*

---

[12] See footnote 5 for the definitions of $VaR^L_\alpha$ and $VaR^U_\alpha$.

[13] Moreover, the generator is unique as long as the risk $Y$ satisfy $ess\ \inf(Y) > -\infty$.

### 5.4.2 Spectral Measures

In the study of spectral measures, we will follow Acerbi and Tasche (2002b) and return to the initial P/L interpretation, namely, $X$ represents the profits associated to a certain position.

As we saw before, ES, given by

$$ES_p(X) = -\frac{1}{p}\int_0^p q_X(u)\,du \tag{5.13}$$

is a coherent measure that solved some of the problems related to VaR, and it can be interpreted as the (negative) average of the $(p \cdot 100)\,\%$ values of the left tail of the P/L distribution.

The expression in equation (5.13) can be expressed in the equivalent form

$$ES_p(X) = -\int_0^1 \phi_{ES_p}(u)\,q_X(u)\,du$$

with

$$\phi_{ES_p}(u) = \frac{1}{p}\mathbf{1}_{u\leq p} \tag{5.14}$$

from where we can see ES as a weighted average in which the same weight $\frac{1}{p}$ is assigned to any value on the left tail. Spectral measures try to take advantage of this interpretation to generalize ES, by allowing the weights to be a function of the position $u$ at the left tail, while maintaining the coherence of the measure.

In general, it is convenient to consider the weight function $\phi$, which we will call *risk spectrum*, as belonging to the normed space $\mathcal{L}^1([0,1])$.[14] With this assumption, we can now define the *spectral risk measure* $M_\phi$ associated to the risk spectrum $\phi$, by[15]

$$M_\phi(X) = -\int_0^1 q_X(u)\,\phi(u)\,du. \tag{5.15}$$

[14]The elements of $\mathcal{L}^1([0,1])$ are equivalence classes of functions, $\phi : [0,1] \to \mathbb{R}$, which satisfy $\|\phi\| \equiv \int_0^1 |\phi(u)|\,du < \infty$. Two functions $\phi_1$, $\phi_2$ belong to the same equivalence class, and represent the same element of $\mathcal{L}^1([0,1])$, if $\|\phi_1 - \phi_2\| = 0$. In this case, $\phi_1$ and $\phi_2$ define the same risk measure.

[15]For the measure $M_\phi$ to be well defined, we need to restrict the set of random variables to $V_\phi = \{X\,|q_X\phi \in \mathcal{L}^1([0,1])\}$, but it does not pose any inconvenience in real-world application (see Acerbi and Tasche [2002b]).

We say that $\phi \in \mathcal{L}^1([0,1])$ is an *admissible risk spectrum* if $\phi$ satisfies the following properties:

- $\phi$ is non-negative:

$$\int_I \phi(u)\,du \geq 0 \quad \forall I \subset [0,1]$$

- $\phi$ is decreasing:

$$\int_{q-\varepsilon}^{q} \phi(u)\,du \geq \int_{q}^{q+\varepsilon} \phi(u)\,du \ \forall q \in (0,1)\ \forall \varepsilon > 0 : [q-\varepsilon, q+\varepsilon] \subset [0,1]$$

- $\phi$ is normalized:

$$\|\phi\| = \int_0^1 |\phi(u)|\,du = 1$$

The next result tells us that admissible risk spectra is the natural class for working with coherent spectral measures.

**Theorem 5.3** *(Acerbi and Tasche, 2002b; Theorem 4.1) The spectral risk measure $M_\phi$ of equation (5.15) is a coherent risk measure if and only if $\phi$ is an admissible risk spectrum.*

As a first example of the power of spectral risk measures, we can obtain the coherence of ES as a direct consequence of Theorem 5.3, simply by considering, as can be easily proven, that $\phi_{ES_p}$ of equation (5.14) is an admissible risk spectrum.

Considering that admissible risk spectra are decreasing, Theorem 5.3 allows for an interpretation of coherent measures as those risk measures that "assigns bigger weights to worse cases" (Acerbi and Tasche, 2002b). According to this interpretation, the risk spectrum $\phi$ can be considered as a *risk aversion function* representing the subjective attitude of an investor toward risk, and could open a new approach to risk management with tailor-made spectral measures adapted to different P&L distributions shapes (Acerbi and Tasche, 2002b).

As VaR is not a coherent measure, by Theorem 5.3, we cannot find an admissible risk spectrum $\phi$ such that $M_\phi = VaR$. Nevertheless, we can consider $\phi_{VaR_p}(u) = \delta(u-p)$, where $\delta$ is a Dirac delta function, as a limiting case for which we can write

$$M_{\phi_{VaR_p}}(X) = -\int_0^1 q_X(u)\,\delta(u-p)\,du = -q_X(p) = VaR_p(X).$$

This formal calculation allows us to reinforce the interpretation of VaR as a risk measure that assigns weights zero to the values on the $p$-left tail and an "infinite weight" to the threshold value of the tail.

The following result, which is a characterization of spectral risk measures, provides new and interesting properties of this type of measures.

**Theorem 5.4** *(**Kusuoka, 2001; Theorem** 7) The measure $\rho$ is a coherent spectral risk measure if and only if it is a law invariant and comonotonic additive coherent risk measure.*

Because of this theorem, coherent spectral measures present two properties which are crucial for risk measures, namely, law invariance and comonotonic additivity. As we saw before, law invariance is a necessary property for a risk measure to be estimable from empirical data. Moreover, spectral risk measures present a characteristic, analogous to property d) of Proposition 5.6 for CVaR, which can be applied to non-parametric estimation.

**Theorem 5.5** *(**Acerbi and Tasche, 2002b; Theorem** 5.3) Let $M_\phi$ be the spectral risk measure generated by the admissible risk spectrum $\phi$. Then*

$$M_\phi(X) = -\lim_{n\to\infty}\sum_{i=1}^{n} X_{i:n}\phi_i,$$

*where $\phi_i \equiv \frac{\phi(i/n)}{\sum_{k=1}^{n}\phi(k/n)}$ and $X_{i:n}$ are the ordered statistics, $X_{1:n} \le \cdots \le X_{n:n}$, associated to $X_1, \ldots, X_n$, which is a sample drawn from independent copies of $X$.*

As we did in the previous section, we conclude this section by presenting an example of spectral risk measures.

**Example 5.2** *(**Exponential Spectral Risk Measure**) The risk aversion function given by*

$$\phi(u) = \frac{ke^{-ku}}{1-e^{-k}}$$

*with $k > 0$, is an admissible risk spectrum. The associated risk measure*

$$M_\phi = -\frac{k}{1-e^{-k}}\int_0^1 e^{-ku} q_X(u)\, du$$

*is called exponential spectral risk measure and, by Theorem 5.3 is a coherent risk measure.*[16]

## 5.5 NOTES

The definition of risk measure is taken from Liu and Wang (2021). The properties of risk measures are standard and can be found in any related text. Other important properties of risk measures not addressed here are convexity, which together with translation invariance and monotonicity gives rise to convex measures (see, for example, Prigent [2007]); and elicitability, closely related to backtesting (Liu and Wang, 2021).

Additional properties of quantile functions, as well as examples and applications, can be found in Petters and Dong (2016). Various risk measures different from VaR and CVaR appear in the literature. Among them we can highlight the Worst Conditional Expectation (WCE; Artzner et al., 1999b), which is the smallest coherent risk measure dominating VaR (Acerbi and Tasche, 2002a) and the Entropic Value-at-Risk (EVaR), a coherent measure introduced in Ahmadi-Javid (2011).

Our study of estimation methods is heavily based on McNeill et al. (2005). This reference also provides a description of backtesting, an illustrative example, and an extensive list of related references.

The discussion of tail risk measures is based on Liu and Wang (2021), while that of spectral risk measures is based on Acerbi and Tasche (2002b), Kusuoka (2001), and Dowd et al. (2008). An important class of risk measures not discussed here is *distortion measures* (Denneberg, 1990), which can be considered as distorted expectations of the random variable representing the risk. Distortion risk measures are translation invariant, positively homogeneous, monotone and comonotonic additive; and have VaR and CVaR as particular cases. Furthermore, a distortion risk measure is coherent if and only if the distortion function is concave (see Balbás et al. [2009] and references therein).

[16]The risk aversion function $\phi$ of this example can be derived from an exponential utility function, with $k$ the Arrow-Pratt coefficient of absolute risk aversion (Dowd et al., 2008). See also this reference for different examples of spectral measures and their properties.

CHAPTER 6

# Factor Models and Factor Investing

Factor models can be considered as an application of the Arbitrage Pricing Theory (APT) theoretical framework developed in Chapter 3. They are based on the assumption that the expected excess return of a portfolio can be obtained as a linear function of certain factors.

The emergence of this branch of portfolio management dates to the publication of Fama and French (1993), which was the first work to present a factor model. The Fama and French model included only three factors: market, size, and value. Since then, the field of factor models has grown continuously in both the academic and professional worlds.

In the academic field, the study of factor models has been developed fundamentally in two ways. The first consists of determining what types of factors are most appropriate in a multifactor model, which has led to a classification of models into statistical, macroeconomic, and cross-sectional models. The second refers to the determination of which are the relevant factors to include in the model. This search has led to the identification of a high number of possible factors (a "zoo of factors" according to Cochrane [2011]), composed of more than 300 (Harvey et al. [2016]), which complicates practitioner's decision about which factors to use.

On the other hand, the appearance of this type of models has given rise, in the industry, to the development of a modern style of portfolio management, known by *factor investing*, which, in terms of portfolio allocation, places emphasis on the risk factors, and not on individual assets. According to this approach, "assets have risk premiums not because the assets themselves earn risk premiums; assets are bundles of factor risks, and it is the exposures to the underlying factor risks that earn risk premiums" (Ang, 2014).

In this chapter, we examine single and multifactor models, as well as the concepts of factor risk and performance attribution, and provide insights into the contributions and limitations of these models. We also discuss the integration of machine learning techniques to further refine factor analysis and investment strategies.

## 6.1 SINGLE AND MULTIFACTOR MODELS

In Chapter 3 we presented the Capital Asset Pricing Model (CAPM) of Sharpe (1964), Lintner (1965), and Mossin (1966), which was determined by the expression (see equation [3.35])

$$R_i = R_0 + \beta_i^M \left(R_{p,M} - R_0\right),$$

where $R_i$ is the expected return of the i-th asset, $R_0$ is the return of the riskless asset, $\beta_i^M$ is the beta of the i-th asset and $R_{p,M}$ is the expected return of the market portfolio. The interpretation of the CAPM is that the expected excess return of an asset is proportional to its beta.

As we already explained in Section 3.6, shortly after the presentation of the CAPM, empirical studies began to emerge rejecting its results, and it is now considered an outdated model (quoting Ang [2014]: "the CAPM is well known to be a spectacular failure").

The Arbitrage Pricing Theory (APT) of Ross (1976), appeared as an alternative to the CAPM, which postulated that the excess asset returns were given by a *strict factor model* of the form

$$\mathbf{e} = \mathbf{a} + \mathbf{B}\mathbf{f} + \boldsymbol{\varepsilon},$$

where $\mathbf{e} = \left(e_1, \ldots, e_n\right)^T$ is the vector of excess asset returns; $\mathbf{a} = \left(a_1, \ldots, a_n\right)^T$ is a vector of constants; $\mathbf{B} = (\beta_{ij})_{n\times k}$ is a matrix of constants, known as *factor loadings* or *betas* of the assets; $\mathbf{f} = \left(f_1, \ldots, f_k\right)^T$ is a random vector of *factors, with* $k < n$; and $\boldsymbol{\varepsilon} = \left(\varepsilon_1, \ldots, \varepsilon_n\right)^T$ is a random vector of *residuals* or *idiosyncratic risks*, verifying certain assumptions (see Section 3.3). For most purposes of this chapter, we will work with the following simplest version, without residuals, which we will call *noiseless factor model*

$$\mathbf{e} = \mathbf{E} + \mathbf{B}\mathbf{f}, \tag{6.1}$$

where $\mathbf{E} = \mathbf{R} - R_0\mathbf{1}$ is the vector of excess expected returns, which allowed us to obtain exact results in the APT. One of these results, already proved in Chapter 3, is that the CAPM can also be understood as a factor model, with a single factor corresponding to the expected excess return of the market portfolio (see equation [3.45]). Thus, the appearance of the APT opened new avenues for the explanation of the expected excess return beyond the failed attempt with the single-factor CAPM.

Depending on the type of factors considered, three types of factor models are usually distinguished: statistical models, macroeconomic models, and cross-sectional models.

### 6.1.1 Statistical Models

Unlike the other two types of models, in statistical models the factors are considered unobservable or latent and will be determined by statistical methods, which makes them difficult to interpret. The main statistical factor model is the Principal Component Analysis (PCA), which we will briefly explain in what follows.[1]

PCA allows us to explain the total variability in a set of data with a new set of variables, which are a linear combination of the original ones, called *principal components*. The main advantage of PCA is that the principal components are ordered in decreasing order in terms of the proportion of the total variance that they explain. This fact allows a large part of the total variance to be explained by a number of principal components smaller than the original number of variables, thus reducing the dimensionality of the problem. In our case, the PCA will allow us to explain, approximately, the covariance structure between the returns, given by the $n \times n$ covariance matrix $\Sigma$, by means of only $k$ principal components, with $k < n$. In addition, we will obtain estimates of the betas of the assets using these $k$ principal components.[2]

As $\Sigma$ is a symmetric and positive definite matrix, it is diagonalizable, with eigenvalues $\lambda_1 \geq \cdots \geq \lambda_n > 0$. Thus, we can write the matrix $\Sigma$ in the form

$$\boldsymbol{\Sigma} = U \boldsymbol{\Lambda} U^T, \tag{6.2}$$

where $\boldsymbol{\Lambda} = diag(\lambda_1, \ldots, \lambda_n)$, and $\mathbf{U} = (\mathbf{U}_1 | \cdots | \mathbf{U}_n)$ is an orthogonal matrix whose $i$-th column, $\mathbf{U}_i$, is an eigenvector associated to the eigenvalue $\lambda_i$, i.e., $\boldsymbol{\Sigma} U_i = \lambda_i \mathbf{U}_i$. If the eigenvectors $\mathbf{U}_i$ are normalized, $||\mathbf{U}_i|| = 1$, $i = 1, \ldots, n$, then $\mathbf{U}\mathbf{U}^T = \mathbf{I}$, where $\mathbf{I}$ is the identity matrix. We can define, for $i = 1, \ldots, n$, the new variables $y_i = \mathbf{U}_i^T \mathbf{e}$, called *principal components*, which explain the same variance as the original variables and satisfy that $\lambda_i (\sum_{j=1}^{n} \lambda_j)^{-1}$ is the proportion of the total variance explained by the $i$-th principal component.

To see how we can obtain estimates of the betas of our model from PCA, consider the noiseless factor model of equation (6.1). It is not difficult to show that, in this case, we have

$$\boldsymbol{\Sigma} = \mathbf{B}\mathbf{B}^T, \tag{6.3}$$

[1] A detailed analysis of PCA, as well as its application to factor models can be found in Johnson and Wichern (2007).

[2] It is possible to obtain estimates of the betas by means of maximum likelihood estimation under the assumption of normally distributed f and $\varepsilon$ (see Johnson and Wichern [2007]).

where $\mathbf{B}$ is a $n \times k$ matrix. As $\lambda_1 \geq \cdots \geq \lambda_n$, if we consider only the first $k$ eigenvalues, we are explaining $\left(\sum_{j=1}^{k} \lambda_j\right)\left(\sum_{i=1}^{n} \lambda_i\right)^{-1}$ of the total variance, and we can replace $\mathbf{U}$ and $\mathbf{\Lambda}$ in equation (6.2) by $\mathbf{U}_k = (\mathbf{U}_1 | \cdots | \mathbf{U}_k)$ and $\mathbf{\Lambda}_k = diag(\lambda_1, \ldots, \lambda_k)$, and write the approximated expression of $\mathbf{\Sigma}$, as

$$\mathbf{\Sigma} = \mathbf{U}_k \mathbf{\Lambda}_k \mathbf{U}_k^T = \mathbf{U}_k \mathbf{\Lambda}_k^{1/2} \mathbf{\Lambda}_k^{1/2} \mathbf{U}_k^T = \left(\mathbf{U}_k \mathbf{\Lambda}_k^{1/2}\right)\left(\mathbf{U}_k \mathbf{\Lambda}_k^{1/2}\right)^T, \tag{6.4}$$

where $\mathbf{\Lambda}_k^{1/2}$ is the square root of $\mathbf{\Lambda}_k$. Joining equations (6.3) and (6.4), we see that we can obtain an estimate of $\mathbf{B}$ as $\widehat{\mathbf{B}} = \mathbf{U}_k \mathbf{\Lambda}_k^{1/2}$.[3] Once the matrix $\widehat{\mathbf{B}}$ has been calculated, the estimated values of the factors can be obtained by ordinary least squares or by the regression method (see Johnson and Wichern [2007] for details).

### 6.1.2 Macroeconomic Models

Intuitively, macroeconomic variables such as the rate of growth or inflation should influence asset returns. Although the study of the relationship between these variables and asset returns dates back to Fama (1981), the first works to study this relationship using factor models were Chan et al. (1985) and Chen et al. (1986). The first of these papers had as its objective the study of the "size effect," while the second sought to determine which of these factors systematically affected performance. Both works used the same macroeconomic factors:

- The monthly growth rate of industrial production (led by one period).
- The change in expected inflation.
- The unanticipated inflation.
- The difference (returns of low-grade corporate bonds) – (returns of long-term government bonds).
- The difference (returns of long-term government bonds) – (returns of short-term Treasury bills).

In their conclusions, Chen et al. (1986) affirm that these five factors are significant in explaining the expected returns. Furthermore, other variables studied, such as innovations in real per capita consumption and oil price changes, did not present significant effects.

---

[3]In fact, there is an indeterminacy on the value of $\widehat{\mathbf{B}}$, since if we consider $\widehat{\mathbf{B}}^* = \widehat{\mathbf{B}}\mathbf{L}$, with $\mathbf{L}$ an orthogonal $k \times k$ matrix, $\mathbf{L}\mathbf{L}^T = \mathbf{I}$, we have $\widehat{\mathbf{B}}^*(\widehat{\mathbf{B}}^*)^T = \widehat{\mathbf{B}}\widehat{\mathbf{B}}^T$. Moreover, if we define $\mathbf{f}^* = \mathbf{L}^T\mathbf{f}$, then $\widehat{\mathbf{B}}^*\mathbf{f}^* = \widehat{\mathbf{B}}\mathbf{f}$ and the models determined by $\left(\widehat{\mathbf{B}}^*, \mathbf{f}^*\right)$ and $(\widehat{\mathbf{B}}, \mathbf{f})$ are indistinguishable. This fact is known as *rotational indeterminacy*.

In a work similar to the previous ones, Connor and Korajczyk (1991) use the same macroeconomic variables as Chan et al. (1985) and Chen et al. (1986), but substituting the change in expected inflation for unexpected unemployment and incorporating equal- and value-weighted stock indices. They studied the relationship between the macroeconomic series and factors extracted from monthly equity returns using the asymptotic principal-components procedure of Connor and Korajczyk (1986, 1987). Connor and Korajczyk (1991) find a high value of the adjusted coefficient of determination, $\bar{R}^2$, for the series of equal- and value-weighted stock indices (99.4% and 95.4%, respectively), but very low values of $\bar{R}^2$ for the purely macroeconomics series, such as unexpected unemployment (8.6%), unexpected inflation (6.3%), and unexpected change in industrial production (1.6%). Therefore, we can conclude that there seems to be a weak relationship between asset returns and the macroeconomic series studied in Chan et al. (1985) and Chen et al. (1986), at least at a monthly frequency.

However, in a later work, Ball et al. (2009) obtain a strong relationship between macroeconomic aggregates and asset returns at an annual frequency. This discrepancy with the results of Connor and Korajczyk (1991) may be due to a higher signal-to-noise ratio in the lead–lag relationship between returns and macroeconomic series at an annual frequency. This poses some difficulties for estimating macroeconomic risk models: Many individual assets do not have a sufficiently long time series to estimate the relation between their annual returns and macroeconomic series with reasonable accuracy (Connor et al., 2010).

The previously mentioned problem is added to others, related to the identification of the macroeconomic variables that influence returns. Firstly, the observation intervals for asset prices and macroeconomic variables are quite different, namely, while asset prices can be observed at intraday frequencies, macroeconomic data is offered with frequencies ranging from monthly to annual or even longer. Second, it is sometimes difficult to know when macroeconomic data affects asset returns, leading to contemporaneous, lagged, or leading specifications. Finally, we must consider the problem associated with reverse causality from asset returns to macroeconomic variables, with causality existing in both directions (Connor et al., 2010).

From the analysis of the literature related to macroeconomic factor models, we can conclude, citing Flannery and Protopapadakis (2002), that "the hypothesis that macroeconomic developments exert important effects on equity returns has strong intuitive appeal but little empirical support." This statement is supported by other works such as Chen et al. (1986) and Chan et al. (1998).

### 6.1.3 Cross-sectional Models

One of the disadvantages of macroeconomic models is that their factors are not tradeable, that is, it is not possible to build factor mimicking portfolios. This fact prevents the investor from obtaining the returns associated with the factors by investing directly in them, which is the objective of factor investing. On the other hand, *cross-sectional factor models*, also called *dynamic factor models*, *fundamental models*, or *characteristic-based factor models*, propose that the explanatory factors of the expected returns are tradeable, that is, it is possible to build factor mimicking portfolios in which one can directly invest.[4]

Fama and French (1993) is considered the first work to propose cross-sectional models. Today it continues to be an important reference framework in the portfolio management industry and that is why we will dedicate a more in-depth study to it.

**Fama and French (1993)** In a previous paper, Fama and French (1992), these authors study the effect of different factors (e.g., market portfolio, size, earnings-price ratio, leverage and book-to-market equity) on the average stock returns by means of the cross-section regressions of Fama and MacBeth (1973). The main result of the study is that only two of these variables, size and book-to-market equity, explain the joint effect, making the rest of the variables redundant. According to the authors' own words: "In a nutshell, market $\beta$ seems to have no role in explaining the average returns on NYSE, AMEX and NASDAQ stocks for 1963–1990, while size and book-to-market equity capture the cross-sectional variation in average stock returns that is related to leverage and E/P."[5]

Fama and French (1993) can be considered an extension of the 1992 paper, which uses the market portfolio and mimicking portfolios for size and book-to-market equity to explain monthly asset returns, through the time-series regression approach of Black (1972). Looking at the previous quote from Fama and French (1992), the inclusion of market beta

[4]This fact has given rise to the emergence of the so-called *smart beta products*, which allow investors to invest directly in certain factors or styles, such as value, low volatility, and so on.

[5]A possible explanation for this fact consists of the possibility that market betas are dynamic. In fact, there is evidence in the literature that market betas vary across the business cycle (Keim and Stambaugh [1986], Fama and French [1989], Chen [1991]), which has led to the consideration of one-factor models, with the excess market return as the only factor, in which the market beta depends on a vector of macroeconomic variables (Connor et al., 2010).

among the Fama and French (1993) factors does not seem reasonable. Although we will see the reason later when we go into more depth in the model, the consideration of excess market return as a factor in the model is supported by theoretical equilibrium considerations presented in Fama (1996).

Fama reinterprets the intertemporal CAPM (ICAPM) of Merton (1973), by considering that, like CAPM investors, ICAPM investors dislike wealth uncertainty, but they are also concerned with hedging more specific aspects of future consumption-investment opportunities. Therefore, ICAPM multifactor-efficient portfolios combine a Mean-Variance (MV) efficient portfolio with hedging portfolios that mimic uncertainty about the future consumption-investment $s$ state variables of concern to investors. The result of his analysis is the following generalization of the CAPM

$$R_i = R_0 + \beta_i^M \left(R_{p,M} - R_0\right) + \sum_{j=1}^{s} \beta_{ij} \left(R_{p,j} - R_0\right),$$

where $R_{p,j}$ is the expected return of the $j$-th state-variable mimicking portfolio, and $\beta_{ij}$ is the sensitivity of the excess return of the $i$-th asset to the excess return of the $j$-th portfolio. If we consider the rest of the factors in Fama and French (1993) as state variables, the previous equation serves as the theoretical foundation of the model within the ICAPM.[6]

Before presenting the Fama and French (1993) model, we will analyze in more detail the role played in it by the two factors that accompany market beta: the size and value factors.

**Size Factor** The size effect refers to the fact that small firms perform better than large firms, after adjusting for their betas. The size factor was discovered by Banz (1981) and Reinganum (1981). In the first of the two works cited, it is stated that the size effect had been occurring for at least forty years before its publication, but shortly after these works were published, the size factor began to decrease in intensity until it practically disappeared during the period 1989–2011 (Fama and French, 2012). Comparable results are obtained in Cazalet and Roncalli (2014) for the period 1995–2013. However, more recent works show that the size effect has shown an increasing

[6]This theoretical justification was not used by Fama and French (1993) since the paper where it is presented is from a later date.

trend in recent years, which points to the existence of cycles in cross-sectional factors (Ang, 2023).

**Value Factor** The value factor is related to the empirical fact that stocks with a high book-to-market ratio (i.e., value stocks) outperform stocks with a low book-to-market ratio (i.e., growth stocks).[7] Although value investing has been used since the first half of the twentieth century, the first reference in academic literature is Basu (1977).[8] The evidence in favor of the value factor was later recognized in Fama and French (1992) for US stock markets, and in Fama and French (1998) for twelve of thirteen major international markets. The value factor produced gains consistently during the second half of the twentieth century and the first decade of the twenty first century, except for some periods such as the recession of the early 1990s and the financial crisis of 2007–2008 (Ang, 2014). However, the value factor recently had its worst drawdown from 2017–2022, confirming the existence of trends and cyclical components in cross-sectional factors (Ang, 2023).

**The Model** Fama and French (1993) propose that the expected excess returns of stocks are explained solely by market, size and value factors, that is,

$$\mathbb{E}\left(r_i\right) - R_0 = \beta_i^M \left(\mathbb{E}\left(r_M\right) - R_0\right) + \beta_i^{SMB} \mathbb{E}\left(r_{SMB}\right) + \beta_i^{HML} \mathbb{E}\left(r_{HML}\right),$$

where $r_i$, $R_0$ and $r_M$ are, respectively, the returns of the $i$-th stock, the riskless asset and the market portfolio. The remaining variables, $r_{SMB}$ and $r_{HML}$ are, respectively, the returns of the mimicking portfolios for the size factor Small Minus Big (SMB) and the value factor High Minus Low book-to-market ratios (HML). To evaluate their three-factor model, they run the regression

$$r_i - R_0 = \alpha_i^{FF} + \beta_i^M \left(r_M - R_0\right) + \beta_i^{SMB} r_{SMB} + \beta_i^{HML} r_{HML} + \varepsilon_i^{FF}. \qquad (6.5)$$

To obtain the mimicking portfolios for the size and value factors, Fama and French divide the stocks into two groups (i.e., small and big) with respect to the size factor, and into three groups (i.e., value, neutral, and growth) with

[7]The book-to-market ratio is the quotient between the value of each share according to the company's balance sheet and its market price.

[8]In the 1934 classic *Security Analysis* by Benjamin Graham and David Dodd, it was already explained how to identify stocks with a low price relative to their fundamental value.

respect to the value factor.[9] The SMB and HML mimicking portfolios are then given by

$$SMB = \frac{1}{3}(SV + SN + SG) - \frac{1}{3}(BV + BN + BG)$$
$$HML = \frac{1}{2}(SV + BV) - \frac{1}{2}(SG + BG),$$

where $S$ and $B$ represent small and big stocks; and $V$, $N$ and $G$ stand for value, neutral, and growth stocks, respectively.

To evaluate their model, they perform the additional regression

$$r_i - R_0 = \alpha_i^{CAPM} + \beta_i^M (r_M - R_0) + \varepsilon_i^{CAPM}.$$

According to their results, $\alpha_i^{CAPM} \neq 0$, $\alpha_i^{FF} = 0$, and the betas in equation (6.5) are significant. Moreover, they obtain an increment of the average $R^2$ from $R^2_{CAPM} = 77.9\%$ to $R^2_{FF} = 93.1\%$, validating their hypothesis.

The Fama-French model has been supported by a wealth of empirical evidence (see Section 6.4 for some references) and has become a widely used tool in the portfolio management industry. However, its empirical conclusions are not exempt from criticism and have not found consensus in the academic community. For example, Black (1993), argues that the Fama and French conclusions are due to data snooping, and states: "I think most of the Fama and French results are attributable to data mining, especially when they reexamine 'effects' that people have been examined for years."[10] Similar criticisms can be found in Kothari et al. (1995) and Jagannathan and McGrattan (1995).

Another limitation of the model refers to the possibility that there are other factors that contribute to the generation of excess return but not specified in it. Precisely this circumstance gave rise to the Carhart (1997) model, which extends the Fama and French (1993) model with the inclusion of the momentum factor.

**Carhart (1997)** Predicting future returns based on past returns has long attracted the attention of financial professionals. In the academic field, we have to go back to Levy (1967) to find the first paper that claimed that the

[9]The breakpoint for the size factor is the median market value, whereas the value factor has the 30-th and 70-th percentiles of the book-to-market ratio as breakpoints. The dataset is composed of stocks listed on the New York Stock Exchange (NYSE), American Stock Exchange (AMEX) and National Association of Securities Dealers Automated Quotation (NASDAQ) from 1963 to 1991.

[10]In fact, Black's criticism referred to Fama and French (1992), but its content also applies to the methodology of Fama and French (1993).

strategy of buying stocks with substantially high prices compared to their average in recent weeks produces abnormal returns. Although Levy's result was later discredited by Jensen and Benington (1970) for selection bias, it gave rise to the study of what we know today as the momentum factor.

**Momentum Factor** The effect studied in Levy (1967) disappeared from academic literature until it was taken up in Jegadeesh and Titman (1993), giving rise to what is now known as *momentum factor*, which can be described as "the phenomenon that winner stocks continue to win and losers continue to lose" (Ang, 2014). Since the publication of Jegadeesh and Titman (1993), a considerable number of papers have appeared supporting the relevance of the momentum factor (see, among others, Chan et al. [1996], Rouwenhorst [1998], Lewellen [2015], or Asness et al. [2013]).

The strategy based on the momentum factor, consisting of buying the stocks that have obtained the highest returns (i.e., winners) and shorting the stocks with the worst returns (i.e., losers), has presented accumulated profits from 1965 to 2011 that are an order of magnitude larger than those of the size and value factors. Although the behavior of accumulated returns represents a clear advantage of the momentum strategy with respect to size and value, it also presents the disadvantage of periodic crashes, due to its nature as a positive feedback strategy (momentum investors buy stocks that have performed well recently, which leads to them continuing to have high yields, thus fueling a cycle that cannot last indefinitely; Ang [2014]). Moreover, the momentum factor has a higher volatility than the size and value factors, and momentum strategies present high negative skewness (Daniel et al., 2012).

**The Model** The Carhart (1997) model emerged as a consequence of the inability of the Fama and French (1993) model to explain cross-sectional variation in momentum-sorted portfolio returns. Carhart took as a starting point the three-factor model of Fama and French and added a new term that accounted for the momentum factor; hence it is also known as the Fama-French-Carhart model. It is given by the expression

$$r_i - R_0 = \alpha_i^C + \beta_i^M \left(r_M - R_0\right) + \beta_i^{SMB} r_{SMB} + \beta_i^{HML} r_{HML} + \beta_i^{WML} r_{WML} + \varepsilon_i^C,$$

where $r_{WML}$ is the return of the mimicking portfolio for the momentum factor Winners Minus Losers (WML), which is constructed as the equal-weight average of firms with the highest 30% eleven-month returns lagged one month minus the equal-weight average of firms with the lowest 30% eleven-month returns lagged one month.

Carhart's model allows us to explain almost entirely the persistence in the mean and risk-adjusted returns of equity mutual funds discovered by

Hendricks et al. (1993). In Fama and French (2012), a study is carried out of the effectiveness of the Fama and French (1993) and Carhart (1997) models in international markets with global and local models. In the case of global models, none of them provide good results, while in the case of local models, the authors conclude: "For Europe and Japan, nothing much is gained or lost in switching from local three-factor to four-factor models, so if it is desirable to settle on one model, local four-factor models can be the choice for Europe, Japan, and North America."

Results such as that of Fama and French (2012) limit the gains obtained by moving from the three-factor model to the four-factor model when predicting excess expected returns. However, in other areas such as the study of mutual fund performance, the Carhart model has replaced the Fama and French model (see, for example, Barras et al. [2010] or Fama and French [2010]).

Before leaving this section, in which we have presented the main types of factor models, it would be interesting to know the results of an empirical study that compares the explanatory power of the three types of models. This study was carried out with US equities in Connor (1995), which concluded that the statistical and cross-sectional models substantially outperform the macroeconomic models, with the cross-sectional models being slightly superior to the statistical ones. Specifically, Connor obtained a total explanatory power of 10.9% for the macroeconomic models, 39.0% for the statistical models, and 42.6% for the cross-sectional models.

## 6.2 FACTOR RISK AND PERFORMANCE ATTRIBUTION

As we have seen previously, some factors, once selected, present certain intrinsic risks. Thus, for example, in the case of cross-sectional factors, they present a risk related to the existence of trends and cycles (Ang, 2023); to which is added, in the case of the momentum factor, the presence of periodic crashes due to its positive feedback nature. To this type of specific risks, we must add the consideration of the risk arising from the selection of the factors to be included, which we call *factor risk*.

The first of these types of risks would be related to what type of factors to include in the model. As we have commented previously, there is empirical evidence that cross-sectional models give the best results, but even choosing this type of models, the problem of redundancies between factors can arise. These may lead to problems with estimates and a reduction in the interpretability of the factor exposures (Coqueret and Guida, 2023). Fama and French (2015) highlighted this problem by showing that the value factor is redundant when the model also includes the market, size, profitability, and investment factors.[11] Other works have studied which combination of factors is most likely given the empirical data (see, for example, De Moor et al. [2015] or Barillas and Shanken [2018]).

Another related problem is the optimal number of factors to be included in a model, about which the literature presents different conclusions, ranging from works that defend the use of models with a small number of latent factors (Kelly et al., 2019) to those that promote the use of at least 15 factors due to transaction costs (DeMiguel et al., 2020). Others, such as Green et al. (2017), point to a time-varying number of factors.

One of the areas of portfolio management in which factor risk has an impact is that of performance attribution, understood as "a technique used to quantify the excess return of a portfolio against its benchmark into the active decisions of the investment decision process" (Bacon, 2008). Specifically, we will analyze the effect of the missing factors in the information ratio, a fundamental tool of performance attribution, based on the multifactor model of Ding and Martin (2017).

Consider an actively managed portfolio, $\mathbf{w}_p$, with return $r_p$ and expected return $R_p = \mathbb{E}[r_p]$; and a benchmark portfolio, $\mathbf{w}_B$, with return $r_B$ and expected return $R_B = \mathbb{E}\left[r_B\right]$. The return of the portfolio $\mathbf{w}_p$ in excess of the return of $\mathbf{w}_B$ is $r_{pB} \equiv r_p - r_B$, and the expected excess return is $R_{pB} = \mathbb{E}[r_{pB}] = R_p - R_B$. The standard deviation of the excess return, also known as the *tracking error* of the active portfolio, is given by $\sigma_{pB} = \sqrt{\mathbb{E}[(r_{pB} - R_{pB})^2]}$.

The information ratio of a portfolio $\mathbf{w}_p$, $IR_p$, was introduced in Grinold (1989), and it is defined as the expected excess return of the actively managed portfolio divided by its tracking error:

$$IR_p = \frac{R_{pB}}{\sigma_{pB}}.$$

The *information ratio*, *IR*, of a portfolio manager is considered as the maximum information ratio that they can attain over all available portfolios:

$$IR = \max_{\mathbf{w}_p} \left\{ IR_p \right\}.$$

Grinold and Kahn (2000) show that the maximum value added by the portfolio manager is proportional to the square of their information ratio.

[11]The investment factor is measured as the quotient (growth of total assets)/(total assets) and profitability as (revenues – (cost and expenses))/(equity).

This property has led to the information ratio being widely regarded as a quantitative measure of an active portfolio manager's performance.[12] In the same work, Grinold and Kahn obtain the so-called *Fundamental Law of Active Portfolio Management*, represented by the following approximate expression of the information ratio

$$IR = IC\sqrt{BR},$$

where $IC$ is the manager's *information coefficient*, which is the correlation between forecasts and actual outcomes, and $BR$ is the number of independent forecasts of exceptional returns made by year.

Ding and Martin (2017) criticize Grinold and Kahn's derivation of the Fundamental Law and propose an alternative model that generalizes their result and eliminates its limitations. In what follows, we will present the fundamentals of the model of Ding and Martin, and their results regarding the consequences of missing factors in the information ratio.

The *beta-adjusted active return of portfolio* $\mathbf{w}_{p,t}$, is defined as

$$r_{A,t} = r_{p,t} - \beta_{p,t} r_{B,t},$$

where $r_{p,t}$ is the portfolio excess return at time $t$, and $\beta_{p,t} = \sum_{i=1}^{n} w_{p,it}\beta_i$ is the *portfolio beta relative to the benchmark*. The *active weights* are defined as the weights of portfolio $\mathbf{w}_{p,t}$ relative to the benchmark $\mathbf{w}_{B,t}$:

$$w_{A,it} = w_{p,it} - w_{B,it}.$$

If, as usual, portfolios are fully invested, that is, $\sum_{i=1}^{n} w_{p,it} = \sum_{i=1}^{n} w_{B,it} = 1$, then $\sum_{i=1}^{n} w_{A,it} = 0$. (Active weights are dollar neutral.) Moreover, we have the following result.

**Proposition 6.1** *The active return of the portfolio, $r_{A,t}$, can be seen as the return of a portfolio whose weights are the active weights, $w_{A,it}$, and whose individual returns are the residual returns $\omega_{it}$:*

$$r_{A,t} = \sum_{i=1}^{n} w_{A,it}\omega_{it} = \mathbf{w}_{A,t}^T \boldsymbol{\omega}_t, \tag{6.6}$$

*where $\boldsymbol{\omega}_t = (\omega_{1t}, \ldots, \omega_{nt})^T$.*

[12] According to Grinold and Kahn (2000), $IR$ values 0.50, 0.75, and 1.00 correspond, respectively, to good, very good, and exceptional portfolio managers.

*Proof.* Equation (6.6) is consequence of the following chain of equalities:

$$\begin{aligned} r_{A,t} &= r_{p,t} - \beta_{p,t} r_{B,t} = r_{p,t} - r_{B,t} - \beta_{p,t} r_{B,t} + \beta_{B,t} r_{B,t} \\ &= \sum_{i=1}^{n} w_{p,it} r_{it} - \sum_{i=1}^{n} w_{B,it} r_{it} - \sum_{i=1}^{n} w_{p,it} \beta_i r_{B,t} + \sum_{i=1}^{n} w_{B,it} \beta_i r_{B,t} \\ &= \sum_{i=1}^{n} \left( w_{p,it} - w_{B,it} \right) \left( r_{it} - \beta_i r_{Bt} \right) = \sum_{i=1}^{n} w_{A,it} \omega_{it}, \end{aligned}$$

where in the second step we have applied that the benchmark beta relative to the benchmark is 1, that is, $\beta_{B,t} = 1$. ■

The *conditional expected residual return*, $\alpha_{it}$, and the *conditional covariance of errors in the forecast*, $\Omega_{ijt}$, are given in matrix form by

$$\begin{aligned} \boldsymbol{\alpha}_t &= \mathbb{E}\left[ \boldsymbol{\omega}_t \,| I_{t-1} \right] \\ \boldsymbol{\Omega}_t &= \mathbb{E}\left[ \left( \boldsymbol{\omega}_t - \boldsymbol{\alpha}_t \right) \left( \boldsymbol{\omega}_t - \boldsymbol{\alpha}_t \right)^T | I_{t-1} \right], \end{aligned}$$

where $I_{t-1}$ is the random information available at time $t-1$. Note that from the first equation, we have $\mathbb{E}\left[ \boldsymbol{\alpha}_t \right] = \mathbb{E}\left[ \mathbb{E}\left[ \boldsymbol{\omega}_t \,| I_{t-1} \right] \right] = \mathbb{E}\left[ \boldsymbol{\omega}_t \right] = 0$.

The following result provides the conditional expectation and variance of the active portfolio return, $r_{A,t}$, in terms of $\boldsymbol{\alpha}_t$ and $\boldsymbol{\Omega}_t$. We state it without proof, since it is a direct consequence of equation (6.6).

**Proposition 6.2** *It is satisfied that*

$$\begin{aligned} \alpha_{A,t} &\equiv \mathbb{E}\left[ r_{A,t} \,| I_{t-1} \right] = \mathbf{w}_{A,t} \boldsymbol{\alpha}_t \\ \sigma_{A,t}^2 &\equiv var\left[ r_{A,t} \,| I_{t-1} \right] = \mathbf{w}_{A,t}^T \boldsymbol{\Omega}_t \mathbf{w}_{A,t}. \end{aligned}$$

The original version of the Fundamental Law of Active Portfolio Management was obtained by Grinold and Kahn solving an expected quadratic utility optimization program. In our case, we have the following optimization problem

$$\begin{aligned} &\underset{\mathbf{w}_{A,t}}{\arg\max} \quad U_t = \alpha_{A,t} - \frac{1}{2} \lambda \sigma_{A,t}^2 = \mathbf{w}_{A,t} \alpha_t - \frac{1}{2} \lambda \mathbf{w}_{A,t}^T \boldsymbol{\Omega}_t \mathbf{w}_{A,t} \\ &s.t. \qquad \mathbf{w}_{A,t} \mathbf{1} = 0, \end{aligned} \tag{6.7}$$

where $\lambda$ is a risk aversion parameter. Before to present the Fundamental Law of Active Portfolio Management under the multifactor model, we need to introduce the definitions of the conditional information ratio of a portfolio and the conditional information ratio of the manager under this framework, which are respectively, $IR_{p,t} \equiv \frac{\alpha_{A,t}}{\sigma_{A,t}}$ and $IR_t \equiv \frac{\alpha^*_{A,t}}{\sigma^*_{A,t}}$, where $\alpha^*_{A,t}$ and $\sigma^*_{A,t}$ are the values of $\alpha_{A,t}$ and $\sigma_{A,t}$ obtained with the solution $\mathbf{w}^*_{A,t}$ of the program in equation (6.7).

**Proposition 6.3** *The conditional information ratio, $IR_t$, is given by*

$$IR_t = \sqrt{\boldsymbol{\alpha}_t^T \boldsymbol{\Omega}_t^{-1} (\boldsymbol{\alpha}_t - \varkappa \mathbf{1})},$$

*where* $\varkappa = \frac{\boldsymbol{\alpha}_t^T \boldsymbol{\Omega}_t^{-1} \mathbf{1}}{\mathbf{1}^T \boldsymbol{\Omega}_t^{-1} \mathbf{1}}$.

*Proof.* The solution of the program in equation (6.7) is given by

$$\mathbf{w}^*_{A,t} = \lambda^{-1} \left( \boldsymbol{\Omega}_t^{-1} \boldsymbol{\alpha}_t - \varkappa \boldsymbol{\Omega}_t^{-1} \mathbf{1} \right), \tag{6.8}$$

which replaced in $\sigma_{A,t} = \sqrt{\mathbf{w}^T_{A,t} \boldsymbol{\Omega}_t \mathbf{w}_{A,t}}$ gives

$$\lambda = \left( \sigma^*_{A,t} \right)^{-1} \sqrt{\boldsymbol{\alpha}_t^T \boldsymbol{\Omega}_t^{-1} \boldsymbol{\alpha}_t - \varkappa \mathbf{1}^T \boldsymbol{\Omega}_t^{-1} \boldsymbol{\alpha}_t},$$

and we can write the optimal portfolio active weights as

$$\mathbf{w}^*_{A,t} = \sigma^*_{A,t} \frac{\boldsymbol{\Omega}_t^{-1} (\boldsymbol{\alpha}_t - \varkappa \mathbf{1})}{\sqrt{\boldsymbol{\alpha}_t^T \boldsymbol{\Omega}_t^{-1} (\boldsymbol{\alpha}_t - \varkappa \mathbf{1})}}.$$

Thus, the conditional information ratio is

$$IR_t = \frac{\alpha^*_{A,t}}{\sigma^*_{A,t}} = \frac{\mathbf{w}^*_{A,t} \boldsymbol{\alpha}_t}{\sigma^*_{A,t}} = \frac{\left( \boldsymbol{\alpha}_t^T - \varkappa \mathbf{1}^T \right) \boldsymbol{\Omega}_t^{-1} \boldsymbol{\alpha}_t}{\sqrt{\boldsymbol{\alpha}_t^T \boldsymbol{\Omega}_t^{-1} (\boldsymbol{\alpha}_t - \varkappa \mathbf{1})}} = \sqrt{\boldsymbol{\alpha}_t^T \boldsymbol{\Omega}_t^{-1} (\boldsymbol{\alpha}_t - \varkappa \mathbf{1})}$$

■

The multifactor model in Ding and Martin (2017) is given by

$$\tilde{\boldsymbol{\omega}}_t = \mathbf{Z}_{t-1} \mathbf{f}_t + \boldsymbol{\varepsilon}_t, \tag{6.9}$$

where

- $\tilde{\boldsymbol{\omega}}_t = \left( \tilde{\omega}_{1t}, \ldots, \tilde{\omega}_{nt} \right)^T = \boldsymbol{\Lambda}_t^{-1/2} \boldsymbol{\omega}_t$ is a random vector of standardized residual returns at time $t$, with $\boldsymbol{\Lambda}_t = diag\left( \sigma^2_{r_{1t}}, \ldots, \sigma^2_{r_{nt}} \right)$ and

$\sigma^2_{r_{it}} = var\left[r_{it}\,|I_{t-1}\right]$. As the $\omega_{it}$ are centered random variables, we have that $var\left[\widetilde{\omega}_{it}\right] = 1$, $i = 1, \ldots, n$.

- $\mathbf{f}_t = \left(f_{1t}, \ldots, f_{kt}\right)^T$ is a random vector of factors at time $t$ whose values are not known at time $t-1$.
- $\mathbf{Z}_{t-1} = \left(Z_{ij,t-1}\right)_{n\times k}$ is a random matrix of factor exposures.
- $\varepsilon_t = \left(\varepsilon_{1t}, \ldots, \varepsilon_{nt}\right)^T$ is an error vector.

Under this model, and with some additional assumptions, the authors conclude that the factors are the correlations of exposures with the standardized residual returns, and thus, they can identify the factors $f_{it}$ as the information coefficients, $IC_{it}$, and write $\mathbf{IC}_t = \mathbf{f}_t$. Furthermore, Ding and Martin arrive at a result for the information ratio, which we present here without proof, referring the reader to the original paper.

**Proposition 6.4** *(Ding and Martin, 2019) The Fundamental Law of Active Management under the multifactor model in equation (6.9) is given by*

$$IR = \sqrt{\mathbf{IC}^T\left(\frac{1}{n}\sigma^2_{\tilde{\varepsilon}}\mathbf{I} + \mathbf{\Sigma}_{\mathrm{IC}}\right)^{-1}\mathbf{IC}},$$

*where*

$$\mathbf{IC} = \mathbb{E}\left[\mathbf{IC}_t\right]$$
$$\left(\mathbf{\Sigma}_{\mathrm{IC}}\right)_{ij} = cov\left(IC_i, IC_j\right)$$
$$\sigma^2_{\tilde{\varepsilon}} = 1 - \sum_{j=1}^{k}\left(\sigma^2_{\mathrm{IC},k} + IC_k^2\right),$$

*with $\sigma^2_{\mathrm{IC},k}$ the diagonal elements of $\mathbf{\Sigma}_{\mathrm{IC}}$ and $IC_k$ the elements of* $\mathbf{IC}$.

As an immediate consequence of Proposition 6.4, we obtain the following asymptotic result.

**Corollary 6.1** *When the number of assets goes to infinity the information ratio is*

$$IR = \sqrt{\mathbf{IC}^T\mathbf{\Sigma}_{\mathrm{IC}}^{-1}\mathbf{IC}}. \tag{6.10}$$

To assess the effect of missing factors in the information ratio, consider $n \to \infty$ and two subgroups of factors, with information coefficients $\mathrm{IC}_{1t}$ and $\mathrm{IC}_{2t}$. The covariance matrix $\boldsymbol{\Sigma}_{\mathrm{IC}}$ will be given by

$$\boldsymbol{\Sigma}_{\mathrm{IC}} = \begin{bmatrix} \boldsymbol{\Sigma}_{11} & \boldsymbol{\Sigma}_{12} \\ \boldsymbol{\Sigma}_{12}^T & \boldsymbol{\Sigma}_{22} \end{bmatrix},$$

and the asymptotic information ratio of equation (6.10) will read as

$$\begin{aligned} IR &= \sqrt{\begin{pmatrix} \mathrm{IC}_1^T & \mathrm{IC}_2^T \end{pmatrix} \begin{pmatrix} \boldsymbol{\Sigma}_{11} & \boldsymbol{\Sigma}_{12} \\ \boldsymbol{\Sigma}_{12}^T & \boldsymbol{\Sigma}_{22} \end{pmatrix}^{-1} \begin{pmatrix} \mathrm{IC}_1 \\ \mathrm{IC}_2 \end{pmatrix}} \\ &= \sqrt{\mathrm{IC}_1^T \boldsymbol{\Sigma}_{11}^{-1} \mathrm{IC}_1 + \left(\mathrm{IC}_2 - \boldsymbol{\Sigma}_{12}^T \boldsymbol{\Sigma}_{11}^{-1} \mathrm{IC}_1\right)^T \mathrm{E}^{-1} \left(\mathrm{IC}_2 - \boldsymbol{\Sigma}_{12}^T \boldsymbol{\Sigma}_{11}^{-1} \mathrm{IC}_1\right)}, \end{aligned}$$

where $\mathrm{E} = \boldsymbol{\Sigma}_{22} - \boldsymbol{\Sigma}_{12}^T \boldsymbol{\Sigma}_{11}^{-1} \boldsymbol{\Sigma}_{12}$ is positive definite, and a formula for the inverse of partitioned matrices has been used.

If the portfolio manager uses a factor model with only the factors in the first group, they will obtain the information ratio $IR_1 = \sqrt{\mathrm{IC}_1^T \boldsymbol{\Sigma}_{11}^{-1} \mathrm{IC}_1}$, that satisfies $IR_1 \leq IR$, with strict inequality unless $\mathrm{IC}_2 = 0$ and $\boldsymbol{\Sigma}_{12} = 0$. Thus, if these equalities do not hold, the information ratio obtained by the manager will be strictly smaller than that obtained with the full factor model.

## 6.3 MACHINE LEARNING IN FACTOR INVESTING

The models that we have studied so far in this chapter operate in low-dimensional settings, that is, a few explanatory factors together with tens of test assets over a time interval of decades. However, in recent years the number of factors and assets under consideration has been increasing, and with it, the dimensionality of the models has also increased.[13] As we already saw in Chapter 2, this setting of large data sets together with high dimensionality is the appropriate environment for machine learning techniques.

In the field of returns prediction, a wide typology of machine learning techniques has been applied, such as regularized linear methods (Chinco et al., 2019), dimension reduction (Kelly et al., 2019), decision trees

[13]See, for example, Kelly et al. (2019), which uses 36 characteristics for 12,813 firms over more than 50 years.

(Bryzgalova et al., 2019) or deep learning (Feng et al., 2023).[14] In this section, we will only discuss those techniques most related to factor models, such as regularized linear methods and dimension reduction methods.

The *linear regression model* is given by

$$\mathbf{y} = \mathbf{X}\boldsymbol{\beta} + \boldsymbol{\varepsilon}, \tag{6.11}$$

where $\mathbf{y}$ is the $n$-vector of outputs, $\mathbf{X}$ is a $n \times k$ matrix of predictors, $\boldsymbol{\beta}$ a $k$-vector of parameters to be estimated, and $\boldsymbol{\varepsilon}$ a $n$-vector with the error terms. The ordinary least squares (OLS) estimation method of the model consists of finding the value of $\boldsymbol{\beta}$ that minimizes the loss function, $L(\boldsymbol{\beta})$, given by the sum of the squared residuals, $L(\boldsymbol{\beta}) = \|\boldsymbol{\varepsilon}\|_2^2 = \|\mathbf{y} - \mathbf{X}\boldsymbol{\beta}\|_2^2$, where $\|\mathbf{x}\|_2^2 \equiv \sum_{i=1}^{n} x_i^2$, for any $n$-vector $\mathbf{x}$. Thus, the OLS estimator of $\boldsymbol{\beta}$, is given by

$$\boldsymbol{\beta}^* = \arg\min_{\boldsymbol{\beta}} \left\{ \|\mathbf{y} - \mathbf{X}\boldsymbol{\beta}\|_2^2 \right\}.$$

When the number of predictors is comparable to the number of observations, the linear model tends to overfit the training data. To avoid this problem, regularization techniques are applied, consisting of maintaining small values of the parameters by adding an extra term to the loss function.

One general regularization technique, called *elastic net* (Zou and Hastie, 2005) is determined by the optimization program

$$\boldsymbol{\beta}^* = \arg\min_{\boldsymbol{\beta}} \left\{ \|\mathbf{y} - \mathbf{X}\boldsymbol{\beta}\|_2^2 + \lambda \left[ (1-\alpha) \|\boldsymbol{\beta}\|_1 + \alpha \|\boldsymbol{\beta}\|_2^2 \right] \right\},$$

where $\|\mathbf{x}\|_1 = \sum_{i=1}^{n} x_i$ for any $x \in \mathbb{R}^n$, $\lambda > 0$ is a Lagrange multiplier, and $\alpha \in [0,1]$. The case $\alpha = 0$ corresponds to least absolute shrinkage and selection operator (LASSO) regularization, whereas $\alpha = 1$ leads to ridge regression (see Section 2.4.3). The parameter $\lambda$ controls the intensity of the penalization, that is, as $\lambda$ increases, the regression coefficients approach zero. This effect is more pronounced in LASSO regularization, reducing coefficients to zero very quickly, while ridge regression is smoother, reaching zero asymptotically for all coefficients.

The previous techniques address high dimensionality using variable selection (i.e., LASSO) or shrinking coefficients (i.e., ridge regression). Another way to manage the problem is to apply dimension reduction methods to reduce the number of predictors and make them uncorrelated. The main dimension reduction techniques within linear regression are *principal component regression* (PCR) and *partial least squares* (PLS).

[14]For a more extensive list of references see, for example, Rapach and Zhou (2020), Giglio et al. (2022), Coqueret and Guida (2023), or Bagnara (2024).

PCR simply replaces the predictor variables in equation (6.11) with the principal components (PCs) obtained from the PCA. Since the PCs are not correlated by construction, there is no multicollinearity. Dimension reduction is obtained by selecting only the first $k$ PCs that explain most of the variance of the predictors. The problem with PCR is that it ignores the covariation between the predictors and the explained variable.

In contrast, PLS looks for those linear combinations of the predictors that have maximum covariance with the dependent variable, with the condition that each linear combination is uncorrelated with the previous ones.

Following Gu et al. (2020), both methods can be expressed in terms of the following variation of equation (6.11):

$$\mathbf{y} = \mathbf{X}\boldsymbol{\Omega}\boldsymbol{\theta} + \tilde{\boldsymbol{\varepsilon}}, \tag{6.12}$$

where $\boldsymbol{\Omega} = \left(\mathbf{w}_1 | \cdots | \mathbf{w}_l\right)$ is a $k \times l$ matrix; $\boldsymbol{\theta}$ is a $l$-vector of parameters to be estimated, with $l < k$, expressing the dimension reduction; and $\tilde{\boldsymbol{\varepsilon}}$ the $n$-vector with the error terms.[15]

Under this framework, PCR obtains recursively the weight vectors, $\mathbf{w}_1^*, \ldots, \mathbf{w}_l^*$, as the solution of the program

$$\begin{aligned} \mathbf{w}_j^* &= \arg\max_{\mathbf{w}} \, var\left(\mathbf{X}\mathbf{w}\right) \\ s.t. \quad & \mathbf{w}^T\mathbf{w} = 1 \\ & cov\left(\mathbf{X}\mathbf{w}, \mathbf{X}\mathbf{w}_m\right) = 0 \quad m = 1, \ldots, j-1, \end{aligned} \tag{6.13}$$

whereas in the PLS method, the weight vectors $\mathbf{w}_j^*$ are given by

$$\begin{aligned} \mathbf{w}_j^* &= \arg\max_{\mathbf{w}} \, cov^2\left(\mathbf{y}, \mathbf{X}\mathbf{w}\right) \\ s.t. \quad & \mathbf{w}^T\mathbf{w} = 1 \\ & cov\left(\mathbf{X}\mathbf{w}, \mathbf{X}\mathbf{w}_m\right) = 0 \quad m = 1, \ldots, j-1. \end{aligned} \tag{6.14}$$

Given the solution $\boldsymbol{\Omega}^* = \left(\mathbf{w}_1^* | \cdots | \mathbf{w}_l^*\right)$ of the programs in equations (6.13) or (6.14), $\boldsymbol{\theta}$ is estimated by OLS regression of $\mathbf{y}$ on $\mathbf{X}\boldsymbol{\Omega}$.

Gu et al. (2020) use a set of more than 900 predictors to perform a comparative analysis of different machine learning methods to measure asset risk premia. They obtain a negative value for the out-of-sample R-squared in the case of OLS regression, showing the inefficiency of this method with a high number of predictors. Elastic net regression increases the $R^2$ value to 0.11% per month, while PCR and PLS further increase $R^2$ to 0.26% and

[15] $l$ is a hyperparameter that can be determined adaptively from the validation sample.

0.27%, respectively, showing the improvement provided by the introduction of machine learning methods when the number of predictors is high.

In a more recent study, Noguer and Zoonekynd (2022) study the performance of different machine learning models (simple, LASSO, and restricted linear regressions; xgboost; and artificial neural networks). Surprisingly, they find that the simple linear model (i.e., unpenalized and unconstrained) outperforms the other models, although it presents extremely high turnover. They also propose an end-to-end model that maximizes the information ratio and that can be interpreted as a form of reinforcement learning. This model has superior performance and the lowest turnover.

## 6.4 NOTES

The exposition of statistical models is based on Connor et al. (2010) and Johnson and Wichern (2007). The main references used for macroeconomic models have been Connor et al. (2010), Cazalet and Roncalli (2014), and the original papers. Another useful reference is Ang (2014). The main sources for the presentation of cross-sectional models have been Cazalet and Roncalli (2014) and Ang (2014). Other interesting references are Connor et al. (2010), Petters and Dong (2016) and Coqueret and Guida (2023). The Fama and French (1993) model has been empirically contrasted in markets of different developed countries, such as the United States (Jensen et al., 1997), Davis et al., (2000) or Japan (Chan and Chen, 1991), and also in emerging markets (see, for example, Drew et al. [2003] for its application in Chinese markets). Recently, new factors different from those introduced in Fama and French (1993) and Carhart (1997), have come into play, such as low volatility (Ang et al., 2006), liquidity (Pástor and Stambaugh, 2000) or quality (Piotroski, 2000). References to more factors can be found in Harvey et al. (2016) and Cazalet and Roncalli (2014).

The section dedicated to risk factor and performance attribution is fundamentally based on Ding and Martin (2017). Additional references related to the information ratio and the Fundamental Law are Goodwin (1998), Grinold and Kahn (2000), and Clarke et al. (2006). A general reference for performance attribution is Bacon (2008).

Our study of machine learning techniques in factor investing partially follows Gu et al. (2020) and Jolliffe (2002). Other interesting references are Giglio et al. (2022), Coqueret and Guida (2023), and Bagnara (2024).

CHAPTER 7

# Market Impact, Transaction Costs, and Liquidity

Most mathematical models used in Finance assume, explicitly or implicitly, the existence of idealized frictionless markets. Thus, for example, it is usually assumed that there is a unique market price for each asset, at which any desired quantity of shares can be traded, immediately, and without incurring any costs. However, the reality of the markets does not conform to these assumptions.

Before closing a trade, there will be different buy and sell orders with different prices and quantities, which will sometimes make it not possible to complete a trade at a single price, since the trade itself will lead to a change in the price. This phenomenon is known as market impact, and together with other factors, it leads to any trading activity having associated costs, known as transaction costs. Furthermore, it is not always possible to conduct a trade with the desired immediacy, giving rise to the existence of illiquid assets or markets.

We will dedicate this chapter to the study of these three market frictions: market impact, transaction costs, and illiquidity; as well as their effects on portfolio optimization. In addition, we will address the problem of portfolio optimization in a multi-period context, giving rise to optimal trading strategies, to which we will also incorporate the consideration of transaction costs.

## 7.1 MARKET IMPACT MODELS

*Market impact* can be defined as "the link between the volume of an order (either market order or metaorder), and the price moves during and after the execution of this order" (Jaisson, 2015; Jusselin and Rosenbaum, 2020).[1] The importance of market impact in trading is expressed in Bouchaud (2010)

[1]A metaorder is a large transaction "typically split into small pieces and executed incrementally" (Farmer et al., 2013).

as follows: "It is also a dour reality for traders for whom price impact is tantamount to a cost: their second buy trade is on average more expensive than the first because of their own impact (and vice-versa for sells)." Market impact leads to the appearance of execution costs that increase with the volume of transactions and decrease the profits associated with investment strategies.

In the literature, a distinction is usually made between *temporary market impact* and *permanent market impact*. In the first case, the variation in price will revert over time returning to the value at the beginning of the transaction. The permanent market impact is assumed to be associated with relevant information held by the trade initiator, and the new price will remain after liquidation. Different market impact models consider only one or both types of impact, with different particularities.

The first model to explain the presence of market impact was proposed in Kyle (1985). In Kyle's model, three types of traders (i.e., an insider, noise traders, and a market maker) trade one asset. At equilibrium, the change in the price of the asset is proportional to the volume traded, a result that we can express as

$$\tilde{S}_t = S_t + \psi \frac{\Delta\theta}{\Delta t}, \tag{7.1}$$

where $S_t$ is the best quote for the risky asset, that represents the price at which an investor can trade a minimal amount without affecting prices; $\tilde{S}_t$ is the price per share at which the order is filled; and $\Delta\theta$ is the number of shares traded over the time interval $\Delta t$ ($\Delta\theta > 0$ for buying and $\Delta\theta < 0$ for selling). The parameter $\psi$ is a measure of market's illiquidity or, put another way, $1/\psi$ measures the depth of the market, that is, the order flow necessary to induce prices to rise or fall by one dollar. When $\psi = 0$ (infinite depth), there is no market impact, and we recover the frictionless setting. In Kyle's model the market impact is linear in volume and permanent in time.

In a multidimensional setting, in which $n$ assets are traded, with prices $S_1, \ldots, S_n$, the previous equation will take the form

$$\tilde{\mathbf{S}}_t = \mathbf{S}_t + \frac{1}{\Delta t}\boldsymbol{\Psi}\boldsymbol{\Delta\theta}, \tag{7.2}$$

where $\tilde{\mathbf{S}}_t$ and $\mathbf{S}_t$ are the vector versions of $\tilde{S}_t$ and $S_t$, $\boldsymbol{\Psi}$ is a symmetric positive-definite matrix (the multidimensional version of $\psi$), and $\boldsymbol{\Delta\theta} = (\Delta\theta_1, \ldots, \Delta\theta_n)^T$ is the vector with the number of shares traded for each asset (Gârleanu and Pedersen, 2013; Moreau et al., 2017).

Guasoni and Weber (2017) point out that the market impact specification of Kyle's model, equation (7.1), is neither scale-preserving, nor invariant with respect to stock splits, and propose the following variant that solves these problems:

$$\tilde{S}_t = S_t\left(1 + \psi\frac{S_t\Delta\theta}{X_t\Delta t}\right),$$

where $X_t$ is the investor's wealth at time $t$. This formulation maintains the linear relationship between volume and market impact, but with the additional property that the percentage change in the execution price is proportional to the fraction of wealth traded, $S_t\Delta\theta/X_t$.

Liu et al. (2017) expand the market impact proposed in Guasoni and Weber (2017), including an additional term:

$$\tilde{S}_t = S_t\left(1 + \varepsilon\, sgn(\Delta\theta) + \psi\frac{S_t\Delta\theta}{X_t\Delta t}\right),$$

where $\varepsilon$ is the relative bid-ask spread, that is, a higher ask price $(1+\varepsilon)S_t$ for purchases and a lower bid price $(1-\varepsilon)S_t$ for sales. When $\varepsilon, \psi \to 0$ we recover the frictionless case.

All market impact models presented so far, which propose a linear relationship with the traded volume, do not agree with the empirical evidence, which indicates a strictly concave relationship between market impact and volume, determined by a powerlaw with exponent approximately equal to 0.5 (Almgren et al. [2005], Moro et al. [2009], and Bershova and Rakhlin [2013]). This empirical fact is known as the *square root law*. Other works, such as Bouchaud et al. (2004), point to a temporary market impact with a decay over time that follows a power-law.

To accommodate the two factors (a temporary and nonlinear market impact on volume), Gatheral (2010) proposes the following general expression for market impact:

$$S_t = S_0 + \int_0^t f(\dot{x}_s)\, G(t-s)\, ds + \int_0^t \sigma dW_t,$$

where $S_t$ is the stock price at time $t$, $\dot{x}_s$ is the rate of trading in dollars at time $s < t$, $\sigma$ is the constant volatility, and $W_t$ a Brownian motion. The function $f$ is the *instantaneous market impact function*, which express the relationship between market impact and volume; and $G$, the *decay kernel*, controls the way in which the market impact decays over time. Gatheral only considers permanent impact and, unlike Liu et al. (2017), does not include any term corresponding to the transitory effect of the bid-ask spread.

Another interesting contribution of Gatheral (2010) is the introduction of the so-called *principle of no-dynamic-arbitrage*, by which price manipulation, understood as a round-trip trade whose expected cost is negative, is not possible.[2]

Among the results in Gatheral (2010), we can highlight the following:

- Nonlinear permanent impact is inconsistent with the principle of no-dynamic-arbitrage.[3]
- No-dynamic-arbitrage together with any reasonable instantaneous market impact function excludes exponentially decay of market impact as a realistic assumption.
- Power-law decay of market impact may be compatible with realistic shapes of the market impact function.
- If $G(\tau) = \tau^{-\gamma}$ and $f(v) \propto v^{\delta}$ (i.e., power-laws for decay and market impact), dynamic no-arbitrage imposes that $\gamma + \delta \geq 1$.

Subsequent empirical research (see, for example, Tóth et al. [2011]) has shown that, for metaorders, the temporal profile of market impact can be decomposed into two phases: a concave transient phase during execution and a decay phase where the price decreases toward a long-term permanent level after the execution in completed. Moreover, the transient part seems to be well described by a power-law with exponent about 0.5 (Bouchaud, 2010; Tóth et al., 2011; Bacry et al., 2015).

Jusselin and Rosenbaum (2020) present a no-arbitrage model that accommodates the empirical results detailed previously in which order flow is modeled through Hawkes processes.[4]

## 7.2 MODELING TRANSACTION COSTS

So far we have studied portfolio optimization models without frictions, which implicitly consider that there is a single market price at which the portfolio manager can sell or buy any number of shares to vary the composition of her portfolio. As we have seen previously, these assumptions do not correspond to reality. Furthermore, the trading activity entails costs, called

[2]Under the framework of Gatheral (2010), a round-trip is a strategy $x_t$ satisfying $\int_0^T \dot{x}_t dt = 0$.

[3]This result was originally obtained by Huberman and Stanzl (2004).

[4]A Hawkes process $N$ is a self-exciting point process where intensity $\lambda_t$ is defined by

$$\lambda_t = \mu + \int_0^t \phi(t-s)\, dN_s,$$

with $\mu$ a positive constant and $\phi$ a non-negative locally integrable function. See Bacry et al. (2015) for an overview of Hawkes processes in finance.

*transaction costs*, which until now we have not considered. These costs can take part of the profits of an investment strategy, or even, as we will see later, lead to a situation in which the optimal strategy is not to trade.

The importance of transaction costs in portfolio management has been stated in Grinold and Kahn (2000) as follows: "They can be the investment management version of death by a thousand cuts. A top-quantile manager with an information ratio of 0.5 may lose half her returns because of transaction costs. They are important."

We can distinguish two types of transaction costs: fixed costs and variable costs (Qian et al., 2007; Almgren et al., 2005). Fixed costs are related to trade commissions and bid-ask spreads.[5]

- **Trade commissions** are usually quoted at some cost per share, regardless of whether it is a buy or a sell order.[6] The transaction costs associated with trade commissions are proportional to the amount of assets traded.
- The **bid-ask spread** gives rise to another type of fixed cost since the investor receives less when selling and pay more when buying. As the cost is associated with each share, it will also be proportional to the number of assets traded.

Variable transaction costs include market impact and opportunity costs.

- As we have already seen, **market impact** refers to the change in price due to investor's trading activity and occurs when the order size exceeds the quote depth currently available. As we will see, the relationship between transaction costs and market impact will depend on the type of impact considered. A market impact linear on the volume traded will result in quadratic transaction costs. In the more realistic case of power-law impacts, we will obtain more complex nonlinear transactions costs.
- **Opportunity costs** are related to the impact on returns of orders that have not been executed. For example, if an investor uses a limit order to buy a stock, and the stock price remains above the limit order price, the trade will not be executed and the investor will lose the opportunity

[5]The bid-ask spread is the difference between the highest price that a buyer is willing to pay for an asset and the lowest price that a seller is willing to accept.

[6]We are assuming here, for simplicity, the same unit costs for buying and selling. For an analysis including different unit costs see, for example, Pogue (1970) or Chen et al. (2019).

to profit from that upward movement.[7] Opportunity costs are difficult to model and we will not consider them in our study.

To include transaction costs in the Mean-Variance (MV) model, we will consider them as a function of the portfolio weights, $w_i$. In the case of fixed costs, since there is no price changes involved, the associated transaction costs, $CT_F(\mathbf{w})$, can be obtained as the sum of the costs associated with the trade of each asset:

$$CT_F(\mathbf{w}) = \sum_{i=1}^{n} \gamma_i |\Delta w_i| = \mathbf{\Gamma}^T |\mathbf{\Delta w}|,$$

where $\mathbf{\Gamma} = (\gamma_1, \ldots, \gamma_n)^T$, with $\gamma_i$ some positive constants, $|\mathbf{\Delta w}| = (|\Delta w_1|, \ldots, |\Delta w_n|)^T$ and $|\Delta w_i| = |w_i - w_{i0}|$, where $w_{i0}$ and $w_i$ are, respectively, the initial and final weights of the $i$-th asset in the portofolio.[8]

For variable transaction costs, $CT_V(\mathbf{w})$, we have to consider the vector of variation in prices, $\mathbf{\Delta S} = \tilde{\mathbf{S}}_t - \mathbf{S}_t$, and write

$$CT_V(\mathbf{w}) = \mathbf{\Delta w}^T \mathbf{\Delta S}.$$

Considering equation (7.2) and assuming that $\frac{\Delta\theta}{\Delta t} \propto \mathbf{\Delta w}$, we obtain[9]

$$CT_V(\mathbf{w}) = \mathbf{\Delta w}^T \mathbf{\Psi} \mathbf{\Delta w}.$$

In this chapter, we will consider the following reformulation of the Markowitz MV problem, known as *risk aversion formulation* (Fabozzi et al., 2007):

---

[7]A *limit order* is an order to trade a certain number of shares at the best available price subject to the condition that the price does not exceed a certain limit specified in the order. In contrast, a *market order* is a mandate to trade immediately at the best available price.

[8]If we only consider trades with the same initial and final total wealth $W$, we have $\Delta w_i = \frac{\Delta\theta_i S_i}{W}$, with $S_i$ the asset price. The fixed cost associated to the $i$-th asset is $CT_F(w_i) = \beta_i \Delta\theta_i = \frac{\beta_i W}{S_i} \Delta w_i$, and thus, $\gamma_i = \frac{\beta_i W}{S_i}$, where $\beta_i$ is the fixed cost of trading one unit of the $i$-th asset.

[9]The assumption $\frac{\Delta\theta}{\Delta t} \propto \mathbf{\Delta w}$ can be considered as a valid approximation in the case in which the total wealth $W$ does not change with trades, and $\frac{S_i}{W} \simeq \frac{S_j}{W}$ (see footnote 8).

$$
\begin{aligned}
\max \quad & \mathbf{w}^T\mathbf{R} - \frac{\lambda}{2}\mathbf{w}^T\boldsymbol{\Sigma}\mathbf{w} \\
s.t. \quad & \mathbf{w}^T 1 = 1.
\end{aligned}
\tag{7.3}
$$

This reformulation allows us to interpret the optimization problem as the maximization of the expected return of the portfolio, but with a risk penalty proportional to its variance. The intensity of the penalization is determined by $\lambda > 0$, the risk aversion index.

Taking advantage of the risk aversion formulation, we can include transaction costs as additional penalties in the form

$$
\begin{aligned}
\max \quad & \mathbf{w}^T\mathbf{R} - \frac{\lambda}{2}\mathbf{w}^T\boldsymbol{\Sigma}\mathbf{w} - \boldsymbol{\Gamma}^T\left|\Delta\mathbf{w}\right| - \frac{1}{2}\Delta\mathbf{w}^T\boldsymbol{\Psi}\Delta\mathbf{w} \\
s.t. \quad & \mathbf{w}^T 1 = 1,
\end{aligned}
\tag{7.4}
$$

which includes fixed and variable transaction costs. The program in equation (7.4) is a quadratic programming problem that should be solved, in general, by numerical techniques. However, to obtain more intuition about the influence of transaction costs on portfolio optimization, and following Qian et al. (2007), we will study different unconstrained versions of program in equation (7.4).

### 7.2.1 Single Asset

In this case, we consider that the investor holds a fraction $w$ of their total wealth $W$ in a risky asset, and the remaining part, $W - wW$, in a riskless asset. The optimal value of $w$ in the presence of transaction costs, $w^*$, is given by $w^* = \arg\ \max\ U(w)$, where

$$
U(w) = wR - \frac{\lambda}{2}\sigma^2 w^2 - \gamma\left|\Delta w\right| - \frac{1}{2}\psi\left(\Delta w\right)^2. \tag{7.5}
$$

When there are no transaction costs, $\gamma = \psi = 0$, the expression in equation (7.5) reduces to the unconstrained and single asset version of equation (7.3), and in this case, the optimal value is

$$
w^* = \frac{R}{\lambda\sigma^2} \equiv \widetilde{w}.
$$

The following results provide the optimal values of the weights for the cases of only quadratic costs and only linear costs.

**Proposition 7.1** *The optimal weight in the case of a single asset with quadratic transaction costs is given by*

$$w^* = \frac{R + \psi w_0}{\lambda\sigma^2 + \psi}. \tag{7.6}$$

*Moreover, when $w_0 = \tilde{w}$ it is optimal not to trade, and when $w_0 \neq \tilde{w}$, for any finite value of the quadratic costs, it will always be optimal to trade.*

*Proof.* Taking $\gamma = 0$ in (7.5) we have

$$U(w) = wR - \frac{\lambda}{2}\sigma^2 w^2 - \frac{1}{2}\psi(\Delta w)^2.$$

and applying $U'(w) = 0$, we obtain the expression the equation (7.6). On the other hand, $\frac{\partial w^*}{\partial \psi} = \frac{\lambda\sigma^2 w_0}{(\lambda\sigma^2+\psi)^2}$. Thus, when $w_0 = \tilde{w}$, we have $w^* = w_0$, which does not vary with transaction costs. When $w_0 > \tilde{w}$, $w^* < w_0$, and $w^*$ is strictly increasing with $\psi$. In the remaining case, $w_0 < \tilde{w}$, then $w^* > w_0$ and $w^*$ is strictly decreasing with $\psi$. In both cases, the value $w^* = w_0$ is only reached when $\psi \to \infty$. Therefore, excluding the case with $w_0 = \tilde{w}$, it is always optimal to invest. ■

**Remark 7.1** *Taking $\psi = 0$ in equation (7.6), we recover $w^* = \tilde{w}$, which is the solution of the unconstrained problem for a single asset without transaction costs.*

**Proposition 7.2** *The optimal weight in the case of a single asset with linear transaction costs is given by*

$$w^* = \begin{cases} \dfrac{R-\gamma}{\lambda\sigma^2} & \text{if } \Delta\tilde{w} > \dfrac{\gamma}{\lambda\sigma^2} \\ w_0 & \text{if } |\Delta\tilde{w}| \leq \dfrac{\gamma}{\lambda\sigma^2}, \\ \dfrac{R+\gamma}{\lambda\sigma^2} & \text{if } \Delta\tilde{w} < -\dfrac{\gamma}{\lambda\sigma^2} \end{cases} \tag{7.7}$$

*where $\Delta\tilde{w} = \tilde{w} - w_0$. Moreover, for initial weights $w_0 \in \left[\frac{R-\gamma}{\lambda\sigma^2}, \frac{R+\gamma}{\lambda\sigma^2}\right]$, it is optimal not to trade.*

*Proof.* Taking $\psi = 0$ in (7.5) we obtain

$$U(w) = wR - \frac{\lambda}{2}\sigma^2 w^2 - \gamma\,|w - w_0|.$$

From this expression, it is not difficult to show that

$$U(w) = U(w_0 + \Delta w) = U(w_0) + \left[\lambda\sigma^2 \Delta\widetilde{w}\Delta w - \frac{\lambda}{2}\sigma^2 (\Delta w)^2 - \gamma |\Delta w|\right].$$

As $U(w_0)$ is a constant, maximizing $U(w)$ is equivalent to maximizing

$$\widetilde{U}(\Delta w) = U(w) - U(w_0) = \lambda\sigma^2 \Delta\widetilde{w}\Delta w - \frac{\lambda}{2}\sigma^2 (\Delta w)^2 - \gamma |\Delta w|. \quad (7.8)$$

We consider three different cases for the initial weight.
$\underline{w_0 = \widetilde{w}}$: In this case, we have $\Delta\widetilde{w} = 0$, and then

$$\widetilde{U}(\Delta w) = -\frac{\lambda}{2}\sigma^2 (\Delta w)^2 - \gamma |\Delta w|.$$

As $\widetilde{U}(\Delta w) \leq 0\ \forall \Delta w$, the maximum is reached at $\Delta w = 0$, that is, $w^* = w_0$.
$\underline{w_0 < \widetilde{w}}$: Now we have $\Delta\widetilde{w} > 0$ and then, by equation (7.8), in order to reach a maximum it is necessary that $\Delta w > 0$. In the opposite case, $\Delta w \leq 0$, $\widetilde{U}(\Delta w)$ is nonpositive, and then the optimum correspond to $\Delta w = 0$, that is, $w^* = w_0$. When $\Delta w > 0$, equation (7.8) reads

$$\widetilde{U}(\Delta w) = \lambda\sigma^2 \Delta\widetilde{w}\Delta w - \frac{\lambda}{2}\sigma^2 (\Delta w)^2 - \gamma \Delta w,$$

which is differentiable. The first-order condition, $\widetilde{U'}(\Delta w) = 0$, gives

$$\Delta w^* = \frac{\lambda\sigma^2\Delta\widetilde{w} - \gamma}{\lambda\sigma^2} = \Delta\widetilde{w} - \frac{\gamma}{\lambda\sigma^2},$$

thus, the optimal weight is

$$w^* = \Delta\widetilde{w} - \frac{\gamma}{\lambda\sigma^2} + w_0 = \frac{R - \gamma}{\lambda\sigma^2}$$

as long as the condition $\Delta w^* > 0$ is satisfied, that is, $\Delta\widetilde{w} > \frac{\gamma}{\lambda\sigma^2}$.
$\underline{w_0 > \widetilde{w}}$: Similarly to the previous case, we have $\Delta w < 0$ ($\Delta w \geq 0$ leads to $w^* = w_0$), and $\Delta w^* = \Delta\widetilde{w} + \frac{\gamma}{\lambda\sigma^2}$. Then $w^* = \frac{R+\gamma}{\lambda\sigma^2}$ when $\Delta\widetilde{w} < -\frac{\gamma}{\lambda\sigma^2}$. The no-trade region correspond to $w^* = w_0$, that is, $|\Delta\widetilde{w}| \leq \frac{\gamma}{\lambda\sigma^2}$, which can be rewritten as $-\frac{\gamma}{\lambda\sigma^2} \leq \widetilde{w} - w_0 \leq \frac{\gamma}{\lambda\sigma^2}$, from where we obtain $\frac{R-\gamma}{\lambda\sigma^2} \leq w_0 \leq \frac{R+\gamma}{\lambda\sigma^2}$. ■

**Remark 7.2** *Taking $\gamma = 0$ in equation (7.7), we recover $w^* = \widetilde{w}$, which is the solution of the unconstrained problem for a single asset without transaction costs.*

Unlike the case of quadratic transaction costs, where there was only one value of the initial weight ($w_0 = \widetilde{w}$) for which the optimal solution was not to trade, when transaction costs are linear, there is a whole interval of no trade, centered at $w_0 = \widetilde{w}$, and with length proportional to transaction costs. This situation is more general, and also holds in dynamic models with linear transaction costs, as we will see in Section 7.3.

### 7.2.2 Multiple Assets

The optimization problem is now the unconstrained version of equation (7.4), namely, to maximize

$$U(\mathbf{w}) = \mathbf{w}^T\mathbf{R} - \frac{\lambda}{2}\mathbf{w}^T\boldsymbol{\Sigma}\mathbf{w} - \boldsymbol{\Gamma}^T|\Delta\mathbf{w}| - \frac{1}{2}\Delta\mathbf{w}^T\boldsymbol{\Psi}\Delta\mathbf{w}. \tag{7.9}$$

For the case of only quadratic costs, we have the following result.

**Proposition 7.3** *The vector with the optimal weights in the case of multiple assets and quadratic costs is given by*

$$\mathbf{w}^* = (\lambda\boldsymbol{\Sigma} + \boldsymbol{\Psi})^{-1}(\mathbf{R} + \boldsymbol{\Psi}\mathbf{w}_0). \tag{7.10}$$

*Proof.* Making $\boldsymbol{\Gamma} = 0$ in (7.9) and taking gradient, we get

$$\frac{\partial U}{\partial \mathbf{w}} = \mathbf{R} - \lambda\boldsymbol{\Sigma}\mathbf{w} - \boldsymbol{\Psi}(\mathbf{w} - \mathbf{w}_0).$$

Solving the equation $\frac{\partial U}{\partial \mathbf{w}} = 0$, we obtain (7.10). ■

**Remark 7.3** *Taking* $\boldsymbol{\Psi} = 0$ *in (7.10), we recover* $\mathbf{w}^* = (\lambda\boldsymbol{\Sigma})^{-1}\mathbf{R}$, *which is the solution of the unconstrained problem for multiple assets without transaction costs.*

When only linear costs are considered, the problem has no analytical solution in general. However, it is possible to transform the problem so that it can be solved using quadratic programming techniques.

**Proposition 7.4** *The optimization problem with multiple assets and linear transaction costs can be reformulated as the maximization of*

$$U(\overline{\mathbf{w}}) = \overline{\mathbf{w}}^T\overline{\mathbf{R}} - \frac{\lambda}{2}\overline{\mathbf{w}}^T\overline{\boldsymbol{\Sigma}}\overline{\mathbf{w}},$$

*where*

$$\overline{\mathbf{w}} = \begin{bmatrix} \mathbf{w}_B \\ \mathbf{w}_S \end{bmatrix}$$

$$\overline{\mathbf{R}} = \begin{bmatrix} \mathbf{R} - \lambda\mathbf{\Sigma}\mathbf{w}_0 - \mathbf{\Gamma} \\ -\mathbf{R} + \lambda\mathbf{\Sigma}\mathbf{w}_0 - \mathbf{\Gamma} \end{bmatrix}$$

$$\overline{\mathbf{\Sigma}} = \begin{bmatrix} \mathbf{\Sigma} & -\mathbf{\Sigma} \\ -\mathbf{\Sigma} & \mathbf{\Sigma} \end{bmatrix}$$

*and* $\mathbf{w}_B, \mathbf{w}_S \geq 0$ *are, respectively, the buy and sell vectors.*

*Proof.* With the help of the vectors $\mathbf{w}_B$ and $\mathbf{w}_S$, we can write $\mathbf{w} = \mathbf{w}_0 + \mathbf{w}_B - \mathbf{w}_S$ and $|\mathbf{\Delta w}| = \mathbf{w}_B + \mathbf{w}_S$. Replacing these values in equation (7.9), with $\mathbf{\Psi} = 0$, we have

$$\begin{aligned} U(\mathbf{w}) = U(\mathbf{w}_0) &+ \mathbf{w}_B^T(\mathbf{R} - \lambda\mathbf{\Sigma}\mathbf{w}_0 - \mathbf{\Gamma}) + \mathbf{w}_S^T(-\mathbf{R} + \lambda\mathbf{\Sigma}\mathbf{w}_0 - \mathbf{\Gamma}) \\ &- \frac{\lambda}{2}\left(\mathbf{w}_B^T\mathbf{\Sigma}\mathbf{w}_B - 2\mathbf{w}_B^T\mathbf{\Sigma}\mathbf{w}_S + \mathbf{w}_S^T\mathbf{\Sigma}\mathbf{w}_S\right) \end{aligned}$$

or, equivalently

$$U(\overline{\mathbf{w}}) = U(\mathbf{w}_0) + \overline{\mathbf{w}}^T\overline{\mathbf{R}} - \frac{\lambda}{2}\overline{\mathbf{w}}^T\overline{\mathbf{\Sigma}}\overline{\mathbf{w}}.$$

The term $U(\mathbf{w}_0)$ is a constant that can be removed from the optimization problem. ∎

In the case of a single asset with linear transaction costs, we saw that a no-trade interval exists. In the multidimensional case with linear costs, there is also a no-trade region (i.e., a multi-dimensional parallelogram; see Dybvig and Pezzo [2020]).

## 7.3 OPTIMAL TRADING STRATEGIES

So far, we have studied portfolio optimization in a single period setting. In this section, we will see how it is possible to extend the optimization process to the consideration of multiple periods, which will give rise to *optimal trading strategies*. The first work to extend the MV model to a multiperiod setting (in continuous time) was probably Richardson (1989). The incorporation of transaction costs into portfolio selection occurred in Magill and Constantinides (1976). These authors used linear transaction costs and obtained the existence of no-trade regions.

The first multiperiod MV model to include (quadratic) transaction costs was Gârleanu and Pedersen (2013). According to these authors, the optimal trading strategy is obtained by maximizing the present value of all future expected excess returns, penalized for risks and trading costs. Using dynamic programming, they find a closed-form expression, which provides the optimal updated portfolio as a linear combination of the current portfolio and an "aim portfolio", given by a weighted average of the current and the (expected) future Markowitz portfolios.[10]

Mei et al. (2016) extend the model in Gârleanu and Pedersen (2013) by allowing the consideration of different transaction costs, such as linear, quadratic, and even the more realistic ones derived from power-law market impact. Due to the generality of their analysis and the importance of their results, in what follows, we will present the model of Mei et al. (2016) in more detail. The results will be stated without proof, for which we refer the reader to the original paper.

### 7.3.1 Mei, DeMiguel, and Nogales (2016)

The general framework of this model is described by the following optimization program, whose solution will be the optimal trading strategy:

$$\max_{\{\mathbf{x}_t\}_{t=1}^{T}} \sum_{t=1}^{T} \left[ (1-\rho)^t \left( \mathbf{x}_t^T \mu - \frac{\lambda}{2} \mathbf{x}_t^T \boldsymbol{\Sigma} \mathbf{x}_t \right) - (1-\rho)^{t-1} \varkappa \left\| \boldsymbol{\Psi}^{1/p} \left( \mathbf{x}_t - \mathbf{x}_{t-1} \right) \right\|_p^p \right], \tag{7.11}$$

where:

- $\mathbf{x}_t$ is the $n$-vector that contains the number of shares of each of the $n$ risky assets held in period $t$.
- $T$ is the investment horizon.
- $\rho$ is the discount rate.
- $\mu$ and $\boldsymbol{\Sigma}$ are, respectively, the $n$-vector of means and the $n \times n$ covariance matrix of price changes (in excess of the risk-free asset price), which are assumed to be independently and identically distributed.
- $\lambda$ is the absolute risk-aversion parameter.
- $\varkappa$ is the transaction costs parameter.

[10] In this section, by the name "Markowitz portfolio", we will refer to the optimal portfolio in the absence of transaction costs; see the text.

- $\boldsymbol{\Psi}$ is the $n \times n$ symmetric and positive definite transaction costs matrix.
- $\|\mathbf{x}\|_p = \left(\sum_{i=1}^{n} |x_i|^p\right)^{1/p}$ is the $p$-norm of the $n$-vector $\mathbf{x} = (x_1, \ldots, x_n)^T$.

The matrix $\boldsymbol{\Psi}^{1/p}$ is defined as $\boldsymbol{\Psi}^{1/p} = \mathbf{Q}^T\mathbf{D}^{1/p}\mathbf{Q}$, where $\boldsymbol{\Psi} = \mathbf{Q}^T\mathbf{D}\mathbf{Q}$ is the spectral decomposition of $\boldsymbol{\Psi}$ as a symmetric positive definite matrix. The term with $\left\|\boldsymbol{\Psi}^{1/p}(\mathbf{x}_t - \mathbf{x}_{t-1})\right\|_p^p$ can lead to linear ($p = 1$, $\boldsymbol{\Psi} = \mathbf{I}$), quadratic ($p = 2$), and more realistic ($1 < p < 2$) transaction costs.[11] Following Mei et al. (2016), we will call the costs of the latter case *market impact transaction costs*.

One of the problems related to dynamic MV models is that they present the so-called *time inconsistency problem*, whereby the initially generated optimal strategy may no longer be optimal at some point between the current moment and the investment horizon (see Dai et al. [2010] and Björk et al. [2014]). This is because the Bellman optimality principle does not hold, and dynamic programming is not directly applicable (for dynamic programming and the optimality principle, see Section 8.1).

One of the first works to recognize time inconsistency and propose a time-consistent dynamic MV model was Basak and Chabakauri (2010), but these authors did not consider transaction costs. The problem with proportional transaction costs was solved in Dai et al. (2010).

One of the advantages of the model of Mei et al. (2016) is that, as the authors themselves prove, the optimal trading strategy obtained from equation (7.11) is time consistent (Mei et al., 2016; Proposition 1).

**Proportional Transaction Costs** The optimization program in equation (7.11) can be written in this case as

$$\max_{\{\mathbf{x}_t\}_{t=1}^{T}} \sum_{t=1}^{T} \left[ (1-\rho)^t \left( \mathbf{x}_t^T \boldsymbol{\mu} - \frac{\lambda}{2} \mathbf{x}_t^T \boldsymbol{\Sigma} \mathbf{x}_t \right) - (1-\rho)^{t-1} \varkappa \left\| \boldsymbol{\Psi}^{1/p} (\mathbf{x}_t - \mathbf{x}_{t-1}) \right\|_1 \right].$$

The optimal trading strategy solution of this program is to trade in the first period and not trade in the rest of the periods ($\mathbf{x}_1 = \cdots = \mathbf{x}_T$). The optimal portfolio in the first period is obtained from the program

$$\begin{aligned} \min_{\mathbf{x}_1} \quad & (\mathbf{x}_1 - \mathbf{x}_0)^T \boldsymbol{\Sigma} (\mathbf{x}_1 - \mathbf{x}_0) \\ s.t. \quad & \|\boldsymbol{\Sigma}(\mathbf{x}_1 - \tilde{\mathbf{x}})\|_\infty \le \frac{\varkappa \rho}{\lambda (1-\rho)\left[1 - (1-\rho)^T\right]}, \end{aligned} \tag{7.12}$$

[11] Mei et al. (2016) recognize that a realistic model would require the presence of diverse types of transaction costs, but in that case it is not possible to obtain analytic solutions.

where $\mathbf{x}_0$ is the initial portfolio, $\tilde{\mathbf{x}} = \lambda^{-1}\boldsymbol{\Sigma}^{-1}\mu$ is the Markowitz portfolio (the optimal portfolio in absence of transaction costs), and $\|\mathbf{x}\|_\infty = \max_i |x_i|$.

The program in equation (7.12) is a quadratic programming problem that can be efficiently solved with numerical techniques. The inequality in equation (7.12) determines the no-trade region, which is a multidimensional parallelogram centered around the Markowitz portfolio.

**Market Impact Costs** This case corresponds to $p \in (1,2)$ and, therefore, the optimization program is the original expression in equation (7.11). In this situation, it is no longer possible to provide a closed-form solution, but we can describe some properties.

In the event that the initial portfolio $x_0$ is the Markowitz portfolio $\tilde{x}$, the optimal strategy is not to trade. If the initial portfolio does not match the Markowitz portfolio then it is optimal to trade, in any period, toward the boundary of the *rebalancing region*, given in period $t$ by

$$\frac{\left\|\sum_{s=t}^{T}(1-\rho)^{s-t}\boldsymbol{\Psi}^{1/p}\boldsymbol{\Sigma}\left(\mathbf{x}_s-\tilde{\mathbf{x}}\right)\right\|_q}{p\left\|\boldsymbol{\Psi}^{1/p}\left(\mathbf{x}_t-\mathbf{x}_{t-1}\right)\right\|_p^{p-1}} \leq \frac{\varkappa}{\lambda(1-\rho)},$$

where $q$ satisfies $\frac{1}{p}+\frac{1}{q}=1$. Furthermore, the rebalancing region shrinks over time and converges to the Markowitz portfolio (which always remains in the rebalancing region) when the investment horizon tends to infinity.

**Quadratic Transaction Costs** The optimal portfolio strategy in this case, which corresponds to equation (7.11) with $p = 2$, is given by a linear system of equations that can be solved numerically (see Mei et al. [2016], Theorem 3). At each period, the optimal portfolio is a combination of the Markowitz portfolio, the previous period portfolio, and the next period portfolio. Moreover, as in the case with market impact costs, the optimal portfolio converges to the Markowitz portfolio when $T \to \infty$.

Mei et al. (2016) also conduct an empirical study, for each type of transaction costs, of the utility losses associated with the following portfolio policies:

- *Target portfolio policy*, consisting of trading to the Markowitz portfolio in the first period and not trading thereafter. This policy corresponds to the absence of transaction costs.

- *Static portfolio policy*, trading in each period to the solution of the one-period model with transaction costs, which correspond to a myopic investor.
- *Multiperiod portfolio policy*, which considers the multiperiod nature of the problem and the transaction costs. This policy corresponds to the model of Mei et al. (2016).

The numerical results show that the utility losses associated with the target and static policies can be large, for all the types of transaction costs, relative to the multiperiod portfolio policy.

Another interesting work related to optimal trading strategies is the one presented in Skaf and Boyd (2009). Instead of considering a multiperiod MV model, these authors aim to minimize the expected mean-square deviation of final wealth from a given desired value over a finite time horizon. Moreover, they include in their model the possibility of incorporating linear transaction costs and additional constraints. We will describe briefly, and without proof, the main results of this paper.

### 7.3.2 Skaf and Boyd (2009)

These authors consider a portfolio determined, at time $t$, by the vector $\mathbf{W}_t = (W_{1t}, \ldots, W_{nt})^T$ of portfolio holdings (in dollars), with $t = 1, \ldots, T+1$. The trades executed at the beginning of period $t$ (in dollars) are described by the vector $\mathbf{u}_t = (u_{1t}, \ldots, u_{nt})^T$, where $u_{it} > 0$ corresponds to purchases of the $i$-th asset, and $u_{it} < 0$ corresponds to sales. The vector of portfolio holdings after the trades, is given by $\mathbf{W}_t^* = \mathbf{W}_t + \mathbf{u}_t$; and at the beginning of the next period, by $\mathbf{W}_{t+1} = \mathbf{A}_t\mathbf{W}_t^* = \mathbf{A}_t(\mathbf{W}_t + \mathbf{u}_t)$, where $\mathbf{A}_t = diag(\mathbf{r}_t)$, with $\mathbf{r}_t$ the vector of asset returns.

The solution of the optimization problem, that is, the trading policy, will be given by a set of functions $\varphi_1, \ldots, \varphi_T : \mathbb{R}^n \to \mathbb{R}^n$ with $\mathbf{u}_t = \varphi_t(\mathbf{W}_t)$, satisfying $(\mathbf{W}_t, \mathbf{u}_t) \in \mathcal{C}_t$, $t = 1, \ldots, T$, where $\mathcal{C}_t \subset \mathbb{R}^{2n}$ is the constraint set for period $t$.

The simplest unconstrained case without transaction costs corresponds to

$$\mathcal{C}_t = \mathcal{C}_t^{unc} = \left\{(\mathbf{W}_t, \mathbf{u}_t) \,|\, \mathbf{1}^T\mathbf{u}_t = 0\right\}, \quad t = 1, \cdots, T,$$

where it has only been considered the self-financing condition $\mathbf{1}^T\mathbf{u}_t = 0$. When linear transaction costs are considered, the self-financing condition will be replaced by

$$\mathbf{1}^T\mathbf{u} + \varkappa_b^T\mathbf{u}^+ + \varkappa_s^T\mathbf{u}^- = 0, \tag{7.13}$$

where $\varkappa_b, \varkappa_s \succeq 0$ are, respectively, the vectors of buying and selling transaction costs rates, and $\mathbf{u}^+, \mathbf{u}^-$ are, respectively, the positive and negative parts of $\mathbf{u}$, defined by $\mathbf{u}^+ = \left(u_1^+, \ldots, u_n^+\right)^T$ and $\mathbf{u}^- = \left(u_1^-, \ldots, u_n^-\right)^T$, with $u_i^+ = \max(u_i, 0)$ and $u_i^- = \max(-u_i, 0)$. The interpretation of the constraint in equation (7.13) is that the total gross trading profit, $-\mathbf{1}^T\mathbf{u}$, equals the total transaction costs from buying and selling.[12]

**Unconstrained Case** In this case, we have to find the solution of the program

$$\begin{aligned} \min \quad & \mathbb{E}\left[\left(W_{T+1} - W^{des}\right)^2\right] \\ s.t. \quad & \left(\mathbf{W}_t, \mathbf{u}_t\right) \in \mathcal{C}_t^{unc}, \quad t = 1, \ldots, T, \end{aligned}$$

where $W_{T+1} = \mathbf{1}^T\mathbf{W}_{T+1}$ is the final wealth, and $W^{des}$ is the desired final wealth. Skaf and Boyd show that the optimal policy solution of this unconstrained case is given by

$$\varphi_t(\mathbf{z}) = \mathbf{K}_t\left(\mathbf{z} - \mathbf{g}_t\right), \quad t = 1, \ldots, T, \tag{7.14}$$

where $\mathbf{z} = \mathbf{x}_t$, $\mathbf{K}_t = \left(\mathbf{1}^T\mathbf{P}_t^{-1}\mathbf{1}\right)^{-1}\left(\mathbf{P}_t^{-1}\mathbf{1}\mathbf{1}^T - \mathbf{I}\right)$ and $\mathbf{g}_t = W_{t+1}^{tar}\mathbf{P}_t^{-1}\mathbf{R}_t$, with $\mathbf{R}_t = \mathbb{E}\left(\mathbf{r}_t\right)$, $\mathbf{P}_t = \mathbf{\Sigma}_t + \mathbf{R}_t\mathbf{R}_t^T$ and $W_{t+1}^{tar} = W^{des}\prod_{\tau=t}^{T}\mathbf{1}^T\mathbf{P}_\tau^{-1}\mathbf{R}_\tau$. Moreover, it can be shown that each post-trade portfolio is on the MV one-period frontier, and $W_t^{tar}$ determines the point of the frontier in period $t$.

Skaf and Boyd propose two different (suboptimal) trading policies when the constraint set is not $\mathcal{C}_t^{unc}$. *Projected affine policies* project the optimal unconstrained policy of equation (7.14) onto the constraint set:

$$\mathbf{u}_t = \arg\min_{(\mathbf{W}_t, \mathbf{v}) \in \mathcal{C}_t} \|\mathbf{v} - \mathbf{K}_t\left(\mathbf{W}_t - \mathbf{g}_t\right)\|_2.$$

On the other hand, *control-Lyapunov policies* are determined by

$$\mathbf{u}_t = \arg\min_{(\mathbf{W}_t, \mathbf{v}) \in \mathcal{C}_t} \mathbf{V}_t^*\left(\mathbf{W}_t + \mathbf{v}\right),$$

where $\mathbf{V}_t^*(\mathbf{x})$ is the optimal objective value of the unconstrained truncated problem started in $\mathbf{W}_t^* = \mathbf{x}$ at time period $t$.[13]

[12]We have removed the time subscripts to simplify the notation.

[13]One interesting property of the control-Lyapunov policies is that, under some circumstances, they give rise to a cone of portfolios, which is a no-trade zone.

**Linear Transaction Costs** Under projected affine policies, the problem with linear transaction costs can be solved analytically. The program in this case is

$$\begin{aligned} \min \quad & \|\mathbf{v} - \mathbf{u}_t^{unc}\|_2 \\ s.t. \quad & (\mathbf{W}_t, \mathbf{v}) \in \mathcal{C}_t^{tran}, \quad t = 1, \ldots, T, \end{aligned} \tag{7.15}$$

where $\mathbf{u}_t^{unc} = \mathbf{K}_t(\mathbf{W}_t - \mathbf{g}_t)$ is the optimal trade vector for the unconstrained problem, and

$$\mathcal{C}_t^{tran} = \left\{(\mathbf{W}_t, \mathbf{u}_t) \,|\, \mathbf{1}^T\mathbf{u}_t + \varkappa_b^T\mathbf{u}_t^+ + \varkappa_s^T\mathbf{u}_t^- = 0\right\}.$$

The solution of the problem (7.15) is given by

$$u_t = \varphi_t(\mathbf{x}_t) = \left[\mathbf{u}_t^{unc} - \lambda(1 + \varkappa_b)\right]^+ - \left[\mathbf{u}_t^{unc} - \lambda(1 - \varkappa_s)\right]^-,$$

where $\lambda$ is obtained by solving the equation

$$\mathbf{1}^T\mathbf{u}_t + \varkappa_b^T\mathbf{u}_t^+ + \varkappa_s^T\mathbf{u}_t^- = 0.$$

Skaf and Boyd perform a simulation exercise generating a thousand return realizations and, for each realization, they simulate the portfolio evolution with different constraints and trading policies. For the case of linear transaction costs, they find that both the control-Lyapunov and the projected affine policies perform very well, being the latter slightly worse.

## 7.4 LIQUIDITY CONSIDERATIONS IN PORTFOLIO OPTIMIZATION

Liquidity is one of the most important and elusive concepts in Finance. Quoting Rogers and Singh (2010): "After credit risk, liquidity risk is probably the next most important risk faced by the finance industry; and yet the study of liquidity is far less advanced." Informally, liquidity can be understood as "the asset's ability to be sold as soon as possible without causing a significant price movement" (Roncalli, 2020).

From the point of view of market microstructure, the functioning of liquidity is as follows (Petters and Dong, 2016). The order limits, which cannot be matched, currently form what is known as the *liquidity pool*, and the orders that compose the pool are called *nonmarketeable orders*. If a new order cannot be matched currently, it is nonmarketeable and *adds liquidity* to the market; while if that new order can be matched immediately, the size of the pool is reduced, and we say that the order *takes liquidity* from the market.

To determine how liquidity affects portfolio optimization, we will study the modifications introduced in some of the main models that we have presented in this book (i.e., MV, CAPM, APT), when considering the effects of liquidity.

### 7.4.1 MV and Liquidity

González and Rubio (2011) consider the impact of liquidity in the MV model and study the simultaneous trade-off between mean-variance and liquidity. Their results provide strong support for the impact of liquidity on portfolio choice.

To measure the illiquidity of a portfolio, these authors use the Amihud (2002) *illiquidity ratio*, defined for the $i$-th asset as

$$A_i = \frac{|r_i|}{v_i},$$

where $r_i$ and $v_i$ are, respectively, the return and the dollar volume traded of the $i$-th asset. The illiquidity of the portfolio $\mathbf{w}$ will be given by $A_p = \mathbf{w}^T\mathbf{A}$, where $\mathbf{A} = (A_1, \ldots, A_n)^T$ is the vector of Amihud ratios.

González and Rubio (2011) propose the following extension of the MV model in the risk aversion formulation:

$$\begin{aligned} \max_{\mathbf{w}} \quad & \mathbf{w}^T\mathbf{R} - \frac{\lambda}{2}\mathbf{w}^T\Sigma\mathbf{w} + \frac{\eta}{A_p} \\ s.t. \quad & \mathbf{w}^T\mathbf{1} = 1 \\ & \mathbf{w} \geq 0, \end{aligned} \tag{7.16}$$

where $\eta \geq 0$ represents the preference for liquidity.[14]

The authors solve problem in equation (7.16) for different values of the parameters $\lambda > 0$ and $\eta \geq 0$. The results show that when liquidity preference is not imposed ($\eta = 0$), investors are willing to accept higher liquidity in their portfolios, and achieve higher Sharpe ratios for reasonable values of risk aversion ($\gamma < 10$). Furthermore, their optimal portfolios have lower levels of liquidity than in the case with $\eta > 0$.

[14]The specific way of introducing the liquidity term, $\frac{\eta}{A_p}$, can be justified assuming a negative exponential CARA utility function and normally distributed returns (see Appendix in González and Rubio [2011]).

### 7.4.2 CAPM and Liquidity

*Liquidity risk* can be defined as "the risk stemming from the lack of marketability of an investment that cannot be bought or sold quickly enough to prevent or minimize a loss" (McNeill et al., 2005). According to economic theory, there should be a premium for bearing the risk of holding illiquid assets. Various works have verified the existence of this illiquidity risk premium, finding that the expected return of an asset increases with the cost of illiquidity (Amihud and Mendelson, 1986; Brennan and Subrahmanyam, 1996). Furthermore, empirical studies have confirmed that the influence of liquidity does not exclusively refer to the expected return of individual assets, but also affects the market as a whole, showing commonality in liquidity (Chordia et al., 2000; Hasbrouck and Seppi, 2001; Huberman and Halka, 2001).

Acharya and Pedersen (2005) present a theoretical model, known as *liquidity-adjusted CAPM*, that explains these and some other empirical facts related to liquidity. Specifically, these authors present an equilibrium model in an economy of overlapping generations in which risk-averse agents trade assets whose liquidity varies randomly over time. Their main result, which we state without proof, is the following.

**Proposition 7.5** ***(Acharya and Pedersen, 2005)*** *The equilibrium conditional expected net return of the i-th security is given by*

$$\mathbb{E}_t\left(r^i_{t+1} - c^i_{t+1}\right) = R_0 + \lambda_t \frac{cov_t\left(r^i_{t+1} - c^i_{t+1}, r^M_{t+1} - c^M_{t+1}\right)}{var\left(r^M_{t+1} - c^M_{t+1}\right)}, \tag{7.17}$$

*where:*

- $r^i_{t+1} = \frac{D^i_t + P^i_t}{P^i_{t-1}}$ *is the asset's return in period t, with* $D^i_t$ *the dividend paid in period t, and* $P^i_t$ *the ex-dividend share price in the same period.*
- $c^i_t = \frac{C^i_t}{P^i_{t-1}}$ *is the relative illiquidity cost, with* $C^i_t$ *the illiquidity cost at period t.*
- $R_0$ *is the risk-free real return.*
- $S^i$ *is the total number of shares of the i-th security.*
- $r^M_t = \frac{\sum_{i=1}^{I} S^i(D^i_t + P^i_t)}{\sum_{i=1}^{I} S^i P^i_{t-1}}$ *is the market return in period t, with I the number of shares of the i-th asset.*
- $c^M_t = \frac{\sum_{i=1}^{I} S^i C^i_t}{\sum_{i=1}^{I} S^i P^i_{t-1}}$ *is the relative market illiquidity cost at period t.*
- $\lambda_t = \mathbb{E}_t\left(r^M_{t+1} - c^M_{t+1} - R_0\right)$ *is the risk premium.*

Observing equation (7.17), we can conclude that the introduction of illiquidity costs gives rise to a modification of the CAPM, with conditional expectations, and obtained by replacing the returns of each asset and the market by the respective returns net of illiquidity costs (see equation [3.35]).

On the other hand, rewriting equation (7.17) in the form

$$\mathbb{E}_t\left(r_{t+1}^i\right) - R_0 = \mathbb{E}_t\left(c_{t+1}^i\right) + \frac{\lambda_t}{var\left(r_{t+1}^M - c_{t+1}^M\right)}\left[cov_t\left(r_{t+1}^i, r_{t+1}^M\right)\right.$$
$$\left. + cov_t\left(c_{t+1}^i, c_{t+1}^M\right) - cov_t\left(r_{t+1}^i, c_{t+1}^M\right) - cov_t\left(c_{t+1}^i, r_{t+1}^M\right)\right],$$

we have that the expected excess return is the sum of three terms. The first is the expected relative illiquidity cost (Amihud and Mendelson, 1986). The second, as in the standard CAPM, is the term linear in the market beta. The third term contains the effect of three covariances that can be interpreted as three forms of liquidity risk, which are the following:

- $cov_t\left(c_{t+1}^i, c_{t+1}^M\right)$: The expected return increases with the covariance between the illiquidity of the asset and the illiquidity of the market. The explanation is that the investor requires compensation for holding an asset that becomes illiquid when the overall market becomes less liquid. This effect is related to the commonality in liquidity risk mentioned previously.
- $cov_t\left(r_{t+1}^i, c_{t+1}^M\right)$: The covariance between an asset's return and market liquidity negatively impacts its expected return. The reason is that an investor can accept an asset with a lower return as long as the asset provides a high return in times of market illiquidity. This effect provides a theoretical explanation for the empirical fact that the average return on stocks with high sensitivities to market liquidity exceeds that for stocks with low sensitivities (Pástor and Stambaugh, 2003).
- $cov_t\left(c_{t+1}^i, r_{t+1}^M\right)$: The covariance between the illiquidity of an asset and the market return also negatively affects the expected return of the asset. An investor is willing to accept a lower expected return on an asset that remains liquid in a down market. The reason is that when the market goes down, the investor becomes poorer and, therefore, the possibility of selling the asset quickly and at low cost is valuable.

Using the illiquidity measure of Amihud (2002), Acharya and Pedersen (2005) find that the liquidity-adjusted CAPM outperforms the standard

CAPM both in terms of $R^2$ for cross-sectional returns and for $p$-values in specification tests.

### 7.4.3 APT and Liquidity

The existence of a liquidity risk premium led Pástor and Stambaugh (2003) to empirically assess whether there is a risk factor associated with the sensitivity to changes in market liquidity. To do this, they took the model of Carhart (1997) as a base, to which they added a new factor that represents innovations in aggregate liquidity. The construction of the factor with liquidity innovations in Pástor and Stambaugh (2003) follows a series of steps that we illustrate here.

1. The liquidity of the $i$-th asset in month $t$, $\hat{\gamma}_{i,t}$, is obtained as the OLS estimate of $\gamma_{i,t}$ in the regression

$$r^e_{i,d+1,t} = \theta_{i,t} + \phi_{i,t} r_{i,d,t} + \gamma_{i,t} sign\left(r^e_{i,d,t}\right) v_{i,d,t} + \varepsilon_{i,d+1,t},$$

   where:

   - $r_{i,d,t}$ is the return on the $i$-th stock on day $d$ in month $t$.
   - $r^e_{i,d,t} = r_{i,d,t} - r_{m,d,t}$, with $r_{m,d,t}$ the return on the Center for Research in Security Prices (CRSP) value-weighted market return on day $d$ in month $t$.[15]
   - $v_{i,d,t}$ is the dollar volume for the $i$-th stock on day $d$ in month $t$.

   The rational behind this formulation of an asset's liquidity is that a contemporaneous "order flow", given by the term $sign\left(r^e_{i,d,t}\right) v_{i,d,t}$, should be followed by a partially reversed future return if the stock is not perfectly liquid. The authors assume that the greater the stock's illiquidity, the greater the expected reversal for a given dollar volume. Thus, negative values of $\hat{\gamma}_{i,t}$ should be found, and greater in absolute value when the liquidity is low, as in Campbell et al. (1993).

2. The liquidity measure for individual assets, $\hat{\gamma}_{i,t}$, is transformed into the market wide measure $\hat{\gamma}_t$, given by

$$\hat{\gamma}_t = \frac{1}{n} \sum_{i=1}^{n} \hat{\gamma}_{i,t},$$

   where $n$ is the number of stocks.

[15]CRSP is the Center for Research in Security Prices at the University of Chicago, from where all the individual-stock returns and volume data used in the paper were taken.

3. The differences in the monthly liquidity measures are averaged and scaled according to the following expression:

$$\Delta\hat{\gamma}_t = \left(\frac{m_t}{m_1}\right)\frac{1}{n_t}\sum_{i=1}^{n_t}\left(\hat{\gamma}_{i,t} - \hat{\gamma}_{i,t-1}\right),$$

where:

- $m_t$ is the total dollar value at the end of month $t-1$ of the stocks included in the average in month $t$.
- $m_1$ is the total dollar value at the first month in the sample.
- $n_t$ is the number of stocks with available data in months $t$ and $t-1$.

4. The difference $\Delta\hat{\gamma}_t$ is regressed on its lag as well as the lagged value of the scaled level series:

$$\Delta\hat{\gamma}_t = a + b\Delta\hat{\gamma}_{t-1} + c\left(\frac{m_{t-1}}{m_1}\right)\hat{\gamma}_{t-1} + u_t$$

5. Finally, the innovation in liquidity, $LIQ_t$, is obtained as the fitted residual, $\hat{u}_t$, divided by 100:

$$LIQ_t = \frac{1}{100}\hat{u}_t.$$

Once the aggregate liquidity factor has been computed, Pástor and Stambaugh (2003) incorporate it into the Carhart (1997) model (see Chapter 6), in the form

$$r_i - R_0 = \alpha_i + \beta_i^M\left(r_M - R_0\right) + \beta_i^{SMB} r_{SMB} + \beta_i^{HML} r_{HML} + \beta_i^{WML} r_{WML}$$
$$+\beta_i^{LIQ} LIQ_t + \varepsilon_i,$$

where $\beta_i^{LIQ}$ measures the asset's comovement with aggregate liquidity.

The authors estimate $\beta_i^{LIQ}$ by adding the liquidity factor to three different models: a one-factor model with only the market factor (CAPM), the Fama and French (1993) model, and the Carhart (1997) model. Then, they sort stocks by their estimated liquidity betas to form 10 (value-weighted) portfolios and obtain the alpha for each of the decile portfolios. Their results show that alpha is increasing with liquidity sensitivity. Specifically, the difference in expected return between the last decile portfolio and the first decile portfolio is 6.4% per year for the CAPM, 9.23% for the Fama-French model, and 7.48% for the Carhart model. Similar and even stronger results are found for equally weighted portfolios. These results lead the authors to conclude that the liquidity factor is priced with a positive premium, that is, "stocks with higher sensitivity to aggregate liquidity shocks offer higher expected returns" (Pástor and Stambaugh, 2003).

## 7.5 NOTES

The models presented in the section dedicated to market impact have been taken from the original papers cited in the text. We have discussed only those models based on market microstructure. For other market impact models based on linear factors (trade-based or asset-based), see Fabozzi et al. (2007) and references therein. A recent monograph on market impact is Webster (2023).

The study of transaction costs is inspired by Qian et al. (2007). Other interesting references are Grinold and Kahn (2000), Fabozzi et al. (2007), Connor et al. (2010), and Chen et al. (2019).

Regarding optimal trading strategies with transaction costs, the references used have been those already indicated in the text. The strategies presented have been obtained within discrete time models. An alternative approach based on dynamic programming techniques can be found in Grinold (2006). Among the continuous-time models for optimal strategies, we can highlight Grinold and Kahn (2000) and Qian et al. (2007), who apply techniques of calculus of variations; or Dai et al. (2010) who transform the optimization problem into a double-obstacle problem.

The main references used when discussing the role of liquidity in portfolio optimization appear already referenced in the text. Other useful references have been Cazalet and Roncalli (2014), Ang (2014), and Petters and Dong (2016). In the text, we have only mentioned those liquidity measures that are used in the presented models. Alternative measures of liquidity can be found, for example, in Connor et al. (2010) and Roncalli (2020). A study identifying the best liquidity proxies is Fong et al. (2017).

# PART Three

# Dynamic Models and Control

CHAPTER 8

# Optimal Control

## 8.1 DYNAMIC PROGRAMMING

Dynamic Programming (DP) is a fundamental approach in optimal control theory, as artfully presented in the volumes Bertsekas (2012a), and Bertsekas (2012b). It is quite useful in portfolio optimization. It breaks down complex problems into simpler subproblems and solves them recursively.

The core of DP is Bellman's Principle of Optimality:

$$V(x,t) = \max_{u}\left\{F(x,u,t) + V\left(f(x,u,t),t+1\right)\right\} \tag{8.1}$$

where $V(x,t)$ is the value function, $x$ is the state, $u$ is the control, $t$ is time, $F$ is the immediate reward function, and $f$ is the state transition function.

For a finite horizon problem with $T$ periods, we solve backward:

$$V_T\left(x_T\right) = g\left(x_T\right) \tag{8.2}$$

$$V_t\left(x_t\right) = \max_{u_t}\left\{F\left(x_t,u_t,t\right) + V_{t+1}\left(f\left(x_t,u_t,t\right)\right)\right\},\ t = T-1,\ldots,0 \tag{8.3}$$

where $g\left(x_T\right)$ is the terminal reward function.

In continuous time, the Hamilton-Jacobi-Bellman (HJB) equation emerges:

$$-\frac{\partial V}{\partial t} = \max_{u}\left\{F(x,u,t) + \nabla V \cdot f(x,u,t)\right\} \tag{8.4}$$

with boundary condition $V(x,T) = g(x)$.

## 8.2 APPROXIMATE DYNAMIC PROGRAMMING

When exact solutions are computationally infeasible, Approximate Dynamic Programming (ADP) provides practical alternatives (see Powell [2011]).

**Value Function Approximation** We approximate the value function:

$$\widetilde{V}(x, t; \theta) \approx V(x, t), \tag{8.5}$$

where $\theta$ are parameters of the approximation (e.g., weights in a neural network).

**Q-Learning** Q-Learning is a model-free ADP method that learns the Q-function:

$$Q(x, u) = F(x, u) + \gamma \max_{u'} Q\left(f(x, u), u'\right). \tag{8.6}$$

The update rule is:

$$Q(x, u) \leftarrow (1 - \alpha) Q(x, u) + \alpha \left[F(x, u) + \gamma \max_{u'} Q\left(f(x, u), u'\right)\right], \tag{8.7}$$

where $\alpha$ is the learning rate and $\gamma$ is the discount factor.

**Policy Gradient Methods** Policy gradient methods directly optimize the policy $\pi_\theta(u|x)$:

$$\nabla_\theta J(\theta) = \mathbb{E}\tau \sim \pi\theta \left[\sum_{t=0}^{T} \nabla_\theta \log \pi_\theta\left(u_t|x_t\right) \cdot R_t\right], \tag{8.8}$$

where $J(\theta)$ is the expected return and $R_t$ is the cumulative reward from time $t$.

## 8.3 THE HAMILTON-JACOBI-BELLMAN EQUATION

The Hamilton-Jacobi-Bellman (HJB) equation is a central result in optimal control theory, providing a necessary condition for optimality in continuous-time optimization problems (see Bertsekas [2012a]). It is a nonlinear partial differential equation (PDE) that characterizes the optimal value function. Furthermore, it is a backward equation, solved from the terminal time $T$ to the initial time 0. The maximization in the HJB equation determines the optimal control $u^*(x, t)$ as a function of the current state and time. If a smooth solution to the HJB equation exists, it provides both necessary and sufficient conditions for optimality.

**Derivation of the HJB Equation** Consider the following continuous-time optimal control problem:

$$\max_{u(\cdot)} \int_0^T F(x(t), u(t), t)\, dt + g(x(T)) \tag{8.9}$$

subject to the dynamics:

$$\frac{dx}{dt} = f(x(t), u(t), t), \quad x(0) = x_0, \tag{8.10}$$

where $x(t) \in \mathbb{R}^n$ is the state vector, $u(t) \in \mathbb{R}^m$ is the control vector, $F$ is the running cost, $g$ is the terminal cost, and $f$ represents the system dynamics.

Let $V(x, t)$ be the value function, representing the optimal cost-to-go from state $x$ at time $t$:

$$V(x, t) = \max_{u(\cdot)} \left\{ \int_t^T F(x(s), u(s), s)\, ds + g(x(T)) \right\}. \tag{8.11}$$

To derive the HJB equation, we use the principle of optimality and consider a small time interval $[t, t + dt]$:

$$V(x, t) = \max_{u(\cdot)} \left\{ \int_t^{t+dt} F(x(s), u(s), s)\, ds + V\big(x(t + dt), t + dt\big) \right\}. \tag{8.12}$$

Expanding the integral and value function using Taylor series:

$$V(x, t) = \max_{u(\cdot)} \left\{ F(x, u, t)\, dt + V(x, t) + \frac{\partial V}{\partial t} dt + \nabla_x V \cdot f(x, u, t)\, dt + o(dt) \right\}. \tag{8.13}$$

Subtracting $V(x, t)$ from both sides, dividing by $dt$, and taking the limit as $dt \to 0$:

$$0 = \max_{u(\cdot)} \left\{ F(x, u, t) + \frac{\partial V}{\partial t} + \nabla_x V \cdot f(x, u, t) \right\}. \tag{8.14}$$

Rearranging terms gives the HJB equation:

$$-\frac{\partial V}{\partial t} = \max_{u(\cdot)} \{ F(x, u, t) + \nabla_x V \cdot f(x, u, t) \} \tag{8.15}$$

with the boundary condition:

$$V(x, T) = g(x). \tag{8.16}$$

**Verification Theorem** The Verification Theorem is a fundamental result in optimal control theory (see Fleming and Soner [2006]) that provides a powerful method for solving stochastic control problems, particularly in the context of portfolio optimization and asset management. This theorem establishes a crucial link between the HJB equation, which characterizes the optimal value function, and the existence of an optimal control strategy. By offering conditions under which a solution to the HJB equation corresponds to the true value function and optimal control, the Verification Theorem serves as a bridge between the theoretical formulation of a control problem and its practical solution. This result is particularly valuable in quantitative finance, where it enables practitioners to derive optimal investment strategies by solving the associated HJB equation, subject to certain regularity conditions. The theorem not only confirms the optimality of a candidate solution but also provides a constructive method for obtaining the optimal control, making it an indispensable tool in the arsenal of quantitative portfolio managers and financial engineers.

Theorem 8.1 *(Verification Theorem) Let $\widetilde{V}(x,t)$ be a solution to the HJB equation. If $\widetilde{V}(x,t)$ is continuously differentiable in x and t, then there exists an admissible control $u^*(x,t)$ that attains the maximum in the HJB equation, and if the resulting state trajectory $x^*(t)$ is unique, then*

$$\widetilde{V}(x,t) = V(x,t),$$

*and $u^*(x,t)$ is the optimal control.*

The HJB equation is difficult to solve analytically, especially for high-dimensional problems. Numerical methods for solving the HJB equation often suffer from the *curse of dimensionality*. The value function may not be differentiable everywhere, leading to the need for weaker solution concepts like viscosity solutions.

## 8.4 SUFFICIENTLY SMOOTH PROBLEMS

For some optimal control problems, the solution can be obtained by considering variations of the total cost functional (see Yong and Zhou [1999] for further details). This approach is particularly useful when the problem is sufficiently smooth, allowing us to derive the necessary conditions for optimality. However, before diving into these difficult cases, we study the simpler case of differentiable solutions to the HJB equation.

**Variational Approach** Consider the optimal control problem:

$$\min_u J[u] = \int_0^T F(x(t), u(t), t)\, dt + g(x(T)) \tag{8.17}$$

subject to the dynamics:

$$\frac{dx}{dt} = f(x(t), u(t), t), \quad x(0) = x_0, \tag{8.18}$$

where $x(t) \in \mathbb{R}^n$, $u(t) \in \mathbb{R}^m$, and $F$, $g$, and $f$ are sufficiently smooth functions.

To find the optimal control, we consider variations in the control and state:

$$u_\epsilon(t) = u(t) + \epsilon\eta(t) \tag{8.19}$$

$$x_\epsilon(t) = x(t) + \epsilon\xi(t), \tag{8.20}$$

where $\eta(t)$ is an arbitrary function and $\xi(t)$ satisfies the variational equation:

$$\frac{d\xi}{dt} = \frac{\partial f}{\partial x}\xi + \frac{\partial f}{\partial u}\eta. \tag{8.21}$$

The first variation of the cost functional is:

$$\delta J = \frac{d}{d\epsilon}J[u_\epsilon]\Big|_{\epsilon=0} = \int_0^T \left(\frac{\partial F}{\partial x}\xi + \frac{\partial F}{\partial u}\eta\right) dt + \frac{\partial g}{\partial x}(x(T))\,\xi(T). \tag{8.22}$$

Now, introduce the adjoint variable $\lambda(t)$ satisfying:

$$\frac{d\lambda}{dt} = -\frac{\partial F}{\partial x} - \lambda^T\frac{\partial f}{\partial x}, \quad \lambda(T) = \frac{\partial g}{\partial x}(x(T))^T. \tag{8.23}$$

**Pontryagin Maximum Principle** Using the adjoint variable, we can rewrite the first variation as:

$$\delta J = \int_0^T \left(\frac{\partial F}{\partial u} + \lambda^T\frac{\partial f}{\partial u}\right)\eta dt. \tag{8.24}$$

For optimality, $\delta J = 0$ for all variations $\eta(t)$. This leads to the Pontryagin Maximum Principle:

$$H(x^{\prime}u^{\prime}\lambda, t) = \min_u H(x^*, u, \lambda, t), \tag{8.25}$$

where the Hamiltonian $H$ is defined as:

$$H(x, u, \lambda, t) = F(x, u, t) + \lambda^T f(x, u, t). \tag{8.26}$$

**Necessary Conditions for Optimality** The necessary conditions for optimality are:

1. State equation:

$$\frac{dx'}{dt} = \frac{\partial H}{\partial \lambda} = f(x', u^*, t). \tag{8.27}$$

2. Adjoint equation:

$$\frac{d\lambda}{dt} = -\frac{\partial H}{\partial x} = -\frac{\partial F}{\partial x} - \lambda^T \frac{\partial f}{\partial x}. \tag{8.28}$$

3. Optimality condition:

$$\frac{\partial H}{\partial u} = \frac{\partial F}{\partial u} + \lambda^T \frac{\partial f}{\partial u} = 0. \tag{8.29}$$

4. Transversality condition:

$$\lambda(T) = \frac{\partial g}{\partial x}(x^*(T))^T. \tag{8.30}$$

**Connection to the HJB Equation** The Pontryagin Maximum Principle is closely related to the Hamilton-Jacobi-Bellman (HJB) equation. In fact, if the value function $V(x, t)$ is sufficiently smooth, we can show that:

$$\lambda(t) = \nabla V(x^*(t), t)^T. \tag{8.31}$$

This connection allows us to interpret the adjoint variable as the gradient of the value function along the optimal trajectory.

The variational approach provides necessary conditions for optimality without requiring the solution of a PDE. It can be applied to problems with control constraints by modifying the optimality condition. However, it may not provide sufficient conditions for optimality in all cases. For problems with state constraints or non-smooth dynamics, additional considerations may be necessary.

## 8.5 VISCOSITY SOLUTIONS

Viscosity solutions provide a generalized framework for solving partial differential equations (PDEs) like the HJB equation, especially when classical smooth solutions do not exist. A viscosity solution is a type of weak solution that accommodates the non-smooth nature of the solution while satisfying the PDE in a generalized sense. In particular, the min or max operators often lead to solutions that are not smooth. Rather, solutions can be continuous but not differentiable everywhere. This is because the min or max operators can introduce points of non-differentiability where the control policy changes. For a detailed and expansive discussion see Bardi and Capuzzo-Dolcetta (2009).

We are interested in viscosity solutions because the HJB equation may lack classical solutions due to discontinuities in the value function non-differentiability at certain points, or singularities in the optimal control. Viscosity solutions offer a weaker (i.e., *more general*) notion of solution that can manage these issues while still providing uniqueness and stability properties.

**Definition of Viscosity Solutions** Consider the HJB equation in the general form:

$$F(x, V(x), \nabla V(x)) = 0, \quad x \in \Omega. \tag{8.32}$$

where $V$ is the value function, $\nabla V$ is its gradient, and $\Omega$ is the domain. A continuous function $V$ is a viscosity solution if:

1. For any $\phi \in C^1(\Omega)$ such that $V - \phi$ has a local maximum at $x_0 \in \Omega$:

$$F\left(x_0, V\left(x_0\right), \nabla\phi\left(x_0\right)\right) \leq 0. \tag{8.33}$$

2. For any $\psi \in C^1(\Omega)$ such that $V - \psi$ has a local minimum at $x_0 \in \Omega$:

$$F\left(x_0, V\left(x_0\right), \nabla\psi\left(x_0\right)\right) \geq 0. \tag{8.34}$$

Viscosity solutions have the following properties:

1. **Existence:** Under mild conditions on $F$, viscosity solutions exist for a wide class of boundary value problems.
2. **Uniqueness:** Viscosity solutions are unique under appropriate boundary conditions.
3. **Stability:** Viscosity solutions are stable under uniform convergence.
4. **Consistency:** If a classical solution exists, it is also a viscosity solution.

Several numerical schemes have been developed to approximate viscosity solutions, including finite difference schemes, semi-Lagrangian schemes, and Markov chain approximations. These methods must satisfy consistency, stability, and monotonicity properties to converge to the viscosity solution.

**Application to Optimal Control** In the context of optimal control, the value function $V(x,t)$ of the HJB equation:

$$\frac{\partial V}{\partial t} + \min_u \{F(x,u) \cdot \nabla V + C(x,u)\} \tag{8.35}$$

$$\frac{du}{dt} = F(x,u) \tag{8.36}$$

is often interpreted as a viscosity solution. Note that this allows handling non-smooth optimal control problems, prove existence and uniqueness of solutions in a wider class of problems, and develop convergent numerical schemes for approximating the value function.

**Subdifferentials in Viscosity Solutions** Subdifferentials play a crucial role in the theory of viscosity solutions, especially when dealing with non-smooth value functions.

For a function $V : \mathbb{R}^n \to \mathbb{R}$, the subdifferential of $V$ at a point $x_0$ is defined as:

$$\partial V(x_0) = p \in \mathbb{R}^n : V(x) - V(x_0) \geq p \cdot (x - x_0) + o(|x - x_0|) \text{ as } x \to x_0. \tag{8.37}$$

The elements of $\partial V(x_0)$ are called subgradients.

**Connection to Viscosity Solutions** In the context of viscosity solutions, we define:

1. The first-order superjet:

$$D^+ V(x_0) = p \in \mathbb{R}^n : \limsup_{x \to x_0} \frac{V(x) - V(x_0) - p \cdot (x - x_0)}{|x - x_0|} \leq 0. \tag{8.38}$$

2. The first-order subjet:

$$D^- V(x_0) = \left\{ p \in \mathbb{R}^n : \liminf_{x \to x_0} \frac{V(x) - V(x_0) - p \cdot (x - x_0)}{|x - x_0|} \geq 0 \right\}. \tag{8.39}$$

These concepts are used in the definition of viscosity sub- and supersolutions.

**Example: Optimal Control with Absolute Value Cost** Consider a simple optimal control problem:

$$\min_{u(\cdot)} \int_0^T |x(t)| + \frac{1}{2} u(t)^2 \, dt \tag{8.40}$$

subject to:

$$\dot{x}(t) = u(t), \quad x(0) = x_0. \tag{8.41}$$

The HJB equation for this problem is:

$$-\frac{\partial V}{\partial t}(x,t) + \frac{1}{2}\left(\frac{\partial V}{\partial x}(x,t)\right)^2 - |x| = 0 \tag{8.42}$$

with terminal condition $V(x, T) = 0$. The optimal control is given by:

$$u^*(x,t) = -\frac{\partial V}{\partial x}(x,t). \tag{8.43}$$

However, due to the absolute value term, the value function is not differentiable at $x = 0$. We can use subdifferentials to characterize the solution:

1. For $x > 0$: $\frac{\partial V}{\partial x}(x,t) = 1 - (T - t)$.
2. For $x < 0$: $\frac{\partial V}{\partial x}(x,t) = -1 + (T - t)$.
3. At $x = 0$: $\partial V(0,t) = [-1 + (T - t), 1 - (T - t)]$.

The value function is:

$$V(x,t) = \begin{cases} x - \frac{1}{2}(T-t)^2 + (T-t)|x|, & \text{if } |x| \geq T - t \\ \frac{1}{2}\frac{x^2}{(T-t)}, & \text{if } |x| < T - t \end{cases} \tag{8.44}$$

$$u^*(x,t) = \begin{cases} -(1 - (T-t)), & \text{if } x > T - t \\ -(1 + (T-t)), & \text{if } x < -(T-t) \\ -\frac{x}{T-t}, & \text{if } |x| < T - t. \end{cases} \tag{8.45}$$

This example demonstrates how subdifferentials can be used to characterize the solution of an optimal control problem with a non-smooth cost function. The subdifferential at $x = 0$ captures the "kink" in the value function, allowing us to describe the optimal control even at points of non-differentiability.

Viscosity solutions provide a powerful framework for analyzing and solving optimal control problems, especially when classical solutions fail to exist. They allow us to prove existence and uniqueness results for a wide class of problems, develop stable numerical schemes, and manage non-smooth and constrained optimal control problems. Understanding viscosity solutions is crucial for tackling complex, real-world optimal control problems in finance, engineering, and other fields.

## 8.6 APPLICATIONS TO PORTFOLIO OPTIMIZATION

Portfolio optimization is a cornerstone application of optimal control theory and the HJB equation in finance. This section explores both classical smooth solutions and more complex scenarios that may require viscosity solutions.

### 8.6.1 Classical Merton Problem

The Merton problem, introduced by Robert C. Merton in 1969 (Merton, 1969a), is a fundamental model in continuous-time finance.

**Problem Setup** Consider an investor allocating wealth between a riskless asset (bond) and a risky asset (stock). Let:

- $X(t)$ be the total wealth at time $t$.
- $\pi(t)$ be the proportion of wealth invested in the risky asset.
- $r$ be the risk-free rate.
- $\mu$ and $\sigma$ be the drift and volatility of the risky asset.

The wealth process evolves according to:

$$dX(t) = \left[rX(t) + (\mu - r)\,\pi(t)\,X(t)\right]dt + \sigma\pi(t)\,X(t)\,dW(t). \tag{8.46}$$

The objective is to maximize expected utility of terminal wealth:

$$\max_{\pi(\cdot)} \mathbb{E}\left[U(X(T))\right], \tag{8.47}$$

where $U(x) = \frac{x^{1-\gamma}}{1-\gamma}$ is the Constant Relative Risk Aversion (CRRA) utility function, and $\gamma > 0, \gamma \neq 1$ is the risk aversion parameter.

**HJB Equation** Define the value function:

$$V(x,t) = \max_{\pi(\cdot)} \mathbb{E}\left[U(X(T))\,|X(t) = x\right]. \tag{8.48}$$

The HJB equation for this problem is:

$$\frac{\partial V}{\partial t} + rx\frac{\partial V}{\partial x} + \max_{\pi}\left[(\mu - r)\,\pi x\frac{\partial V}{\partial x} + \frac{1}{2}\sigma^2\pi^2x^2\frac{\partial^2 V}{\partial x^2}\right] = 0 \tag{8.49}$$

with terminal condition $V(x, T) = U(x)$.

**Optimal Portfolio Allocation** The first-order condition for the maximum in the HJB equation yields:

$$\pi^*(x,t) = -\frac{(\mu - r)}{\sigma^2 x} \cdot \frac{\frac{\partial V}{\partial x}}{\frac{\partial^2 V}{\partial x^2}}. \tag{8.50}$$

For the CRRA utility, we can guess a solution of the form:

$$V(x,t) = \frac{x^{1-\gamma}}{1-\gamma}f(t). \tag{8.51}$$

Substituting this into the HJB equation and solving, we find:

$$\pi^* = \frac{\mu - r}{\gamma\sigma^2}. \tag{8.52}$$

The optimal portfolio allocation $\pi^*$ is constant and independent of wealth and time. It increases with the Sharpe ratio $(\mu - r)/\sigma$ and decreases with risk aversion $\gamma$.

### 8.6.2 Multi-asset Portfolio with Transaction Costs

Now, let us consider a more complex problem with transaction costs, which may require viscosity solutions. See Davis and Norman (1990a) and Shreve and Soner (1994a) for multi-asset portfolio optimization, the former presenting portfolio selection problem with proportional transaction costs, and the latter utilizing viscosity solutions of the a non-smooth HJB.

**Problem Setup** Consider a portfolio with one risk-free asset and $n$ risky assets. Let:

- $X_0(t)$ be the amount in the risk-free asset.
- $X_i(t)$ be the amount in risky asset $i$, $i = 1, \ldots, n$.
- $\lambda_i^+$ and $\lambda_i^-$ be the proportional transaction costs for buying and selling asset $i$.

The wealth process now includes transaction costs:

$$dX_0 = rX_0 dt - \sum_{i=1}^{n} (1 + \lambda_i^+)\, dL_i + \sum_{i=1}^{n} (1 - \lambda_i^-)\, dM_i \tag{8.53}$$

$$dX_i = \mu_i X_i dt + \sigma_i X_i dW_i + dL_i - dM_i, \quad i = 1, \ldots, n, \tag{8.54}$$

where $L_i$ and $M_i$ are cumulative purchase and sale processes for asset $i$.

**Non-smooth HJB Equation** The value function now depends on the entire portfolio composition:

$$V(x_0, x_1, \ldots, x_n, t) = \max_{L_i, M_i} \mathbb{E}\left[ U\left( X_0(T) + \sum_{i=1}^{n} X_i(T) \right) | X_i(t) = x_i \right]. \tag{8.55}$$

The HJB equation becomes a variational inequality:

$$\max\left\{ \frac{\partial V}{\partial t} + \mathcal{L}V, \max_i \left\{ (1 - \lambda_i^-) \frac{\partial V}{\partial x_0} - \frac{\partial V}{\partial x_i} \right\}, \max_i \left\{ -(1 + \lambda_i^+) \frac{\partial V}{\partial x_0} + \frac{\partial V}{\partial x_i} \right\} \right\} = 0, \tag{8.56}$$

where $\mathcal{L}$ is the differential operator corresponding to the uncontrolled dynamics.

**Viscosity Solution Characterization** The value function $V$ is generally not smooth due to the presence of transaction costs. We interpret it as a viscosity solution to the HJB equation. The solution typically has three regions:

1. **No-trade region:** Where it is optimal to hold the current portfolio
2. **Buy region:** Where it is optimal to purchase more of certain assets
3. **Sell region:** Where it is optimal to sell some assets

The boundaries between these regions are generally not smooth, necessitating the use of viscosity solutions.

Practical implementation often relies on numerical methods, such as finite difference schemes adapted for viscosity solutions, policy iteration methods, and Markov chain approximations

These methods must be carefully designed to converge to the viscosity solution of the HJB equation.

### 8.6.3 Risk-sensitive Portfolio Optimization

Finally, let us consider a risk-sensitive formulation, which incorporates risk aversion directly into the objective. See Bielecki and Pliska (1999) for a comprehensive treatment of risk-sensitive asset management in continuous time, and Fleming and Sheu (2006) for an exposition of risk-sensitive portfolio optimization in both full and partial information settings, that provides a rigorous mathematical treatment of the problem, including the derivation and analysis of the risk-sensitive HJB equation.

**Problem Setup** The objective is now to maximize:

$$\max_{\pi(\cdot)} -\frac{1}{\theta} \log \mathbb{E}\left[\exp\left(-\theta X(T)\right)\right], \tag{8.57}$$

where $\theta > 0$ is the risk-sensitivity parameter.

**Risk-Sensitive HJB Equation** The corresponding HJB equation is:

$$\frac{\partial V}{\partial t} + rx\frac{\partial V}{\partial x} + \max_{\pi}\left[(\mu - r)\,\pi x\frac{\partial V}{\partial x} + \frac{1}{2}\sigma^2\pi^2x^2\frac{\partial^2 V}{\partial x^2} - \frac{\theta}{2}\sigma^2\pi^2x^2\left(\frac{\partial V}{\partial x}\right)^2\right] = 0. \tag{8.58}$$

**Analysis of Optimal Strategy** The optimal portfolio allocation is:

$$\pi^*(x,t) = \frac{\mu - r}{\sigma^2\left(\theta x + \gamma\right)}, \tag{8.59}$$

where $\gamma = -x\frac{\partial^2 V}{\partial x^2}/\frac{\partial V}{\partial x}$ is the local risk aversion.

**Comparison with Classical Results** Unlike the Merton problem, the optimal allocation depends on wealth and time. As $\theta \to 0$, we recover the classical Merton solution. For $\theta > 0$, the allocation is more conservative, and the solution captures both risk aversion and sensitivity to large deviations

This risk-sensitive approach provides a more nuanced view of optimal portfolio allocation, accounting for the investor's attitude toward extreme outcomes. In conclusion, optimal control theory and the HJB equation provide powerful tools for addressing a wide range of portfolio optimization problems, from classical smooth cases to complex scenarios involving transaction costs and risk sensitivity. The use of viscosity solutions extends these methods to manage non-smooth value functions, making them applicable to many real-world financial optimization problems.

### 8.6.4 Optimal Portfolio Allocation with Transaction Costs

In portfolio optimization with transaction costs (see Magill and Constantinides [1976]), the HJB equation often includes terms that account for the costs associated with buying or selling assets. The value function can exhibit kinks at points where the optimal strategy switches from buying to selling or vice versa. The HJB equation is given by

$$V_t + \sup_{\pi} \left\{ \pi^T (\mu - r1)\, V_x + \frac{1}{2} \pi^T \Sigma \pi V_{xx} - \lambda \|\pi\| \right\} = 0, \tag{8.60}$$

where $V$ is the value function, $\pi$ is the portfolio allocation, $\mu$ is the vector of expected returns, $r$ is the risk-free rate, $\Sigma$ is the covariance matrix of returns, and $\lambda$ represents transaction costs.

The transaction costs ($\lambda\|\pi\|$) introduce non-smoothness at the boundaries of regions where different trading actions are optimal.

### 8.6.5 American Option Pricing

In the context of American options, the early exercise feature leads to a value function that is typically non-smooth at the exercise boundary. See Jaillet et al. (1990) for related treatment of American options using a variational approach.

The HJB equation is given by

$$\max \left\{ V_t + rV - \frac{1}{2} \sigma^2 S^2 V_{SS} - (r - q)\, S V_S, S - K \right\} = 0, \tag{8.61}$$

where $V$ is the value function of the option, $S$ is the underlying asset price, $K$ is the strike price, $r$ is the risk-free interest rate, $q$ is the dividend yield, and $\sigma$ is the volatility of the underlying asset. The value function $V$ exhibits non-smoothness at the exercise boundary, where the option holder is indifferent between holding and exercising the option.

### 8.6.6 Portfolio Optimization with Constraints

In portfolio optimization problems with constraints (such as no-short selling or leverage constraints, see Cvitanić and Karatzas [1992]), the value function can be non-smooth at the boundaries defined by these constraints.

The HJB equation is given by

$$V_t + \sup_{\pi \in \mathcal{A}} \left\{ \pi^T (\mu - r1)\, V_x + \frac{1}{2} \pi^T \Sigma \pi V_{xx} \right\} = 0, \tag{8.62}$$

where $\mathcal{A}$ is the set of admissible portfolios (e.g., $\mathcal{A} = \{\pi \mid \pi_i \geq 0, \sum \pi_i \leq 1\}$ for no-short selling and full investment constraints). The optimal portfolio strategy may change abruptly at the boundaries of the constraint set $\mathcal{A}$, leading to non-smoothness in the value function.

### 8.6.7 Mean-variance Portfolio Optimization

When considering mean-variance optimization, the HJB equation involves a trade-off between the expected return and the variance of the portfolio, leading to potential non-smoothness in the value function. See Zhou and Li (2000a) for a related treatment of continuous-time mean-variance portfolio selection using a stochastic linear-quadratic (LQ) control approach.

The HJB equation is given by

$$V_t + \sup_{\pi} \left\{ \pi^T (\mu - r\mathbf{1}) V_x - \frac{\gamma}{2} \pi^T \Sigma \pi \right\} = 0, \tag{8.63}$$

$\gamma$ is the risk aversion parameter. The value function may exhibit non-smooth behavior at points where the optimal trade-off between return and risk changes.

To visualize and numerically approximate such non-smooth value functions, techniques like finite difference methods, dynamic programming, and Monte Carlo simulations are often employed (see Kushner and Dupuis [2013] for a masterful exposition in numerical methods). For instance, in the case of American options, the finite difference method with an explicit scheme can be used to discretize the PDE and visualize the non-smoothness at the exercise boundary. As these examples illustrate, non-smoothness in value functions often arises due to the presence of constraints, transaction costs, or early exercise features, which are common in financial optimization problems.

### 8.6.8 Schrödinger Control in Wealth Management

In Halperin (2024), Halperin addresses the challenge of optimizing contributions in financial planning, focusing on scenarios such as an individual saving for retirement. The primary objective is to determine an optimal and feasible schedule of periodic installments into an investment portfolio designed to meet a specific financial goal.

Given the inherent randomness of portfolio returns, the practical application of this problem involves finding an optimal contribution scheme that achieves the goal with some confidence bounds. The approach introduces a semi-analytical method for a continuous-time version of this problem, utilizing a controlled backward Kolmogorov equation (BKE) to describe the tail probability of the terminal wealth under a given contribution policy.

The controlled BKE is solved semi-analytically since it reduces the BKE to a controlled Schrödinger equation and applies an algebraic method to solve it. The numerical approach finds semi-analytical solutions simultaneously for all values of control parameters on a small grid and employs standard two-dimensional spline interpolation to represent all satisficing solutions of the original plan optimization problem.

Halperin finds that satisficing solutions do not represent a single point in the space of control variables. Instead, they form continuous contour lines, or efficient frontiers, within this space. This result provides a more nuanced and flexible approach to financial planning optimization.

The problem is formulated as follows: Let $\Pi_t$ be the portfolio value at time $t$, evolving according to the stochastic differential equation:

$$d\Pi_t = (r\Pi_t + u_t)\,dt + \sigma\Pi_t dW_t, \tag{8.64}$$

where $r$ is the risk-adjusted return, $\sigma$ is the portfolio volatility, $W_t$ is a standard Brownian motion, and $u_t$ is the contribution rate at time $t$. The contribution policy is parameterized as:

$$u_t = u_0 e^{\xi t}, \tag{8.65}$$

with $u_0$ being the initial contribution and $\xi$ the growth rate. The objective is to find optimal values of $u_0$ and $\xi$ such that:

$$P\left[\Pi_T < \hat{\Pi} | \Pi_t = w\right] \leq \alpha, \tag{8.66}$$

where $\hat{\Pi}$ is a target wealth at terminal time $T$, and $\alpha$ is a given confidence level.

Halperin demonstrates that the wealth management problem can be reformulated as a quantum control problem with the Morse potential. This is achieved through a series of variable transformations:

$$v_t = \frac{2}{\sigma^2}\frac{u_t}{\Pi_t}, \quad x_t = -\log v_t. \tag{8.67}$$

Leading to the Schrödinger equation:

$$\hbar\frac{\partial\Psi(x,t)}{\partial t} = \left(-\frac{\hbar^2}{2}\frac{\partial^2}{\partial x^2} + U(x)\right)\Psi(x,t), \tag{8.68}$$

where $U(x)$ is the Morse potential:

$$U(x) = D_0\left(1 - \frac{1}{g}e^x\right)^2 + U_0. \tag{8.69}$$

A semi-analytical solution to both the forward Fokker-Planck equation (FPE) and BKE using an eigenvalue decomposition method. The solution is expressed in terms of generalized Laguerre polynomials:

$$\Psi(x,t) = \sum_{n=0}^{\infty} w_n(t) f_n(x), \tag{8.70}$$

where $f_n(x)$ are basis functions constructed using Supersymmetric (SUSY) quantum mechanics techniques.

The efficient frontiers for the wealth management problem are shown to be analogous to Markowitz portfolio theory. These are contour lines of constant probability on the surface of the BKE tail probability $p(y, 0|\xi)$, viewed as a function of control parameters $y$ and $\xi$. While the provided practical numerical scheme for computing optimal contribution policies requires discretization of the control space $(u_0, \xi)$, provides a method of computation of the BKE tail probability on this grid, then uses 2D cubic spline interpolation for arbitrary inputs, and plotting contour levels to visualize efficient frontiers. This approach reduces the original stochastic control problem to a combination of semi-analytical calculations and standard numerical techniques, offering both computational efficiency and insights into the problem's structure.

## 8.7 NOTES

The foundations of dynamic programming in optimal control theory were laid by Bellman (1957). For a comprehensive treatment of dynamic programming and its applications, see Bertsekas (2012a) and Bertsekas (2012b).

Approximate dynamic programming methods, including value function approximation, Q-learning, and policy gradient methods, are well-covered in Powell (2011). For a deep dive into reinforcement learning techniques, which share many similarities with approximate dynamic programming, refer to Sutton and Barto (2018).

The Hamilton-Jacobi-Bellman (HJB) equation is a cornerstone of continuous-time optimal control. Its derivation and applications are thoroughly discussed in Fleming and Soner (2006). The verification theorem, which provides sufficient conditions for optimality, is detailed in Yong and Zhou (1999).

For a rigorous treatment of the calculus of variations and Pontryagin's maximum principle, see Liberzon (2011). The connection between the maximum principle and the HJB equation is explored in Bardi and Capuzzo-Dolcetta (2009).

Viscosity solutions, introduced to manage non-smooth optimal control problems, are comprehensively covered in Crandall et al. (1992). Their application to finance is well-documented in Pham (2009).

The classical Merton problem, a foundational work in continuous-time portfolio optimization, was introduced in Merton (1969b) and further developed in Merton (1971).

For portfolio optimization with transaction costs, Davis and Norman (1990b) provides a seminal treatment using the HJB approach. The application of viscosity solutions to this problem is explored in Shreve and Soner (1994b).

Risk-sensitive portfolio optimization, which incorporates higher moments of the return distribution, is discussed in Bielecki and Pliska (2005). For a comparison with classical results, see Fleming and McEneaney (1995).

American option pricing as an optimal stopping problem is treated in Peskir and Shiryaev (2006). The connection between option pricing and optimal control is further explored in Touzi (2012).

Portfolio optimization with constraints, including no-short-selling and drawdown constraints, is addressed in Cvitanić and Karatzas (1992) and Elie and Touzi (2008), respectively.

For a comprehensive treatment of mean-variance portfolio optimization in continuous time, refer to Zhou and Li (2000b).

Recent advancements in applying machine learning techniques to optimal control problems in finance can be found in Bühler et al. (2019) and Han et al. (2018).

CHAPTER 9

# Markov Decision Processes

Markov Decision Processes (MDPs) are a fundamental framework in the fields of operations research, control theory, and reinforcement learning (see Krishnamurthy [2016] for a comprehensive treatment of MPDs and partially observed MPDs). They provide a mathematical model for sequential decision-making under uncertainty, where an agent interacts with an environment over time. The key characteristic of MDPs is the Markov property, which posits that the future state of the system depends only on the current state and action, not on the history of previous states and actions. The MDP model relies on important components such as the agent, states, actions, rewards, and optimum policies. An agent is a system that makes decisions and performs actions. It works in an environment that describes the many states that the agent is in, as it transitions from one to another. MDP defines the method by which specific states and an agent's activities lead to other states. Furthermore, the agent earns incentives according to the actions it takes and the state it achieves (i.e., present state). The policy for the MDP model discloses the agent's next action based on its present status. In the Figure 9.1, we can visualize the MDP model framework.

Figure 9.1 illustrates the MDP loop, where $S$ is the state space ($s \in S$), $A$ is the action space ($a \in A$), $P\left(s_{t+1} \mid s_t, a_t\right)$ is the transition probability of the agent occupying state $s_{t+1}$ by taking action $a_t$ given that it is in state $s_t$, and $R\left(s_t\right)$ is the reward given by the environment to the agent when in state $s_t$.

MDPs find applications in various domains, including robotics, inventory management, healthcare, and finance. Their ability to model complex, dynamic systems with stochastic elements makes them particularly useful for problems involving optimization under uncertainty. In these scenarios, an agent must make a series of decisions to maximize some notion of cumulative reward or minimize a cost function.

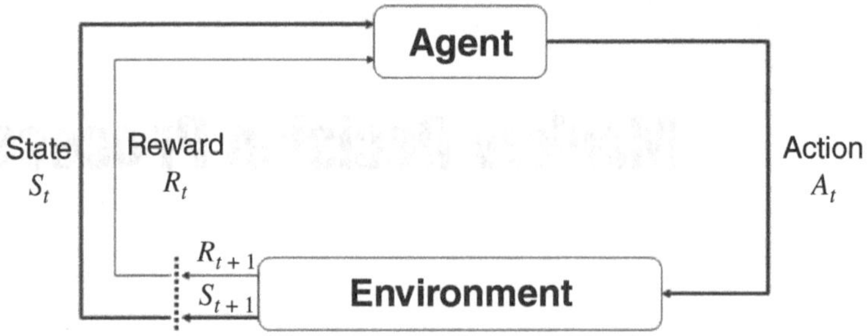


**FIGURE 9.1** **MDP Framework:** Schematic representation of how the components (i.e., agent, states, actions, and rewards) of the MDP model are connected and interact.

In the realm of quantitative portfolio management, MDPs offer a powerful framework for addressing the inherent challenges of financial markets (Barberis, 2000, Brandt and Santa-Clara, 2006, and Moallemi and Sağlam, 2013). Portfolio managers face a dynamic environment characterized by changing market conditions, varying asset returns, and evolving risk profiles. The sequential nature of investment decisions, coupled with the uncertainty of market movements, aligns well with the MDP paradigm.

MDPs enter quantitative portfolio management in several ways:

**Asset Allocation:** MDPs can model the decision process of dynamically allocating capital across different asset classes or individual securities. The state space might represent market conditions and portfolio composition, while actions correspond to rebalancing decisions. See Iyengar and Liang (2005) for a more in-depth treatment.

**Risk Management:** By incorporating risk measures into the reward function, MDPs can help managers balance return objectives with risk constraints over time. See Bielecki et al. (2005) for more details.

**Trading Strategies:** For more active management styles, MDPs can be used to develop and optimize trading strategies, considering factors such as market impact, transaction costs, and liquidity. See Bertsimas and Lo (1998) for a stochastic programming formulation amenable to MDPs.

**Multi-Period Portfolio Optimization:** MDPs naturally extend single-period optimization models to account for the temporal aspect of investment decisions, allowing for more realistic and forward-looking portfolio construction. See Mei et al. (2016).

As we delve into the subsequent sections, we will explore the various formulations of MDPs, their mathematical properties, and specific applications to portfolio optimization problems. This will provide a comprehensive understanding of how this powerful framework can be leveraged to enhance decision-making in quantitative finance.

## 9.1 FULLY OBSERVED MDPs

Fully Observed Markov Decision Processes (MDPs) form the foundation of the MDP framework (see Puterman [2009] for a general reference). In this setting, the agent has complete information about the current state of the system at each decision point. Let us formally define the components of a fully observed MDP and discuss their relevance to portfolio optimization.

A fully observed MDP is defined by a tuple $(S, A, P, R, \gamma)$, where $S$ is the state space, representing all configurations of the system. $A$ is the action space, encompassing all decisions the agent can make. $P : S \times A \times S \rightarrow [0, 1]$ is the transition probability function, where $P(s'|s, a)$ gives the probability of transitioning to state $s'$ given that action $a$ is taken in state $s$. $R : S{\times}A \rightarrow \mathbb{R}$ is the reward function, specifying the immediate reward (or cost) of acting $a$ in state $s$. $\gamma \in [0, 1]$ is the discount factor, which balances the importance of immediate versus future rewards.

In the context of portfolio optimization, the state space $S$ might include market indicators (e.g., interest rates, volatility indices, etc.), current portfolio holdings, and other relevant financial metrics. The action space $A$ could represent portfolio rebalancing decisions, such as buying or selling specific assets. The transition probabilities $P$ capture the stochastic nature of financial markets, modeling how the portfolio and market conditions evolve based on the chosen actions. The reward function $R$ typically relates to portfolio performance metrics like returns or risk-adjusted measures (e.g., Sharpe ratio). The discount factor $\gamma$ reflects the time preference of the investor, with values closer to 1 indicating a greater emphasis on long-term performance.

The goal in a fully observed MDP is to find an optimal policy $\pi^* : S \rightarrow A$ that maximizes the expected cumulative discounted reward:

$$V^{\pi^*}(s) = \max_{\pi} \mathbb{E}\left[\sum_{t=0}^{\infty} \gamma^t R\left(s_t, \pi\left(s_t\right)\right) \mid s_0 = s\right], \tag{9.1}$$

where $V^{\pi^*}(s)$ is the optimal value function, representing the maximum expected cumulative reward starting from state $s$.

For portfolio optimization, this translates to finding the best sequence of investment decisions that maximizes the expected long-term portfolio performance, given the current market conditions and portfolio state.

Key challenges in applying fully observed MDPs to portfolio optimization include:

1. **Dimensionality:** The state and action spaces can be extremely large, especially when considering multiple assets or complex market indicators.

2. **Continuous spaces:** Financial variables are often continuous, requiring techniques like function approximation or discretization.
3. **Non-stationarity:** Financial markets evolve over time, potentially violating the stationary assumption of standard MDPs.
4. **Model uncertainty:** Accurately specifying transition probabilities and reward functions in financial markets is challenging due to their complex and dynamic nature.

Despite these challenges, fully observed MDPs provide a powerful framework for modeling and solving sequential decision-making problems in portfolio management. They allow for the incorporation of risk preferences, transaction costs, and other practical constraints while maintaining a principled approach to optimization under uncertainty.

## 9.2 PARTIALLY OBSERVED MDPs

While fully observed MDPs provide a powerful framework, they often fall short in capturing the realities of financial markets, where complete information is rarely available. Partially Observed Markov Decision Processes (POMDPs) extend the MDP framework to scenarios where the agent cannot directly observe the true state of the system (see Krishnamurthy [2016] for a general reference). This model is particularly relevant for portfolio optimization, given the inherent uncertainties and hidden factors in financial markets.

A POMDP is defined by a tuple $(S, A, O, T, Z, R, \gamma)$, where $S$, $A$, $R$, and $\gamma$ are defined as in the fully observed MDP. $O$ is the set of observations. $T : S \times A \times S \to [0, 1]$ is the state transition function, where $T(s'|s, a)$ gives the probability of transitioning to state $s'$ given action $a$ in state $s$. $Z$ : $S{\times}A{\times}O \to [0, 1]$ is the observation function, where $Z\left(o|s', a\right)$ gives the probability of observing $o$, given that action $a$ was taken and resulted in state $s'$. In Figure 9.2, we have an example of a POMDP applied to the financial sector, representing a simple problem with two states {Bull Market and Bear Market}, three actions {Buy, Sell, and Hold}, and two observations {Corporate Profit Growth and Decline in Corporate Profits}.

Figure 9.2 depicts a POMDP, where $S$ = {Bull Market, Bear Market}, $A$ = {Buy, Sell and Hold}, and $O$ = {Corporate Profit Growth, Decline in Corporate Profits}. In the context of portfolio optimization, POMDPs can model scenarios where:

- The true state of the market (e.g., regime, liquidity conditions, etc.) is not directly observable.

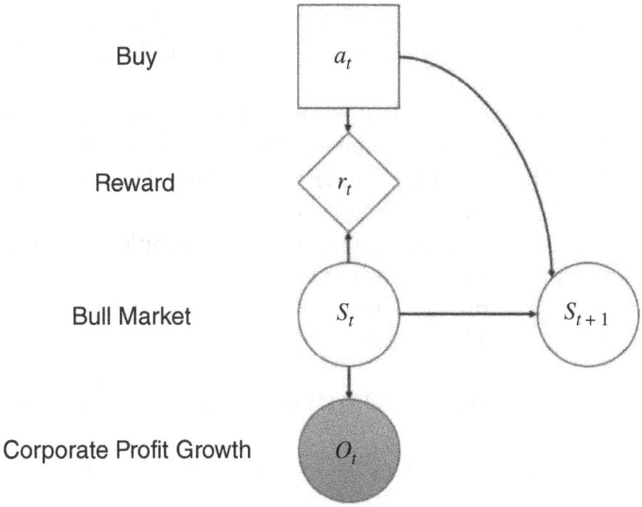


**FIGURE 9.2** Example of POMDP.

- There is uncertainty about the true value or future performance of assets.
- The impact of exogenous factors (e.g., geopolitical events, policy changes, etc.) is not fully known.

The key difference in POMDPs is that the agent maintains a belief state $b(s)$, which is a probability distribution over states. The belief state is updated after each action and observation using Bayes's rule:

$$b'(s') = \frac{Z(o|s',a)\sum_{s\in S} T(s'|s,a)b(s)}{\sum_{s'\in S} Z(o|s',a)\sum_{s\in S} T(s'|s,a)b(s)} \tag{9.2}$$

The goal in a POMDP is to find an optimal policy $\pi^*$ that maximizes the expected cumulative discounted reward, now defined over belief states:

$$V^*(b) = \max_a \left[ R(b,a) + \gamma \sum_{o\in O} P(o|b,a)\, V^*\left(b_{a,o}\right) \right], \tag{9.3}$$

where $R(b,a) = \sum_{s\in S} b(s)\, R(s,a)$ is the expected immediate reward, and $b_{a,o}$ is the updated belief state after taking action $a$ and observing $o$.

Solving POMDPs is computationally challenging, especially for large state spaces common in finance. Several approaches have been developed:

1. **Value Iteration over Belief MDPs:** This approach transforms the POMDP into a continuous-state MDP over belief states.
2. **Policy Iteration with Finite-State Controllers:** This method represents policies as finite-state machines.
3. **Point-Based Value Iteration:** This technique samples a finite set of belief points to approximate the value function.
4. **Monte Carlo Planning:** These methods use sampling to estimate the value of actions in belief states.

In portfolio optimization, POMDPs can be applied to various problems:

- **Asset Allocation under Uncertainty:** When the true state of the market or the risk/return characteristics of assets are not fully observable.
- **Dynamic Trading Strategies:** When market impact or liquidity conditions are uncertain.
- **Risk Management:** When the full extent of potential risks or correlations between assets is not known.

Despite their computational challenges, POMDPs offer a more realistic framework for modeling the uncertainties inherent in financial decision-making. They allow portfolio managers to explicitly account for incomplete information and to design strategies that balance exploration (gathering more information) and exploitation (maximizing returns based on current beliefs).

## 9.3 INFINITE HORIZON PROBLEMS

Infinite horizon problems in MDPs deal with scenarios where the decision-making process continues indefinitely (Krishnamurthy, 2016; Puterman, 2009). This framework is relevant for long-term portfolio management strategies where there is no predetermined end date. Furthermore, infinite horizon problems can model long-term asset allocation strategies, perpetual fund management, or continuous trading strategies in liquid markets. See Campbell et al. (2004) for a treatment of strategic asset allocation in a continuous-time setting. The authors develop a model for long-term investors who face time-varying investment opportunities. In these problems, the goal is to find a stationary optimal policy that maximizes the expected discounted sum of rewards over an infinite time horizon.

The value function for an infinite horizon problem is defined as:

$$V^{\pi}(s) = \mathbb{E}_{\pi}\left[\sum_{t=0}^{\infty} \gamma^{t} R(s_t, a_t) \mid s_0 = s\right], \tag{9.4}$$

where $\gamma \in [0, 1]$ is the discount factor, which ensures that the sum converges.

- **Stationarity:** The optimal policy is independent of time, depending only on the current state.
- **Discounting:** Future rewards are typically discounted to reflect the time value of money and to ensure convergence.
- **Convergence:** Under certain conditions, value iteration and policy iteration algorithms are guaranteed to converge to the optimal policy.

The Bellman equation for the optimal value function in infinite horizon problems is:

$$V^{*}(s) = \max_{a}\left[R(s, a) + \gamma \sum_{s' \in S} P(s'|s, a) V^{*}(s')\right]. \tag{9.5}$$

Two primary methods for solving infinite horizon MDPs are:

1. **Value Iteration:** This algorithm iteratively updates the value function:

   $$V_{k+1}(s) = \max_{a}\left[R(s, a) + \gamma \sum_{s' \in S} P(s'|s, a) V_{k}(s')\right]. \tag{9.6}$$

   In Value Iteration, we start with an initial estimate of the value function $V_0(s)$ for all states $s$. The algorithm then iteratively improves this estimate. At each iteration $k$, for each state $s$, we consider all actions $a$. For each action, we compute the expected immediate reward plus the discounted future value (based on the previous iteration's value estimates). We select the action that maximizes this sum, and this becomes the new value estimate for state $s$.
   The takeaways are that the value function $V_k(s)$ changes in each iteration. The action $a$ that maximizes the expression is implicitly defining a policy, but this policy may change in each iteration. The algorithm continues until the change in the value function between iterations is smaller than a predefined threshold.
2. **Policy Iteration:** This method alternates between policy evaluation and policy improvement:
   - *Evaluation:* $V^{\pi}(s) = R(s, \pi(s)) + \gamma \sum_{s' \in S} P(s'|s, \pi(s)) V^{\pi}(s')$.
   - *Improvement:* $\pi'(s) = \operatorname{argmax}_a \left[R(s, a) + \gamma \sum_{s' \in S} P(s'|s, a) V^{\pi}(s')\right]$.

Policy Iteration consists of two alternating steps:

1. **Policy Evaluation:** Given a policy $\pi$, we compute its value function $V^{\pi}(s)$. This involves solving a system of linear equations (one for each state) or iteratively applying the evaluation equation until convergence.
2. **Policy Improvement:** Using the computed value function $V^{\pi}(s)$, we define a new policy $\pi'$ that chooses the action maximizing the expected return in each state. This new policy is guaranteed to be at least as good as the previous one.
   The takeaway is that in the evaluation step, we compute the exact value function for the current policy. In the improvement step, we define a new policy based on this value function. The algorithm alternates between these steps until the policy no longer changes.

In broad terms, to implement these algorithms:

1. For Value Iteration:
   i. Initialize $V_0(s)$ arbitrarily for all states.
   ii. Repeat until convergence:
      - For each state, compute the new value using the equation.
      - Update all state values simultaneously.
   iii. Extract the optimal policy from the final value function.
2. For Policy Iteration:
   i. Start with an arbitrary policy $\pi_0$.
   ii. Repeat until convergence:
      - Evaluate the current policy (solve the system of equations).
      - Improve the policy using the computed value function.

Both methods converge to the optimal policy, but they may differ in computational efficiency depending on the specific problem structure. There will be more to say about these methods in the chapter on reinforcement learning.

Challenges in applying infinite horizon MDPs to portfolio optimization include:

- **Curse of dimensionality:** As the number of assets or state variables increases, the state space grows exponentially (see Puterman [2009]). This phenomenon poses a significant challenge in MDPs, particularly in finance and portfolio management. For instance, if we are considering a portfolio with multiple assets, each additional asset exponentially increases the number of states. This rapid growth makes it increasingly difficult to compute and store value functions or policies for all states. It also impacts the efficiency of dynamic programming algorithms, as they need to iterate over all states. In practice, this can lead to computational intractability for high-dimensional problems, necessitating the use of approximation methods or dimensionality reduction techniques.

- **Model uncertainty:** The true transition probabilities and reward function may be unknown or change over time. Bayesian approaches may be warranted. In real-world applications of MDPs, especially in dynamic environments like financial markets, the underlying model parameters are often not fully known or may evolve over time (see Krishnamurthy [2016]). This uncertainty can significantly impact the optimal policy derived from the MDP. Bayesian approaches offer a framework to incorporate this uncertainty by proposing a probability distribution over models. These methods allow for continuous learning and adaptation as new information becomes available. For instance, in a trading MDP, Bayesian techniques could help update beliefs about market dynamics based on observed price movements, potentially leading to more robust decision-making under uncertainty.
- **Computational complexity:** Solving for the optimal policy can be computationally intensive for large state spaces, as the complexity of MDPs is polynomial in time (see Papadimitriou and Tsitsiklis [1987]). This is a critical challenge in MDPs, particularly when dealing with real-world problems that involve numerous states and actions. Traditional methods like value iteration or policy iteration can become prohibitively slow as the state space expands. The time complexity of these algorithms typically grows polynomially with the number of states, which can quickly become impractical for large-scale problems. This limitation has spurred the development of various approximation methods, such as approximate dynamic programming, reinforcement learning techniques like Q-learning, or the use of function approximators to represent value functions or policies. These approaches aim to find near-optimal solutions in reasonable time frames, trading off some degree of optimality for computational feasibility in complex, high-dimensional MDPs.

To address these challenges, various approximate methods have been developed, such as Approximate Dynamic Programming which, as was discussed in Section 8.2, uses function approximation to estimate the value function. There is also Reinforcement Learning (see Chapter 10) where an agent learns the optimal policy through interaction with the environment, without explicit knowledge of the transition probabilities. There is also State

Aggregation, which groups similar states to reduce the state space dimensionality.

In portfolio optimization, infinite horizon MDPs can be used to develop robust, long-term investment strategies that adapt to changing market conditions while maintaining a consistent decision-making framework. They are particularly useful for institutional investors, pension funds, and other entities with long-term investment horizons.

## 9.4 FINITE HORIZON PROBLEMS

Finite horizon problems in Markov Decision Processes deal with scenarios where the decision-making process has a predetermined end point (Puterman, 2009; Krishnamurthy, 2016). In the context of portfolio optimization, this could represent investment strategies with a specific target date, such as saving for retirement or managing a fund with a fixed maturity.

In a finite horizon MDP, the optimal policy and value function depend not only on the current state but also on the time remaining until the terminal period. Let $T$ be the finite time horizon, then, the value function at time $t$ is defined as:

$$V_t^{\pi}(s) = \mathbb{E}_{\pi}\left[\sum_{k=t}^{T-1} \gamma^{k-t} R(s_k, a_k) + \gamma^{T-t} V_T(s_T) \mid s_t = s\right], \tag{9.7}$$

where $V_T(s_T)$ is the terminal value function.

Key characteristics of finite horizon problems include:

- **Time-dependent policies:** The optimal action may depend on both the current state and the remaining time.
- **Backward induction:** Solutions are typically computed starting from the terminal period and working backward.
- **Terminal value:** The final state often has a specific value or reward associated with it.

The Bellman equation for finite horizon problems is:

$$V_t^*(s) = \max_a \left[R(s,a) + \gamma \sum_{s' \in S} P(s'|s,a) V_{t+1}^*(s')\right], \tag{9.8}$$

for $t = 0, 1, \ldots, T-1$, with $V_T^*(s) = V_T(s)$ given as the terminal value function.

The optimal policy at time $t$ is:

$$\pi_t^*(s) = \text{argmax}_a \left[ R(s,a) + \gamma \sum_{s' \in S} P(s'|s,a) V_{t+1}^*(s') \right]. \qquad (9.9)$$

Solving finite horizon MDPs backward induction is used. It is the primary method for solving finite horizon MDPs. The steps are as follows:

1. Start with $V_T^*(s) = V_T(s)$ for all $s \in S$.
2. For $t = T-1, T-2, ..., 0$:
   i. Compute $V_t^*(s)$ using the Bellman equation.
   ii. Determine $\pi_t^*(s)$ for each state.

Some applications of POMDPs to portfolio optimization include:

- **Target-date funds:** Optimizing asset allocation as the target date approaches.
- **Liquidation strategies:** Planning the sale of a large position over a fixed time period.
- **Fixed-term investment products:** Managing portfolios with predefined maturity dates.

Challenges in finite horizon portfolio optimization:

- **Curse of dimensionality:** The state space can grow exponentially with the number of time steps and assets.
- **Model uncertainty:** Transition probabilities and rewards may be difficult to estimate, especially for distant future periods.
- **Time-varying parameters:** Market conditions and investor preferences may change over the investment horizon.

To address these challenges, various techniques can be employed:

- **Approximate Dynamic Programming:** Use function approximation to estimate value functions in high-dimensional state spaces.
- **Scenario-based optimization:** Generate and solve for multiple future scenarios.
- **Rolling horizon approach:** Solve a series of shorter-horizon problems, updating the model as time progresses.

Finite horizon MDPs provide a powerful framework for modeling and solving portfolio optimization problems with specific time constraints. They allow for the incorporation of changing investment objectives and risk preferences over time, making them particularly suitable for lifecycle investing and other time-bound financial planning scenarios.

## 9.5 THE BELLMAN EQUATION

The Bellman equation, named after Richard Bellman, is a fundamental concept in dynamic programming and forms the cornerstone of solving MDPs (see the original presentation by Bellman in Bellman [1952]). It provides a recursive formulation of the value function, enabling us to break down complex sequential decision problems into simpler subproblems.

**Derivation of the Bellman Equation** Let us start with the definition of the value function for a policy $\pi$:

$$V^{\pi}(s) = \mathbb{E}_{\pi}\left[\sum_{t=0}^{\infty} \gamma^t R(s_t, a_t) \mid s_0 = s\right]. \tag{9.10}$$

We can separate the immediate reward from future rewards:

$$\begin{aligned} V^{\pi}(s) &= \mathbb{E}_{\pi}\left[R(s_0, a_0) + \gamma \sum_{t=1}^{\infty} \gamma^{t-1} R(s_t, a_t) \mid s_0 = s\right] \\ &= \mathbb{E}_{\pi}\left[R(s_0, a_0) + \gamma V^{\pi}(s_1) \mid s_0 = s\right]. \end{aligned} \tag{9.11}$$

Expanding this expectation:

$$V^{\pi}(s) = R(s, \pi(s)) + \gamma \sum_{s' \in S} P(s'|s, \pi(s)) V^{\pi}(s'). \tag{9.12}$$

This is the Bellman equation for a given policy $\pi$. For the optimal policy $\pi^*$, we have the Bellman optimality equation:

$$V^*(s) = \max_a \left[R(s, a) + \gamma \sum_{s' \in S} P(s'|s, a) V^*(s')\right]. \tag{9.13}$$

### Important Special Cases

**Deterministic MDPs** In deterministic MDPs, each action leads to a specific next state with probability 1. The Bellman equation simplifies to:

$$V^*(s) = \max_a \left[R(s, a) + \gamma V^*(f(s, a))\right], \tag{9.14}$$

where $f(s, a)$ is the deterministic next state function.

**Finite Horizon Problems** For finite horizon problems with horizon $T$, the Bellman equation becomes time-dependent:

$$V_t^*(s) = \max_a \left[ R(s,a) + \gamma \sum_{s' \in S} P(s'|s,a) V_{t+1}^*(s') \right], \tag{9.15}$$

for $t = 0, 1, ..., T-1$, with the boundary condition $V_T^*(s) = V_T(s)$.

**Average Reward MDPs** In some cases, we are interested in maximizing the average reward per time step. The Bellman equation for average reward MDPs is:

$$h^*(s) + \rho^* = \max_a \left[ R(s,a) + \sum_{s' \in S} P(s'|s,a) h^*(s') \right], \tag{9.16}$$

where $h^*(s)$ is the differential value function and $\rho^*$ is the optimal average reward.

## State, Actions, and the Bellman Equation

**Discrete Spaces** The Q-function, also known as the state-action value function, is a fundamental concept in reinforcement learning and MDPs. It represents the expected cumulative reward of taking a specific action $a$ in a given state $s$, and then following the optimal policy thereafter. The Q-function provides a way to directly compare the value of different actions in a given state, making it particularly useful for decision-making and policy improvement.

The Q-function, is defined as:

$$Q^\pi(s,a) = R(s,a) + \gamma \sum_{s' \in S} P(s'|s,a) V^\pi(s'). \tag{9.17}$$

The Bellman equation for the optimal Q-function is:

$$Q^*(s,a) = R(s,a) + \gamma \sum_{s' \in S} P(s'|s,a) \max_{a'} Q^*(s',a'). \tag{9.18}$$

**Continuous Spaces** For continuous state and action spaces, the Bellman equation becomes an integral:

$$V^*(s) = \max_{a \in A} \left[ R(s,a) + \gamma \int_S P(s'|s,a) V^*(s') \, ds' \right]. \tag{9.19}$$

### Partial Observability

In POMDPs, the agent does not have direct access to the true state of the environment. Instead, it maintains a belief state $b$, which is a probability distribution over states. The Bellman equation for POMDPs is defined over these belief states:

$$V^*(b) = \max_a \left[ R(b,a) + \gamma \sum_{o \in O} P(o|b,a) V^*\left(b_{a,o}\right) \right], \tag{9.20}$$

where $b$ is the current belief state, $a$ is the action taken, $o$ is the observation received,

$$R(b,a) = \sum_{s \in S} b(s) R(s,a) \tag{9.21}$$

is the expected immediate reward,

$$P(o|b,a) = \sum_{s \in S} b(s) \sum_{s' \in S} P(s'|s,a) Z(o|s',a) \tag{9.22}$$

is the probability of observation $o$, and $b_{a,o}$ is the updated belief state after taking action $a$ and observing $o$.

The belief update $b_{a,o}$ is computed using Bayes' rule:

$$b_{a,o}(s') = \frac{Z(o|s',a) \sum_{s \in S} T(s'|s,a) b(s)}{P(o|b,a)}, \tag{9.23}$$

where $Z(o|s',a)$ is the observation probability and $T(s'|s,a)$ is the state transition probability.

In portfolio optimization, POMDPs can model scenarios where the true state of the market (e.g., bull or bear regime) is not directly observable, but must be inferred from noisy indicators. The belief state might represent the probability distribution over different market regimes, and observations could include price movements, economic indicators, or company reports.

### Risk-sensitive MDPs

Standard MDPs optimize the expected cumulative reward, which may not adequately capture an investor's risk preferences. Risk-sensitive MDPs modify the objective to account for the risk associated with different policies. One common approach uses exponential utility:

$$V^*(s) = \max_a \left[ -\frac{1}{\lambda} \log \mathbb{E}\left[ e^{-\lambda (R(s,a) + \gamma V^*(s'))} \right] \right], \tag{9.24}$$

where $\lambda$ is the risk-sensitivity parameter denotes in the following cases:

- $\lambda > 0$: Risk-averse behavior (penalizes variance in returns).
- $\lambda < 0$: Risk-seeking behavior (prefers variance in returns).
- $\lambda \to 0$: Approaches risk-neutral behavior (standard MDP).

This formulation has several important properties as it satisfies the principle of certainty equivalence, it is compatible with dynamic programming, allowing for recursive solution methods, and as $\lambda \to 0$, it converges to the risk-neutral solution.

An alternative formulation incorporates a measure of variability directly:

$$V^*(s) = \max_a \left[ R(s,a) + \gamma \mathbb{E}\left[V^*(s')\right] - \frac{\lambda}{2} \mathrm{Var}\left[R(s,a) + \gamma V^*(s')\right] \right], \quad (9.25)$$

where $\mathrm{Var}[\cdot]$ denotes variance.

In portfolio optimization, risk-sensitive MDPs can model investors with different risk tolerances. For example:

- A conservative pension fund might use a high-positive $\lambda$ to prioritize stable returns.
- A growth-oriented hedge fund might use a negative $\lambda$ to seek out high-risk, high-reward opportunities.
- A balanced fund might use a $\lambda$ close to zero or adjust $\lambda$ based on market conditions.

Solving risk-sensitive MDPs often requires specialized algorithms, as the introduction of risk measures can make the problem nonlinear and potentially non-convex. Techniques such as robust dynamic programming, stochastic approximation, and policy gradient methods are commonly employed in this context.

## 9.6 SOLVING THE BELLMAN EQUATION

Several methods exist for solving the Bellman equation (Puterman, 2009; Powell, 2011; Bertsekas, 2012a; Bertsekas, 2019; and Sutton and Barto, 2018):

- **Value Iteration:** Iteratively apply the Bellman optimality equation until convergence.
- **Policy Iteration:** Alternate between policy evaluation (solving the Bellman equation for a fixed policy) and policy improvement.
- **Linear Programming:** Formulate the Bellman equation as a linear program for finite MDPs.

- **Approximate Dynamic Programming:** Use function approximation to estimate the value function in high-dimensional or continuous spaces.

Here is a detailed algorithm for Value Iteration:

**Algorithm 1:** Value Iteration

Initialize $V_0(s) = 0$ for all $s \in S$.
Choose $\theta > 0$ (convergence threshold).
$k \leftarrow 0$
**Repeat**
  $\Delta \leftarrow 0$
  **for** *each* $s \in S$, **do**
    $v \leftarrow V_k(s)$
    $V_{k+1}(s) \leftarrow \max_a \left[R(s,a) + \gamma \sum_{s' \in S} P(s'|s,a)V_k(s')\right]$
    $\Delta \leftarrow \max(\Delta, |v - V_{k+1}(s)|)$
  $k \leftarrow k+1$
**until**
$\Delta < \theta$ **return** $V_k$

When solving the Bellman equation for portfolio optimization, one should consider the specific characteristics of the financial problem at hand. For instance, in a multi-asset allocation problem, the state space might represent different market conditions and portfolio compositions, while actions correspond to rebalancing decisions. The reward function could incorporate both returns and risk measures, such as the Sharpe ratio or drawdown constraints.

One analytically solvable example that illustrates the application of the Bellman equation in finance is the optimal stopping problem for American option pricing. Consider a simple binomial model for a stock price over two periods. The state space is the possible stock prices, actions are to exercise or hold the option, and the reward is the payoff from exercising. The Bellman equation for this problem is:

$$V(S_t, t) = \max\left\{(K - S_t)^+, e^{-r\Delta t}\mathbb{E}\left[V(S_{t+1}, t+1)\,|S_t\right]\right\}, \tag{9.26}$$

where $S_t$ is the stock price at time $t$, $K$ is the strike price, $r$ is the risk-free rate, and $\Delta t$ is the time step. This equation can be solved backward from the option's expiry, providing both the option price and the optimal exercise strategy.

In more complex portfolio optimization scenarios, analytical solutions are often intractable, and numerical methods such as those listed previously become necessary. These methods allow us to manage multiple assets, transaction costs, and complex market dynamics, providing a powerful framework for deriving optimal investment strategies that balance immediate returns with long-term value, while accounting for the stochastic nature of financial markets and the sequential nature of investment decisions.

## 9.7 EXAMPLES IN PORTFOLIO OPTIMIZATION

### 9.7.1 An MDP in Multi-asset Allocation with Transaction Costs

Consider a portfolio allocation problem across $n$ assets over a finite horizon $T$. Let the state space be $S_t = (w_t, m_t)$, where $w_t \in \mathbb{R}^n$ represents the portfolio weights, and $m_t \in \mathbb{R}^k$ represents the market state (e.g., volatility regimes, economic indicators, etc.). The action space is denoted by $A_t = \Delta w_t \in \mathbb{R}^n$, representing changes in portfolio weights. The transition function is given by

$$w_{t+1} = \frac{\left(w_t + \Delta w_t\right) \circ \left(1 + r_{t+1}\right)}{\sum_{i=1}^{n} \left(w_{t,i} + \Delta w_{t,i}\right)\left(1 + r_{t+1,i}\right)}, \tag{9.27}$$

where $r_{t+1}$ is the vector of asset returns, and $\circ$ denotes element-wise multiplication. The reward function in this case is given by

$$R\left(S_t, A_t\right) = w_t^\top r_t - \lambda w_t^\top \Sigma_t w_t - c^\top |\Delta w_t|, \tag{9.28}$$

where $\Sigma_t$ is the covariance matrix of returns, $\lambda$ is a risk aversion parameter, and $c$ is a vector of transaction costs. Lastly, the Bellman equation is

$$V_t\left(S_t\right) = \max_{A_t} \left[R\left(S_t, A_t\right) + \gamma \mathbb{E}\left[V_{t+1}\left(S_{t+1}\right) | S_t, A_t\right]\right]. \tag{9.29}$$

This MDP captures the trade-off between expected returns, risk, and transaction costs in a multi-period setting. See Boyd et al. (2017) for an exposition on multi-period, multi-asset allocation with transaction costs through the lens of convex optimization.

### 9.7.2 A POMDP for Asset Allocation with Regime Switching

Consider a portfolio allocation problem between stocks and bonds where the market follows a hidden regime-switching process, that is, a jump process between different sets of parameters. See Zhou and Yin (2003a) for a related problem on regime-switching, and Sotomayor and Cadenillas (2009) for an example of POMDPs in dynamic asset allocation.

Let the hidden state space be

$$S = s_{\text{bull}}, s_{\text{bear}},$$

representing bull and bear market regimes. The observation space is denoted by

$$O = o_{\text{high}}, o_{\text{low}},$$

representing high and low observed returns. The action space is given by $A = [0, 1]$, representing the proportion of wealth allocated to stocks, with the remainder in bonds. The transition probabilities are given by $P(s'|s)$, for example,

$$P(s_{\text{bull}}|s_{\text{bull}}), = 0.9$$

$$P(s_{\text{bear}}|s_{\text{bull}}) = 0.1.$$

The observation probabilities are denoted by $Z(o|s)$, e.g.,

$$Z(o_{\text{high}}|s_{\text{bull}}) = 0.7,$$

then $Z(o_{\text{low}}|s_{\text{bull}}) = 0.3$. The reward function in this case is given by

$$R(s, a) = a \cdot r_{\text{stock}}(s) + (1 - a) \cdot r_{\text{bond}}, \tag{9.30}$$

where $r_{\text{stock}}(s)$ is the stock return in state $s$, and $r_{\text{bond}}$ is the (constant) bond return. The Bellman equation for this POMDP is

$$V(b) = \max_a \left[ \sum_{s \in S} b(s) R(s, a) + \gamma \sum_{o \in O} P(o|b, a) V(b_{a,o}) \right], \tag{9.31}$$

where $b$ is the belief state (probability distribution over $S$). This POMDP captures the uncertainty about the true market regime and the need to infer it from noisy observations.

### 9.7.3 An MDP with Continuous State and Action Spaces for Option Hedging with Stochastic Volatility

Consider the problem of dynamically hedging a European call option in a market with stochastic volatility. Let the state space be $S_t = (S_t, v_t, t)$, where $S_t$ is the underlying asset price and $v_t$ is the volatility. The action space is denoted by $A_t = \Delta_t \in \mathbb{R}$, and represents the number of shares of the underlying asset held.

The dynamics of the system are given by the Heston Model

$$dS_t = \mu S_t dt + \sqrt{v_t} S_t dW^{S_t} \tag{9.32}$$

$$dv_t = \kappa(\theta - v_t) dt + \sigma \sqrt{V_t} dW^{v_t}, \tag{9.33}$$

where $dW^{S_t}$ and $dW^{v_t}$ are correlated Brownian motions driving the price and volatility, respectively.

The reward function, which is the negative of the hedging error, is given by

$$R\left(S_t, v_t, t, \Delta_t\right) = -\left|\left(\Delta_t S_t + B_t\right) - C\left(S_t, v_t, t\right)\right|, \tag{9.34}$$

where $B_t$ is the money market account and $C\left(S_t, v_t, t\right)$ is the option price.

The Bellman equation for the value function $V = V(S, v, t)$ for this continuous-state, continuous-action MDP is given by

$$\begin{aligned} 0 = \max_{\Delta_t} \Bigg[ & \frac{\partial V}{\partial t} + \mu S \frac{\partial V}{\partial S} + \kappa(\theta - V)\frac{\partial V}{\partial V} + \frac{1}{2} V S^2 \frac{\partial^2 V}{\partial S^2} \\ & + \frac{1}{2}\sigma^2 V \frac{\partial^2 V}{\partial V^2} + \rho\sigma V S \frac{\partial^2 V}{\partial S \partial V} + R(S, V, t, \Delta_t) \Bigg]. \end{aligned} \tag{9.35}$$

This MDP captures the complex dynamics of option hedging in a stochastic volatility environment. This continuous-state, continuous-action MDP captures the complex dynamics of option hedging in a stochastic volatility environment. Solving this Bellman equation numerically can provide insights into optimal hedging strategies that go beyond traditional delta-hedging approaches. See Riedel (2003) for a treatment of dynamics risk measures, and Kurpiel et al. (1999) for a treatment of hedging with stochastic volatility.

## 9.8 NOTES

The theory of Markov Decision Processes (MDPs) provides a powerful framework for sequential decision-making under uncertainty. For a comprehensive introduction to MDPs, see Puterman (2009).

Partially Observable MPDPs extend MDPs to scenarios where the state is not fully observable. A thorough treatment of POMDPs can be found in Kaelbling et al. (1998) and Krishnamurthy (2016), which was one of the main references in the chapter.

The distinction between infinite and finite horizon problems is crucial in MDPs. For a detailed discussion on infinite horizon problems, refer to Bertsekas (2012b). Finite horizon problems are well-covered in Bertsekas (2012a).

The Bellman equation, a fundamental concept in dynamic programming and MDPs, is derived and explained in depth in Bellman (1957). For important of the Bellman equation, including deterministic MDPs and average reward MDPs, see Howard (1960).

The treatment of state and action spaces, both discrete and continuous, in the context of the Bellman equation is discussed in Sutton and Barto (2018). For continuous state and action spaces, which are particularly relevant in finance, refer to Bertsekas and Tsitsiklis (1996).

Partial observability in MDPs leads to POMDPs, which are extensively covered in Spaan (2012). The application of POMDPs to finance, particularly in the context of regime-switching models, is explored in Zhou and Yin (2003a).

Risk-sensitive MDPs, which incorporate risk measures into the decision-making process, are discussed in Howard and Matheson (1972). For a modern treatment with applications to finance, see Shen et al. (2014).

Various methods for solving the Bellman equation are presented in Powell (2011), including value iteration, policy iteration, and approximate dynamic programming techniques.

In the context of portfolio optimization, MDPs have been applied to multi-asset allocation problems with transaction costs. A seminal paper on this topic is Iyengar and Kang (2005). For a more recent treatment using reinforcement learning techniques, see Jiang et al. (2017).

POMDPs have been used to model asset allocation problems with regime switching, where the underlying market regime is not directly observable. This approach is detailed in Bäuerle and Rieder (2011).

Continuous-time MDPs, which are closely related to stochastic control problems, are particularly relevant for many financial applications. A comprehensive treatment can be found in Pham (2009).

Recent advancements in applying machine learning techniques to solve high-dimensional MDPs in finance are discussed in Bühler et al. (2019) and Kolm and Ritter (2019).

CHAPTER 10

# Reinforcement Learning

Reinforcement Learning (RL) (Sutton and Barto, 2018; Rao and Jelvis, 2022)[1] has emerged as a powerful paradigm in machine learning, with far-reaching applications across various domains. In the context of quantitative finance, and specifically portfolio optimization, RL offers a promising approach to tackle complex, dynamic decision-making problems under uncertainty. Importantly, the RL framework is agnostic to probability distributions and whether they are stationary or nonstationary. RL agents will learn to navigate their environment with sufficient data and training. This chapter explores the fundamental concepts of reinforcement learning and their applications to portfolio optimization.

Fundamentally, RL concerns how agents should take actions in an environment to maximize a cumulative reward. This framework aligns naturally with the objectives of portfolio optimization, where the goal is to make sequential investment decisions that maximize long-term returns while managing risk.

The RL portfolio optimization can be cast as an MDP, defined by the tuple $(\mathcal{S}, \mathcal{A}, \mathcal{P}, \mathcal{R}, \gamma)$, where:

- $\mathcal{S}$ is the state space, representing market conditions and portfolio positions.
- $\mathcal{A}$ is the action space, corresponding to trading decisions.
- $\mathcal{P} : \mathcal{S} \times \mathcal{A} \times \mathcal{S} \to [0, 1]$ is the transition probability function.
- $\mathcal{R} : \mathcal{S} \times \mathcal{A} \times \mathcal{S} \to \mathbb{R}$ is the reward function.

---

[1]Sutton and Barto is the standard reference for RL and will be used throughout this chapter without further explicit citation, except in the applications at the end of the chapter. The book by Rao and Jelvis, dealing specifically with RL in finance, will similarly be referenced without explicit citation, except in the applications at the end of the chapter.

- $\gamma \in [0,1]$ is the discount factor for future rewards. The decay is exponential, so the smaller $\gamma$, the faster the discounting, and the less the agent considers future rewards, that is, the more myopic the policy. Conversely, the closer $\gamma$ is to unity, the more future looking the agent is.

The objective in RL is to find an optimal policy $\pi^* : \mathcal{S} \to \mathcal{A}$ that maximizes the expected cumulative discounted reward:

$$\pi^* = \arg\max_{\pi} \mathbb{E}\left[\sum_{t=0}^{\infty} \gamma^t \mathcal{R}\left(s_t, a_t, s_{t+1}\right) \mid \pi\right], \tag{10.1}$$

where $s_t \in \mathcal{S}$ is the state at time $t$, and $a_t = \pi\left(s_t\right)$ is the action taken according to policy $\pi$. The agent's policy, $\pi(S)$, determines the action to perform in a given state to maximize total rewards. Each state is connected with a value function $V(S)$, which predicts the expected amount of future rewards we may earn in this state by enacting the appropriate policy. In other words, the value function determines how excellent a state is. Reinforcement Learning seeks to understand both policy and value functions. The Venn diagram on the right of Figure 10.1 depicts the relationships between the value function, policy, and whether there is an environment model, or if training is (environment) model-free. On the left of Figure 10.1 is a directed diagram the relationship between the different learning modes in RL.

This chapter will delve into the theoretical foundations of reinforcement learning, exploring its connections to optimal control theory, the crucial components of the RL framework, and the distinction between on-policy and off-policy methods. We will then examine how these concepts can be

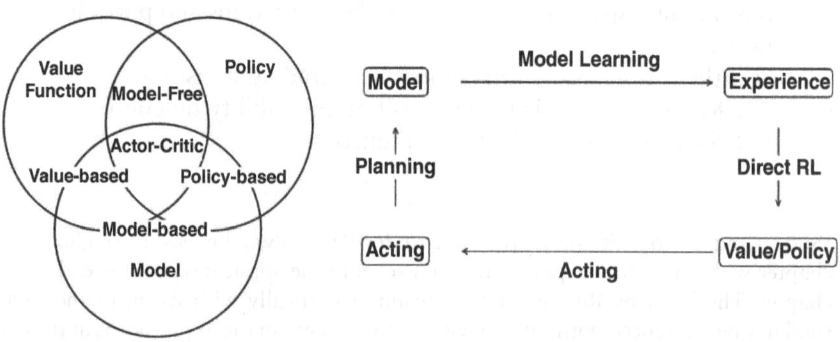


**FIGURE 10.1** Schematic of approaches in RL based on whether the model to be developed is for the value function, policy, or the environment.

applied to the domain of portfolio optimization, addressing challenges such as handling high-dimensional and continuous state and action spaces; dealing with nonstationary and partially observable market environments; balancing exploration and exploitation in financial markets; incorporating risk measures and constraints into the RL framework; and adapting to changing market regimes and investor preferences.

## 10.1 CONNECTIONS TO OPTIMAL CONTROL

Reinforcement Learning and Optimal Control (OC) are closely related fields that deal with sequential decision-making problems (Bertsekas [2019] and Powell [2022] are two excellent references on this topic). While they have developed, with RL emerging from computer science and OC from engineering and applied mathematics, their underlying principles and objectives are quite similar. Understanding these connections can provide valuable insights for applying RL techniques to portfolio optimization.

**Shared Fundamentals** Both RL and OC aim to find an optimal policy or control law that maximizes a cumulative reward or minimizes a cost function over time as the agent's or control policy's dynamics evolve. For most intense and purposes, a cost function can be thought of as the negative of a reward function. The key shared elements include:

- **State Space:** In both frameworks, the system is described by a state $s_t \in \mathcal{S}$ at each time step $t$.
- **Action/Control Space:** Decisions are made from an action space $a_t \in \mathcal{A}$ (in RL) or a control space $u_t \in \mathcal{U}$ (in OC).
- **Transition Dynamics:** The evolution of the system is governed by transition probabilities (in stochastic settings) or deterministic functions.
- **Objective Function:** Both aim to optimize a cumulative reward or cost function.

**The Bellman Equation** A fundamental concept in both RL and OC is the Bellman equation covered in Section 9.5, which provides a recursive formulation of the value function dictating the agent or control dynamics. In the context of RL for portfolio optimization, the Bellman equation for the optimal value function $V^*(s)$ can be written as:

$$V^*(s) = \max_{a \in \mathcal{A}} \left\{ R(s, a) + \gamma \mathbb{E}_{s' \sim P(\cdot|s,a)} \left[ V^*(s') \right] \right\}, \tag{10.2}$$

where $R(s,a)$ is the immediate reward, $\gamma$ is the discount factor, and $P(\cdot|s,a)$ is the transition probability function.

In OC, the analogous Hamilton-Jacobi-Bellman equation for a continuous-time system is (see Section 8.3):

$$-\frac{\partial V}{\partial t}(t,s) = \max_{u \in \mathcal{U}} \{f(t,s,u) \cdot \nabla_s V(t,s) + L(t,s,u)\} \tag{10.3}$$

$$\text{subject to} \quad \frac{ds}{dt} = f(t,s,u), \tag{10.4}$$

where $V(t,s)$ is the value function, $f(t,s,u)$ describes the system dynamics, and $L(t,s,u)$ is the running cost.

### 10.1.1 Policy Iteration

Policy iteration is a fundamental approach in RL for discovering the optimal policy in a given environment. This method operates on the principle of iterative refinement, alternating between policy evaluation and policy improvement steps until convergence to the optimal policy is achieved.

Let us consider a policy $\pi : \mathcal{S} \to \mathcal{A}$ that assigns an action to each state. For any state $s$, the action $\pi(s)$ will be chosen whenever the system is in state $s$. The policy iteration algorithm begins with an arbitrary initial policy, and then proceeds through a series of evaluation and improvement cycles.

The first step in each iteration is policy evaluation. Here, we calculate the value function $V_\pi(s)$ for all states $s \in \mathcal{S}$ under the current policy $\pi$. This value function represents the expected cumulative discounted reward when starting from state $s$ and following policy $\pi$ thereafter. It is defined by the Bellman expectation equation:

$$V_\pi(s) = \mathbb{E}\left[R\left(s,\pi(s),s'\right) + \gamma V_\pi(s')\right], \tag{10.5}$$

where $R\left(s,\pi(s),s'\right)$ is the immediate reward received when transitioning from state $s$ to $s'$ under action $\pi(s)$, and $\gamma$ is the discount factor for future rewards.

Following the evaluation step, we proceed to policy improvement. In this phase, we seek to find a better action for each state by considering all actions and selecting the one that maximizes the expected sum of the immediate reward and the discounted value of the resulting state. This yields a new policy $\pi'$, defined as:

$$\pi'(s) = \arg\max_{a \in \mathcal{A}} \mathbb{E}\left[R\left(s,a,s'\right) + \gamma V_\pi(s')\right]. \tag{10.6}$$

This process of alternating between evaluation and improvement continues until the value function converges to the optimal value function, at which point we have found the optimal policy. The power of policy iteration lies in its ability to systematically explore the state-action space while exploiting known good strategies, gradually refining the policy until optimality is achieved.

In practice, policy iteration can be highly effective for problems with manageable state and action spaces. However, for large-scale problems, approximate methods or variants like value iteration may be employed to balance computational efficiency with the quality of the resulting policy.

In policy iteration, determining convergence to the optimal policy is a key consideration. The process of alternating between policy evaluation and policy improvement continues until we reach a point where further iterations do not yield any improvements. However, in practice, there are several ways to assess convergence.

One common approach is to monitor the changes in the value function between iterations. We can consider the algorithm to have converged when the maximum change in the value function falls below a small threshold $\epsilon$:

$$\max_{s \in \mathcal{S}} |V_{\pi_{k+1}}(s) - V_{\pi_k}(s)| < \epsilon, \tag{10.7}$$

where $V_{\pi_k}(s)$ is the value function for the policy at iteration $k$.

Another indicator of convergence is when the policy itself stops changing between iterations. If $\pi_{k+1}(s) = \pi_k(s)$ for all states $s \in \mathcal{S}$, we have reached a fixed point in the policy space. Theoretically, this fixed point is guaranteed to be the optimal policy.

A more rigorous check for optimality is to verify if the current value function satisfies the Bellman optimality equation for all states:

$$V_\pi(s) = \max_{a \in \mathcal{A}} \left\{ R(s,a) + \gamma \sum_{s' \in \mathcal{S}} P(s'|s,a) V_\pi(s') \right\} \quad \forall s \in \mathcal{S}. \tag{10.8}$$

If this equation holds for all states, then the current policy is optimal.

It is important to note that policy iteration is guaranteed to converge to the optimal policy in a finite number of iterations for finite MDPs. This is because:

1. The policy evaluation step always converges to the true value function for the current policy.
2. The policy improvement step always yields a strictly better policy unless the current policy is already optimal.
3. There are only a finite number of deterministic policies in a finite MDP.

Therefore, the algorithm must eventually reach a point where no further improvements are possible, which corresponds to the optimal policy.

In practice, exact convergence may not be necessary or computationally feasible, especially for large state spaces. Often, we use approximation methods:

- **Truncated policy evaluation:** Instead of running policy evaluation to convergence, we might perform only a fixed number of iterations.
- **Approximate dynamic programming:** For continuous state spaces, we might use function approximation methods to represent the value function.

In these cases, convergence criteria are often based on the stability of the approximate value function or policy, or on performance metrics specific to the problem domain. For portfolio optimization applications, convergence might also be assessed based on the stability of key financial metrics, such as expected returns, risk measures, or the Sharpe ratio of the resulting investment strategy.

### 10.1.2 Value Iteration

Value iteration is another fundamental algorithm in reinforcement learning for finding the optimal policy in an MDP. Unlike policy iteration, which maintains an explicit policy at each step, value iteration focuses on directly computing the optimal value function from which an optimal policy can be derived.

The core idea of value iteration is to iteratively refine the estimate of the optimal value function $V^*(s)$ for all states $s \in \mathcal{S}$. This optimal value function represents the maximum expected cumulative discounted reward that can be achieved starting from state $s$ and following the best possible policy thereafter.

The algorithm begins with an arbitrary initialization of the value function $V_0(s)$ for all states. Then, at each iteration $k$, we update the value function for each state according to the Bellman optimality equation:

$$V_{k+1}(s) = \max_{a \in \mathcal{A}} \left\{ R(s,a) + \gamma \sum_{s' \in \mathcal{S}} P(s'|s,a) V_k(s') \right\}. \tag{10.9}$$

Here, $R(s,a)$ is the immediate reward for taking action $a$ in state $s$, $\gamma$ is the discount factor, and $P(s'|s,a)$ is the probability of transitioning to state $s'$ when taking action $a$ in state $s$.

This update rule encapsulates the principle of dynamic programming, where we consider all actions and subsequent states, choosing the action that maximizes the sum of immediate reward and discounted future value. As the iterations progress, the value function gradually converges to the optimal value function $V^*(s)$.

The convergence of value iteration is guaranteed under certain conditions, typically when the discount factor $\gamma < 1$ or when the MDP has a proper termination condition. In practice, we often terminate the algorithm when the maximum change in the value function between iterations falls below a specified threshold $\epsilon$:

$$\max_{s \in \mathcal{S}} |V_{k+1}(s) - V_k(s)| < \epsilon. \tag{10.10}$$

Once the value function has converged (or the change is sufficiently small), we can extract the optimal policy $\pi^*(s)$ by choosing the action that maximizes the expected value at each state:

$$\pi^*(s) = \arg\max_{a \in \mathcal{A}} \left\{ R(s,a) + \gamma \sum_{s' \in \mathcal{S}} P(s'|s,a) V^*(s') \right\}. \tag{10.11}$$

Value iteration is particularly effective in scenarios where the state transition probabilities and reward function are known. It can converge faster than policy iteration in some cases, especially when starting from a poor initial policy. However, for large state spaces, approximate methods or more advanced techniques like Q-learning may be necessary to manage the computational complexity.

In the context of RL for portfolio optimization, value iteration can be applied to find optimal investment strategies by modeling market states, potential actions (such as buy, sell, or hold decisions), and defining appropriate reward functions based on financial metrics like returns or risk-adjusted performance measures.

### 10.1.3 Continuous vs. Discrete Formulations

While OC traditionally deals with continuous state and action spaces, and RL often operates in discrete spaces, both fields have developed methods for handling both cases:

- **Continuous RL**: Techniques that manage continuous action spaces include:
  - **Deep Deterministic Policy Gradient (DDPG)**: An actor-critic algorithm that combines deep learning with deterministic policy gradients. It uses two neural networks (an actor and a critic) to learn policies in continuous action spaces, making it suitable for complex control tasks.
  - **Soft Actor-Critic (SAC)**: A maximum entropy RL algorithm that balances exploration and exploitation by optimizing a trade-off

between expected return and entropy. SAC is known for its sample efficiency and stability in continuous control tasks.
  - **Proximal Policy Optimization (PPO):** A policy gradient method that uses clipped probability ratios to ensure stable learning. PPO is known for its simplicity and good performance across a wide range of continuous control tasks.
  - **Twin-delayed Deep Deterministic Policy Gradient (TD3):** An extension of DDPG that addresses function approximation error in actor-critic methods. It uses two critics to reduce overestimation bias and delayed policy updates to improve stability.
- **Discrete OC:** Methods that manage discrete state or action spaces include:
  - **Discrete-time optimal control:** Formulates the control problem in discrete time steps, often using dynamic programming approaches like value iteration or policy iteration.
  - **Switched systems:** Deals with hybrid systems, that is, systems that can switch between different discrete modes, each with its own continuous dynamics. This is particularly relevant for portfolio optimization with distinct market regimes.

For portfolio optimization, this flexibility allows for modeling both discrete trading decisions (e.g., buy/sell/hold) and continuous allocation choices. Continuous RL methods can be applied to determine optimal portfolio weights or trading volumes, while discrete formulations can be used for making binary trading decisions or selecting from a finite set of investment strategies.

The choice between continuous and discrete formulations often depends on the specific requirements of the portfolio optimization problem, such as the granularity of trading decisions, the nature of the assets being traded, and computational considerations. Hybrid approaches that combine elements of both continuous and discrete methods are also possible, potentially offering the best of both worlds for complex portfolio optimization tasks.

**Implications for Portfolio Optimization** The connections between RL and OC offer several advantages for portfolio optimization:

1. **Theoretical Foundations:** OC provides a rigorous mathematical framework that can enhance the theoretical understanding of RL algorithms in financial contexts.

2. **Algorithm Design:** Insights from OC can inspire new RL algorithms tailored for portfolio management tasks.
3. **Interpretability:** The control-theoretic perspective can aid in interpreting and explaining RL-based trading strategies to stakeholders.
4. **Hybrid Approaches:** Combining RL's model-free learning capabilities with OC's model-based techniques can lead to powerful hybrid methods for portfolio optimization.

By leveraging these connections, researchers and practitioners can develop more sophisticated, robust, and theoretically grounded approaches to reinforcement learning in quantitative portfolio optimization.

## 10.2 THE ENVIRONMENT AND THE REWARD FUNCTION

In the context of reinforcement learning for portfolio optimization, the environment and reward function are crucial components that define the problem space and objectives. This section delves into these elements, highlighting their importance and specific considerations for financial applications. We begin by examining the environment in detail, breaking down its key components and characteristics that are essential for modeling the complexities of financial markets.

### 10.2.1 The Environment

The environment in reinforcement learning for portfolio optimization represents the financial market and all relevant factors that influence investment decisions. It encapsulates the dynamics, constraints, and information available to the agent, here the portfolio manager, at each time step. To formalize this concept, we begin by defining the state space, which comprises all the information the agent needs to make informed decisions.

**State Space** The state space $\mathcal{S}$ is defined by:

- **Asset Prices:** A vector $p_t = \left(p_t^1, \ldots, p_t^n\right)$ representing the prices of $n$ assets at time $t$.
- **Portfolio Holdings:** A vector $h_t = \left(h_t^1, \ldots, h_t^n\right)$ indicating the quantity of each asset held at time $t$.
- **Cash Position:** The amount of cash $c_t$ available for trading at time $t$.

- **Market Indicators:** Various financial and economic indicators such as volatility indices, interest rates, and macroeconomic factors.
- **Technical Indicators:** Derived features like moving averages, relative strength index (RSI), etc.
- **Time:** The current time step or date, which can be important for capturing temporal dependencies.

Formally, we can define the state at time $t$ as:

$$s_t = (p_t, h_t, c_t, m_t, i_t, t) \in \mathcal{S}, \tag{10.12}$$

where $m_t$ represents market indicators and $i_t$ represents technical indicators.

**Action Space** The action space $\mathcal{A}$ defines the set of trading decisions. It can be formulated in many ways:

- **Continuous Actions:** A vector $a_t = \left(a_t^1, \ldots, a_t^n\right) \in \mathbb{R}^n$ representing the target portfolio weights or the amount of each asset to buy/sell.
- **Discrete Actions:** A set of predefined actions such as {buy, sell, hold} for each asset, or a discretized version of portfolio weights.

**Transition Dynamics** The transition from one state to another is governed by both the agent's actions and the inherent market dynamics. The transition function $P\left(s_{t+1} | s_t, a_t\right)$ governs these dynamics, which are typically stochastic due to market uncertainties. For example, the evolution of asset prices might be modeled as a stochastic process:

$$p_{t+1}^i = p_t^i \exp\left(\mu_i \Delta t + \sigma_i \sqrt{\Delta t} \epsilon_t^i\right), \tag{10.13}$$

where $\mu_i$ is the drift, $\sigma_i$ is the volatility, $\Delta t$ is the time step, and $\epsilon_t^i \sim \mathcal{N}(0, 1)$ is a standard normal random variable.

**Constraints and Friction** Real-world portfolio optimization often involves various constraints and frictions that need to be incorporated into the environment. These elements are crucial for creating realistic and practical RL models for financial applications.

Transaction costs, TC, are typically modeled as a function of the trading volume. A common formulation is:

$$\text{TC}\left(a_t\right) = \sum_{i=1}^{n} \kappa_i \left|a_t^i\right|, \tag{10.14}$$

where $\kappa_i$ is the transaction cost rate for asset $i$, and $a_t^i$ represents the trading action (i.e., buy/sell volume) for asset $i$ at time $t$. More sophisticated models might include both fixed and variable components:

$$\mathrm{TC}(a_t) = \sum_{i=1}^{n} \left( \phi_i \mathbb{I}_{a_t^i \neq 0} + \kappa_i \left|a_t^i\right| + \eta_i \left(a_t^i\right)^2 \right), \tag{10.15}$$

where $\phi_i$ is a fixed cost, $\mathbb{I}_{a_t^i \neq 0}$ is an indicator function for non-zero trades, and $\eta_i(a_t^i)^2$ represents a quadratic term to model increasing marginal costs for larger trades. For example, if $\kappa_i = 0.1\%$, a trade of \$10,000 in asset $i$ would incur a cost of \$10.

Large trades can affect asset prices, a phenomenon known as market impact (MI). This is often modeled as a function of trade size and market liquidity. A simple linear model might be:

$$\mathrm{MI}\left(a_t^i\right) = \lambda_i \frac{a_t^i}{\mathrm{ADV}_i}, \tag{10.16}$$

where $\lambda_i$ is the market impact factor for asset $i$, and $\mathrm{ADV}_i$ is the average daily volume. More complex models incorporate nonlinear effects and temporal decay:

$$\mathrm{MI}\left(a_t^i, t\right) = \mathrm{sign}\left(a_t^i\right) \cdot \sigma_i \cdot \left( \frac{|a_t^i|}{\mathrm{ADV}_i} \right)^{\alpha} \cdot \left( \frac{T - t + 1}{T} \right)^{\beta}, \tag{10.17}$$

where $\sigma_i$ is the volatility of asset $i$, $\alpha$ and $\beta$ are model parameters, and $T$ is the total execution time. For instance, if $\lambda_i = 0.1$ and $ADV_i = \$1,000,000$, a trade of \$100,000 would cause a price impact of a unit basis point.

Position limits constrain the maximum allowed position in each asset, often expressed as:

$$\left|h_t^i\right| \leq L_i \quad \forall i, t, \tag{10.18}$$

where $h_t^i$ is the holding of asset $i$ at time $t$, and $L_i$ is the position limit for asset $i$. These limits can be absolute values or relative to some benchmark:

$$\left| \frac{h_t^i}{\mathrm{NAV}_t} - w_i^b \right| \leq \delta_i \quad \forall i, t, \tag{10.19}$$

where $\mathrm{NAV}_t$ is the net asset value at time $t$, $w_i^b$ is the benchmark weight for asset $i$, and $\delta_i$ is the allowed deviation. For example, if the benchmark weight for an asset is 5% and $\delta_i = 2\%$, the portfolio weight for that asset must be between 3% and 7%.

Risk constraints impose limits on various portfolio risk measures. For instance, a constraint on portfolio volatility might be:

$$\sqrt{w_t^T \Sigma_t w_t} \leq \sigma_{max}, \tag{10.20}$$

where $w_t$ is the vector of portfolio weights at time $t$, $\Sigma_t$ is the covariance matrix of asset returns, and $\sigma_{max}$ is the maximum allowed portfolio volatility. Similarly, a Value-at-Risk (VaR) constraint could be formulated as:

$$P\left(r_p \leq -\text{VaR}_\alpha\right) \leq \alpha, \tag{10.21}$$

where $r_p$ is the portfolio return, $\text{VaR}_\alpha$ is the Value-at-Risk at confidence level $1-\alpha$. In practice, this might be implemented as a constraint on the historical VaR:

$$\text{VaR}_\alpha\left(w_t\right) = -w_t^T \mu - z_\alpha \sqrt{w_t^T \Sigma_t w_t} \leq VaR_{max}, \tag{10.22}$$

where $\mu$ is the vector of expected returns, $z_\alpha$ is the $z$–score for the chosen confidence level, and $\text{VaR}_{max}$ is the maximum allowed VaR. For instance, with a 99% confidence level ($z$–score $\simeq$ 2.33) and $\text{VaR}_{max}$ = 5%, the portfolio would be constrained to have no more than a 5% loss at the 99th percentile of the return distribution.

In many real-world scenarios, the true state of the environment is not fully observable. This leads to a partially observable Markov decision process formulation, where the agent must make decisions based on incomplete information. Techniques such as recurrent neural networks or attention mechanisms can be employed to manage partial observability in the RL framework.

Financial markets involve multiple actors, and their interactions can significantly impact market dynamics. While single-agent RL is more common in portfolio optimization, multi-agent reinforcement learning (MARL) approaches are gaining attention for modeling complex market ecosystems and strategic interactions between traders.

By carefully designing the environment to capture these various aspects of financial markets, we create a rich and realistic setting for the RL agent to learn effective portfolio optimization strategies.

### 10.2.2 The Reward Function

The reward function is a crucial component in reinforcement learning (RL) for portfolio optimization, as it directly shapes the agent's behavior and defines the optimization objective. In financial contexts, the reward function typically reflects investment goals, risk preferences, and other relevant performance metrics.

In its most general form, the reward function $R : \mathcal{S} \times \mathcal{A} \times \mathcal{S} \rightarrow \mathbb{R}$ maps a state-action-next state tuple to a scalar reward value. For portfolio optimization, we can express this as:

$$R\left(s_t, a_t, s_{t+1}\right) = f(p_t, p_{t+1}, w_t, w_{t+1}, \text{other factors}), \tag{10.23}$$

where $p_t$ and $p_{t+1}$ are vectors of asset prices, and $w_t$ and $w_{t+1}$ are portfolio weights before and after the action $a_t$. Other factors may include transaction costs, risk measures, or external market indicators.

Several reward formulations are commonly used in RL for portfolio optimization:

1. **Portfolio Returns:** The simplest reward function is based on the portfolio's return over the time step:

$$R_t = \sum_{i=1}^{n} w_{t,i} \frac{p_{t+1,i} - p_{t,i}}{p_{t,i}} - \text{TC}\left(a_t\right), \tag{10.24}$$

where $n$ is the number of assets, $w_{t,i}$ is the weight of asset $i$ at time $t$, and $\text{TC}\left(a_t\right)$ represents transaction costs.

2. **Sharpe Ratio:** To balance return and risk, the reward can be based on the Sharpe ratio:

$$R_t = \frac{\mathbb{E}\left[r_p\right] - r_f}{\sigma_p}, \tag{10.25}$$

where $\mathbb{E}\left[r_p\right]$ is the expected portfolio return, $r_f$ is the risk-free rate, and $\sigma_p$ is the portfolio volatility. In practice, this is often calculated over a rolling window.

3. **Sortino Ratio:** Similar to the Sharpe ratio, but penalizing only downside volatility:

$$R_t = \frac{\mathbb{E}\left[r_p\right] - r_f}{\sigma_d}, \tag{10.26}$$

where $\sigma_d$ is the downside deviation.

4. **Maximum Drawdown:** To manage risk, the reward can incorporate the maximum drawdown:

$$R_t = r_t - \lambda \cdot \text{MDD}_t, \tag{10.27}$$

where $r_t$ is the portfolio return, $\text{MDD}_t$ is the maximum drawdown up to time $t$, and $\lambda$ is a risk aversion parameter.

5. **Multi-objective Reward:** Combining multiple objectives:

$$R_t = w_1 \cdot \text{Return}_t + w_2 \cdot \text{Risk}_t + w_3 \cdot \text{Turnover}_t + w_4 \cdot \text{Diversity}_t, \quad (10.28)$$

where $w_i$ are weights for different objectives.

**Considerations in Reward Design** When designing reward functions for RL in portfolio optimization, several factors should be considered:

1. **Time Horizon:** The reward should align with the investment horizon. Short-term rewards may lead to myopic strategies, while long-term rewards can better capture long-term investment goals.
2. **Risk Adjustment:** Pure return-based rewards may lead to excessive risk-taking. Incorporating risk measures helps in developing more balanced strategies.
3. **Transaction Costs:** Including transaction costs in the reward function encourages the development of strategies that balance returns with trading efficiency.
4. **Constraints:** While hard constraints are typically managed in the action space, soft constraints can be incorporated into the reward function as penalties.
5. **Benchmarking:** For relative return strategies, the reward can be defined relative to a benchmark index.
6. **Stability:** The reward function should promote stable strategies, possibly by penalizing large shifts in portfolio composition.

**Challenges in Reward Function Design** Designing an effective reward function for portfolio optimization presents several challenges:

1. **Delayed Consequences:** Financial decisions often have long-term impacts that are not immediately reflected in short-term rewards.
2. **Noise:** Financial markets are inherently noisy, making it difficult to attribute outcomes solely to the agent's actions.
3. **Nonstationarity:** Market dynamics change over time, potentially requiring adaptive reward functions.
4. **Interpretability:** Complex reward functions may lead to strategies that are difficult to interpret or explain to stakeholders.

The choice and design of the reward function significantly impacts the behavior and performance of the RL agent in portfolio optimization.

Careful consideration of financial objectives, risk preferences, and practical constraints, for example, transaction costs, is essential for developing effective and robust investment strategies through reinforcement learning.

## 10.3 AGENTS ACTING IN AN ENVIRONMENT

In the context of reinforcement learning for portfolio optimization, an agent represents the decision-making entity that interacts with the financial market environment. This interaction forms the core of the learning process, where the agent aims to develop an optimal investment strategy over time.

The interaction between the agent and the environment can be described as a continuous loop:

$$s_t \xrightarrow{\text{Agent}} a_t \xrightarrow{\text{Environment}} r_t, s_{t+1} \xrightarrow{\text{Agent}} a_{t+1} \xrightarrow{\text{Environment}} \cdots, \tag{10.29}$$

where $s_t$ is the state at time $t$, $a_t$ is the action taken by the agent, $r_t$ is the reward received, and $s_{t+1}$ is the next state.

**Agent Architecture** The agent's architecture typically consists of several components:

1. **Policy $\pi(a|s)$:** This is the core of the agent, defining the probability of taking action $a$ in state $s$. In portfolio optimization, this could be a function that determines asset allocation based on market conditions:

$$\pi_\theta(a|s) = P(a_t = a|s_t = s, \theta), \tag{10.30}$$

where $\theta$ represents the parameters of the policy (e.g., weights in a neural network).

2. **Value Function $V(s)$ or Action-Value Function $Q(s,a)$:** These functions estimate the expected cumulative reward from a given state or state-action pair:

$$V_\pi(s) = \mathbb{E}_\pi\left[\sum_{k=0}^{\infty} \gamma^k r_{t+k} | s_t = s\right] \tag{10.31}$$

$$Q_\pi(s,a) = \mathbb{E}_\pi\left[\sum_{k=0}^{\infty} \gamma^k r_{t+k} | s_t = s, a_t = a\right]. \tag{10.32}$$

3. **Model (optional):** Some agents maintain an internal model of the environment, predicting state transitions and rewards:

$$\widehat{P}\left(s_{t+1}|s_t, a_t\right), \widehat{R}\left(s_t, a_t, s_{t+1}\right). \tag{10.33}$$

**Types of Agents** Different types of agents can be employed in portfolio optimization:

1. **Value-Based Agents:** These agents learn the optimal action-value function $Q^*(s, a)$ and derive the policy from it. Examples include Q-learning and DQN (Deep Q-Network):

$$\pi(s) = \arg\max_a Q^*(s, a). \tag{10.34}$$

2. **Policy-Based Agents:** These agents directly learn the policy $\pi_\theta(a|s)$. Examples include REINFORCE and PPO (Proximal Policy Optimization):

$$\nabla_\theta J(\theta) = \mathbb{E}_{\pi_\theta}\left[\nabla_\theta \log \pi_\theta(a|s)\, Q_{\pi_\theta}(s, a)\right]. \tag{10.35}$$

3. **Actor-Critic Agents:** These combine value-based and policy-based approaches, learning both a policy (actor) and a value function (critic). Examples include Advantage Actor-Critic (A2C) and Deep Deterministic Policy Gradient (DDPG).

In the context of portfolio optimization, the agent's behavior manifests in several key aspects:

1. **Asset Allocation:** The agent decides how to distribute capital across different assets:

$$w_t = f_\theta(s_t), \tag{10.36}$$

where $w_t$ is the vector of portfolio weights and $f_\theta$ is the agent's decision function.

2. **Risk Management:** The agent learns to balance return and risk, potentially incorporating various risk measures:

$$\text{Risk}_t = g\left(w_t, \Sigma_t\right), \tag{10.37}$$

where $\Sigma_t$ is the covariance matrix of asset returns.

3. **Trading Execution:** The agent determines the timing and size of trades, considering transaction costs:

$$\Delta w_t = h_\theta\left(s_t, w_{t-1}\right), \tag{10.38}$$

where $\Delta w_t$ represents the changes in portfolio weights.

4. **Adaptation to Market Regimes:** The agent learns to recognize and adapt to different market conditions:

$$\pi_\theta\left(a|s\right) = \sum_{i=1}^{K} \alpha_i\left(s\right)\pi_i\left(a|s\right), \tag{10.39}$$

where $\pi_i$ represents sub-policies for different regimes and $\alpha_i(s)$ are state-dependent mixing coefficients.

Designing effective agents for portfolio optimization presents several challenges, such as:

1. **Partial Observability:** Financial markets are often partially observable, requiring agents to infer hidden states or work with incomplete information.
2. **Nonstationarity:** Market dynamics change over time, necessitating agents that can adapt to evolving environments.
3. **Exploration-Exploitation Trade-off:** Balancing the need to explore new strategies with exploiting known profitable strategies is crucial in financial markets.
4. **Sample Efficiency:** Financial data is often limited and expensive, requiring agents that can learn efficiently from limited samples.
5. **Interpretability:** In many financial applications, it is important for the agent's decisions to be interpretable and explainable.

The design of RL agents for portfolio optimization should weigh these factors to create robust, adaptive, and effective investment strategies. The choice of agent architecture, learning algorithm, and behavioral characteristics has a high impact on the performance and reliability of the resulting portfolio management system.

## 10.4 STATE-ACTION AND VALUE FUNCTIONS

In reinforcement learning for portfolio optimization, state-action and value functions play a central part in quantifying the expected performance of strategies and guiding the decision-making process. This section provides a detailed examination of these functions, their properties, and their signifi cance in the context of financial applications. Next, the value function is defined along with some of its properties laid out.

### 10.4.1 Value Functions

The value function $V^{\pi}(s)$ represents the expected return when starting in state $s$ and following policy $\pi$ thereafter. In the context of portfolio optimization, it can be interpreted as the expected cumulative portfolio value or return from a given market state.

For a policy $\pi$, the value function is defined as:

$$V^{\pi}(s) = \mathbb{E}_{\pi}\left[\sum_{k=0}^{\infty} \gamma^k R_{t+k+1} \middle| S_t = s\right], \tag{10.40}$$

where $\gamma \in [0, 1]$ is the discount factor, and $R_t$ is the reward at time $t$.

Importantly, the value function satisfies the Bellman expectation equation:

$$V^{\pi}(s) = \sum_{a} \pi(a|s) \sum_{s',r} p(s', r|s, a)\left[r + \gamma V^{\pi}(s')\right], \tag{10.41}$$

where $p(s', r|s, a)$ is the probability of transitioning to state $s'$ and receiving reward $r$ when taking action $a$ in state $s$.

The optimal value function $V^*(s)$ is defined as:

$$V^*(s) = \max_{\pi} V^{\pi}(s). \tag{10.42}$$

$V^*$, the optimal value functions, satisfies the Bellman optimality equation:

$$V^*(s) = \max_{a} \sum_{s',r} p(s', r|s, a)\left[r + \gamma V^*(s')\right]. \tag{10.43}$$

**Action-Value Functions** The action-value function $Q^{\pi}(s, a)$ represents the expected return starting from state $s$, taking action $a$, and thereafter following policy $\pi$.

For a policy $\pi$, the action-value function is defined as:

$$Q^{\pi}(s, a) = \mathbb{E}_{\pi}\left[\sum_{k=0}^{\infty} \gamma^k R_{t+k+1} \middle| S_t = s, A_t = a\right]. \tag{10.44}$$

The action-value function satisfies:

$$Q^{\pi}(s,a) = \sum_{s',r} p(s',r|s,a)\left[r + \gamma \sum_{a'} \pi(a'|s')Q^{\pi}(s',a')\right]. \tag{10.45}$$

The optimal action-value function $Q^{*}(s,a)$ is defined as:

$$Q^{*}(s,a) = \max_{\pi} Q^{\pi}(s,a). \tag{10.46}$$

It satisfies the Bellman optimality equation for Q-values:

$$Q^{*}(s,a) = \sum_{s',r} p(s',r|s,a)\left[r + \gamma \max_{a'} Q^{*}(s',a')\right]. \tag{10.47}$$

The value and action-value functions are closely related:

$$V^{\pi}(s) = \sum_{a} \pi(a|s)Q^{\pi}(s,a) \tag{10.48}$$

$$Q^{\pi}(s,a) = \sum_{s',r} p(s',r|s,a)\left[r + \gamma V^{\pi}(s')\right]. \tag{10.49}$$

For optimal functions:

$$V^{*}(s) = \max_{a} Q^{*}(s,a). \tag{10.50}$$

That is, an agent might learn $Q^{*}(s,a)$ through experience, and they take the actions that maximize the value when in a particular state $s$.

### 10.4.2 Gradients and Policy Improvement

The concept of policy gradient is central to many reinforcement learning algorithms, particularly in continuous action spaces common in portfolio optimization. The policy gradient theorem provides a framework for directly optimizing the policy without explicitly computing the value function.

**Policy Gradient Theorem** The policy gradient theorem states that the gradient of the expected return with respect to the policy parameters $\theta$ is:

$$\nabla_{\theta} J(\theta) = \mathbb{E}_{\pi_{\theta}}\left[\sum_{t=0}^{\infty} \Psi_t \nabla_{\theta} \log \pi_{\theta}(A_t|S_t)\right], \tag{10.51}$$

where $\Psi_t$ is a placeholder for different advantage estimators. This theorem forms the basis for various policy gradient algorithms, each differing in how they estimate the advantage function.

### Common Policy Gradient Algorithms

1. **REINFORCE:** This algorithm uses $Q^\pi(S_t, A_t)$ as the advantage estimator.

$$\Psi_t = \sum_{k=t}^{\infty} \gamma^{k-t} R_k. \tag{10.52}$$

REINFORCE is simple but often suffers from high variance in gradient estimates.

2. **Advantage Actor-Critic (A2C):** Uses $A^\pi(S_t, A_t) = Q^\pi(S_t, A_t) - V^\pi(S_t)$ as the advantage estimator.

$$\Psi_t = R_t + \gamma V^\pi(S_{t+1}) - V^\pi(S_t). \tag{10.53}$$

A2C reduces variance compared to REINFORCE by subtracting a baseline (the value function).

3. **Temporal Difference Error:** Uses the TD error $\delta_t = R_{t+1} + \gamma V^\pi(S_{t+1}) - V^\pi(S_t)$ as the advantage estimator.

$$\Psi_t = \delta_t. \tag{10.54}$$

This approach is often used in actor-critic methods and can be seen as a special case of A2C.

In portfolio optimization, the state space could include current portfolio weights, market indicators, and other relevant financial data. The action space typically represents portfolio rebalancing decisions, for example, changes in asset weights. The reward function is often based on portfolio returns, possibly adjusted for risk or transaction costs. The policy is a parameterized function that maps states to probability distributions over actions. In continuous action spaces, this is often modeled as a Gaussian distribution with mean given by a neural network.

When applying policy gradient methods to portfolio optimization, there are several challenges and considerations to bear in mind:

1. **Sample Efficiency:** Financial markets often have low signal-to-noise ratios, requiring substantial amounts of data for reliable gradient estimates.
2. **Non-stationarity:** Market dynamics change over time, potentially invalidating learned policies.
3. **Risk Management:** Standard policy gradient methods optimize for expected returns, which may not adequately account for risk.
4. **Interpretability:** The black-box nature of neural network policies can be a concern in financial applications.

5. **Risk-awareness:** Incorporating risk measures into value functions, for example, using risk-sensitive reinforcement learning approaches.
6. **Multi-period optimization:** Balancing short-term and long-term objectives in value function formulation.
7. **Constraints:** Handling portfolio constraints within the value function framework, possibly through constrained MDPs or penalty methods.

To address these challenges, researchers have proposed various modifications:

- **Off-policy learning:** Algorithms like Off-Policy Actor-Critic (Off-PAC) can improve sample efficiency by learning from historical data.
- **Meta-learning:** Techniques like Model-Agnostic Meta-Learning (MAML) can help adapt to changing market conditions.
- **Risk-sensitive RL:** Incorporating risk measures into the objective function, for example, using the Conditional Value at Risk (CVaR).
- **Constrained Policy Optimization:** Enforcing constraints on the policy to ensure certain risk or regulatory requirements are met.

By leveraging these advanced techniques, policy gradient methods can be effectively applied to complex portfolio optimization problems, potentially uncovering profitable strategies that traditional methods might lack.

**Function Approximation** In practical portfolio optimization problems, the state space is often continuous and high-dimensional. Function approximation methods are used to estimate value and action-value functions because they enable the agent to generalize from limited experience to larger state spaces of states and actions:

$$\hat{V}(s,\mathbf{w}) \approx V^{\pi}(s), \quad \hat{Q}(s,a,\mathbf{w}) \approx Q^{\pi}(s,a), \tag{10.55}$$

where $\mathbf{w}$ are the parameters of the function approximator, for example, weights in a neural network.

For value function approximation, the gradient descent update rule is:

$$\mathbf{w}_{t+1} = \mathbf{w}_t + \alpha\left[R_{t+1} + \gamma\hat{V}(S_{t+1},\mathbf{w}_t) - \hat{V}(S_t,\mathbf{w}_t)\right]\nabla_{\mathbf{w}}\hat{V}(S_t,\mathbf{w}_t). \tag{10.56}$$

For Q-learning with function approximation:

$$\mathbf{w}_{t+1} = \mathbf{w}_t + \alpha\left[R_{t+1} + \gamma\max_a\left\{\hat{Q}(S_{t+1},a,\mathbf{w}_t) - \hat{Q}(S_t,A_t,\mathbf{w}_t)\right\}\right]$$
$$\nabla_{\mathbf{w}}\hat{Q}(S_t,A_t,\mathbf{w}_t). \tag{10.57}$$

**Convergence and Stability Analysis** The convergence of value function and policy iteration methods is incredibly important in reinforcement learning. For tabular methods with finite state and action spaces, convergence to the optimal value function and policy is guaranteed under certain conditions.

For function approximation methods, convergence guarantees are more challenging. The so-called deadly triad of function approximation, bootstrapping, and off-policy learning can lead to instability and divergence. Techniques to mitigate these issues include experience replay to break temporal correlations, target networks to stabilize bootstrapping, gradient clipping to prevent large updates, and double Q-learning to reduce overestimation bias.

**Considerations for Portfolio Optimization** In portfolio optimization, when considering value functions, it is important to keep in mind the following constraints:

The effective design and estimation of state-action and value functions are crucial for developing robust and efficient reinforcement learning algorithms for portfolio optimization. These functions serve as the foundation for decision-making processes, guiding the learning agent toward optimal investment strategies in complex and dynamic financial markets.

## 10.5 THE POLICY

In the context of reinforcement learning for portfolio optimization, the policy plays a crucial role in determining the agent's behavior. This section provides a rigorous mathematical treatment of policies, including their formulation, gradients, asymptotic properties, optimality conditions, and learning algorithms.

**Policy Definition and Formulation** We define a policy $\pi$ as a function that maps states to actions:

$$\pi : \mathcal{S} \rightarrow \mathcal{A}, \tag{10.58}$$

where $\mathcal{S}$ is the state space (e.g., market conditions, portfolio composition, etc.) and $\mathcal{A}$ is the action space (e.g., trading decisions).

More formally, we express the policy as a probability distribution over actions given a state:

$$\pi(a|s) = P(A_t = a|S_t = s), \tag{10.59}$$

where $A_t$ and $S_t$ are the action and state at time $t$, respectively.

**Policy Gradients** The policy gradient theorem is central to many reinforcement learning algorithms. It provides a way to compute the gradient of the expected return with respect to the policy parameters. Let $J(\theta)$ be the expected return under policy $\pi_\theta$ parameterized by $\theta$. The policy gradient theorem states:

$$\nabla_\theta J(\theta) = \mathbb{E}_{\pi_\theta}\left[\sum_{t=0}^{T} \nabla_\theta \log \pi_\theta (A_t|S_t)\, Q^{\pi_\theta}(S_t, A_t)\right], \tag{10.60}$$

where $Q^{\pi_\theta}(s, a)$ is the action-value function under policy $\pi_\theta$.

**Asymptotic Analysis and Convergence** The convergence of policy gradient methods can be analyzed using stochastic approximation theory. Under certain conditions, policy gradient methods converge to a local optimum (Sutton et al., 2000). The key convergence theorem states:

**Theorem 10.1.** *Given a policy gradient algorithm with update rule:*

$$\theta_{t+1} = \theta_t + \alpha_t \nabla_\theta \log \pi_\theta (A_t|S_t)\, Q^{\pi_\theta}(S_t, A_t). \tag{10.61}$$

*If the following conditions are met:*

1. $\sum_{t=1}^{\infty} \alpha_t = \infty$ *and* $\sum_{t=1}^{\infty} \alpha_t^2 < \infty$.
2. *The policy is differentiable with respect to its parameters.*
3. *The Markov Decision Process is ergodic.*

*Then $\theta_t$ converges to a local optimum of $J(\theta)$ with probability 1.*

A sketch of the proof is as follows:

1. First, we establish that the expected update is in the direction of the policy gradient. From the policy gradient theorem, we have:

$$\nabla J(\theta) = \mathbb{E}_{\pi_\theta}\left[\nabla_\theta \log \pi_\theta (A|S)\, Q^{\pi_\theta}(S, A)\right]. \tag{10.62}$$

2. Our update rule is a sample-based estimate of this expectation:

$$\theta_{t+1} = \theta_t + \alpha_t \nabla_\theta \log \pi_\theta (A_t|S_t)\, Q^{\pi_\theta}(S_t, A_t). \tag{10.63}$$

3. The ergodicity assumption ensures that our samples will, over time, be drawn according to the stationary distribution of the MDP under policy $\pi_\theta$.
4. The differentiability of the policy ensures that $\nabla_\theta \log \pi_\theta (A|S)$ exists and is well-defined.

5. The conditions on the step sizes $\left(\sum_{t=1}^{\infty} \alpha_t = \infty \text{ and } \sum_{t=1}^{\infty} \alpha_t^2 < \infty\right)$ are standard requirements for stochastic approximation algorithms. They ensure that the step sizes are large enough to overcome initial conditions and noise (first condition) but eventually become small enough to ensure convergence (second condition).
6. Given these conditions, we can apply the theory of stochastic approximation, specifically the Robbins-Monro algorithm. This theory states that under these conditions, the algorithm will converge to a local optimum of the objective function with probability 1.
7. In our case, the objective function is $J(\theta)$, the expected return under policy $\pi_\theta$.

Therefore, we can conclude that $\theta_t$ will converge to a local optimum of $J(\theta)$ with probability 1.

Note: This proof sketch assumes that the MDP is finite, and that certain technical conditions (like bounded rewards) hold. A full, rigorous proof would need to address these details explicitly.

**Optimality Conditions** The optimal policy $\pi^*$ satisfies the Bellman optimality equation:

$$V^*(s) = \max_a \left( R(s,a) + \gamma \sum_{s'} P(s'|s,a) V^*(s') \right), \tag{10.64}$$

where $V^*(s)$ is the optimal value function, $R(s,a)$ is the reward function, $\gamma$ is the discount factor, and $P(s'|s,a)$ is the transition probability.

The optimal policy can be derived from the optimal value function:

$$\pi^*(s) = \underset{a}{\operatorname{argmax}} \left( R(s,a) + \gamma \sum_{s'} P(s'|s,a) V^*(s') \right). \tag{10.65}$$

**Policy Learning Algorithms** Several algorithms can be used to learn the optimal policy:

1. Policy Gradient Methods:

$$\theta_{t+1} = \theta_t + \alpha \nabla_\theta J(\theta). \tag{10.66}$$

2. Actor-Critic Methods:

$$\delta_t = R_{t+1} + \gamma V(S_{t+1}) - V(S_t) \tag{10.67}$$

$$\theta_{t+1} = \theta_t + \alpha \nabla_\theta \log \pi_\theta (A_t|S_t) \delta_t. \tag{10.68}$$

3. Proximal Policy Optimization (PPO):

$$L^{\text{CLIP}}(\theta) = \mathbb{E}_t\left[\min\left(r_t(\theta)\hat{A}_t, \text{clip}\left(r_t(\theta), 1-\epsilon, 1+\epsilon\right)\hat{A}_t\right)\right], \tag{10.69}$$

where

$$r_t(\theta) = \frac{\pi_\theta\left(a_t|s_t\right)}{\pi_{\theta_{\text{old}}}\left(a_t|s_t\right)}, \tag{10.70}$$

and $\hat{A}_t$ is the estimated advantage.

These algorithms provide different approaches to learning optimal policies in reinforcement learning for portfolio optimization, each with its own trade-offs in terms of sample efficiency, stability, and convergence properties.

## 10.6 ON-POLICY METHODS

On-policy methods in reinforcement learning are a class of algorithms where the agent learns the value function and improves the policy based on actions taken according to its current policy. These methods are particularly relevant in portfolio optimization due to their stability and the direct relationship between the learned policy and the agent's behavior.

On-policy methods have several key characteristics:

1. They learn about the policy currently being followed.
2. The policy used to make decisions is also being improved.
3. They typically have good convergence properties but may be less sample-efficient than off-policy methods.

The following is a review of key algorithms for on-policy methods.

**SARSA: State-Action-Reward-State-Action** SARSA is a fundamental on-policy algorithm. For portfolio optimization, it can be used to learn the optimal trading strategy while following the current policy.

The update rule for SARSA is:

$$Q\left(S_t, A_t\right) \leftarrow Q\left(S_t, A_t\right) + \alpha\left[R_{t+1} + \gamma Q\left(S_{t+1}, A_{t+1}\right) - Q\left(S_t, A_t\right)\right], \tag{10.71}$$

where:

- $Q\left(S_t, A_t\right)$ is the action-value function.
- $\alpha$ is the learning rate.

- $R_{t+1}$ is the reward (e.g., portfolio return).
- $\gamma$ is the discount factor.

The policy improvement in SARSA typically follows an $\epsilon$-greedy strategy:

$$\pi(a|s) = \begin{cases} 1 - \epsilon + \frac{\epsilon}{|\mathcal{A}|}, & \text{if } a = \text{argmax}_{a'} Q(s, a') \\ \frac{\epsilon}{|\mathcal{A}|}, & \text{otherwise} \end{cases}, \tag{10.72}$$

where $|\mathcal{A}|$ is the size of the action space.

**REINFORCE: Monte Carlo Policy Gradient** REINFORCE is an on-policy algorithm that directly optimizes the policy without learning a value function. It is particularly useful for portfolio optimization problems with continuous action spaces.

The update rule for REINFORCE is:

$$\theta \leftarrow \theta + \alpha G_t \nabla_\theta \ln \pi_\theta (A_t|S_t), \tag{10.73}$$

where:

- $\theta$ are the policy parameters.
- $G_t = \sum_{k=0}^{T-t} \gamma^k R_{t+k+1}$ is the return from time step $t$.
- $\nabla_\theta \ln \pi_\theta (A_t|S_t)$ is the score function (i.e., policy gradient).

**Proximal Policy Optimization (PPO)** PPO is a popular on-policy algorithm that aims to improve the stability of policy optimization. It is particularly effective for high-dimensional portfolio optimization problems.

The objective function for PPO (in its clipped version) is:

$$L^{CLIP}(\theta) = \mathbb{E}_t\left[\min\left(r_t(\theta)\widehat{A}_t, \text{clip}\left(r_t(\theta), 1-\epsilon, 1+\epsilon\right)\widehat{A}_t\right)\right], \tag{10.74}$$

where:

- $r_t(\theta) = \frac{\pi_\theta(A_t|S_t)}{\pi_{\theta_{old}}(A_t|S_t)}$ is the probability ratio.
- $\widehat{A}_t$ is the estimated advantage function.
- $\epsilon$ is a hyperparameter, typically around 0.2.

There are some advantages and challenges to on-policy methods.

Advantages

- **Stability:** On-policy methods tend to be more stable as they do not suffer from the extrapolation errors that can occur in off-policy methods.
- **Simplicity:** The update rules are often simpler and more intuitive.
- **Convergence:** On-policy methods often have stronger theoretical convergence guarantees.

Challenges

- **Sample Efficiency:** On-policy methods may require more samples to converge compared to off-policy methods.
- **Exploration:** Balancing exploration and exploitation can be challenging, especially in the context of financial markets where exploration can be costly.
- **Continuous Action Spaces:** Some on-policy methods struggle with continuous action spaces, which are common in portfolio optimization.

In the context of portfolio optimization, on-policy methods can be applied taking the state space as market conditions, current portfolio weights, or risk factors. Action spaces include portfolio rebalancing decisions, for example, buy, sell, hold for each asset. The reward function is the portfolio return, possibly adjusted for risk or transaction costs. The policy is the probability distribution over rebalancing actions given the current state. The goal is to learn a policy that maximizes the expected cumulative (discounted) portfolio return while managing risk and transaction costs. On-policy methods provide a robust framework for learning optimal trading strategies in dynamic market conditions, making them valuable tools in quantitative portfolio management.

## 10.7 OFF-POLICY METHODS

Off-policy methods in reinforcement learning involve learning the value function or policy using data generated by some other policy. This distinction allows for greater flexibility and efficiency in learning, particularly when exploration and exploitation need to be balanced optimally.

Off-policy methods have several distinct characteristics:

1. They can learn about one policy while following another.
2. Off-policy methods are typically more sample-efficient than on-policy methods.

3. They allow for the reuse of data collected from different policies or even from different tasks.

The following discusses key algorithms for off-policy methods.

**Q-Learning** Q-Learning is a foundational off-policy algorithm. It learns the optimal action-value function independently of the policy being followed. This property is particularly useful in portfolio optimization where the agent can learn optimal trading strategies from historical market data.

The update rule for Q-Learning is:

$$Q(S_t, A_t) \leftarrow Q(S_t, A_t) + \alpha \left[ R_{t+1} + \gamma \max_{a'} Q(S_{t+1}, a') - Q(S_t, A_t) \right], \tag{10.75}$$

where:

- $Q(S_t, A_t)$ is the action-value function.
- $\alpha$ is the learning rate.
- $R_{t+1}$ is the reward (e.g., portfolio return).
- $\gamma$ is the discount factor.

Q-Learning updates are based on the greedy action selection from the next state, which decouples the learning policy from the behavior policy.

**Deep Q-Networks (DQN)** Deep Q-Networks (DQNs) extend Q-Learning to manage high-dimensional state spaces by using neural networks as function approximators. This approach is highly relevant for portfolio optimization with complex state representations, such as historical price data, technical indicators, and macroeconomic variables. The original paper (Mnih et al., 2013) was applied to Q-learning to learn control policies by having an agent play Atari videogames, the data being raw pixels.

The Q-update in DQN is given by:

$$\theta \leftarrow \theta + \alpha \left[ R_{t+1} + \gamma \max_{a'} Q(S_{t+1}, a'; \theta^-) - Q(S_t, A_t; \theta) \right] \nabla_\theta Q(S_t, A_t; \theta), \tag{10.76}$$

where:

- $\theta$ are the parameters of the Q-network.
- $\theta^-$ are the parameters of the target network, updated periodically.

DQN employs experience replay and target networks to stabilize training, both critical for learning effective trading policies in dynamic financial markets.

**Double Q-Learning** Double Q-Learning (Hasselt, 2010) addresses the overestimation bias in Q-Learning by decoupling the action selection from the target value computation. This algorithm can improve the stability and accuracy of learned Q-values in portfolio optimization.

The update rule for Double Q-Learning is:

$$Q(S_t, A_t) \leftarrow Q(S_t, A_t) + \alpha \left[ R_{t+1} + \gamma Q\left( S_{t+1}, \underset{a'}{\operatorname{argmax}}\, Q(S_{t+1}, a'; \theta); \theta^- \right) - Q(S_t, A_t) \right]. \quad (10.77)$$

**Deterministic Policy Gradient (DPG)** Deterministic Policy Gradient (Silver et al., 2014) is an off-policy algorithm suited for continuous action spaces, making it highly applicable for portfolio-rebalancing decisions. DPG directly optimizes a deterministic policy by following the gradient of the expected return.

The policy update in DPG is given by:

$$\nabla_{\theta^\mu} J \approx \mathbb{E}_{s \sim \rho^\beta} \left[ \nabla_a Q\left(s, a | \theta^Q\right) \nabla_{\theta^\mu} \mu\left(s | \theta^\mu\right) \right], \quad (10.78)$$

where $\theta^\mu$ are the policy parameters, $\theta^Q$ are the Q-function parameters, and $\rho^\beta$ is the state distribution under behavior policy $\beta$.

The Deep Deterministic Policy Gradient (DDPG) extends DPG by incorporating deep neural networks, enabling it to scale to high-dimensional state and action spaces. It combines the benefits of DQN and DPG, using a replay buffer and target networks to stabilize training.

The actor and critic updates in DDPG are:

$$\theta^Q \leftarrow \theta^Q + \alpha_Q [R_{t+1} + \gamma Q(S_{t+1}, \mu(S_{t+1} | \theta^{\mu^-}) | \theta^{Q^-}) - Q(S_t, A_t | \theta^Q)] \nabla_{\theta^Q} Q(S_t, A_t | \theta^Q) \quad (10.79)$$

$$\theta^\mu \leftarrow \theta^\mu + \alpha_\mu \mathbb{E}_{s \sim \rho^\beta} \left[ \nabla_a Q\left(s, \mu\left(s | \theta^\mu\right) | \theta^Q\right) \nabla_{\theta^\mu} \mu\left(s | \theta^\mu\right) \right]. \quad (10.80)$$

**Advantage Weighted Regression (AWR)** Advantage Weighted Regression (Peng et al., (2019) is an off-policy actor-critic algorithm that updates the policy by weighted regression, using advantage estimates to reweight sampled actions. This method balances exploration and exploitation, which is essential for effective portfolio optimization.

The policy update rule for AWR is:

$$\theta \leftarrow \underset{\theta}{\operatorname{argmax}} \mathbb{E}_{(s,a)\sim\beta}\left[\exp\left(\frac{1}{\beta}A(s,a)\right)\log\pi_\theta(a|s)\right], \tag{10.81}$$

where:

- $A(s,a)$ is the advantage estimate.
- $\beta$ is a temperature parameter.

**Advantages of Off-policy Methods**

- **Sample Efficiency:** Off-policy methods can be more sample-efficient by reusing past experiences.
- **Exploration:** These methods can learn optimal policies while following an exploratory policy.
- **Flexibility:** Off-policy methods are flexible in terms of data usage and can leverage data from various sources.

**Challenges**

- **Stability:** Off-policy methods can be less stable due to the mismatch between behavior and target policies.
- **Complexity:** Implementing and tuning off-policy algorithms can be complex.
- **Bias-Variance Tradeoff:** Balancing bias and variance in the value function estimates is challenging.

In portfolio optimization, off-policy methods are applied with similar identifications as on-policy methods. The goal is to learn a policy that maximizes the expected cumulative (discounted) portfolio return while managing risk and transaction costs. Off-policy methods are powerful tools for learning trading strategies from historical market data, enabling robust portfolio management in dynamic and uncertain financial environments.

## 10.8 APPLICATIONS TO PORTFOLIO OPTIMIZATION

### 10.8.1 Mean-variance Optimization

Consider a financial market with $n$ assets. Let $\mu \in \mathbb{R}^n$ be the vector of expected returns and $\Sigma \in \mathbb{R}^{n\times n}$ the covariance matrix of returns. The objective is to maximize the mean-variance utility of the portfolio. See Wu and Li (2024) for a similar application of RL to mean-variance optimization, and Jiang et al. (2024) for a deep RL approach to mean-variance portfolio optimization.

**Problem Formulation** The mean-variance optimization problem is formulated as:

$$\pi^* = \max_{\pi \in \mathcal{A}} \left( \pi^T \mu - \frac{\gamma}{2} \pi^T \Sigma \pi \right), \tag{10.82}$$

where $\pi \in \mathbb{R}^n$ is the portfolio allocation vector, $\mathcal{A}$ is the set of admissible portfolios, and $\gamma > 0$ is the risk aversion parameter.

**Reinforcement Learning Approach** Define the state space as $\mathcal{S} = \mathbb{R}^n$ (the portfolio weights) and the action space as $\mathcal{A} = \mathbb{R}^n$ (the changes in portfolio weights). The reward function is given by:

$$r_t = \pi_t^T \mu - \frac{\gamma}{2} \pi_t^T \Sigma \pi_t. \tag{10.83}$$

The agent's goal is to learn a policy $\pi_t = \pi(s_t)$ that maximizes the cumulative reward. Using a Q-learning approach, the Q-function is updated as:

$$Q(s_t, a_t) \leftarrow Q(s_t, a_t) + \alpha \left( r_t + \gamma \max_{a'} Q(s_{t+1}, a') - Q(s_t, a_t) \right), \tag{10.84}$$

where $\alpha$ is the learning rate and $\gamma$ is the discount factor.

### 10.8.2 Reinforcement Learning Comparison with Mean-variance Optimization

This example is a summary of S. Sood and Balch (2023) where the authors present a comparison between deep reinforcement learning strategies and traditional mean-variance optimization. See Table 10.1 for the comparison.

**TABLE 10.1** Performance comparison of DRL and MVO approaches as reported in Sood and Balch (2023).

| Metric | DRL | MVO |
|---|---|---|
| Annual return | 0.1211 | 0.0653 |
| Cumulative returns | 0.1195 | 0.0650 |
| Annual volatility | 0.1249 | 0.1460 |
| Sharpe ratio | 1.1662 | 0.6776 |
| Calmar ratio | 2.3133 | 1.1608 |
| Stability | 0.6234 | 0.4841 |

(*Continued*)

**TABLE 10.1** (*Continued*)

| Metric | DRL | MVO |
|---|---|---|
| Max drawdown | -0.3296 | -0.3303 |
| Omega ratio | 1.2360 | 1.1315 |
| Sortino ratio | 1.7208 | 1.0060 |
| Skew | -0.4063 | -0.3328 |
| Kurtosis | 2.7054 | 2.6801 |
| Tail ratio | 1.0423 | 0.9448 |
| Daily value at risk | -0.0152 | -0.0181 |

This paper compares Deep Reinforcement Learning (DRL) and Mean-Variance Optimization (MVO) for portfolio allocation in the US equities market, focusing on optimizing risk-adjusted returns.

The DRL approach is based on

- Environment: Market replay using S&P 500 sector index data.
- State space: $S_t \in \mathbb{R}^{(n+1)\times T}$, where $n$ is the number of assets, $T = 60$ day lookback

$$S_t = \begin{bmatrix} w_1 & r_{1,t-1} & \cdots & r_{1,t-T+1} \\ \vdots & \vdots & \ddots & \vdots \\ w_n & r_{n,t-1} & \cdots & r_{n,t-T+1} \\ w_c & \text{vol}_{20} & \dfrac{\text{vol}_{20}}{\text{vol}_{60}} & \text{VIX}_t \end{bmatrix},$$

  where $w_i$ are portfolio weights, $r_{i,t}$ are log returns.
- Action space: Portfolio weights $w \in \mathbb{R}^n$, $\sum w_i = 1$, $0 \leq w_i \leq 1$.
- Reward: Differential Sharpe ratio (DSR)

$$D_t = \frac{B_{t-1}\Delta A_t - \frac{1}{2}A_{t-1}\Delta B_t}{\left(B_{t-1} - A_{t-1}^2\right)^{3/2}},$$

  where $A_t$ and $B_t$ are exponential moving averages of returns and squared returns.
- Algorithm: Proximal Policy Optimization (PPO).

In MVO, the estimation a 60-day lookback window was used and covariance estimation leveraged Ledoit-Wolf (Ledoit and Wolf, 2003) shrinkage to maximize Sharpe ratio

$$\max_{w} \frac{\mu^T w - R_f}{\left(w^T \Sigma w\right)^{1/2}},$$

subject to

$$\sum w_i = 1, 0 \leq w_i \leq 1.$$

The DRL approach outperformed MVO in several metrics:

- Higher annual returns (12.11% vs 6.53% )
- Higher Sharpe ratio (1.1662 vs 0.6776)
- Lower portfolio turnover
- More consistent returns across different market regimes

### 10.8.3 G-Learning and GIRL

In Dixon and Halperin (2020), the authors consider a discrete-time process. The investor keeps wealth in $N$ assets, with $\mathbf{x}_t$ being the vector of dollar values of positions in different assets at time $t$, and $\mathbf{u}_t$ being the vector of changes in these positions. The first asset ($n = 1$) is a risk-free bond, and other assets are risky with uncertain returns $\mathbf{r}_t$ whose expected values are $\bar{\mathbf{r}}_t$. The covariance matrix of returns is $\Sigma_r$ of size $(N-1) \times (N-1)$.

The relevant variables are the state variable $\mathbf{x}_t$ (vector of dollar values of positions), the action variable $\mathbf{u}_t$ (vector of changes in positions), and the cash installment $c_t$ (related to $\mathbf{u}_t$ by $\sum_{n=1}^{N} u_{tn} = c_t$).

The one-step reward is defined as

$$R_t\left(\mathbf{x}_t, \mathbf{u}_t\right) = -\sum_{n=1}^{N} u_{tn} - \lambda \mathbb{E}_t\left[\left(\hat{P}_{t+1} - \left(1 + \mathbf{r}_t\right)^T \left(\mathbf{x}_t + \mathbf{u}_t\right)\right)^2\right] - \mathbf{u}_t^T \Omega \mathbf{u}_t, \tag{10.85}$$

where $\hat{P}_{t+1}$ is the target portfolio value at $t+1$, $\lambda$ is a penalty parameter, and $\Omega$ is a transaction cost matrix

The target portfolio is given by:

$$\hat{P}_{t+1} = (1-\rho) B_t + \rho\eta \mathbf{1}^T \mathbf{x}_t, \tag{10.86}$$

where $B_t$ is a benchmark, $\rho$ is a mixing parameter, and $\eta$ is a growth parameter.

The G-function (entropy-regularized Q-function) is

$$G_t^{\pi}\left(\mathbf{x}_t,\mathbf{u}_t\right) = R_t\left(\mathbf{x}_t,\mathbf{u}_t\right) + \gamma \mathbb{E}_{t,\mathrm{u}}\left[F_{t+1}^{\pi}\left(\mathbf{x}_{t+1}\right)\right], \tag{10.87}$$

where $F_t^{\pi}\left(\mathbf{x}_t\right)$ is the free energy function. The optimal policy is given by

$$\pi\left(\mathbf{u}_t|\mathbf{x}_t\right) = \pi_0\left(\mathbf{u}_t|\mathbf{x}_t\right) e^{\beta\left(G_t^{\pi}(\mathbf{x}_t,\mathbf{u}_t)-F_t^{\pi}(\mathbf{x}_t)\right)}, \tag{10.88}$$

where $\pi_0$ is a reference policy and $\beta$ is the inverse temperature parameter.

We assume quadratic forms for the G-function and F-function written as

$$G_t^{\pi}\left(\mathbf{x}_t,\mathbf{u}_t\right) = \mathbf{x}_t^T Q_t^{(xx)}\mathbf{x}_t + \mathbf{u}_t^T Q_t^{(ux)}\mathbf{x}_t + \mathbf{u}_t^T Q_t^{(uu)}\mathbf{u}_t + \mathbf{x}_t^T Q_t^{(x)} + \mathbf{u}_t^T Q_t^{(u)} + Q_t^{(0)} \tag{10.89}$$

and

$$F_t^{\pi}\left(\mathbf{x}_t\right) = \mathbf{x}_t^T F_t^{(xx)}\mathbf{x}_t + \mathbf{x}_t^T F_t^{(x)} + F_t^{(0)} \tag{10.90}$$

The reference policy $\pi_0$ is assumed to be Gaussian and given by

$$\pi_0\left(\mathbf{u}_t|\mathbf{x}_t\right) = \mathcal{N}\left(\bar{\mathbf{u}}_t + \bar{\mathbf{v}}_t\mathbf{x}_t, \Sigma_p\right). \tag{10.91}$$

The optimal policy is also Gaussian:

$$\pi\left(\mathbf{u}_t|\mathbf{x}_t\right) = \mathcal{N}\left(\tilde{\mathbf{u}}_t + \tilde{\mathbf{v}}_t\mathbf{x}_t, \tilde{\Sigma}_p\right), \tag{10.92}$$

where:

$$\tilde{\Sigma}_p^{-1} = \Sigma_p^{-1} - 2\beta Q_t^{(uu)} \tag{10.93}$$

$$\tilde{\mathbf{u}}_t = \tilde{\Sigma}_p\left(\Sigma_p^{-1}\bar{\mathbf{u}}_t + \beta Q_t^{(u)}\right) \tag{10.94}$$

$$\tilde{\mathbf{v}}_t = \tilde{\Sigma}_p\left(\Sigma_p^{-1}\bar{\mathbf{v}}_t + \beta Q_t^{(ux)}\right). \tag{10.95}$$

The algorithm then proceeds backward in time, or backpropagating, updating the G-function and F-function parameters at each step:

$$Q_t^{(xx)} = R_t^{(xx)} + \gamma\left(A_t^T\bar{F}_{t+1}^{(xx)}A_t + \tilde{\Sigma}_r \circ \bar{F}_{t+1}^{(xx)}\right) \tag{10.96}$$

$$Q_t^{(ux)} = R_t^{(ux)} + 2\gamma\left(A_t^T\bar{F}_{t+1}^{(xx)}A_t + \tilde{\Sigma}_r \circ \bar{F}_{t+1}^{(xx)}\right) \tag{10.97}$$

$$Q_t^{(uu)} = R_t^{(uu)} + \gamma\left(A_t^T\bar{F}_{t+1}^{(xx)}A_t + \tilde{\Sigma}_r \circ \bar{F}_{t+1}^{(xx)}\right) - \Omega \tag{10.98}$$

$$Q_t^{(x)} = R_t^{(x)} + \gamma A_t^T\bar{F}_{t+1}^{(x)} \tag{10.99}$$

$$Q_t^{(u)} = R_t^{(u)} + \gamma A_t^T \bar{F}_{t+1}^{(x)} \tag{10.100}$$

$$Q_t^{(0)} = R_t^{(0)} + \gamma F_{t+1}^{(0)}, \tag{10.101}$$

where $A_t = \text{diag}\left(1 + \bar{\mathbf{r}}_t\right)$ and

$$\tilde{\Sigma}_r = \begin{bmatrix} 0 & 0 \\ 0 & \Sigma_r \end{bmatrix}.$$

The F-function parameters are updated by

$$F_t^{(xx)} = Q_t^{(xx)} + \frac{1}{2\beta}\left(U_t^T \overline{\Sigma}_p^{-1} U_t - \bar{\mathbf{v}}_t^T \Sigma_p^{-1} \bar{\mathbf{v}}_t\right) \tag{10.102}$$

$$F_t^{(x)} = Q_t^{(x)} + \frac{1}{\beta}\left(U_t^T \overline{\Sigma}_p^{-1} W_t - \bar{\mathbf{v}}_t^T \Sigma_p^{-1} \bar{\mathbf{u}}_t\right) \tag{10.103}$$

$$F_t^{(0)} = Q_t^{(0)} + \frac{1}{2\beta}\left(W_t^T \overline{\Sigma}_p^{-1} W_t - \bar{\mathbf{u}}_t^T \Sigma_p^{-1} \bar{\mathbf{u}}_t\right) - \frac{1}{2\beta}\left(\log|\Sigma_p| + \log|\overline{\Sigma}_p|\right), \tag{10.104}$$

where

$$U_t = \beta Q_t^{(ux)} + \Sigma_p^{-1} \bar{\mathbf{v}}_t \tag{10.105}$$

$$W_t = \beta Q_t^{(u)} + \Sigma_p^{-1} \bar{\mathbf{u}}_t \tag{10.106}$$

$$\overline{\Sigma}_p = \Sigma_p^{-1} - 2\beta Q_t^{(uu)}. \tag{10.107}$$

The optimal cash contribution $c_t$ is Gaussian distributed with mean:

$$\bar{c}_t = \mathbf{1}^T\left(\bar{\mathbf{u}}_t + \bar{\mathbf{v}}_t \mathbf{x}_t\right). \tag{10.108}$$

This formulation provides a semi-analytical solution to the portfolio optimization problem using G-learning, allowing for efficient computation of optimal policies and cash contributions in a goal-based wealth management framework.

**Summary of Experiments** The authors conducted experiments to evaluate their G-Learner and GIRL algorithms for goal-based wealth management over a 7.5-year investment horizon with quarterly rebalancing. They simulated a portfolio initially worth 1,000 USD, equally allocated among

99 stocks and a risk-free bond, with realistic transaction costs and a compounding benchmark. Asset returns were modeled using a modified CAPM with weak predictability, and 1,000 simulation paths were generated. The G-Learner algorithm, evaluated with arbitrarily chosen parameters, outperformed an equally weighted, never-rebalanced portfolio, achieving superior Sharpe ratios with minimal training time. Subsequently, GIRL was employed to imitate the G-Learner, successfully learning parameters close to the G-Learner's and producing portfolio returns that closely tracked its performance. Although GIRL achieved a slightly lower Sharpe ratio due to small errors in learned parameters, it converged efficiently in about 200 iterations. Based on these results, the authors concluded that the G-Learner algorithm can effectively improve upon a benchmark equally weighted portfolio strategy, even with weak predictability in asset returns, by successfully harvesting the predictive power of the *alpha-model.*

Furthermore, they demonstrated that GIRL can accurately infer the reward function parameters of a G-Learner agent, effectively imitating its behavior. The authors arrived at these conclusions by comparing Sharpe ratios, analyzing the similarity between G-Learner and GIRL portfolio returns, evaluating GIRL's accuracy in learning G-Learner parameters, and demonstrating the computational efficiency of both algorithms. These findings suggest that the proposed algorithms can effectively optimize wealth management strategies and learn from observed behavior, even in the presence of noisy financial data and weak predictability, pointing to potential applications in robot-advising where GIRL could be used to imitate the best human investors.

### 10.8.4 Continuous-time Penalization in Portfolio Optimization

In García-Galicia et al. (2019), the authors introduce a continuous-time reinforcement learning approach for portfolio management, incorporating time penalization. The core of the mathematical framework is built upon a continuous-time Markov decision process (CTMDP) model. In this model, the portfolio problem is characterized by a finite state space $S = s_1, \ldots, s_N$ and a finite action space $A = a_1, \ldots, a_M$. The dynamics of the system are governed by a transition rate matrix $\Lambda = \left[\lambda_{ijk}\right]$, where $\lambda_{ijk}$ represents the transition rate from state $s_i$ to $s_j$ given action $a_k$. The model is completed by a utility function $U : S \times K \rightarrow \mathbb{R}$, defined over the set of admissible state-action pairs $K = (s, a) | s \in S, a \in A(s)$. At the heart of the paper lies the mean-variance portfolio optimization problem, elegantly formulated as:

$$\Phi(c) = E(c) - \frac{\xi}{2} Var(c) \rightarrow \max_{c \in C_{adm}} . \tag{10.109}$$

Here, $c$ represents the portfolio strategy, and $C_{adm}$ denotes the set of admissible strategies. This formulation encapsulates the fundamental trade-off in portfolio management: maximizing expected returns while minimizing variance (risk). The paper's key contribution is its reinforcement learning approach to solving this optimization problem. The approach is built on three main pillars. First, it employs maximum likelihood estimation to estimate the transition rates of the CTMDP:

$$\hat{\lambda}ijk\,(t) = \frac{\eta ijk\,(t)}{Y_{ik}\,(t)}. \tag{10.110}$$

In this equation, $\eta_{ijk}\,(t)$ counts the number of transitions from state $s_i$ to $s_j$ under action $a_k$, while $Y_{ik}\,(t)$ measures the total time spent in state $s_i$ while taking action $a_k$. Secondly, the approach estimates utility values using a similar counting mechanism:

$$\hat{U}ijk\,(t) = \frac{Uijk\,(t)}{\eta_{ijk}\,(t)}. \tag{10.111}$$

Finally, the approach employs a proximal optimization method to compute the optimal policy:

$$c^* = \arg\min_{c \in C_{adm}} \left\{ \frac{\delta_n}{2} |c - c^*|^2_{\text{diag}(\Gamma_1,\ldots,\Gamma_M)} + \gamma_n \left( \Phi\,(c) - \Phi\,(c_n) \right) \right\}. \tag{10.112}$$

This optimization problem balances the desire to maximize the objective function $\Phi\,(c)$ with the need to stay close to the current policy estimate, as reflected in the quadratic penalty term.

**Numerical Experiments** To demonstrate the efficacy of their approach, the authors present a comprehensive numerical example. This example considers a system with eight states and three actions, a complex scenario that allows for meaningful insights. The reinforcement learning algorithm estimates transition probability matrices $\hat{p}j|ik$ for each action, as well as utility matrices $\hat{u}ij1$, $\hat{u}ij2$, and $\hat{u}ij3$. The paper provides a series of illuminating convergence plots that track the evolution of key metrics as the learning process unfolds. These include the convergence of portfolio strategies, expected returns, and variance. Particularly noteworthy is the convergence plot for the objective function $\Phi\,(c)$, which provides a clear visualization of how the algorithm progressively improves its performance over time. The authors also present mean square error plots for both the transition and utility matrices. These plots offer valuable insights into the learning process, showing how the algorithm's estimates of these crucial parameters improve with more data and iterations. Collectively, these numerical results provide strong evidence for the effectiveness of the proposed approach. They demonstrate that the algorithm successfully learns optimal portfolio strategies, while accounting for the complexities introduced by transaction costs and time penalization. This ability to manage such realistic constraints represents a significant advancement in the field of algorithmic portfolio management.

### 10.8.5 Reinforcement Learning for Utility Maximization

Consider a utility maximization problem where the agent aims to maximize the expected utility of terminal wealth. See Rao and Jelvis (2022) for an in-depth treatment of utility-maximizing agents.

The utility function $U(W_T)$ is typically chosen as a concave function.

**Problem Formulation** The objective is:

$$\max_{\pi_t} \mathbb{E}\left[U\left(W_T\right)\right], \tag{10.113}$$

where $W_T$ is the terminal wealth and $\pi_t$ is the portfolio allocation at time $t$.

The wealth dynamics are given by:

$$dW_t = \pi_t^T \left(dX_t - rW_t dt\right), \tag{10.114}$$

where $dX_t$ is the vector of asset returns and $r$ is the risk-free rate.

**Reinforcement Learning Approach** The state space is $\mathcal{S} = \mathbb{R}$ (current wealth), and the action space is $\mathcal{A} = \mathbb{R}^n$ (portfolio weights). The reward function at each time step is:

$$r_t = U\left(W_t\right). \tag{10.115}$$

Using a policy gradient method, the policy $\pi_\theta$ is parameterized by $\theta$. The objective is to maximize the expected return:

$$J(\theta) = \mathbb{E}_{\pi_\theta}\left[\sum_{t=0}^{T} \gamma^t r_t\right]. \tag{10.116}$$

The policy is updated using the gradient ascent:

$$\theta \leftarrow \theta + \alpha \nabla_\theta J(\theta), \tag{10.117}$$

where $\alpha$ is the learning rate.

### 10.8.6 Continuous-time Portfolio Optimization with Transaction Costs

Consider a continuous-time portfolio optimization problem with proportional transaction costs (see Wang and Zhou [2019] for a related problem).

**Problem Formulation** The objective is to maximize the expected utility of terminal wealth, considering transaction costs. The optimization problem is:

$$\max_{\pi_t} \mathbb{E}\left[U\left(W_T\right)\right], \tag{10.118}$$

subject to the wealth dynamics stochastic differential equation:

$$dW_t = \pi_t^T\left(dX_t - rW_t dt\right) - \lambda\|\pi_t\|dt, \tag{10.119}$$

where $\lambda$ represents transaction costs.

**Reinforcement Learning Approach** The state space is $\mathcal{S} = \mathbb{R}$ (current wealth), and the action space is $\mathcal{A} = \mathbb{R}^n$ (portfolio weights). The reward function is:

$$r_t = U\left(W_t\right) - \lambda\|\pi_t\|. \tag{10.120}$$

Using an actor-critic method, the actor updates the policy parameters $\theta$ to maximize the expected return, while the critic estimates the value function $V\left(s_t\right)$.

The policy update is:

$$\theta \leftarrow \theta + \alpha \nabla_\theta \log \pi_\theta\left(a_t|s_t\right)\left[r_t + \gamma V\left(s_{t+1}\right) - V\left(s_t\right)\right], \tag{10.121}$$

where $\alpha$ is the learning rate.

The value function is updated as:

$$V\left(s_t\right) \leftarrow V\left(s_t\right) + \beta\left[r_t + \gamma V\left(s_{t+1}\right) - V\left(s_t\right)\right], \tag{10.122}$$

where $\beta$ is the learning rate for the critic.

These examples demonstrate how reinforcement learning can be applied to solve various mathematical portfolio optimization problems. The RL approaches leverage techniques such as Q-learning, policy gradients, and actor-critic methods to find optimal policies in complex financial environments.

## 10.9 NOTES

Reinforcement Learning (RL) provides a powerful framework for sequential decision-making under uncertainty, with strong connections to optimal control theory. For a comprehensive introduction to RL, see Sutton and Barto (2018), which was extensively referenced in this chapter.

The connection between RL and optimal control, particularly through the Bellman equation, is explored in depth in Bertsekas (2019). For a discussion on continuous vs. discrete formulations and their implications for portfolio optimization, refer to Moody and Saffell (2001).

The design of the environment and reward function is crucial in RL. For insights into state space, action space, and transition dynamics in financial contexts, see Jiang et al. (2017). The challenges in designing appropriate reward functions for portfolio optimization are discussed in Fischer (2018).

Various agent architectures and types are employed in RL. For a discussion on value-based, policy-based, and actor-critic agents in financial applications, refer to Zhang et al. (2020). The application of these agent types to various aspects of portfolio management is explored in Kolm and Ritter (2019).

State-action and value functions form the backbone of many RL algorithms. The policy gradient theorem and its applications are well-explained in Silver et al. (2014). For a detailed analysis of function approximation in RL, especially in high-dimensional settings relevant to finance, see Tsitsiklis and Van Roy (1997).

Policy definition, formulation, and learning are central to RL. Policy gradient methods and their convergence properties are thoroughly discussed in Kakade (2002). For asymptotic analysis and optimality conditions in the context of financial applications, refer to Bäuerle and Rieder (2011).

On-policy methods like SARSA and REINFORCE are covered in detail in Sutton and Barto (2018). For a deep dive into Proximal Policy Optimization (PPO) and its applications, see Schulman et al. (2017).

Off-policy methods, including Q-learning and its variants, are extensively covered in Mnih et al. (2015). For insights into Deterministic Policy Gradient (DPG) and its applications to continuous control problems, which are particularly relevant in finance, refer to Silver et al. (2014).

The application of RL to mean-variance optimization is explored in Almahdi and Yang (2017). For RL approaches to utility maximization in portfolio management, see Hens et al. (2018).

Continuous-time portfolio optimization with transaction costs is a challenging problem well-suited to RL approaches. For a comprehensive treatment, refer to Jiang and Xu (2017). Recent advancements in applying deep RL to portfolio optimization, including handling market frictions and adapting to changing market regimes, are discussed in Zhang et al. (2020) and Wang et al. (2021). Though not about finance, the paper by Padakandla et al. (2019) introduces Context Q-learning, a novel reinforcement learning algorithm designed for nonstationary environments where the underlying MDP changes over time. The proposed method combines Q-learning with an online change detection algorithm to learn and store policies for different environmental contexts, demonstrating improved performance over existing approaches in random MDPs.

There are some reviews of RL in portfolio optimization, for instance, Boutyour and Idrissi (2023) that reviews many applications of RL and contrasts recent approaches. There is also Meng and Khushi (2019), where the authors reviewed articles on stock and foreign exchange prediction or trading with RL. They found that while many studies demonstrated statistically significant profitability using RL compared to baseline models, several key issues and unrealistic assumptions were prevalent. Many studies did not account for transaction costs, liquidity issues, or bid/ask spreads, which have significant impacts in real-world trading. This was born out by the author's research, that transaction costs, including the bid/ask spread, have a significant impact on the profitability of RL algorithms. Studies that considered transaction costs showed a substantial decrease in profitability, highlighting the need for realistic assumptions in model evaluations. Furthermore, there was a lack of performance comparisons between RL and other sophisticated machine learning or deep learning models. In addition, it was found that substantial changes in price patterns between training and test data (distributional shift) could lead RL models to show no meaningful levels of profitability.

A more contemporary view of RL in finance incorporates multimodal models (Avramelou et al., 2024), that is, artificial intelligence models that are capable of processing structured data (e.g., time series), and unstructured data (e.g., text, images, and video). The authors incorporate sentiment analysis into cryptocurrency prediction and find that sentiment has a noticeable effect on prices and can be leveraged by an RL agent advantageously. Furthermore, they find that multimodal embedding layers (layers that turn positive integers or indexes into dense vectors of fixed size) can improve agent's performance and explainability.

For a broader perspective on the integration of machine learning techniques in quantitative finance, including RL, see Dixon et al. (2020).

PART

# Four

# Machine Learning and Deep Learning

CHAPTER 11

# Deep Learning in Portfolio Management

Deep learning is the field within machine learning whose learning algorithms are neural networks with more than one hidden layer (Goodfellow et al., 2016; Bishop and Bishop, 2023; Zhang et al., 2023; and Prince, 2023).[1] In quantitative portfolio optimization, deep learning techniques offer powerful approaches to asset allocation, risk management, and strategy development. The reader would be well-advised to consider the pros and cons of using deep learning in their work before deciding to proceed with a deep learning model. We present reasons for and against using deep learning in portfolio optimization. Figure 11.1 depicts a schematic of a Deep Neural Network (DNN) and how neurons might be connected. Layers of neural networks require nonlinear activation functions to give the network its expressive power.

## 11.1 NEURONS AND ACTIVATION FUNCTIONS

Artificial neurons, or simply neurons, are the computational units of DNNs. The neuron's role in a DNN is to integrate the information incoming from the previous layer of the network weighted according to which neuron a signal comes from. See Figure 11.2 for a schematic of the process.

Activation functions are nonlinear functions applied to the integration of neurons in a layer, that is, all neurons in a layer are subject to the same activation function. Typical activation functions are:

[1]Similarly to the chapter on reinforcement learning, these will be our base references for this chapter and will be referenced without explicit citation in the general and standard topics of deep learning.

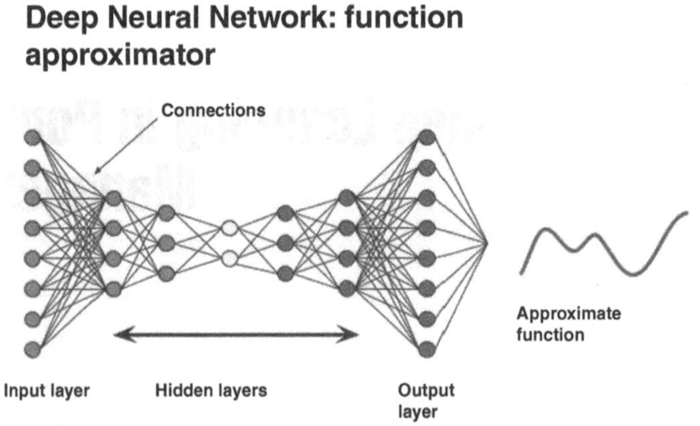


**FIGURE 11.1** Deep Neural Network: Depiction of a DNN. Data is fed into the input layer and is transformed through the layers until the output or final layer when the function approximation is returned.

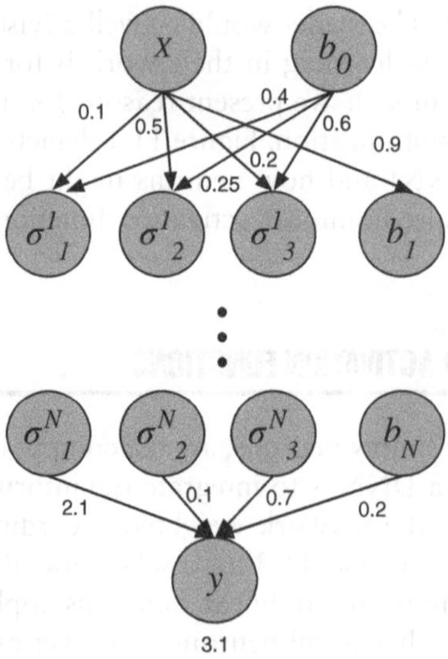


**FIGURE 11.2** **DNN with weights, biases, and activations:** In this representation, the DNN is already trained, and the weights are the numbers shown next to their corresponding arrow that represents a connection. The $\{\sigma^n\}_{n=1}^{N}$ are the activation functions, which are fixed for each layer but can vary unrestricted from layer to layer. The biases are depicted by $\{b_n\}_{n=0}^{N}$.

1. **Sigmoid Function**
   The sigmoid function, also known as the logistic function, is defined as:
   $$\sigma(x) = \frac{1}{1+e^{-x}}.$$
2. **Hyperbolic Tangent (Tanh) Function**
   The hyperbolic tangent function is defined as:
   $$\tanh(x) = \frac{e^x - e^{-x}}{e^x + e^{-x}}$$
   or equivalently,
   $$\tanh(x) = 2\sigma(2x) - 1.$$
3. **Rectified Linear Unit (ReLU)**
   The ReLU function is defined as:
   $$\text{ReLU}(x) = \max(0, x).$$
4. **Leaky ReLU**
   The Leaky ReLU function introduces a small slope for negative values and is defined as:
   $$\text{Leaky ReLU}(x) = \begin{cases} x & \text{if } x \geq 0 \\ \alpha x & \text{if } x < 0 \end{cases},$$
   where $\alpha$ is a small positive constant.
5. **Parametric ReLU (PReLU)**
   The Parametric ReLU function is similar to Leaky ReLU but allows the slope for negative values to be learned. It is defined as:
   $$\text{PReLU}(x) = \begin{cases} x & \text{if } x \geq 0 \\ \alpha x & \text{if } x < 0 \end{cases},$$
   where $\alpha$ is a learnable parameter.
6. **Exponential Linear Unit (ELU)**
   The ELU function is defined as:
   $$\text{ELU}(x) = \begin{cases} x & \text{if } x \geq 0 \\ \alpha(e^x - 1) & \text{if } x < 0 \end{cases},$$
   where $\alpha$ is a positive constant.

7. **Swish**
   The Swish function is defined as:

$$\text{Swish}(x) = x \cdot \sigma(x) = \frac{x}{1 + e^{-x}},$$

8. **Softmax**
   The Softmax function is used primarily in the output layer for classification tasks and is defined as:

$$\text{Softmax}(x_i) = \frac{e^{x_i}}{\sum_{j=1}^{K} e^{x_j}},$$

   where $K$ is the number of classes and $x_i$ is the input to the $i$-th neuron.

## 11.2 NEURAL NETWORKS AND FUNCTION APPROXIMATION

Deep learning is concerned with function approximation and neural networks are used to approximate complex nonlinear functions. Some theoretical results exist that show the capacity of DNNs to approximate functions to arbitrary precision. Perhaps the most important such theorem is the Universal Approximation Theorem.

### Universal Approximation Theorem

**Statement** The Universal Approximation Theorem is a fundamental result which states that a neural network with a single hidden layer can approximate any continuous function on a compact subset of $\mathbb{R}^n$ to arbitrary precision, given sufficient neurons in the hidden layer.

**Theorem 11.1 (Universal Approximation Theorem)** *Let $\sigma : \mathbb{R} \to \mathbb{R}$ be a bounded, continuous, nonconstant function. Let $I_m$ denote the m-dimensional unit cube $[0,1]^m$. The space of continuous functions on $I_m$ is denoted by $C(I_m)$. Then, given any $\varepsilon > 0$ and any function $f \in C(I_m)$, there exist an integer N, real constants $v_i, b_i \in \mathbb{R}$ and real vectors $w_i \in \mathbb{R}^m$ ($i = 1, \ldots, N$) such that we may define:*

$$F(x) = \sum_{i=1}^{N} v_i \sigma\left(w_i^T x + b_i\right)$$

*as an approximate realization of the function f; that is,*

$$|F(x) - f(x)| < \varepsilon$$

*for all $x \in I_m$.*

*Proof.* The proof consists of several steps:

1. First, we show that the class of neural networks is dense in $C(I_m)$ with respect to the uniform norm.
2. We use the Stone-Weierstrass theorem, which states that if $\mathcal{A}$ is an algebra of real-valued continuous functions on a compact Hausdorff space $X$, and if $\mathcal{A}$ separates points in $X$ and contains a non-zero constant function, then $\mathcal{A}$ is dense in $C(X)$ with respect to the uniform norm.
3. We define $\mathcal{N}$ as the set of all functions of the form:

$$G(x) = \sum_{i=1}^{N} v_i \sigma\left(w_i^T x + b_i\right),$$

   where $N$ is any positive integer, $v_i, b_i \in \mathbb{R}$, and $w_i \in \mathbb{R}^m$.
4. We show that $\mathcal{N}$ satisfies the conditions of the Stone-Weierstrass theorem:

   **Lemma 11.1** *$\mathcal{N}$ is an algebra of functions.*

   *Proof.* $\mathcal{N}$ is closed under addition and scalar multiplication by construction. To show it is closed under multiplication, consider $G_1, G_2 \in \mathcal{N}$. Their product can be expressed as a sum of terms of the form $v_i v_j \sigma\left(w_i^T x + b_i\right) \sigma\left(w_j^T x + b_j\right)$, which can be approximated arbitrarily closely by functions in $\mathcal{N}$ due to the non-constancy of $\sigma$. ■

   **Lemma 11.2** *$\mathcal{N}$ separates points in $I_m$.*

   *Proof.* For any two distinct points $x, y \in I_m$, we can find a hyperplane separating them. This hyperplane corresponds to a function in $\mathcal{N}$ that takes different values at $x$ and $y$. ■

   **Lemma 11.3** *$\mathcal{N}$ contains a non-zero constant function.*

   *Proof.* Since $\sigma$ is nonconstant, there exist $a, b \in \mathbb{R}$ such that $\sigma(a) \neq \sigma(b)$. Then the function $G(x) = \frac{\sigma\left(w^T x + a\right) - \sigma\left(w^T x + b\right)}{\sigma(a) - \sigma(b)}$ is in $\mathcal{N}$ and is constant with value 1. ■

5. By the Stone-Weierstrass theorem, $\mathcal{N}$ is dense in $C(I_m)$. This means that for any $f \in C(I_m)$ and any $\varepsilon > 0$, there exists a function $F \in \mathcal{N}$ such that $|F(x) - f(x)| < \varepsilon$ for all $x \in I_m$.

This completes the proof of the Universal Approximation Theorem. ■

We will present other similar theorems, but forgo their full proof, providing only a sketch.

### Deep Networks and Compositional Functions

Deep networks, with multiple hidden layers, can approximate not only continuous functions but also compositional functions (i.e., a function of functions composed with other functions) more efficiently than shallow networks. This is formalized in the following theorem:

**Theorem 11.2 (Approximation by DNNs).** *Let $f : [0,1]^n \to \mathbb{R}$ be a continuous function that can be represented as a composition of functions $f = f_1 \circ f_2 \circ \cdots \circ f_L$. For any $\epsilon > 0$, there exists a neural network with L hidden layers such that the network function $F(x)$ satisfies*

$$\sup_{x \in [0,1]^n} |f(x) - F(x)| < \epsilon.$$

**Sketch of Proof** The proof for deep networks follows similar steps as the Universal Approximation Theorem but emphasizes the compositional structure of the target function:

1. **Constructing Compositional Functions:** Show that each component function $f_i$ can be approximated by a shallow network using the Universal Approximation Theorem.
2. **Layer-wise Approximation:** Build a deep network by stacking the shallow networks that approximate each component function $f_i$.
3. **Uniform Convergence:** Demonstrate that the resulting deep network converges uniformly to the target function $f(x)$ by ensuring that each layer approximates the corresponding component function to the desired precision.

### Approximation with ReLU Activation Functions

The Rectified Linear Unit (ReLU) activation function $\text{ReLU}(x) = \max(0, x)$ is a popular choice in deep learning due to its easy implementation at the function and gradient level. The following theorem extends the Universal Approximation Theorem to networks with ReLU activations.

**Theorem 11.3 (Universal Approximation with ReLU)** *Let $f : [0,1]^n \to \mathbb{R}$ be a continuous function. For any $\epsilon > 0$, there exists a ReLU neural* *network with a finite number of neurons such that the network function* $F(x)$ *satisfies*

$$\sup_{x \in [0,1]^n} |f(x) - F(x)| < \epsilon.$$

#### Proof Sketch

1. **Piecewise Linear Approximation:** Show that ReLU networks can approximate piecewise linear functions by leveraging the linear segments created by the ReLU activation.
2. **Density of Piecewise Linear Functions:** Demonstrate that piecewise linear functions are dense in the space of continuous functions on a compact set.
3. **Uniform Approximation:** Construct a ReLU network that uniformly approximates the target function $f(x)$ using these piecewise linear functions, ensuring the approximation is within the desired precision.

## 11.3 REVIEW OF SOME IMPORTANT ARCHITECTURES

We now provide a comprehensive review of important deep learning architectures, with a focus on their applications in quantitative portfolio optimization. We will explore the mathematical foundations, key properties, and relevant theorems for each architecture.

### Feedforward Neural Networks (FNNs)

Feedforward Neural Networks, also known as Multilayer Perceptrons (MLPs), are the foundational architecture in deep learning.

**Mathematical Formulation** For an $L$-layer FNN, we can define:

$$h^{(l)} = f^{(l)}\left(W^{(l)}h^{(l-1)} + b^{(l)}\right), \tag{11.1}$$

where $h^{(l)}$ is the output of layer $l$, $W^{(l)}$ is the weight matrix, $b^{(l)}$ is the bias vector, and $f^{(l)}$ is the activation function for layer $l$.

One of the most important results for FNNs is the Universal Approximation Theorem. This theorem ensures that FNNs can approximate any continuous function on a compact subset of $\mathbb{R}^m$ to arbitrary precision.

**Application in Portfolio Optimization** In quantitative portfolio optimization, FNNs can be used for:

1. **Predicting asset returns:** FNNs can forecast future asset returns based on historical data and other relevant features. The input is typically a vector $x \in \mathbb{R}^n$ containing historical returns (e.g., daily returns for the past 20 trading days), technical indicators (e.g., moving averages, relative strength index), fundamental data (e.g., price-to-earnings ratio, book-to-market ratio), and macroeconomic variables (e.g., interest rates, GDP growth). The output is a scalar $y \in \mathbb{R}$ representing the predicted return for the next time period (e.g., next day, next week, next month). The model can be represented as an FNN $f_\theta : \mathbb{R}^n \to \mathbb{R}$ with parameters $\theta$, such that $\hat{y} = f_\theta(x)$. It is typically trained to minimize the mean squared error: $\mathcal{L}(\theta) = \frac{1}{m} \sum_{i=1}^{m} \left(y_i - f_\theta(x_i)\right)^2$, where $m$ is the number of training samples.
2. **Estimating risk factors:** FNNs can estimate risk factors that drive asset returns, extending traditional factor models like the Fama-French model. The input is a vector $x \in \mathbb{R}^n$ containing asset-specific features (e.g., market capitalization, book-to-market ratio), market-wide indicators (e.g., volatility index, credit spreads), and economic indicators (e.g., inflation rate, unemployment rate). The output is a vector $y \in \mathbb{R}^k$ representing the estimated loadings on $k$ risk factors. The model can be formulated as an FNN $f_\theta : \mathbb{R}^n \to \mathbb{R}^k$ with parameters $\theta$, such that $\hat{y} = f_\theta(x)$. It can be trained using a combination of supervised learning (when factor loadings are known) and unsupervised learning (to discover latent factors). A possible loss function could be

$$\mathcal{L}(\theta) = \frac{1}{m} \sum_{i=1}^{m} \|y_i - f_\theta(x_i)\|^2 + \lambda \cdot \mathcal{R}(\theta),$$

where the regularization term, $\mathcal{R}(\theta)$, encourages sparsity or orthogonality in the learned factors.
3. **Approximating complex nonlinear relationships between financial variables:** FNNs can capture intricate, nonlinear relationships between various financial variables, which is useful for pricing derivatives or estimating complex risk measures. The input is a vector $x \in \mathbb{R}^n$ containing relevant financial variables, such as asset prices, interest rates, volatility measures, time to maturity (for derivatives), and strike price (for options). The output can be a scalar or vector $y \in \mathbb{R}^k$ representing the target variable(s), such as option price, Value at Risk (VaR), or Expected Shortfall (ES). The model is an FNN $f_\theta : \mathbb{R}^n \to \mathbb{R}^k$ with parameters $\theta$, such that $\hat{y} = f_\theta(x)$. It can be trained to minimize an appropriate

loss function, depending on the specific task. For example, for option pricing:

$$\mathcal{L}(\theta) = \frac{1}{m}\sum_{i=1}^{m}\left(y_i - f_\theta\left(x_i\right)\right)^2 + \lambda \cdot \text{Regularization}\,(\theta),$$

where $y_i$ represents the observed market prices of options.

FNNs offer the advantage of capturing complex, nonlinear relationships without requiring explicit feature engineering or making strong assumptions about the underlying data-generating process. However, care must be taken to prevent overfitting, especially when dealing with financial time series data, which can be noisy and nonstationary. Techniques such as regularization, dropout, and proper cross-validation are important for developing robust models in these contexts.

### Convolutional Neural Networks (CNNs)

CNNs are particularly effective for processing grid-like data, such as time series of asset prices or returns in finance.

**Mathematical Formulation** The core operation in a CNN is the convolution:

$$(f * g)\,(t) = \int f(x)\,g\,(t - x)dx. \tag{11.2}$$

In discrete form, for a 1D convolution:

$$(f * g)(i) = \sum_j f(j)\,g(i - j) \tag{11.3}$$

#### Key Properties

1. **Parameter sharing:** This property refers to the use of the same filter (or kernel) across various positions of the input. In a CNN, each filter is applied to every position of the input, which means the weights of the filter are shared across the entire input space. This significantly reduces the number of parameters compared to FFNs, as the same set of weights is reused multiple times. Parameter sharing not only decreases the model's memory footprint but also improves its ability to generalize by enforcing the learning of position-invariant features.
2. **Local connectivity:** In CNNs, each neuron in a layer is connected only to a small, localized region of the input from the previous layer,

known as the receptive field. This is in contrast to fully connected networks where each neuron is connected to every neuron in the previous layer. Local connectivity allows the network to focus on learning local patterns and spatial hierarchies in the data. It is particularly effective for data with spatial or temporal structure, such as images or time series, where nearby elements are more strongly correlated than distant ones.

3. **Equivariance to translation:** This property means that if the input is translated (i.e., shifted), the output of the convolutional layer will be translated by the same amount. In other words, if a pattern appears in a different position in the input, the CNN will still detect it, producing the same response but at a different position in the output. This is essential for tasks where the position of a feature in the input should not affect its detection or interpretation, such as object recognition in images or pattern detection in financial time series. Equivariance to translation helps CNNs to be robust to positional variations in the input data.

### Application in Portfolio Optimization

- **Detecting patterns in price movements:** CNNs are well-suited for this task due to their ability to capture local patterns and spatial hierarchies in data through the different kernel sizes in each layer. The input typically consists of a 2D array where rows represent different assets and columns represent time steps, with each cell containing price or return data. For example, a $50 \times 100$ input array might represent 50 assets over 100 time steps. The CNN can be designed to output trading signals (e.g., buy, hold, sell) for each asset or a vector of predicted returns. The network's convolutional layers can automatically learn to detect relevant patterns such as trend reversals, breakouts, or specific chart patterns. Success can be measured by the accuracy of the predictions (for classification tasks) or by financial metrics such as Sharpe ratio or returns when the model is used in a simulated trading environment.
- **Analyzing cross-sectional data of multiple assets:** CNNs can effectively process substantial amounts of cross-sectional data to identify patterns across different assets. The input could be a 2D array where rows represent assets and columns represent various features (e.g., price-to-earnings ratio, market cap, momentum). For instance, a $1{,}000 \times 50$ input array might represent 1,000 stocks with 50 features each. CNN can be trained to output rankings; clustering is or expected returns of assets. The convolutional layers can capture interactions between distinctive features and assets, potentially identifying complex, nonlinear relationships. Success can be measured by the performance of a

portfolio constructed based on the model's outputs, evaluated using metrics like information ratio or factor model alpha.

- **Processing alternative data sources:** CNNs excel at processing alternative data, like images, making them ideal for extracting information from alternative data sources. For satellite image analysis, the input would be the raw image data, typically represented as a 3D tensor (height × width × color channels). For example, a $256 \times 256 \times 3$ input might represent a satellite image of an oil storage facility. The CNN can be trained to output predictions of commodity supply, demand, or prices. The convolutional layers can learn to recognize relevant features in the images, such as the number of vehicles in a parking lot or the fill levels of oil tanks. A useful performance metric is the accuracy of the predictions compared to official reports or by the profitability of trading strategies based on these predictions.

CNNs leverage their ability to automatically learn hierarchical features from structured data. The convolutional layers function as trainable feature extractors, often eliminating the need for manual feature engineering. However, care must be taken to avoid overfitting, especially given the often noisy and nonstationary nature of financial data. Techniques such as regularization, data augmentation, and proper cross-validation are important for developing robust models. Additionally, interpretability techniques like feature visualization or attribution methods can be employed to understand what patterns the CNN is detecting, which is particularly important in financial applications where model transparency is often required.

### Recurrent Neural Networks (RNNs)

RNNs are designed to work with sequential data (i.e., that changes over time), making them particularly suitable for time series analysis in finance.

**Mathematical Formulation** The basic RNN formulation is:

$$h_t = f\left(Wx_t + Uh_{t-1} + b\right), \tag{11.4}$$

where $h_t$ is the hidden state at time $t$, $x_t$ is the input at time $t$, $W$ and $U$ are weight matrices, and $b$ is a bias vector.

**Long Short-Term Memory (LSTM)** LSTMs are a type of RNN designed to capture long-term dependencies. The LSTM architecture includes a memory cell $c_t$ and three gates: input gate $i_t$, forget gate $f_t$, and output gate $o_t$.

$$f_t = \sigma(W_f \cdot [h_{t-1}, x_t] + b_f) \tag{11.5}$$

$$i_t = \sigma(W_i \cdot [h_{t-1}, x_t] + b_i) \tag{11.6}$$

$$\tilde{c}_t = \tanh(W_c \cdot [h_{t-1}, x_t] + b_c) \tag{11.7}$$

$$c_t = f_t \circ c_{t-1} + i_t \circ \tilde{c}_t \tag{11.8}$$

$$o_t = \sigma(W_o \cdot [h_{t-1}, x_t] + b_o) \tag{11.9}$$

$$h_t = o_t \circ \tanh(c_t), \tag{11.10}$$

where $\sigma$ is the sigmoid function and $\circ$ denotes the Hadamard (elementwise) product.

#### Application in Portfolio Optimization

- **Predicting future asset returns based on historical data:** RNNs and LSTMs are useful for this task due to their ability to process sequential data and maintain an internal state. The input typically consists of a sequence of feature vectors, where each vector represents the state of an asset or market at a particular time step. For example, an input sequence might be $\{x_t\}_{t=1}^{T}$ where $x_t \in \mathbb{R}^n$ includes features like past returns, trading volume, and various technical indicators. The network can be designed to output predicted returns for the next time step or for multiple steps ahead. The recurrent nature of these networks allows them to capture long-term dependencies and trends in the data. Success can be measured by prediction accuracy metrics like Mean Squared Error (MSE) or Mean Absolute Error (MAE), as well as financial metrics like Sharpe ratio or cumulative returns when the predictions are used in a trading strategy.
- **Modeling the dynamics of risk factors over time:** RNNs and LSTMs can effectively model how risk factors evolve and interact over time. The input could be a sequence of risk factor realizations, where each element in the sequence is a vector representing the values of several risk factors at a given time. For instance, $\{r_t\}_{t=1}^{T}$, where $r_t \in \mathbb{R}^k$ represents $k$ risk factors at time $t$. The network can be trained to predict future risk factor values or to model the joint distribution of risk factors. LSTMs, in particular, are good at capturing both short-term and long-term dependencies in the risk factor dynamics. The output could be point estimates of future risk factor values or parameters of a distribution. Success can be evaluated by the accuracy of risk predictions, the performance of risk-adjusted portfolios constructed using these predictions, or the improvement in risk measures like Value at Risk (VaR) or Expected Shortfall (ES).

- **Capturing complex temporal dependencies in financial time series:** RNNs and LSTMs excel at discovering and leveraging complex temporal patterns in data. The input for this application is typically a multivariate time series, where each time step contains multiple features related to one or more financial instruments. For example, $\{f_t\}_{t=1}^{T}$, where $f_t \in \mathbb{R}^m$ includes features like price, volume, order book data, and macroeconomic indicators. The network can be designed to perform tasks like anomaly detection, regime change identification, or forecasting of multiple related variables. The ability of LSTMs to selectively remember or forget information makes a great choice for identifying long-term trends and cyclical patterns. The output could be binary signals (e.g., regime change detection), multi-class classifications (e.g., market state identification), or multiple time series predictions. Success can be measured by task-specific metrics like classification accuracy or prediction error, as well as by the performance improvement of trading or risk management strategies that incorporate these insights.

RNNs and LSTMs leverage their ability to process sequential data and maintain an internal state, which allows them to capture temporal dependencies of varying lengths. This is particularly valuable in financial applications where both short-term and long-term patterns can be significant. However, these models can be challenging to train due to issues like vanishing or exploding gradients, especially for exceedingly long sequences. Techniques such as careful initialization, gradient clipping, and using variants like Gated Recurrent Units (GRUs) or attention mechanisms can help mitigate these issues. GRUs are a simplified version of LSTMs, featuring two gates (reset and update) instead of three, which can make them faster to train and equally effective for many tasks. They achieve a similar ability to capture long-term dependencies but with a simpler structure, making them an attractive alternative in some financial modeling scenarios. Moreover, the black-box nature of these models can be a concern in regulated financial environments. Therefore, techniques for improving interpretability, such as attention visualization or analyzing cell states, are often employed alongside these models.

### Transformer Architecture

Transformers, introduced by Vaswani et al. in the seminal paper Vaswani et al. (2017), have become increasingly important in various domains, including finance and are the backbone of large language models or LLMs for short.

**Mathematical Formulation** The key to transformers is the self-attention mechanism. For a given set of queries Q, keys K, and values V, the scaled dot-product attention is computed as:

$$\text{Attention}\left(Q, K, V\right) = \text{softmax}\left(\frac{QK^T}{\sqrt{d_k}}\right)V, \tag{11.11}$$

where $d_k$ is the dimension of the keys.

**Multi-Head Attention** Transformers use multi-head attention, which allows the model to jointly attend to information from different representation subspaces:

$$\text{MultiHead}\left(Q, K, V\right) = \text{Concat}\left(\text{head}_1, \ldots, \text{head}_h\right) W^Q, \tag{11.12}$$

where each head is computed as:

$$\text{head}_i = \text{Attention}\left(QW_i^Q, KW_i^K, VW_i^V\right). \tag{11.13}$$

### Application in Portfolio Optimization

- **Capturing Complex Relationships between multiple Assets:** Transformers excel at modeling interactions between different elements in a sequence, making them well-suited for analyzing multiple assets simultaneously. The input typically consists of a sequence of feature vectors, where each vector represents the state of multiple assets at a particular time step. For example, $\{x_t\}_{t=1}^T$, where $x_t \in \mathbb{R}^{n \times m}$ represents $n$ features for $m$ assets at time $t$. The self-attention mechanism allows the model to dynamically weigh the importance of different assets and time periods. The output could be predictions of future returns, risk measures, or optimal portfolio weights. The multi-head attention mechanism enables the model to capture several types of relationships simultaneously, potentially identifying complex, nonlinear interactions between assets. Success can be measured by the accuracy of predictions, the performance of constructed portfolios (e.g., Sharpe ratio, alpha), or improvements in risk-adjusted returns compared to traditional methods.
- **Analyzing long-term dependencies in financial time series:** The Transformer's ability to manage long sequences without the vanishing gradient problems of RNNs makes it particularly useful for analyzing long-time dependencies, for example, a long market run on a certain trend. The input is typically a long sequence of market data, potentially including price, volume, and other technical or fundamental indicators.

For instance, $\{f_t\}_{t=1}^{T}$, where $f_t \in \mathbb{R}^k$ represents $k$ features at time $t$, and $T$ could be (*e.g.*, several years of daily data). The positional encoding in Transformers allows the model to understand the temporal order while still processing the entire sequence in parallel. The output could be predictions of future market states, identification of long-term cycles, or detection of regime changes. The attention weights can provide insights into which historical periods are most relevant for predictions. Success can be evaluated by prediction accuracy, the profitability of long-term trading strategies based on the model's outputs, or improvements in long-horizon risk forecasts.

- **Processing text data for sentiment analysis:** Transformers have revolutionized natural language processing tasks on text data, making them ideal for analyzing financial reports or the news. The input is typically a sequence of tokens (words or sub-words) from financial news articles, earnings call transcripts, or social media posts. For example, $\{w_1, w_2, ..., w_n\}$, where each $w_i$ is a token in the text. The Transformer can be pre-trained on a large corpus of financial texts, and then fine-tuned for specific tasks. The output could be sentiment scores (positive, negative, neutral), predicted market impact, or extraction of key financial metrics. The self-attention mechanism allows the model to capture context and nuances in language that are crucial for accurate sentiment analysis. Success can be measured by sentiment classification accuracy, correlation of sentiment scores with market movements, or improvements in trading strategies that incorporate text analysis. Additionally, the attention weights can provide interpretability by highlighting which parts of the text were most influential in the model's decision.

Transformers leverage their attention mechanism to dynamically focus on relevant parts of the input, whether it is different assets, time periods, or words in a text. This flexibility allows them to capture complex, long-range dependencies that might be missed by other architectures. However, transformers can be computationally intensive, especially for exceptionally long sequences, and may require substantial amounts of data for effective training. Techniques like sparse attention or efficient transformer variants (e.g., Reformer, Longformer) can be employed to manage longer sequences more efficiently. Moreover, while the attention weights provide some level of interpretability, additional techniques may be needed to fully explain the model's decisions in a financial context. As with other deep learning models in finance, careful validation and back testing are crucial to ensure the model's generalization to out-of-sample data and changing market conditions.

### Generative Adversarial Networks (GANs)

GANs consist of two networks, a generator $G$ and a discriminator $D$, trained simultaneously through adversarial training in a zero-sum game. In essence, $G$ generates a sample that is given to $D$ to classify as a real datum or a generated one. As the generator learns the underlying distribution of the data, the better it becomes at fooling the discriminator. Concurrently, the discriminator will try to learn to distinguish real from generated data. The netter the discriminator gets, the worse off the generator is, and vice versa. An equilibrium can be reached when the generator produces samples that the discriminator deems as equally likely to be from the generated or real data.

**Mathematical Formulation** The GAN objective can be formulated as a minimax game:

$$\min_G \max_D V(D, G) = \mathbb{E}_{x \sim p_{\text{data}}(x)} \left[\log D(x)\right] + \mathbb{E}_{z \sim p_z(z)} \left[\log(1 - D(G(z)))\right], \tag{11.14}$$

where $p_{\text{data}}$ is the real data distribution and $p_z$ is a prior on input noise variables.

**Wasserstein GAN** Wasserstein GANs (WGANs) use the Wasserstein distance instead of the Jensen-Shannon divergence, leading to more stable training:

$$\min_G \max_{D \in \mathcal{D}} \mathbb{E}_{x \sim p_{\text{data}}(x)} [D(x)] - \mathbb{E}_{z \sim p_z(z)} [D(G(z))], \tag{11.15}$$

where $\mathcal{D}$ is the set of 1-Lipschitz functions.

#### Application in Portfolio Optimization

- **Generating Synthetic Financial Data for Stress Testing:** A GAN achieves this by training on historical financial data to learn the underlying distribution of asset returns. The input to the GAN typically consists of random noise vectors, while the output is synthetic financial data that mimics real market behavior. The success of the GAN can be measured by comparing the statistical properties (e.g., mean, variance, skewness, kurtosis) of the generated data with the actual historical data. Additionally, visual inspections and metrics like the Kolmogorov-Smirnov test can be used to evaluate the similarity between the synthetic and real data distributions.
- **Augmenting Limited Datasets in Quantitative Strategy Development:** In this application, the GAN is used to expand small datasets by generating additional synthetic data points. The input to the GAN is random noise, and the output is new, realistic-looking financial data that

can be added to the existing dataset. Success can be measured by the performance of quantitative strategies developed using the augmented dataset compared to those developed using the original limited dataset. Metrics such as the Sharpe ratio, maximum drawdown, and backtest performance can be used to evaluate the effectiveness of the augmented data in improving strategy robustness and generalizability.

- **Modeling complex, multi-modal distributions of asset returns:** GANs are particularly effective at capturing and generating data from complex, multimodal distributions, which are common in financial markets. The input to the GAN is again random noise, and the output is data that reflects the multimodal nature of asset returns, including features such as fat tails and volatility clustering. Success can be measured by how well the generated data captures these complex distributional characteristics compared to real market data. Techniques such as visual inspection of return distributions, comparison of higher-order moments, and specific financial metrics like Value at Risk (VaR) and Conditional Value at Risk (CVaR) can be used to assess the fidelity of the modeled distributions.

## 11.4 PHYSICS-INFORMED NEURAL NETWORKS

Physics-informed neural networks (PINNs) were originally conceived as a deep-learning-based way to solve nonlinear parabolic partial differential equations (PDEs) that arise in physics. The simplicity of the methods, however, lends itself to be adapted to solving ordinary and stochastic differential equations (ODEs, SDEs, respectively), extending their scope beyond physics. This chapter will present an overview of PINNs and their use in solving PDEs and SDEs in finance. The seminal paper for PINNs is Raissi et al. (2019) and will be referenced extensively in this section. We will also make extensive reference of Noguer i Alonso and Antolin Camarena (2023), especially for PINNs' Bayesian interpretation and their application to finance.

### Framework for PINNs

Physics-Informed Neural Networks (PINNs) combine the expressiveness of neural networks with the constraints imposed by physical laws. The general framework for PINNs can be described as follows:

1. **Define the governing equations:** Let $\mathcal{N}[u](\mathbf{x}, t) = 0$ be the PDE of interest, where $u$ is the solution, $\mathbf{x}$ is the spatial variable, and $t$ is time.
2. **Neural network approximation:** Define a neural network $\hat{u}(\mathbf{x}, t; \theta)$ to approximate the solution $u$, where $\theta$ represents the network parameters.

3. **Loss function:** Construct a loss function that incorporates both the data and the physics:

$$\mathcal{L}(\theta) = \mathcal{L}_{\text{data}}(\theta) + \mathcal{L}_{\text{PDE}}(\theta), \tag{11.16}$$

where:

$$\mathcal{L}_{\text{data}}(\theta) = \frac{1}{N_d} \sum_{i=1}^{N_d} \left| \hat{u}\left(\mathbf{x}_i, t_i; \theta\right) - u_i \right|^2 \tag{11.17}$$

$$\mathcal{L}_{\text{PDE}}(\theta) = \frac{1}{N_f} \sum_{i=1}^{N_f} \left| \mathcal{N}\left[\hat{u}\right]\left(\mathbf{x}_i, t_i; \theta\right) \right|^2. \tag{11.18}$$

Here, $N_d$ is the number of data points, and $N_f$ is the number of collocation points used to enforce the PDE.

4. **Training:** Minimize the loss function with respect to $\theta$ using gradient-based optimization algorithms.

The key advantage of PINNs is their ability to incorporate physical constraints directly into the learning process, potentially improving generalization and reducing the amount of data required for training.

### Bayesian Interpretation of PINNs

The PINN architecture has a Bayesian interpretation, where the loss, $L$ can be considered as the negative log-posterior for $f_\theta$. The fit-to-data comes from the likelihood function and the physics-informed loss is the prior information available on $f_\theta$. Thus, in a Bayesian framework, for data $X$, we have:

$$\overset{\text{posterior}}{p\left(f_\theta | X\right)} = \frac{\overset{\text{likelihood}}{p\left(X | f_\theta\right)} \overset{\text{prior}}{p\left(f_\theta | \mathcal{D}\right) p\left(\mathcal{D}\right)}}{\underset{\text{evidence}}{p\left(X\right)}}, \tag{11.19}$$

where the prior is a distribution over differential operators $\mathcal{D}$ known to describe the dynamics of the function $f_\theta$, *i.e.*, that satisfy

$$\mathcal{D} f_\theta = 0, \quad L_{\text{physics}} = \left| \mathcal{D} f_\theta \right|^2. \tag{11.20}$$

For many dynamical problems, $\mathcal{D}$ is known in general form. It is the parameters that specify it that need to be found. In the case that the operator is known exactly, $p(\mathcal{D}) = \delta(\mathcal{D})$, meaning that there is no uncertainty about $\mathcal{D}$.

In the more general case, we do not precisely know the parameters, $\lambda$, that specify the operator. This means that the operator itself becomes stochastic as there is now need for a distribution over $\lambda$ to describe our uncertainty in the dynamics of the system. For such cases, we may write

$$p(f_\theta, \mathcal{D}_\lambda, \lambda) = p(f_\theta|\mathcal{D}_\lambda, \lambda)\, p(\mathcal{D}_\lambda|\lambda)\, p(\lambda). \tag{11.21}$$

The advantage afforded by PINNs in this case is that operator or system parameters can be fit with data. Thus, PINNs allow dynamics to be learned in a data-driven fashion.

Lastly, note that in the Bayesian view, the prior imposes a regularization constraint on estimation since it will penalize solutions that stray far from what is already known about the parameters, and that do not satisfy the data via the likelihood function. In this sense, the well-known fact about PINNs that imposing physical dynamics as a constraint acts as a regularization term for the neural network arises naturally. This term, represented by $L_{\text{physics}}$, will penalize functions that poorly satisfy the dynamics, but that also satisfy the data model poorly. Thus, a regularized function will be forced to satisfy both constraints.

## Partial Differential Equations in Finance

In quantitative finance, partial differential equations (Evans, 2010), or PDEs for short, play a key role in modeling the behavior of financial instruments. One of the most fundamental PDEs in finance is the Black-Scholes-Merton equation (BSME). See Black et al. (1972) and Merton (1973) for the seminal papers on the BSME.

**Black-Scholes-Merton Model** The Black-Scholes-Merton model describes the price evolution of a European option. The PDE for this model is given by:

$$\frac{\partial V}{\partial t} + \frac{1}{2}\sigma^2 S^2 \frac{\partial^2 V}{\partial S^2} + rS\frac{\partial V}{\partial S} - rV = 0, \tag{11.22}$$

where $V(S, t)$ is the option price as a function of the underlying asset price $S$ and time $t$, $\sigma$ is the volatility of the underlying asset, and $r$ is the risk-free interest rate

To apply PINNs to solve this PDE, we define the differential operator $\mathcal{N}$ as

$$\mathcal{N}[V] = \frac{\partial V}{\partial t} + \frac{1}{2}\sigma^2 S^2 \frac{\partial^2 V}{\partial S^2} + rS\frac{\partial V}{\partial S} - rV. \tag{11.23}$$

The neural network $V_\theta(S, t)$ approximates the option price, and the loss function becomes:

$$\mathcal{L}(\theta) = \mathcal{L}_{\text{data}}(\theta) + \mathcal{L}_{\text{BSM}}(\theta) + \mathcal{L}_{\text{BC}}(\theta), \tag{11.24}$$

where $\mathcal{L}_{\mathrm{BSM}}(\theta)$ enforces the Black-Scholes-Merton PDE, and $\mathcal{L}_{\mathrm{BC}}(\theta)$ ensures the boundary conditions are satisfied, such as the payoff at expiration:

$$\mathcal{L}_{\mathrm{BC}}(\theta) = \frac{1}{N_b} \sum_{i=1}^{N_b} \left| V_\theta\left(S_i, T\right) - \max\left(S_i - K, 0\right) \right|^2, \tag{11.25}$$

for a European call option with strike price $K$ and expiration time $T$.

**Vasicek Model** The Vasicek model (Vasicek, 1977) is a mathematical model describing the evolution of interest rates. It is used in pricing interest rate derivatives and bonds. The model assumes that the instantaneous interest rate follows an Ornstein-Uhlenbeck (mean-reverting) process.

The stochastic differential equation (SDE) for the Vasicek model is

$$dr_t = a\left(b - r_t\right) dt + \sigma dW_t, \tag{11.26}$$

where $r_t$ is the instantaneous interest rate at time $t$, $a$ is the speed of mean reversion, $b$ is the long-term mean level, $\sigma$ is the volatility, and $W_t$ is a Wiener process.

The corresponding (Fokker-Planck) PDE for the price $V(r,t)$ of a zero-coupon bond under the Vasicek model is:

$$\frac{\partial V}{\partial t} + \frac{1}{2}\sigma^2 \frac{\partial^2 V}{\partial r^2} + a\left(b - r\right) \frac{\partial V}{\partial r} - rV = 0. \tag{11.27}$$

To apply PINNs to solve this PDE, we define the differential operator $\mathcal{N}$ as

$$\mathcal{N}[V] = \frac{\partial V}{\partial t} + \frac{1}{2}\sigma^2 \frac{\partial^2 V}{\partial r^2} + a\left(b - r\right) \frac{\partial V}{\partial r} - rV. \tag{11.28}$$

The neural network $V_\theta(r,t)$ approximates the bond price, and the loss function becomes

$$\mathcal{L}(\theta) = \mathcal{L}_{\mathrm{data}}(\theta) + \mathcal{L}_{\mathrm{Vasicek}}(\theta) + \mathcal{L}_{\mathrm{BC}}(\theta), \tag{11.29}$$

where $\mathcal{L}_{\mathrm{Vasicek}}(\theta)$ enforces the Vasicek PDE:

$$\mathcal{L}_{\mathrm{Vasicek}}(\theta) = \frac{1}{N_f} \sum_{i=1}^{N_f} \left| \mathcal{N}\left[V_\theta\right]\left(r_i, t_i; \theta\right) \right|^2 \tag{11.30}$$

and $\mathcal{L}_{\mathrm{BC}}(\theta)$ ensures the boundary condition is satisfied, such as the bond price at maturity:

$$\mathcal{L}_{\mathrm{BC}}(\theta) = \frac{1}{N_b} \sum_{i=1}^{N_b} \left| V_\theta\left(r_i, T\right) - 1 \right|^2, \tag{11.31}$$

where $T$ is the maturity time of the zero-coupon bond.

The PINN approach to solving the Vasicek model PDE offers several advantages:

1. PINNs can manage high-dimensional problems more efficiently than traditional numerical methods. For example, a typical numerical scheme for solving PDEs is the finite element method where the memory requirements scale exponentially in the grid dimension.
2. PINNs naturally incorporate both the PDE constraints and the boundary conditions.
3. PINNs provide a continuous solution over the entire domain, allowing for easy computation of Greeks (sensitivities).
4. The trained PINN can be evaluated (inference/forward pass), typically in a few milliseconds or less on commodity hardware, for each set of input parameters, facilitating real-time pricing and risk management.

By incorporating the Vasicek model into the PINN framework, we can efficiently price interest rate derivatives and analyze the term structure of interest rates, providing valuable insights for fixed income portfolio management and risk assessment.

## Stochastic Differential Equations in Finance

Stochastic Differential Equations are fundamental in modeling the dynamics of financial markets, capturing the inherent randomness and volatility (see, e.g., Øksendal [2014] for a formal treatment and Särkkä and Solin [2019] for an applied view). PINNs can be adapted to solve SDEs, providing a powerful tool for financial modeling and risk management.

**Heston Model** The Heston model (Heston, 1993) is a popular stochastic volatility model in finance. It describes the evolution of an asset price and its variance using a system of coupled SDEs:

$$\begin{aligned} dS_t &= \mu S_t dt + \sqrt{v_t} S_t dW_t^S \\ dv_t &= \kappa (\theta - v_t)\, dt + \sigma \sqrt{v_t} dW_t^v, \end{aligned} \tag{11.32}$$

where $S_t$ is the asset price at time $t$, $v_t$ is the variance at time $t$, $\mu$ is the drift of the asset price, $\kappa$ is the mean reversion speed of variance, $\theta$ is the long-term mean of variance, $\sigma$ is the volatility of variance, and $W_t^S$ and $W_t^v$ are Wiener processes with correlation $\rho$.

To apply PINNs to the Heston model, we can formulate the problem as follows:

**1. Define two neural networks:** $S_t^{\theta_S}$ and $v_t^{\theta_v}$ to approximate $S_t$ and $v_t$ respectively.

**2. Construct the loss function:**

$$\mathcal{L}(\theta_S, \theta_v) = \mathcal{L}_{\text{data}}(\theta_S, \theta_v) + \mathcal{L}_{\text{SDE}}(\theta_S, \theta_v), \tag{11.33}$$

where $\mathcal{L}_{\text{SDE}}(\theta_S, \theta_v)$ enforces the SDE constraints:

$$\begin{aligned}\mathcal{L}_{\text{SDE}}(\theta_S, \theta_v) = {} & \mathbb{E}\left[\left|\frac{dS^{\theta_S}}{dt} - \mu S^{\theta_S}\right|^2\right] + \mathbb{E}\left[\left|\frac{dv^{\theta_v}}{dt} - \kappa\left(\theta - v^{\theta_v}\right)\right|^2\right] + \\ & \mathbb{E}\left[\left|\left(S_{t+\Delta t}^{\theta_S} - S_t^{\theta_S}\right)^2 - v_t^{\theta_v} S_t^{\theta_S 2} \Delta t\right|^2\right] + \\ & \mathbb{E}\left[\left|\left(v_{t+\Delta t}^{\theta_v} - v_t^{\theta_v}\right)^2 - \sigma^2 v_t^{\theta_v} \Delta t\right|^2\right].\end{aligned} \tag{11.34}$$

The last two terms in $\mathcal{L}_{\text{SDE}}$ enforce the quadratic variation of the processes, which is essential for capturing the stochastic nature of the model.

**3. Train the neural networks:** Minimize the loss function using stochastic gradient descent or other optimization algorithms.

This PINN approach to solving the Heston model allows for efficient simulation and pricing of derivatives under stochastic volatility, potentially offering advantages over traditional numerical methods in terms of computational efficiency and accuracy.

**Bates Model** The Bates model (Bates, 2015) extends the Heston stochastic volatility model by incorporating jump-diffusion. This model is used for pricing options on assets that exhibit both continuous price changes and sudden, discontinuous jumps.

The Bates model is described by the following system of SDEs:

$$\begin{aligned} dS_t &= \left(r - \lambda \mu_J\right) S_t dt + \sqrt{v_t} S_t dW_t^S + J_t S_t dN_t \\ dv_t &= \kappa\left(\theta - v_t\right) dt + \sigma \sqrt{v_t} dW_t^v, \end{aligned} \tag{11.35}$$

where $S_t$ is the asset price at time $t$, $v_t$ is the variance at time $t$, $r$ is the risk-free interest rate, $\lambda$ is the jump intensity (average number of jumps per year), $\mu_J$ is the expected jump size, $\kappa$ is the mean reversion speed of variance, $\theta$ is the long-term mean of variance, $\sigma$ is the volatility of variance, $W_t^S$ and

$W_t^v$ are Wiener processes with correlation $\rho$, $J_t$ is the jump size, typically log-normally distributed, that is,

$$\log(1+J_t) \sim N\left(\log(1+\mu_J) - \frac{1}{2}\sigma_J^2, \sigma_J^2\right), \tag{11.36}$$

and $N_t$ is a Poisson process with intensity $\lambda$.

To apply PINNs to the Bates model, we can formulate the problem as follows:

1. **Define two neural networks:** $S_t^{\theta_S}$ and $v_t^{\theta_v}$ to approximate $S_t$ and $v_t$ respectively.
2. **Construct the loss function:**

$$\mathcal{L}(\theta_S, \theta_v) = \mathcal{L}_{\text{data}}(\theta_S, \theta_v) + \mathcal{L}_{\text{SDE}}(\theta_S, \theta_v) + \mathcal{L}_{\text{jump}}(\theta_S), \tag{11.37}$$

where $\mathcal{L}_{\text{SDE}}(\theta_S, \theta_v)$ enforces the SDE constraints:

$$\begin{aligned}\mathcal{L}_{\text{SDE}}(\theta_S, \theta_v) = {} & \mathbb{E}\left[\left|\frac{dS^{\theta_S}}{dt} - (r - \lambda\mu_J)S^{\theta_S}\right|^2\right] + \mathbb{E}\left[\left|\frac{dv^{\theta_v}}{dt} - \kappa\left(\theta - v^{\theta_v}\right)\right|^2\right] + \\ & \mathbb{E}\left[\left|\left(S_{t+\Delta t}^{\theta_S} - S_t^{\theta_S}\right)^2 - v_t S_t^{\theta_S 2}\Delta t\right|^2\right] + \\ & \mathbb{E}\left[\left|\left(v_{t+\Delta t}^{\theta_v} - v_t^{\theta_v}\right)^2 - \sigma^2 v_t^{\theta_v}\Delta t\right|^2\right]\end{aligned} \tag{11.38}$$

and $\mathcal{L}_{\text{jump}}(\theta_S)$ accounts for the jump component:

$$\mathcal{L}_{\text{jump}}(\theta_S) = \mathbb{E}\left[\left|\log\left(S_{t+\Delta t}^{\theta_S}\right) - \log\left(S_t^{\theta_S}\right) - N\left(\log(1+\mu_J) - \frac{1}{2}\sigma_J^2, \sigma_J^2\right)\right|^2\right], \tag{11.39}$$

where the expectation is taken over simulated jump events.
3. **Train the neural networks:** Minimize the loss function using stochastic gradient descent or other optimization algorithms.

The PINN approach to solving the Bates model offers several advantages:

1. It can manage the complex interactions between stochastic volatility and jump-diffusion more efficiently than traditional numerical methods.
2. It provides a continuous solution over the entire domain, allowing for easy computation of Greeks and risk measures.

3. The trained network can be quickly evaluated for different input parameters, facilitating real-time pricing and risk management.
4. It can naturally incorporate both historical data and the model constraints, potentially leading to more accurate and robust predictions.

Implementing the Bates model using PINNs allows for efficient pricing of options and other derivatives in markets with both continuous and discontinuous price movements. This approach can be particularly valuable in capturing the effects of rare but significant events (jumps) on option prices, while also accounting for stochastic volatility. The flexibility of the PINN framework makes it well-suited to manage such complex models, providing a powerful tool for quantitative analysts and risk managers in the financial industry.

## 11.5 APPLICATIONS TO PORTFOLIO OPTIMIZATION

The models we have discussed, when implemented using Physics-Informed Neural Networks (PINNs), can be powerful tools for quantitative portfolio optimization. Here, we present two applications that leverage these models to enhance portfolio management strategies.

### 11.5.1 Dynamic Asset Allocation Using the Heston Model

The Heston model, with its ability to capture stochastic volatility, can be used to develop a dynamic asset allocation strategy that adapts to changing market conditions. See Pan et al. (2018) for more on this topic.

**Problem Formulation** Consider a portfolio consisting of a risky asset (modeled by the Heston model) and a risk-free asset. The objective is to maximize the expected utility of terminal wealth over a fixed investment horizon $T$.

The value of the portfolio $X_t$ evolves according to:

$$dX_t = \left[\alpha_t \left(\mu - r\right) X_t + rX_t\right] dt + \alpha_t \sqrt{v_t} X_t dW_t^1, \tag{11.40}$$

where $\alpha_t$ is the proportion of wealth invested in the risky asset at time $t$.

The optimization problem can be formulated as:

$$\max_{\alpha_t} \mathbb{E}\left[U\left(X_T\right)\right], \tag{11.41}$$

subject to the Heston model dynamics for the risky asset and variance processes.

#### PINN Implementation

1. **Define neural networks:** $X^{\theta_X}(t, S_t, v_t)$ to approximate the portfolio value and $\alpha^{\theta_\alpha}(t, S_t, v_t)$ to approximate the optimal allocation strategy.
2. **Construct the loss function:**
$$\mathcal{L}(\theta_X, \theta_\alpha) = \mathcal{L}_{\text{HJB}}(\theta_X, \theta_\alpha) + \mathcal{L}_{\text{BC}}(\theta_X) + \mathcal{L}_{\text{utility}}(\theta_X, \theta_\alpha), \quad (11.42)$$
where $\mathcal{L}_{\text{HJB}}$ enforces the Hamilton-Jacobi-Bellman equation, $\mathcal{L}_{\text{BC}}$ ensures boundary conditions, and $\mathcal{L}_{\text{utility}}$ maximizes the expected utility.
3. **Train the neural networks:** Minimize the loss function. This approach allows for a flexible, adaptive asset allocation strategy that accounts for stochastic volatility, potentially leading to improved risk-adjusted returns.

### 11.5.2 Option-based Portfolio Insurance Using the Bates Model

The Bates model, which incorporates both stochastic volatility and jumps (Bates, 1988), can be used to implement a sophisticated option-based portfolio insurance (OBPI) strategy.

**Problem Formulation** Consider a portfolio that needs to be protected against downside risk while still allowing for upside potential. The goal is to determine the optimal mix of a risky asset (modeled by the Bates model), a risk-free asset, and a put option on the risky asset.

The portfolio value $P_t$ at time $t$ is given by:

$$P_t = \alpha_t S_t + \beta_t B_t + \gamma_t \Pi(S_t, K, T), \quad (11.43)$$

where $\alpha_t$, $\beta_t$, and $\gamma_t$ are the allocations to the risky asset, risk-free asset, and put option respectively, and $\Pi(S_t, K, T)$ is the price of a put option with strike $K$ and maturity $T$.

The optimization problem is to maximize expected return while ensuring the portfolio value does not fall below a certain floor $F$:

$$\max_{\alpha_t, \beta_t, \gamma_t} \mathbb{E}[P_T] \quad (11.44)$$

subject to $P_t \geq F$ for all $t$.

#### PINN Implementation

1. **Define neural networks:** $P^{\theta_P}(t, S_t, v_t)$ to approximate the portfolio value and $\alpha^{\theta_\alpha}(t, S_t, v_t)$, $\beta^{\theta_\beta}(t, S_t, v_t)$, $\gamma^{\theta_\gamma}(t, S_t, v_t)$ to approximate the optimal allocation strategies.

2. **Use a PINN:** Solve the Bates model PDE for option pricing, obtaining $\Pi^{\theta_\Pi}(S_t, v_t, t)$.
3. **Construct the loss function:**

$$\mathcal{L}(\theta_P, \theta_\alpha, \theta_\beta, \theta_\gamma, \theta_\Pi) = \mathcal{L}_{\text{dynamics}}(\theta_P, \theta_\alpha, \theta_\beta, \theta_\gamma, \theta_\Pi) + \mathcal{L}_{\text{floor}}(\theta_P) + \mathcal{L}_{\text{return}}(\theta_P), \quad (11.45)$$

where $\mathcal{L}_{\text{dynamics}}$ ensures the portfolio evolution follows the Bates model, $\mathcal{L}_{\text{floor}}$ enforces the floor constraint, and $\mathcal{L}_{\text{return}}$ maximizes the expected return.
4. **Train the neural networks:** Minimize the loss function. This OBPI strategy, implemented using PINNs and the Bates model, can provide downside protection while allowing for participation in market upside, accounting for both stochastic volatility and potential jumps in the underlying asset price.

Both of these applications demonstrate how PINNs can be used to solve complex portfolio optimization problems that incorporate sophisticated financial models. The PINN approach allows for flexible, adaptive strategies that can manage the nonlinearities and high-dimensionality inherent in these problems, potentially leading to improved portfolio performance and risk management.

### 11.5.3 Factor Learning Approach to Generative Modeling of Equities

Reference Gopal (2024) introduces NeuralFactors, a novel machine learning approach to factor analysis for generative modeling of equity returns, where a neural network outputs factor exposures and factor returns, trained using the same methodology as variational autoencoders. Gopal addresses the problem of modeling the joint distribution of stock returns, which is crucial for risk forecasting and portfolio optimization. The method allows for the discovery of latent factors without predefined factor portfolios. The problem is to model the conditional distribution of returns is $p(r_{t+1}|F_t)$, where $r_{t+1}$ represents the returns at time $t+1$, and $F_t$ is the historical information up to time $t$. The method uses a variational autoencoder (VAE) framework for generative modeling, where the latent space represents market factors, and the decoder combines these with learned factor exposures.

Gopal compares NeuralFactors against baseline models such as Probabilistic Principal Component Analysis (PPCA) and previous deep learning approaches. The model's performance is evaluated on negative log-likelihood, covariance forecasting, Value at Risk (VaR) analysis, and portfolio optimization tasks using S&P 500 constituent data from 1996 to 2023. Results show that NeuralFactors outperforms baseline models in terms of log-likelihood performance, covariance estimation, and portfolio optimization. The model demonstrates competitive performance in generating realistic synthetic data and risk analysis.

NeuralFactors models the joint distribution of returns using a latent variable model:

$$z_{t+1} \sim t_{\nu_z}\left(\mu_z, \sigma_z\right) \tag{11.46}$$

$$r_{i,t+1} \sim p(r_{i,t+1}|z_{t+1}, F_t) \quad \text{for } i = 1 \text{ to } N_{t+1}, \tag{11.47}$$

where $z_{t+1} \in \mathbb{R}^F$ represents $F$ latent factors. The conditional distribution of returns is modeled as:

$$p\left(r_{i,t+1}|z_{t+1}, F_t\right) = p\left(r_{i,t+1}|t_{\nu_{i,t}}\left(\alpha_{i,t} + \beta_{i,t}^T z_{t+1}, \sigma_{i,t}\right)\right). \tag{11.48}$$

Here, $\alpha_{i,t}$, $\beta_{i,t}$, $\sigma_{i,t}$, and $\nu_{i,t}$ are outputs of neural networks processing historical data $F_t$.

The model is trained using variational inference, optimizing the evidence lower bound (ELBO):

$$\log p(r_{t+1}|F_t) \geq \mathbb{E}_{z_{t+1} \sim q(z_{t+1}|r_{t+1}, F_t)} \left[\sum_{i=1}^{N_{t+1}} \log p\left(r_{i,t+1}|z_{t+1}, F_t\right) + p\left(z_{t+1}\right) - q\left(z_{t+1}\right)\right]. \tag{11.49}$$

Gopal uses the Conditional Importance Weighted Autoencoder (CIWAE) loss to reduce bias in the variational approximation:

$$\log p(r_{t+1}|F_t) \geq \mathbb{E}_{z_1, \ldots, z_k \sim q(z|r_{t+1}, F_t)} \left[\log \frac{1}{k} \sum_{j=1}^{k} \frac{p\left(r_{t+1}|F_t, z_j\right) p\left(z_j|F_t\right)}{q\left(z_j|r_{t+1}, F_t\right)}\right]. \tag{11.50}$$

For inference, the model samples from the prior distribution $t_{\nu_z}\left(\mu_z, \sigma_z\right)$ and uses the decoder to generate returns.

Model evaluation is done using several metrics, including negative log-likelihood (NLL):

$$\text{NLL}_{\text{joint},t} = -\frac{1}{N_{t+1}} \log p\left(\left\{r_{i,t+1}\right\}_{i=1}^{N_{t+1}} |F_t\right) \tag{11.51}$$

$$\text{NLL}_{\text{ind},t} = -\sum_i \frac{1}{N_{t+1}} \log p(r_{i,t}|F_t). \tag{11.52}$$

For covariance forecasting, they use mean squared error (MSE) and Box's M test statistic on whitened returns. Value-at-Risk (VaR) analysis employs calibration error as defined by Kuleshov et al. (2018).

Gopal finds that NeuralFactors outperforms baseline models in NLL metrics, with $\mathrm{NLL}_{\mathrm{joint}} = 0.556$ on the test set compared to 0.620 for the next best model. In portfolio optimization, the authors use mean-variance optimization:

$$\underset{w \in \mathbb{R}^N, \|w\|_1 = L}{\operatorname{argmax}} \ \mathbb{E}_{r_{T+1}} \left[ w^T r_{T+1} \right] - \frac{\lambda}{2} \mathrm{Var}_{r_{T+1}} \left[ w^T r_{T+1} \right]. \tag{11.53}$$

NeuralFactors achieves the highest Sharpe ratios in most configurations, with a long-only $L = 1$ strategy yielding a Sharpe ratio of 1.04 on the test set, outperforming other models and demonstrating its effectiveness in practical financial applications.

## 11.6 THE CASE FOR AND AGAINST DEEP LEARNING

### The Case For Deep Learning

Traditional portfolio optimization techniques, like mean-variance optimization, may not scale well with high-dimensional data. Deep neural networks excel at handling high-dimensional input spaces. DNNs can capture arbitrary dependencies among a large number of assets, identifying intricate patterns that might be missed by classical methods.

Financial markets exhibit complex nonlinear and dynamic behaviors. DNNs are inherently nonlinear through the use of nonlinear activation functions and can approximate any real function. This makes them suitable for modeling the nonlinear dependencies in asset returns and covariances. This flexibility allows for the construction of more robust and adaptive portfolio strategies.

Deep learning models can automatically learn and extract relevant features from raw data, reducing the need for manual feature engineering. This capability is particularly useful in finance, where identifying relevant factors can be challenging. By learning hierarchical representations, deep learning models can uncover hidden structures in financial data, potentially leading to better portfolio decisions.

The incorporation of alternative data sources, such as social media sentiment, news articles, and satellite images, has become increasingly important in modern finance. Deep learning models are well-suited to process and integrate these diverse data types, providing a more comprehensive view of market conditions and enhancing the decision-making process.

### The Case Against Deep Learning

One of the main criticisms of deep learning models is their lack of interpretability. In finance, understanding the rationale behind investment decisions is central to risk management and regulatory compliance. Deep learning models are often referred to as black boxes, because they provide limited insights into their decision-making or inference process, making it difficult to justify and trust their recommendations.

Deep learning models are prone to overfitting, especially when applied to financial data with its inherent noise and nonstationarity. Overfitting occurs when a model learns the training data so well that the model captures noise as if it were a signal, leading to poor generalization. This issue can result in suboptimal or even detrimental portfolio strategies when deployed in real-world scenarios due to distributional drift or the training data that is not sufficiently representative of real data.

Training deep learning models requires significant computational resources, including powerful GPUs and large memory capacities. This resource intensity can be a barrier for many practitioners and institutions. Additionally, depending on the model, the training time might be long compared to quickly changing market conditions.

Deep learning models require large amounts of high-quality (high signal-to-noise ratio, representative of true distribution, etc.) data for training. In finance, obtaining such data can be difficult due to limited historical records, missing values, and inconsistencies. Moreover, the quality of the data is paramount, as noisy or biased data can lead to poor model performance and unreliable portfolio strategies.

The use of deep learning in quantitative portfolio optimization presents both promise and drawbacks. While deep learning models offer advanced capabilities in handling high-dimensional data, capturing nonlinear relationships, and integrating alternative and unstructured data sources, they also face significant hurdles related to interpretability, overfitting, computational complexity, and data requirements.

A balanced approach that combines the strengths of deep learning with traditional quantitative methods may offer the most robust solution. By leveraging deep learning for feature extraction and nonlinear modeling while maintaining transparency and interpretability through classical techniques, it is possible to develop more effective and trustworthy portfolio optimization strategies.

## 11.7 NOTES

Deep Learning has emerged as a powerful tool in various domains, including portfolio management. For a comprehensive and up-to-date account of deep learning with engaging narrative, see Prince (2023). For a somewhat more rigorous introduction to deep learning, see Goodfellow et al. (2016) and Bishop and Bishop (2023).

The Universal Approximation Theorem, a fundamental result in neural network theory, is discussed in depth in Hornik (1991). For recent developments in approximation theory for deep networks, particularly with ReLU activation functions, refer to Lu et al. (2017).

Feedforward Neural Networks (FNNs) and their applications in finance are well-covered in Heaton et al. (2017). For a detailed treatment of Convolutional Neural Networks (CNNs) and their potential in financial time series analysis, see Sezer et al. (2020).

Recurrent Neural Networks (RNNs), particularly Long Short-Term Memory (LSTM) networks, have shown promise in capturing temporal dependencies in financial data. For an overview and applications, refer to Fischer (2018).

The transformer architecture, which has revolutionized natural language processing, is increasingly being applied to financial time series. For the original paper introducing transformers, see Vaswani et al. (2017). An application to financial forecasting can be found in Jiang (2020).

Generative Adversarial Networks (GANs) have found interesting applications in finance, particularly in scenario generation and risk management. The original GAN paper is Goodfellow et al. (2014), while financial applications are explored in Wiese et al. (2020).

Physics-Informed Neural Networks (PINNs) represent a novel approach to solving differential equations, with potential applications in financial modeling. The foundational work on PINNs is presented in Raissi et al. (2019). For applications in finance, particularly in option pricing, see Horváth et al. (2021).

The Black-Scholes-Merton model, a cornerstone of option pricing theory, is presented in Black (1972). The Vasicek model for interest rates is introduced in Vasicek (1977).

Stochastic volatility models, such as the Heston model in Heston (1993) and the Bates model in Bates (2015), provide more realistic descriptions of asset price dynamics and are increasingly being studied using deep learning approaches.

Dynamic asset allocation using deep learning, particularly in the context of the Heston model, is explored in Bühler et al. (2019). For option-based portfolio insurance strategies using advanced models like the Bates model, refer to Cont and Kan (2013).

While deep learning has shown remarkable success in many areas of finance, it's important to consider both its strengths and limitations see López de Prado (2018) and Dixon et al. (2020). The work by López de Prado highlights the algorithms in machine learning that are important in finance, rather than simply "hard" machine learning. Notably, this text also lays out an organizational approach to the machine learning pipeline meant to nudge funds to adopt such organization for improved returns. There have been some changes in philosophy regarding the type of information mining that the text states, that is "nugget mining,"[2] but otherwise the proposed organization has remained a solid foundation to emulate.

[2]In allusion to how gold is mined in modern times as contrasted with how it used to be mined centuries ago.

CHAPTER 12

# Graph-based Portfolios

## 12.1 GRAPH THEORY-BASED PORTFOLIOS

Graph theory provides a novel approach to portfolio optimization by representing assets as nodes and their relationships (e.g., correlations) as edges in a graph. This method offers an alternative to traditional optimization techniques, addressing some of their limitations and enhancing diversification and risk management. This chapter synthesizes findings from recent research, particularly the works of Cajas (2023a, 2023b), to evaluate the effectiveness of graph theory in portfolio optimization.

### 12.1.1 Literature Review

Graph theory-based methods have gained traction in finance, with key techniques including Hierarchical Risk Parity (HRP; López de Prado, 2016b), minimum spanning trees (MST; Mantegna, 1999), and triangulated maximally filtered graphs (TMFG; Pozzi et al., 2013). These methods enable the selection of low- and high-correlation assets by analyzing their positions and connections within the network. Cajas (2023b) extends this by introducing additional constraints into traditional convex optimization models, leveraging centrality, and neighborhood measures.

## 12.2 GRAPH THEORY PORTFOLIOS: MST AND TMFG

We applied several graph theory techniques to identify optimal asset combinations and compared their performance to traditional Markowitz optimization.

The primary methods include:

1. **Minimum Spanning Tree** (MST): Simplifies complex networks by connecting all vertices with the minimum number of edges.

2. **Triangulated Maximally Filtered Graph (TMFG):** Provides a network-filtering method that retains the most significant relationships among assets.
3. **Degeneracy Ordering:** Selects assets based on their degree of connectivity within the network, favoring those with fewer connections (i.e., lower degeneracy).
4. **Clique Centrality:** Identifies clusters of highly interconnected assets, favoring those with more connections within these clusters.

### 12.2.1 Equations and Formulas

1. **Adjacency Matrix (A):**

$$A_{ij} = \begin{cases} 1 & \text{if there is an edge between nodes } i \text{ and } j \\ 0 & \text{otherwise} \end{cases}. \tag{12.1}$$

2. **Centrality Measures:**

   (a) **Node's Degree:**

$$D_n = A\mathbf{1}_n. \tag{12.2}$$

   (b) **Eigenvector Centrality:**

$$EC_n = \frac{1}{\lambda_{\max}} A q_{\max}. \tag{12.3}$$

   (c) **Subgraph Centrality:**

$$EE_n = \operatorname{diag}\left(e^A\right) = \operatorname{diag}\left(\sum_{i=0}^{\infty} \frac{A^i}{i!}\right). \tag{12.4}$$

3. **Connection Matrix ($B_k$):**

$$B_k = \mathbf{1}_{\times 1}(A^k + I_n) - I_n. \tag{12.5}$$

4. **Average Centrality Measure of a Portfolio:**

$$CM(x) = C_n' x. \tag{12.6}$$

5. **Percentage Invested in Connected Assets:**

$$CA(x) = \frac{\mathbf{1}_n\left(B_{1,l} \odot |xx'|\right)\mathbf{1}_n'}{\mathbf{1}_n |xx'| \mathbf{1}_n'}. \tag{12.7}$$

6. **Optimization Problems:**

(a) **Centrality Measure Constraint:**

$$\begin{aligned}
&\text{optimize}_x \quad \varphi(x) \\
&\text{subject to} \quad C_n' x = \bar{c} \\
&x \in X.
\end{aligned} \tag{12.8}$$

(b) **Neighborhood Constraint (MIP Approach):**

$$\begin{aligned}
&\text{optimize}_x \quad \varphi(x) \\
&\text{subject to} \quad \left(B_{1,l} + I_n\right) y \leq 1 \\
&x_i \leq b_u y_i \quad \forall i \\
&x_i \geq b_l y_i \quad \forall i \\
&x \in X.
\end{aligned} \tag{12.9}$$

(c) **Neighborhood Constraint (SDP Approach):**

$$\begin{aligned}
&\text{minimize}_{x,X} \quad \mathrm{Tr}(\Sigma X) \\
&\text{subject to} \quad \begin{bmatrix} X & x \\ x' & 1 \end{bmatrix} \succeq 0 \\
&X = X' \\
&B_{1,l} \odot X = 0 \\
&x \in X.
\end{aligned} \tag{12.10}$$

### 12.2.2 Results

To evaluate the performance of graph theory-based methods, we conducted numerical experiments comparing traditional optimization techniques with MST, TMFG, degeneracy ordering, and clique centrality. We used daily adjusted closing prices of 30 assets from the SP 500 for the period from January 1, 2019, to December 30, 2022.

The author calculated the efficient frontier using variance as a risk measure and grouped the weights of the assets by the node's degree in the MST and TMFG. We found that portfolios on the efficient frontier were more concentrated in peripheral assets (i.e., low-degree nodes) when risk aversion was higher.

He compared portfolios optimized using traditional methods with those incorporating graph theory constraints. Portfolios with constraints based on average node degree and neighborhood showed improved diversification and lower investment in connected assets.

We present the following numerical example in Table 12.1 to illustrate the results:

**TABLE 12.1** Comparison of Portfolio Compositions.

| Clusters | Min Variance | MIP Constraint | SDP Constraint |
|---|---|---|---|
| Cluster 1 | 6.13% | 9.29% | 9.49% |
| Cluster 2 | 6.64% | 7.21% | 7.27% |
| Cluster 3 | 32.58% | 31.46% | 30.08% |
| Cluster 4 | 7.03% | 11.33% | 11.71% |
| Cluster 5 | 47.62% | 40.72% | 41.44% |
| $\sigma(x)$ | 1.00% | 1.05% | 1.04% |
| NEC(x) | 2.89 | 3.43 | 3.45 |
| RA(x) | 16.93% | 0.00% | 2.58% |

Table 12.1 shows that adding Mixed Integer Programming (MIP) and Semidefinite Programming (SDP) constraints to the minimum variance portfolio reduces the number of assets but increases diversification per cluster, as indicated by the higher number of effective assets (NEC). The SDP formulation closely matches the standard deviation of the minimum variance portfolio but incurs a slightly higher percentage of related assets (RA) than the MIP formulation.

The integration of graph theory into portfolio optimization addresses several limitations of traditional methods. Graph-based approaches offer superior diversification by considering the centrality and connectivity of assets, which are often overlooked in conventional techniques. These methods provide a more nuanced understanding of asset relationships and dependencies, enhancing portfolio performance in volatile markets.

Graph theory provides a valuable framework for portfolio optimization, offering enhanced diversification and robustness compared to traditional methods. By incorporating centrality and neighborhood constraints, investors can achieve better risk management and asset selection. The findings support the adoption of graph-based methods.

## 12.3 HIERARCHICAL RISK PARITY

Hierarchical Risk Parity (HRP) is a portfolio allocation algorithm presented in López de Prado (2016b) and designed to address some of the issues related to Markowitz's mean-variance modeling.

The HRP algorithm can be divided into three successive stages: tree clustering, quasi-diagonalization, and recursive bisection.

**Tree Clustering** In this stage, an agglomerative clustering algorithm is performed. Each data point is placed initially in its own cluster and at each step, the two most similar clusters are joined into a larger cluster. The algorithm continues until all clusters are members of a single large cluster.

To conduct the algorithm, a measure of similarity (i.e., a distance) between clusters is needed. To obtain it, we start from the matrix of asset returns correlations, $\mathbf{P} = (\rho_{ij})$, with $\rho_{ij} = \frac{cov(r_i, r_j)}{\sigma_i \sigma_j}$. As the correlation is not a proper distance (it can take negative values), López de Prado proposes the transformation

$$d_{ij} = d(r_i, r_j) = \sqrt{\frac{1}{2}(1 - \rho_{ij})},$$

which was originally presented in Mantegna and Stanley (2000).[1] As can be easily seen, $d$ is a strictly decreasing continuous bijection, mapping $[-1, 1]$ onto $[0, 1]$, and then, it can be considered as a rescaling of the correlation, making it not negative. Perfectly anticorrelated values $(\rho_{ij} = -1)$ will be at maximum distance 1, while values with perfect positive correlation $(\rho_{ij} = 1)$ will be at distance 0.

With the newly defined distances $d_{ij}$, we form the matrix $\mathbf{D} = (d_{ij})_{n \times n} = (\mathbf{D}_1 | \cdots | \mathbf{D}_n)$ where $\mathbf{D}_j$ is the column vector of distances to the $j$-th asset. Then, a new matrix $\widetilde{\mathbf{D}}^{(0)} = \left(d_{ij}^{(0)}\right)_{n \times n}$ (the *dissimilarity matrix*) is formed, whose elements are the Euclidean distances, $d_{EUC}$, between the columns of $\mathbf{D}$, which are the initial (singletons) clusters, $C_i^{(0)} = \mathbf{D}_i$, with

$$\tilde{d}_{ij}^{(0)} = d_{EUC}\left(C_i^{(0)}, C_j^{(0)}\right) = \sqrt{\sum_{s=1}^{n} \left(d_{sj} - d_{si}\right)^2}.$$

[1] Actually, $d$ does not define a distance, as can be seen by taking $r_j = 2r_i$, which leads to $\rho_{ij} = 1$ and $d(r_i, r_j) = 0$, although $r_i \neq r_j$. It would be a truly distance in the case in which the returns were standardized random variables with mean zero and variance one (Mantegna and Stanley, 2000).

At the $k$-th step of the agglomerative clustering algorithm, $k = 1, \ldots, n-1$, a new cluster, $C^{(k)} = C_{i^*}^{(k-1)} \cup C_{j^*}^{(k-1)}$, is formed, with $(i^*, j^*) = \arg\min_{i \neq j} \tilde{d}_{ij}^{(k-1)}$. If $k = n - 1$, we end up with only one cluster containing all the original assets, and the algorithm is concluded. If $k < n - 1$, the matrix $\widetilde{\mathbf{D}}^{(k-1)} = \left(\tilde{d}_{ij}^{(k-1)}\right)_{(n-k+1)\times(n-k+1)}$ is updated to $\widetilde{\mathbf{D}}^{(k)} = \left(\tilde{d}_{ij}^{(k)}\right)_{(n-k)\times(n-k)}$, corresponding to the $(n - k)$ remaining clusters $C_1^{(k)}, \ldots, C_{n-k}^{(k)}$, with

$$\tilde{d}_{ij}^{(k)} = \min_{l,m} \left\{ \tilde{d}_{lm}^{(k-1)} \middle| C_l^{(k-1)} \subset C_i^{(k)}, C_m^{(k-1)} \subset C_j^{(k)} \right\}.$$

This method of obtaining the distances between clusters is known as *single linkage*, which is the one used in HRP. It is usual to represent the resulting tree structure as a dendrogram, where the initial assets appear in the horizontal axis, and the distance $\tilde{d}^{(k)}$ between the merged clusters is represented on the vertical axis.

The results of the tree clustering stage are summarized in a *linkage matrix*, $Y_{(n-1)\times 4}$, given by

$$Y = \begin{bmatrix} y_{11} & y_{12} & y_{13} & y_{14} \\ \cdots & \cdots & \cdots & \cdots \\ y_{k1} & y_{k2} & y_{k3} & y_{k4} \\ \cdots & \cdots & \cdots & \cdots \\ y_{(n-1),1} & y_{(n-1),2} & y_{(n-1),3} & y_{(n-1),4} \end{bmatrix},$$

where the $k$-th row includes information about the cluster formed in the $k$-th step: $y_{k1}$, $y_{k2}$ are the two components of the cluster, $y_{k3}$ is the distance $\tilde{d}^{(k)}$ between its components, and $y_{k4}$ is the number of original assets included in the cluster.[2]

**Quasi-Diagonalization** At this stage, the rows and columns of the covariance matrix are rearranged so that the largest values appear near the diagonal.

[2]In López de Prado (2016b), the linkage matrix is obtained with the functionality scipy.cluster.hierarchy of the scipy Python package. In this case, values of $y_{k1}$ or $y_{k2}$ from 0 to $n - 1$ correspond to the original assets. The value $n$ represents the cluster formed in the first step of the algorithm, $n + 1$ represents the cluster formed in the second step, and so on.

As a result of this rearrangement, similar assets are placed together, and dissimilar assets appear far apart. The quasi-diagonalization algorithm takes the linkage matrix from the previous stage as input and works as follows.

The value of $max(y_{(n-1),1}, y_{(n-1),2})$ corresponds to the last cluster formed before finishing the algorithm (see footnote 2), and is replaced by its constituents, which appear in the previous row of the linkage matrix ($y_{(n-2),1}$ and $y_{(n-2),2}$). If the other component is also a cluster, it is replaced by its constituents ($y_{(n-3),1}$ and $y_{(n-3),2}$). The process continues recursively until there are no clusters left. The output is an ordered list of the original assets.[3]

To gain intuition about the underlying cluster structure in the asset portfolio, it is usual to represent the covariance matrix resulting from the quasi-diagonalization stage in the form of a heat-map.

**Recursive Bisection** The reasoning behind this last stage of the HRP algorithm is based on the following result.

**Proposition 12.1.** *If the covariance matrix* $\mathbf{\Sigma}$ *is diagonal, then the global minimum variance portfolio is given by*

$$\mathbf{w} = \frac{1}{\sum_{i=1}^{n} \frac{1}{\sigma_i^2}} \begin{bmatrix} \frac{1}{\sigma_1^2} \\ \vdots \\ \frac{1}{\sigma_1^2} \end{bmatrix}. \tag{12.11}$$

*Proof.* The global minimum portfolio is given by (see equation [3.11], Chapter 3)

$$\mathbf{w}_G = \frac{\mathbf{\Sigma}^{-1}\mathbf{1}}{\mathbf{1}^T\mathbf{\Sigma}^{-1}\mathbf{1}}$$

If $\mathbf{\Sigma}$ is diagonal

$$\mathbf{\Sigma} = \begin{bmatrix} \sigma_1^2 & & 0 \\ & \ddots & \\ 0 & & \sigma_n^2 \end{bmatrix},$$

[3]Note that the result of the quasi-diagonalization algorithm is not unique since each cluster can be ordered in two diverse ways.

and

$$\mathbf{\Sigma}^{-1} = \begin{bmatrix} \frac{1}{\sigma_1^2} & & 0 \\ & \ddots & \\ 0 & & \frac{1}{\sigma_n^2} \end{bmatrix}.$$

Replacing this expression of $\mathbf{\Sigma}^{-1}$ in $\mathbf{w}_G$, we obtain the desired result. ■

As the covariance matrix obtained from the second stage is quasi-diagonal, it is reasonable to perform the allocation assigning weights in inverse proportion to variance. Moreover, if we consider two assets, $n = 2$, then from equation (12.11) the allocation reads

$$w_1 = \frac{\frac{1}{\sigma_1^2}}{\frac{1}{\sigma_1^2} + \frac{1}{\sigma_2^2}} = 1 - \frac{\sigma_1^2}{\sigma_1^2 + \sigma_2^2}; \; w_2 = 1 - w_1, \tag{12.12}$$

and this is the rule that is applied in the recursive bisection algorithm, that we describe in what follows.

The algorithm is initialized with the list of assets, $L_0$, ordered as obtained from the quasi-diagonalization stage, and with unit weights for each asset: $w_i = 1, i = 1, \ldots, n$.

1. Any subset $L_i$ of assets is split into two, $L_i^{(1)}$ and $L_i^{(2)}$, with $L_i^{(1)} \cup L_i^{(2)} = L_i$, $|L_i^{(1)}| = int\left(\frac{1}{2}|L_i|\right)$ and the order is preserved.
2. The allocation is recalculated, multiplying each weight $w_k$ by the factor $\alpha_i$ if $k \in L_i^{(1)}$ or by $(1 - \alpha_i)$ if $k \in L_i^{(2)}$. The split factor $\alpha_i$ is given by

$$\alpha_i = 1 - \frac{\widetilde{V}_i^{(1)}}{\widetilde{V}_i^{(1)} + \widetilde{V}_i^{(2)}},$$

where

$$\widetilde{V}_i^{(j)} = \left(\widetilde{\mathbf{w}}_i^{(j)}\right)^T \mathbf{\Sigma}_i^{(j)} \widetilde{\mathbf{w}}_i^{(j)}$$

with

$$\widetilde{\mathbf{w}}_i^{(j)} = \frac{1}{tr\left[\left(\mathbf{\Sigma}_i^{(j)}\right)^{-1}\right]} \cdot diag\left[\left(\mathbf{\Sigma}_i^{(j)}\right)^{-1}\right]$$

and $\mathbf{\Sigma}_i^{(j)}$ is the covariance matrix between the constituents of the subset $L_i^{(j)}$, for $j = 1, 2$. (Note the analogy between the previous equations and equations [12.11] and [12.12] for the case of a diagonal covariance matrix.)

3. If each subset of assets has only one asset, the algorithm stops, and the final allocation is stored in the vector of weights $\mathbf{w}^T = (w_1, \ldots, w_n)$. Otherwise, the algorithm loops to step 1.

Note that the allocation obtained as the final result of the algorithm always gives rise to a portfolio, that is, $\sum_{i=1}^{n} w_i = 1$. To proof this, it is enough to realize that there will be pairs of weights that contain factors of the type $\alpha_k$ and $1 - \alpha_k$, where $\alpha_k$ is one of the split factors used in the last bisection, and with the other factors equal. By adding these two weights, that factor will disappear. Proceeding recursively from bottom to top, all factors are eliminated, obtaining the desired result.

López de Prado (2016b) uses simulated data to compare the HRP model with the Critical Line Algorithm (CLA) of Markowitz et al. (1993), and Risk Parity with inverse-variance allocation. The in-sample results show that the CLA portfolio is highly concentrated in a few assets, showing vulnerability to idiosyncratic shocks, while the Risk Parity portfolio offers an almost uniform distribution of weights among all assets, ignoring correlations, and making it vulnerable to systemic shocks. The HRP portfolio finds a compromise between both situations, making it more resilient against these types of shocks. The out-of-sample results show a considerable reduction in portfolio variance in the HRP method compared to CLA and Risk Parity.

In addition to the advantages noted above in terms of its empirical application, one of the most interesting properties of the HRP algorithm is that, unlike MV methods, it does not require the inversion of the covariance matrix, so it can work even with non-invertible matrices. Among the deficiencies of HRP revealed in the literature we can highlight the following (Raffinot, 2018b):

- **Chaining:** This is a problem derived from the use of the single linkage criterion and is because it only requires that a single distance be small for two clusters to be merged, ignoring all the other members of the clusters. This can lead to dispersed and not sufficiently compact clusters.
- **Lack of relationship between the first and third stages:** In the recursive bisection, the set of assets is divided into equal parts taking into account the ordering of the quasi-diagonalization stage, but without

taking into account the hierarchical structure obtained in the tree clustering stage.

- **Number of clusters:** In HRP, each asset is considered its own cluster, which can be interpreted as a form of overfitting, which can lead to suboptimal results.

## 12.4 NOTES

The HRP exposition is based on López de Prado (2016b, 2018). Other references used have been Raffinot (2018a) and Kaae and Karppinen (2022). Various works have emerged trying to remedy the problems of the HRP algorithm mentioned above. In Raffinot (2018a), a variation of the HRP model is proposed in which, instead of considering only the single linkage criterion, different agglomerative clustering alternatives are considered, specifically, complete linkage, average linkage, Ward's method and directed bubble hierarchical tree. Furthermore, within each cluster obtained from the dendrogram, an equally weighted allocation is considered. In Kaae and Karppinen (2022), a variant of HRP is proposed, called HRP Topdown, with only two stages: tree clustering with Ward's method as linkage criterion, and inverse-variance weight allocation for clusters arising from tree clustering.

CHAPTER 13

# Sensitivity-based Portfolios

by Alejandro Rodríguez Domínguez

This chapter is adapted by the author of the original paper, *Portfolio optimization based on neural networks sensitivities from assets dynamics respect common drivers*, Rodriguez Dominguez (2023). It introduces a comprehensive framework for modeling asset and portfolio dynamics, integrating this information into portfolio optimization. The focus is on defining the drivers for asset and portfolio dynamics and their optimal selection, utilizing the Commonality Principle to select portfolio drivers optimally as the common drivers.

The chapter begins by modeling portfolio constituent dynamics through Partial Differential Equations (PDEs), with solutions approximated using neural networks. Sensitivities with respect to the common drivers are obtained via Automatic Adjoin Differentiation (AAD) and incorporated into the portfolio optimization process. By embedding portfolio constituents into a sensitivity space regarding their common drivers and employing a distance matrix in this space—termed the Sensitivity Matrix—convex optimization for diversification is addressed. This matrix measures the similarity of the projections of portfolio constituents on a vector space formed by common drivers' returns, optimizing diversification for both idiosyncratic and systematic risks, and adding directionality and future behavior information via returns dynamics.

Hierarchical clustering is performed on the Sensitivity Matrix for portfolio optimization. The resulting clustering tree is used for recursive bisection to determine the weights. Sensitivities' dynamics approximated with neural networks are employed to solve the convex optimization problem, incorporating the hierarchical information of these sensitivities. Public and listed variables are leveraged to achieve maximum idiosyncratic and systematic diversification through the sensitivity space concerning optimal portfolio drivers.

The framework demonstrates superior performance in various experiments compared to all other out-of-sample methods across different markets and real datasets. It addresses critical portfolio management challenges, such as regime changes, non-stationarity, overfitting, and selection bias, providing a robust methodology to enhance performance further.

The true asset dynamics are modeled using differential equations with drivers as exogenous variables, as opposed to traditional risk factors or functions of individual variables. Asset and driver time series are used to approximate the solution of differential equations and partial derivatives with neural networks. This allows for the integration of sensitivity information into portfolio optimization, incorporating true risk and return dynamics approximated with public and listed data instead of statistical risk factors. The result is a vector of average sensitivity values with respect to the common drivers for each constituent, embedded in that vector space.

A distance matrix, the Sensitivity Matrix, is computed in this space and used for portfolio optimization. Hierarchical clustering is performed on a positive semi-definite neighbor of the sensitivity matrix using the single-linkage algorithm and a distance metric based on the sensitivity matrix. Clustered items are sorted by distance, and the Recursive Bisection technique is utilized, employing the clustering tree and clusters' covariances.

The main contributions of this framework are:

1. Incorporating sensitivity dynamics information approximated with neural networks into portfolio optimization.
2. Utilizing hierarchical clustering on the sensitivity matrix to solve the convex optimization problem and incorporating hierarchical information from these sensitivities, named Hierarchical Sensitivity Parity (HSP).
3. Developing a method to achieve maximum idiosyncratic and systematic diversification through the sensitivity space concerning optimal portfolio drivers (common drivers).

This innovative approach offers a robust and dynamic methodology for portfolio optimization, addressing key challenges in the field and providing a significant performance edge in real-world applications.

## 13.1 MODELING PORTFOLIOS DYNAMICS WITH PDEs

Asset dynamics can be modeled by unknown PDEs with independent variables as drivers. For an asset return $a_t$, a vector of lagged drivers returns $D_\tau = \{D_{1\tau}, \ldots, D_{M\tau}\}$ with lag $t - \tau$, assuming the asset dynamics can be modeled by a first-order PDE, which is unknown and analytically unsolvable, and its solution can be represented as a function $F : \mathbb{R}^{3M+1} \Rightarrow \mathbb{R}$:

$$a_t = F\left(\frac{\partial a_t}{\partial D_{1\tau}}, \frac{\partial a_t}{\partial D_{2\tau}}, \ldots, \frac{\partial a_t}{\partial D_{M\tau}}, \frac{\partial D_{1\tau}}{\partial t}, \ldots, \frac{\partial D_{M\tau}}{\partial t}, \frac{\partial a_t}{\partial t}, D_{1\tau}, \ldots, D_{M\tau}\right). \quad (13.1)$$

$F$ can be non-linear, but in the case of being linear it can be expressed as:

$$\begin{aligned} a_t = & \frac{\partial a_t}{\partial D_{1\tau}} + \frac{\partial a_t}{\partial D_{2\tau}} + \ldots + \frac{\partial a_t}{\partial D_{M\tau}} + \frac{\partial D_{1\tau}}{\partial t} + \ldots + \frac{\partial D_{M\tau}}{\partial t} \\ & + \frac{\partial a_t}{\partial t} + D_{1\tau} + \ldots + D_{M\tau}. \end{aligned} \quad (13.2)$$

A PDE solution of the type in equation (13.1) can be approximated with time series data and a neural network because they are universal approximators Cybenko (1989). A description of the functional approximator of a dynamical system like equation (13.2) and its components, following San Roque (1996) is:

$$a[t] = g(a_{t-1}, D_t, \varepsilon_{t-1}) + \varepsilon[t], \quad (13.3)$$

where:

- $g$ is a nonlinear function.
- $a[t]$ is the prediction of asset return at time $t$.
- $a_{t-1} = [a[t-1], a[t-2], \ldots]^T$ is a vector containing the asset returns in times $t-1$ and backward.
- $\boldsymbol{D}_t = [\boldsymbol{D}[t], \boldsymbol{D}[t-1], \ldots]^T$ is a vector containing the exogenous entries at times $t$ and backward (the asset drivers).
- $\varepsilon_{t-1} = [\varepsilon[t], \varepsilon[t-1], \ldots]^T$ is a vector with the White-Noise(WN) realizations at the assets return predictions at time $t-1$ and backward.
- $\varepsilon[t]$ is the WN realization at the assets return predictions at time $t$.

The system that represents the PDE solution in equation (13.2) for this case, can be approximated with a neural network $g = F(\boldsymbol{D}, \boldsymbol{w})$ in which the inputs are, $\boldsymbol{D}_t$ (feed-forward networks), or $\boldsymbol{D}_t$, $a_{t-1}$, $\varepsilon_t$ (recurrent networks), so that different configurations of neural networks can be used to approximate different modeling PDEs. In this chapter, the focus is specifically on feed-forward networks, with inputs, $\boldsymbol{D}_t$, the portfolio drivers, and output, $a[t]$, the prediction of asset returns. Once true dynamics are approximated with exogenous drivers, the sensitivities of the assets with respect to their drivers are obtained via Automatic Differentiation.

## 13.2 OPTIMAL DRIVERS SELECTION: CAUSALITY AND PERSISTENCE

Drivers are selected with two primary objectives: maximizing accuracy in approximating asset and portfolio dynamics and utilizing sensitivity information to project portfolio constituents into a sensitivity space, enabling diversification based on dynamic risk and return data. Drivers are defined as exogenous market or economic variables that influence asset dynamics, allowing for optimal selection for assets and portfolios.

**Definition 13.1** *Drivers Optimality. A driver is optimal for an asset if it is:*

- *Optimal in persistence: the amount of time it remains a driver.*
- *Optimal in selection based on the probability of causality: Since causality cannot be guaranteed, it is considered in terms of probabilities. An optimal driver should maximize the probability of influencing asset dynamics.*

**Definition 13.2** *Specific drivers are the optimal drivers for individual assets (portfolio constituents).*

Optimal driver selection enhances the approximation of asset dynamics and sensitivities. It is essential to use the most common specific drivers among all constituents for portfolio optimization, ensuring the sensitivity space allows for optimal diversification. This common set of drivers also serves as the optimal portfolio drivers based on their defined optimality.

The following theorem and proof are from Rodriguez Dominguez (2023), though seemingly obvious, are crucial for the methodology. They are necessary for improving portfolio dynamics approximation and achieving greater diversification.

**Theorem 13.1** *The Commonality Principle for Portfolio Drivers states that optimal drivers for a portfolio are the specific drivers that are repeatedly selected for the greatest number of portfolio constituents, both in terms of persistence and probability of causality.*

To prove the Commonality Principle, we first need to establish that the common drivers, the most repeatedly selected specific drivers among all constituents, are the most persistent and thus optimal for a portfolio. This proof leverages Modern Portfolio Theory (MPT) (Markowitz, 1952).

*Proof.* Modern portfolio theory and portfolio drivers' persistence: Drivers influence asset risks by determining their dynamics. Risks are categorized as idiosyncratic or systematic, with specific drivers contributing to both types. Most specific drivers of a particular portfolio constituent primarily contribute to its idiosyncratic risk, affecting only that asset. However, some drivers may also contribute to the systematic risk of both this individual asset and other constituents.

In the context of Modern Portfolio Theory (MPT), the total systematic risk explained by focusing on all specific drivers from all constituents is not maximal, as most specific drivers focus solely on idiosyncratic risks. By identifying common drivers across the portfolio, the focus shifts to those specific drivers that maximize systematic risk explanation across all constituents. These common drivers ensure optimal driver persistence as they contribute the maximum amount of systematic risk explanation for the portfolio. ■

To further support the Commonality Principle, it must be proved that the common drivers are the specific drivers for all constituents that exhibit the highest probability of causality for portfolio dynamics. This can be shown by proving that the maximum probability of causality for a portfolio, given any selection of drivers, is achieved by selecting drivers according to the Commonality Principle. Since causality cannot be guaranteed, the probability of causality is utilized in this analysis.

*Proof.* Probabilistic common causality and optimal portfolio drivers:

- Probability of causality for an asset or a portfolio, given a set of drivers, is defined as the probability that their dynamics are caused by this set of drivers.
- Given portfolio constituents $a_1, \ldots, a_N$ of a portfolio $p$, each constituent has associated $M_1, \ldots, M_N$ number of specific drivers. Constituent $a_1$ has $SD_{11}, \ldots, SD_{1M_1}$ specific drivers, $a_2$ has $SD_{21}, \ldots, SD_{1M_2}$, and the same up to $a_N$ with $SD_{N1}, \ldots, SD_{NM_N}$. There exists a probability of causality, probability of the drivers causing the constituents' dynamics at $k$ time steps in the future. Given by the following vector X, using Judea Pearl notation (Neuberg, 2003):

$$P\left(a_{1,t+k} | do\left(\left[SD_{11}, \ldots SD_{1M_1}\right]_t\right)\right) \leq X_1, \ldots,$$
$$P\left(a_{N,t+k} | do\left(\left[SD_{N1}, \ldots SD_{NM_N}\right]_t\right)\right) \leq X_N \tag{13.4}$$

- At a portfolio level, with $\boldsymbol{D}_t = \left[D_1, \ldots D_M\right]_t$ the common drivers for the portfolio as per the commonality principle:

$$P\left(p_{t+k} | \left[D_1, \ldots D_M\right]_t\right) \leq Y \tag{13.5}$$

- To prove the principle (portfolio drivers' optimality) for the probability of causality, the following proposition must be verified surely. It is shown now that it is, but only for the special case that the focus is at a portfolio level, which is coincidentally the only interest in portfolio optimization. $\forall p = [a_1, \ldots, a_N]$ and specific drivers $SD = [SD_{11}, \ldots, SD_{1M_1}, SD_{21}, \ldots, SD_{1M_2} \ldots, SD_{N1}, \ldots, SD_{NM_N}]$ and common drivers $\boldsymbol{D} = [D_1, \ldots D_M]$:

$$\begin{aligned} P\left(p_{t+k} | [D_1, \ldots D_M]_t\right) = \\ P\left(a_{1,t+k} \cap \cdots \cap a_{N,t+k} | [D_1, \ldots D_M]_t\right) > \\ P\left(a_{1,t+k} | [SD_{11}, \ldots SD_{1M_1}]_t\right) * \cdots * P\left(a_{N,t+p} | [SD_{N1}, \ldots SD_{NM_N}]_t\right) = \\ P\left(a_{1,t+k}\right) * \cdots * P\left(a_{N,t+k}\right). \end{aligned} \tag{13.6}$$

- For the proof, the Common Cause Principle (CCP, Reichenbach, 1956) is used: Suppose that events A and B are positively probabilistically correlated:

$$p(A \cap B) > p(A)p(B). \tag{13.7}$$

Reichenbach's Common Cause Principle states that when such a probabilistic correlation between A and B exists, this is because one of the following causal relations exists: A is a cause of B; B is a cause of A; or A and B are both caused by a third factor, C. In the last case, the common cause C occurs prior to A and B, and must satisfy the following four independent conditions:

$$p(A \cap B|C) = p(A|C)p(B|C) \tag{13.8}$$

$$p\left(A \cap B|\overline{C}\right) = p\left(A|\overline{C}\right)p\left(B|\overline{C}\right) \tag{13.9}$$

$$p(A|C) > p\left(A|\overline{C}\right) \tag{13.10}$$

$$p(B|C) > p\left(B|\overline{C}\right). \tag{13.11}$$

$\overline{C}$ denotes the absence of event C (the negation of the proposition that C happens), and it is assumed that neither C nor $\overline{C}$ has probability zero. The condition in equation (13.8) states that A and B are conditionally independent, given C. In Reichenbach's terminology, C screens A off from B. The condition in equation (13.9) states that $\overline{C}$ also screens A off from B. The conditions in equations (13.10) and (13.11) state that A and B are more probable, conditional on C, than conditional on the absence of C. These inequalities are natural consequences of C being a cause of A and of B. Together, the conditions in equations (13.8) through (13.11) mathematically entail equation (13.7). The common cause can thus be understood to explain the correlation in equation (13.7) (Reichenbach, 1956).

- For the general (CCP) case that the correlated effects are random variables like in the portfolio case: Suppose X and Y are random variables that are correlated, ie, there exist $x_i$ and $y_j$ such that

$$p\left(X = x_i \cap Y = y_j\right) \neq p\left(X = x_i\right) p\left(Y = y_j\right). \tag{13.12}$$

Then there exists a set of variables $Z_1, \ldots, Z_M$ so that each variable is the cause of X and Y, and

$$p(X = x_i \cap Y = y_j | Z_1 = z_{k_1}, \ldots, Z_m = z_{k_m}) = p(X = x_i | Z_1 = z_{k_1}, \ldots, Z_m = z_{k_m}) p(Y = y_j | Z_1 = z_{k_1}, \ldots, Z_m = z_{k_m}). \tag{13.13}$$

How the independent conditions are met for the portfolio case it is verified $\forall\, \boldsymbol{p} = [a_1, \ldots, a_N]$, $\forall i, j = 1, \ldots, N$, $i \neq j$, and common drivers $\boldsymbol{D} = [D_1, \ldots D_M]$:

$$p\left(a_i \cap a_j | \mathbf{D}\right) = p\left(a_i | \mathbf{D}\right) p\left(a_j | \mathbf{D}\right) \tag{13.14}$$

$$p\left(a_i \cap a_j | \overline{\mathbf{D}}\right) = p\left(a_i | \overline{\mathbf{D}}\right) p\left(a_j | \overline{\mathbf{D}}\right) \tag{13.15}$$

$$p\left(a_i | \mathbf{D}\right) > p\left(a_i | \overline{\mathbf{D}}\right) \tag{13.16}$$

$$p\left(a_j | \mathbf{D}\right) > p\left(a_j | \overline{\mathbf{D}}\right). \tag{13.17}$$

This mathematically entails:

$$p\left(a_i \cap a_j | \mathbf{D}\right) > p\left(a_i\right) p\left(a_j\right). \tag{13.18}$$

The common drivers (common cause) can thus be understood to explain the correlation between assets in the portfolio. The common cause must occur prior, which is the case for the common portfolio drivers and asset dynamics. The generalization of CCP is given by the Causal Markov Condition (CMC): A variable $a_i$ is independent of every other variable (except $a_i$'s effects) and conditional on all its direct causes. The CMC can be applied to all pairs of portfolio constituents as a generalization of CCP, given the subset of common drivers such that equations (13.14–13.17) holds. For that, it is necessary that the common driver's subset is a direct cause of portfolio constituent dynamics, which can be probabilistic approximated with correlation, by making use of the CCP for the particular case that the common cause (i.e., common drivers) is, at most, the same for all portfolio constituents. If $A$ is a subset of $\boldsymbol{p} = [a_1, \ldots, a_N]$, $\boldsymbol{S_i}$ is the set of specific drivers for asset $a_i$, $\boldsymbol{SD}$ is the set of all specific drivers for the portfolio constituents:

$$\forall a_i \in \boldsymbol{A}, \forall \boldsymbol{S_i} \in \boldsymbol{SD}, P\,(a_i|do\,(\boldsymbol{S_i})) > P\,(a_i|do\,(\sim \boldsymbol{S_i})). \tag{13.19}$$

Then, for the case of two assets: $\boldsymbol{D} = [D_1, \ldots D_M]$:

$$\begin{aligned} &\forall\, a_i, a_j \in A, i, j = 1, \ldots, N, i \neq j, \forall\, S_i, S_j \in SD\,: \\ &\qquad [P(a_i \mid do(S_i)) \;>\; P(a_i \mid do(\sim S_i))] \\ &\qquad \wedge\, [P(a_j \mid do(S_j)) \;>\; P(a_j \mid do(\sim S_j))] \\ &\rightarrow\; [P(a_i \cap a_j|S_X, S_Y) = P(a_i|S_X)P(a_j|S_Y)] = \\ &\qquad [P(a_i \cap Y|S) = P(a_i)P(a_j)], S \equiv S_i \equiv S_j, \end{aligned} \tag{13.20}$$

with $S$ a set of common drivers for constituents $a_i$ and $a_j$. Finally, for any $N$-assets portfolio:

$$\begin{aligned} &\{\forall p = [a_1, \ldots, a_N] \equiv A, \forall\, \{S_1, S_2, \ldots, S_N\} \equiv SD, \\ &\qquad [P(p|do\,(SD)) > P(p|do\,(\sim SD))]\{ \\ &\qquad\qquad \longleftrightarrow \\ &[P(a_1 \cap a_2, \cap \ldots|S_1, S_2, \ldots, S_N) = P(a_1|S_1)P(a_2|S_2), \ldots] \equiv \\ &\qquad [P(a_1 \cap a_2, \cap \ldots|S) = P\,(a_1)\,P\,(a_2)\ldots] \\ &\forall a_1,\, a_2, \ldots a_N \in A, \forall S_1 \equiv S_2 \equiv, \cdots \equiv S_N \equiv S. \end{aligned} \tag{13.21}$$

- In equation (13.19), it is shown that for any $a_i$, there exists a set of specific drivers that cause its dynamics optimally in probability, using Judea Pearl notation (Neuberg, 2003). In equation (13.20), it is shown how for a portfolio of two assets, and its specific drivers' selection, how, if they have the highest probability of causality for the assets' dynamics, the CCP conditions and equation (13.18) are met only if both $S_i$ and $S_j$ are equivalent, as per the commonality principle, and equal to their optimal common drivers in terms of probabilistic causality. This means that the common drivers are the common source of causality of portfolio constituents' dynamics, they are the greatest source in the probability of causality for portfolio dynamics, and they explain the correlation between portfolio constituents, for the two assets case, by applying (Reichenbach, 1956).

- In equation (13.21), the generalization for any combination of assets (portfolio) is shown in (13.21). Here, the implication goes two ways in that, for any portfolio of assets, their common drivers being the source of the highest probability of causality of portfolio dynamics (not their constituents), imply CCP conditions and equation (13.18) are met. But, if CCP and equation (13.18) are met, which occurs only in the case that the common drivers are selected based on the commonality principle, which, in turn, makes the equivalence in sets S possible, CCP conditions and equation (13.18) imply that they are the greatest source in the probability of causality for portfolio dynamics. This is true for any combinations of assets or portfolio ($p$) and common drivers set ($D$) chosen as in the commonality principle. But also, like in equation (13.20), this means that common drivers explain the correlation between portfolio constituents by applying (Reichenbach, 1956). ■

The fact that common drivers explain the correlation between portfolio constituents, as outlined by Reichenbach (1956), justifies the possible selection of common drivers (common causes) as those most correlated with the greatest number of portfolio constituents. This is the simplest driver selection method and has been shown to work effectively in experiments. Other selection methods may also be applicable, but they must adhere to the commonality principle, such as using Bayesian networks to check the CCP independence conditions.

## 13.3 AAD SENSITIVITIES APPROXIMATION

This chapter uses a neural network to approximate asset and portfolio dynamics, modeled by PDEs or stochastic differential equations (SDEs) with drivers as exogenous variables. Sensitivities are approximated using neural networks with Automated Adjoint Differentiation (AAD). However, this framework is suited for any sensitivity approximation due to the generality of the Commonality principle for portfolio drivers.

Neural networks function as feature extractors of dynamics, not solvers of the convex optimization problem. Sensitivities are obtained through derivative-based local methods, particularly Adjoint modeling and AAD. AAD is standard for extracting derivatives and system sensitivities. For example, Huge and Savine (2020) introduced Differential Machine Learning for derivative pricing and hedging. For a recent survey on sensitivity analysis using neural networks, see Pizarroso et al. (2021).

### 13.3.1 Optimal Network Selection

For each portfolio constituent, a neural network is fitted with the constituent as the output and the common drivers as inputs, using historical daily returns. Various architectures are evaluated, differing in layers, neurons, fitting window lengths, and lags between outputs and inputs. The architectures are trained and evaluated using Mean Square Error (MSE), selecting the optimal architecture based on this metric. A multilayer perceptron is used for each portfolio constituent. Figure 13.1 shows this step.

### 13.3.2 Sensitivity Analysis

An optimal architecture is selected for each portfolio constituent, and automatic differentiation approximates the partial derivatives with respect to the common drivers (i.e., sensitivities). These sensitivities are discrete functions with values at each time step of the fitting period. The average value provides a metric for each sensitivity over the computation period. Different functions can summarize this sensitivity information to improve performance (Pizarroso et al., 2021). For each portfolio constituent $a_i$:

$$E\left[a_{it}|D_\tau\right] = F\left(\frac{\partial a_t}{\partial D_{1\tau}}, \frac{\partial a_t}{\partial D_{2\tau}}, \ldots, \frac{\partial a_t}{\partial D_{M\tau}}, \frac{\partial D_{1\tau}}{\partial t}, \ldots, \frac{\partial D_{M\tau}}{\partial t}, \frac{\partial a_t}{\partial t}, D_{1\tau}, \ldots, D_{M\tau}\right) \tag{13.22}$$

is approximated by a neural network $(NN_i)$, and sensitivities with respect to the common drivers $\frac{\partial a_t}{\partial D_{1\tau}}, \frac{\partial a_t}{\partial D_{2\tau}}, \ldots, \frac{\partial a_t}{\partial D_{M\tau}}$, are obtained with AAD. Sensitivities are the partial derivatives defined as $s_{ij}|_{D_\tau}^{NN_i} = \frac{\partial a_{it}}{\partial D_{j\tau}}(\boldsymbol{D}_\tau)$, referring to the sensitivity of the output of the neuron in the output layer of $NN_i$ with respect to the input of the $j^{th}$ neuron in the input layer evaluated in the sample $\boldsymbol{D}_\tau$. It is obtained by applying the chain rule to the partial derivatives of the inner layers.

### 13.3.3 Sensitivity Distance Matrix

Once sensitivities are obtained for all portfolio constituents with respect to the common drivers, they are incorporated into the portfolio optimization.

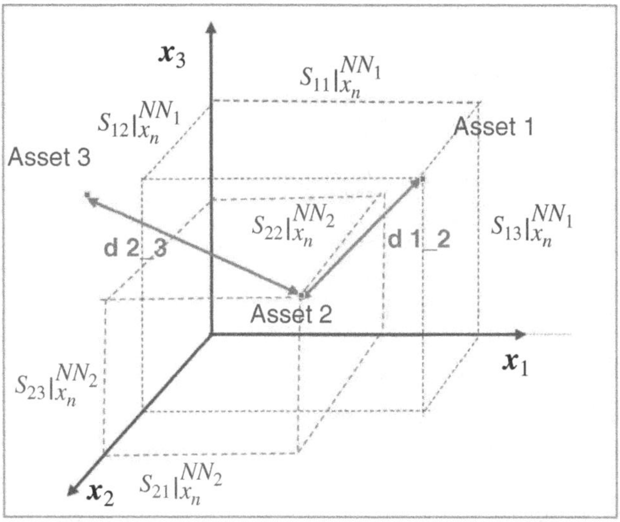


**FIGURE 13.1** Embedded space of sensitivities: Average sensitivities $s_{ij}|_{D_\tau}^{NN_i}$ of asset $i$, $i = 1, \ldots, 3$ and common driver $x_j = D_{j\tau}$, $j = 1, \ldots, 3$ (dashes for asset 2 and smaller dashes for asset 1). Distances are labeled as d 2_3 and d 1_2.

Portfolio constituents, $a_{1t}, \ldots, a_{Nt}$, are embedded in the M-dimensional space of averages of sensitivity values with respect to common drivers, with $M$ being the number of common drivers for the portfolio:

$$\begin{bmatrix} a_{1t} \\ \vdots \\ a_{Nt} \end{bmatrix} = \begin{bmatrix} \frac{\partial a_{1t}}{\partial D_{1\tau}} & \cdots & \frac{\partial a_{1t}}{\partial D_{M\tau}} \\ \vdots & \ddots & \vdots \\ \frac{\partial a_{Nt}}{\partial D_{1\tau}} & \cdots & \frac{\partial a_{Nt}}{\partial D_{M\tau}} \end{bmatrix} \begin{bmatrix} D_{1\tau} \\ \vdots \\ D_{M\tau} \end{bmatrix} \cong \begin{bmatrix} s_{11}|_{D_\tau}^{NN_1} & \cdots & s_{1M}|_{D_\tau}^{NN_1} \\ \vdots & \ddots & \vdots \\ s_{N1}|_{D_\tau}^{NN_N} & \cdots & s_{NM}|_{D_\tau}^{NN_N} \end{bmatrix} \begin{bmatrix} D_{1\tau} \\ \vdots \\ D_{M\tau} \end{bmatrix}. \tag{13.23}$$

In Figure 13.2, three portfolio constituents are represented in a M-dimensional space with $M = 3$, and coordinates given by the average sensitivity values of each constituent (i.e., asset) with respect to the common drivers. Finally, in this space a distance matrix can be computed for any metric.

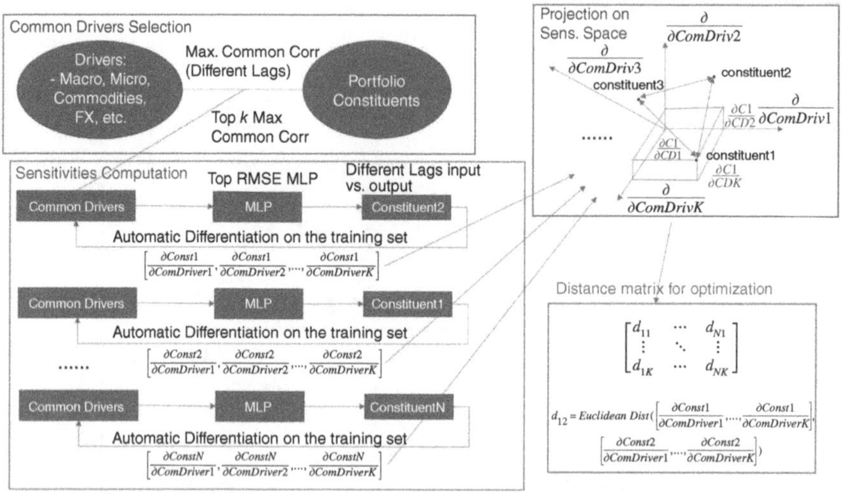


**FIGURE 13.2** Methodology modules: sensitivities are extracted from multilayer perceptrons (MLP) with AAD and used as coordinates in the projective space, each constituent has its own vector. Distance matrix computed in this space.

**Definition 13.3** *Sensitivity Matrix: Distance matrix between portfolio constituents in the embedded space of sensitivity values.*

$$S = \begin{bmatrix} s_{11} & \cdots & s_{1N} \\ \vdots & \ddots & \vdots \\ s_{N1} & \cdots & s_{NN} \end{bmatrix},$$

$$s_{ij} = d\left(\frac{\partial a_{it}}{\partial D_\tau}, \frac{\partial a_{jt}}{\partial D_\tau}\right) = d\left(\vec{\beta}_i, \vec{\beta}_j\right) = d\left(\left[\beta_i^1, \ldots, \beta_i^M\right], \left[\beta_j^1, \ldots, \beta_j^M\right]\right). \quad (13.24)$$

In this work, coordinates of portfolio constituents are the averages (i.e., any other function can be applied) of sensitivity values with respect to the common drivers in the training or test dataset. Sensitivities capture optimal causal and persistence information of constituents' dynamics for the fitting period. By embedding constituents into a sensitivity space, the similarity matrix (i.e., sensitivity matrix) enables comparison of portfolio assets based on their causal and persistent common dynamics. Additionally, the setup supports directional diversification, where risk diversification gains an extra dimension from the true dynamics information of portfolio returns related to public and listed variables, rather than statistical factors. This approach enhances the approximation of directionality or future trajectory in portfolio returns for risk diversification.

## 13.4 HIERARCHICAL SENSITIVITY PARITY

To address the problem of portfolio optimization, it is essential to map risk from the sensitivity space to a chosen risk measure. There are several solutions available. This chapter focuses on Hierarchical Sensitivity Parity, as proposed by Rodriguez Dominguez (2023), which employs hierarchical clustering to map risk from the sensitivity space to volatility measures, assuming that risk hierarchies are maintained. Similar to López de Prado (2016b), who used hierarchical clustering on the correlation matrix, this method applies hierarchical clustering to the sensitivity matrix from 13.24, and uses the hierarchical representation of projections in the sensitivity space to improve diversification. Performance improves by using the nearest positive-definite neighbor of the sensitivity matrix, computed as in Higham (1988).

Single-linkage clustering is then applied to the sensitivity matrix or a positive-definite neighbor one. Clustered items are sorted by distance, ensuring portfolio constituents are close to comparable items and far from dissimilar ones (Quasidiagonalization from Section 12.3). Recursive Bisection from Section 12.3 is then used to compute the weights. The sorted sensitivity matrix helps explore the clustering tree from top to bottom, with two clusters competing for weights at each partition. This method, Hierarchical Sensitivity Parity (HSP), applies recursive bisection with a clustering tree derived from the single-linkage algorithm using the sensitivity matrix or its positive semi-definite neighbor, unlike Hierarchical Risk Parity (HRP) from López de Prado (2016b), which uses a correlation matrix. This allows the inclusion of exogenous information in the form of drivers' dynamics and future trajectories of risk and return into the search for diversification and optimal solutions.

## 13.5 IMPLEMENTATION

### 13.5.1 Datasets

Bloomberg provides two datasets:

- **Driver's Dataset:** This dataset includes 1200 time series data from 2022 to 2022, covering spot and option prices for major FX crosses, government bonds, macroeconomic indicators, principal equity indexes, mutual fund indexes, Credit Default Swap (CDS) prices, futures prices for major commodities, smart beta Exchange Traded Funds (ETFs), main crypto assets, equity index's option implied volatility, and equity sector's ETFs for the US and Europe.

- **Stock Price Dataset:** This dataset includes daily price data for 14 stocks from the Stoxx 600 and SP500 (Europe and US portfolios, respectively), covering different sectors to ensure initial diversification.

### 13.5.2 Experimental Setup

Experiments are conducted with various hyperparameters. The number of common drivers, $M$, is evaluated with values 10, 15, 20, and 30. The correlation window $W_{CD}$ uses 6 and 12 months of daily data for optimal driver selection. The neural networks training window $W_{NN}$ is evaluated with 60, 90, and 125 market days. Any probabilistic method that maximizes the Reichenbach independent conditions (Reichenbach, 1956) for $M$ common drivers is valid. For simplicity, we use the method based on correlations. For correlation thresholds $T_1$ and $T_0$, a ranking rule selects the top $M$ candidates most correlated with the portfolio constituents. Different lags are used in the neural networks for both in-sample and out-of-sample sensitivity approximation.

Two HSP method versions are available: Select allows adjustments based on additional information, while Opt. selects the top $M$ drivers based solely on the highest correlation values. Driver selection can use lag 0 or 1 separately or both simultaneously, resulting in different sets of optimal drivers and performances. Portfolio optimization (i.e., rebalancing) is performed monthly with fixed weights for the next month. Experiments include driver selection on each rebalance date and a scenario where common drivers' selection occurs every six months, fixed for six subsequent rebalances. All backtest performances are measured out-of-sample, with past data used for all modules, models, and computations, ensuring consistency across methods. Equity names are fixed, and weights are restricted between 3% and 10% to avoid concentration.

The study includes various mean-variance optimization techniques (Maximum Sharpe, Minimum Volatility, Quadratic Utility, Target Return, etc.) and the HRP method to evaluate the hypothesis that adding hierarchical sensitivity dynamics information improves performance compared to using hierarchical correlation information as in HRP. Indirect comparisons to other methods using risk factors instead of drivers are made by selecting smart beta ETFs or equity and sector indexes as common drivers. It has been validated that adding risk factors as common drivers results in lower performance than OPT variants. All methods use the same past window for covariance or correlation matrices for optimization, including recursive bisection for HRP and HSP.

### 13.5.3 Short-to-medium Investments

Experiments for the US and Europe portfolios are presented with performance measured using Net Asset Values (NAVs), representing the time series daily dollars under management if the strategy starts with 100 dollars, computed from 01/06/2020 to 01/12/2021. For the proposed method, common drivers are selected on 01/06/2020, 01/01/2021, and 01/07/2021. All rebalances are performed on the 1st of each month with weights fixed for the next 30 days.

**US Portfolio** In Table 13.1, we show returns, volatilities (annualized), and Sharpes for the top mean-variance methods and 1/N only, for the entire period from 01/06/2020 to 01/12/2021. In Figure 13.3, we show NAVs from 02/2021 to 12/2021.

**TABLE 13.1** US portfolio performance metrics for top mean-variance methods and 1/N: Returns, Risks, and Sharpes for full period: 01/06/2020–01/12/2021.

| | Max Sharpe(Mark) | Min Vol(Mark) | QU Mark | 1/N |
|---|---|---|---|---|
| Return | 49% | 44% | 49% | 50% |
| Vol (Ann) | 16% | 15% | 17% | 17% |
| Sharpe | 3,061 | 3,002 | 2,920 | 3,006 |

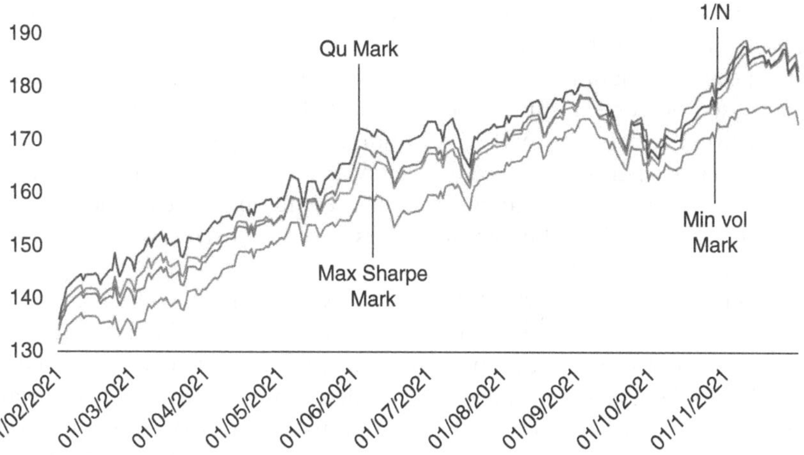


**FIGURE 13.3** NAVs for US portfolio top mean-variance methods and 1/N: NAV starting from 01/06/2020, showing sub-period (02/2021–12/2021).

**TABLE 13.2** US portfolio performance metrics for 1/N, HRP, HSP for different model hyperparameters: Returns, Risk and Sharpes for full period: 01/06/2020–01/12/2021.

| | HSP 6m LAG 1 SELECT | HSP 6m LAG 0 OPT | HSP 6m LAG 1 OPT | 1/N | HRP |
|---|---|---|---|---|---|
| Return | 54% | 55% | 54% | 50% | 52% |
| Vol (Ann) | 17% | 17% | 17% | 17% | 17% |
| Sharpe | 3,157 | 3,340 | 3,116 | 3,0 | 2,954 |

The results now include the proposed method (HSP). Table 13.2 presents the top mean-variance performers, including Max Sharpe, the 1/N method, and HRP. Additionally, the best-performing versions of the proposed method—HSP 6m LAG1 SELECT, HSP 6m LAG0 OPT, and HSP 6m LAG1 OPT—are included, all of which outperform the other methods. Six or twelve months of past data windows for correlations are used for driver selection. Correlation thresholds $T_1$ and $T_0$ for respective lags 1 and 0 ensure sufficient candidates and a similar number of common drivers on all selection dates. The optimal neural network (NN) architecture for fitting and sensitivity computation, as described in Section 13.3.1, is chosen from networks with inputs and outputs having lag 0, lag 1, or both. Different fitting windows of 60, 90, and 125 market days are evaluated to find the optimal configuration.

HSP 6m LAG1 OPT uses a 6-month window for correlation-based driver selection, with only lag 1 between constituents and drivers, to find the optimal configuration. The OPT version uses the full algorithmic selection based on correlation thresholds. The SELECT version tunes the common drivers' selection from the algorithm, considering spurious correlations, stocks that are part of an index driver, and multicollinearity. The ranking of the most commonly correlated drivers is used, taking these restrictions into account. The number of common drivers varies on each selection date due to fluctuating correlations.

Figure 13.4 displays the NAVs for the entire period, while Figure 13.5 focuses on the sub-period from 01/02/2021 to 01/12/2021. Note that the last common driver selection occurred on 01/07/2021, five months prior to the observed underperformance of all models from November 2021 onward (see Figure 13.5). This suggests that the optimal selection of common drivers might have changed within those five months, and more frequent updates, rather than every six months, could potentially have mitigated the observed losses. Despite the overall performance decline, the HSP 6m LAG0 OPT model maintained its performance.

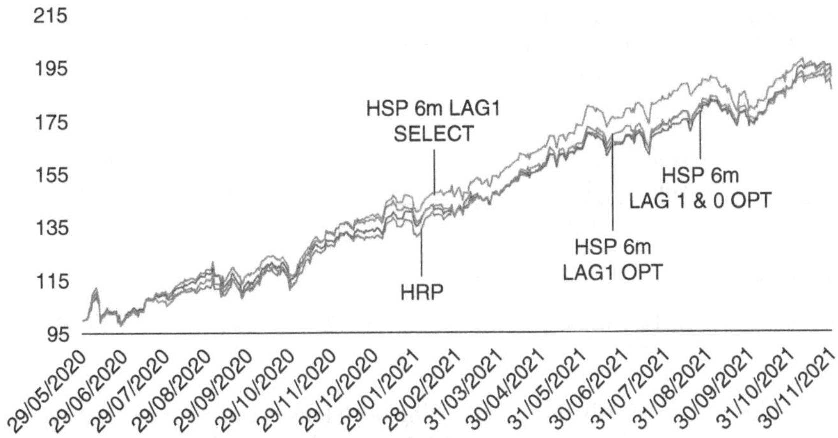


**FIGURE 13.4** NAVs for US portfolio for top mean-variance methods, 1/N, HRP, and HSP for different model hyperparameters: NAV starting from 01/06/2020. Showing the top four performers.

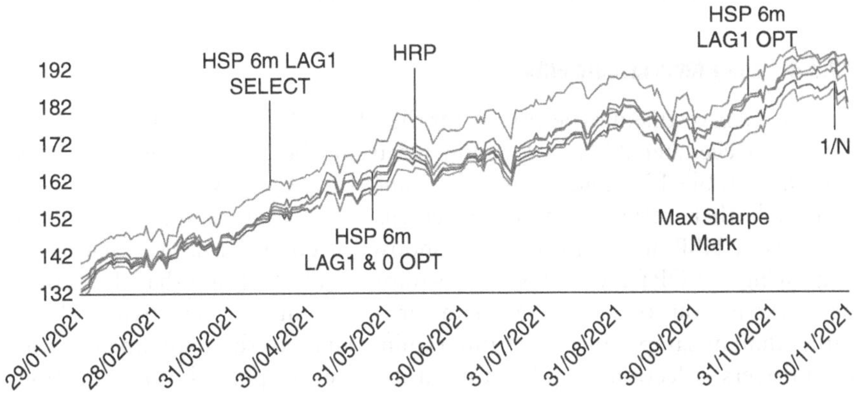


**FIGURE 13.5** NAVs for US portfolio for top mean-variance methods, 1/N, HRP, and HSP for different model hyperparameters: NAV starting from 01/06/2020, zoom of Figure 13.4 showing sub-period from 01/2021.

**Europe Portfolio** The proposed method continues to be the best performer in the EU case. Table 13.3 presents the results for the top mean-variance case, 1/N, HRP, and two variants of the proposed method: HSP 6m LAG1 OPT and HSP 6m LAG0 & 1 SELECT. HSP 6m LAG1 OPT uses a 6-month window and lag 1, employing full algorithmic selection based on correlation thresholds as determined in the US case. HSP 6m LAG0 & 1 SELECT involves modifications to the common drivers' candidates that pass the

**TABLE 13.3** EU portfolio performance metrics for top mean-variance methods, 1/N, HRP, HSP for different model hyperparameters. Returns, Risk and Sharpes for full period: 01/06/2020–01/12/2021.

| | Min vol | Target Ret | 1/N | HRP | HSP 6m LAG 1 OPT | HSP 6m LAG0 & 1 SELECT |
|---|---|---|---|---|---|---|
| Return | 22% | 16% | 25% | 30% | 34% | 30% |
| Vol (Ann) | 17% | 16% | 18% | 19% | 21% | 21% |
| Sharpe | 1,3014 | 0,9688 | 1,3740 | 1,5242 | 1,6494 | 1,433 |

thresholds, as previously described, using both lags 0 and 1 for input drivers. The performances shown in Table 13.3 cover the period from 01/06/2020 to 01/12/2021. The superiority of the proposed method over all others is evident. The comments made in the US experiment subsection apply here as well, indicating potential performance improvements with further optimization of model hyperparameters and flexible configurations.

### 13.5.4 Long-term Investments

Long-term investment experiments for the US portfolio, spanning from June 2015 to December 2021, are conducted using the same methodology. As shown in Table 13.4 and Figures 13.6 and 13.7, the HSP method outperforms all other methods in terms of returns, Sharpe ratios, and NAVs. Both versions of HSP utilize a 6-month window for common driver's selection, employing the OPT method. Out-of-sample results indicate that the neural networks use out-of-sample test data for the averages of sensitivity values, rather than in-sample averages from training data. For this experiment, common drivers' selection is updated monthly on every portfolio optimization (rebalance) date, resulting in improved performance compared to the previous EU and USA cases, as evidenced by the NAV series in Figures 13.6–13.8 and Tables 13.4 and 13.5. In Table 13.5 and Figure 13.8 experiments are shown for two decades (from December 2002 to December 2022).

From the experiments, it is observed that the optimal number of common drivers depends on the number of portfolio constituents. An optimal range of 10–20 yields the best results for a portfolio of fourteen constituents. Fewer drivers result in lost explanatory power, while more drivers introduce multicollinearity issues. Correlation thresholds ensure that all drivers' selection dates have between ten and twenty candidates above the thresholds. Correlation windows of 6 and 12 months are used, with shorter

**TABLE 13.4** US portfolio long-term investments performance metrics for top mean-variance methods, HRP, HSP for different model hyperparameters. Returns, Risk and Sharpes for full period: 06/2015–12/2021.

| | HSP 6m Out-Of-Sample OPT | HSP 6m In-sample OPT | Min Vol | Quadratic Utility | HRP |
|---|---|---|---|---|---|
| Return | 18,9% | 19,3% | 15,3% | 17,2% | 18,1% |
| Vol (Ann) | 21,2% | 21,2% | 19,2% | 20,4% | 21,8% |
| Sharpe | 0,89 | 0,91 | 0,80 | 0,85 | 0,83 |

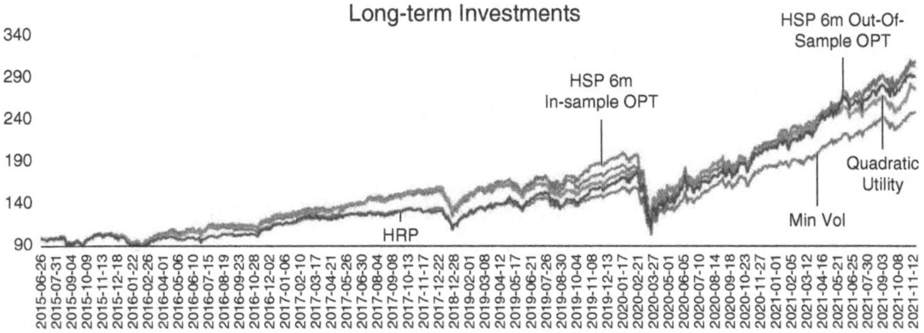


**FIGURE 13.6** NAVs for US portfolio long-term investments for top mean-variance methods, HRP, and HSP for different model hyperparameters. NAV from 06/2015 to 12/2021.

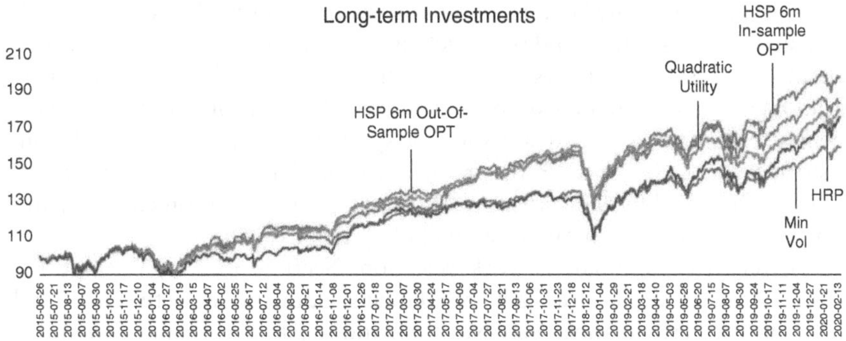


**FIGURE 13.7** NAVs for US portfolio long-term investments zoom of Figure 13.6: from 06/2015 to pre-COVID 03/2020.

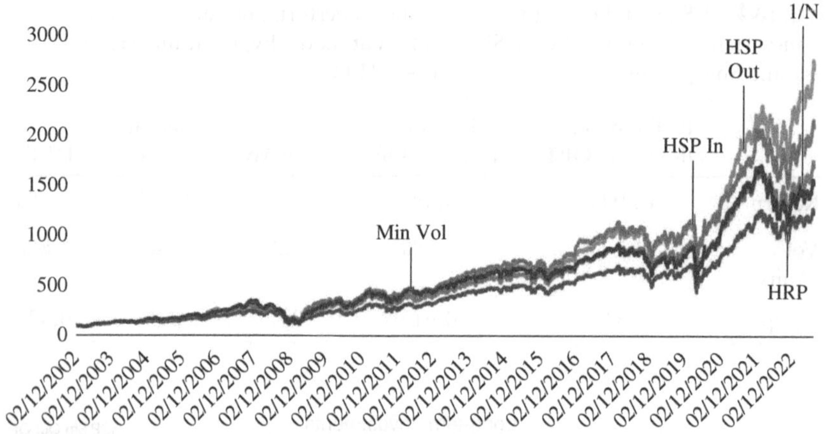


**FIGURE 13.8** Long-term investments. US portfolio long-term investments performance metrics for top mean-variance methods, HRP, and HSP for different model hyperparameters. Two decades: 12/2002–12/2022.

windows adapting better to changing market conditions when drivers' selection remains fixed for future rebalancing dates.

The OPT version of the drivers' selection uses correlation thresholds to achieve the desired number of common driver candidates. Hyperparameters can be tuned based on historical performance. The SELECT version allows truncating the optimal drivers' selection to combine common correlation and other rationales, avoiding issues like multicollinearity. Drivers' selections can be truncated to use any desired set of drivers, which is useful when employing smart beta indexes to utilize precomputed risk factor models listed as ETFs. Other indexes, such as sector-based, geographical, credit quality, or cross-asset drivers, can also be used. Public and listed information from ETFs, funds, and indexes provides accessible and computationally efficient alternatives to hidden statistical or synthetic risk factors derived from historical data. Flexibility in the frequency of updates for common drivers' selection helps address backtest overfitting, market condition changes, and portfolio adjustments at any level, including risk aversion.

In terms of optimal network selection (Section 13.3.1), the optimal fitting window varies for each rebalancing date but is between 3 and 4.5 months. Performance decreases for windows longer than 4.5 months. A consistent lag for all rebalances works better on average than mixing lags. Figures 13.7 present two user options: using the training set for in-sample sensitivities or the test set for out-of-sample sensitivities with different prediction horizons. Users can choose other distance metrics for the sensitivity matrix, though Euclidean distance is used in this chapter. The HSP algorithm

**TABLE 13.5** US portfolio long-term investments performance metrics for top mean-variance methods, HRP, and HSP for different model hyperparameters. Returns, Risk and Sharpes for full period: 12/2002–12/2022.

| | HSP 6m Out-Of-Sample OPT | HSP 6m In-sample OPT | Min Vol | 1/N | HRP |
|---|---|---|---|---|---|
| $NAV_0$ | 100% | 100% | 100% | 100% | 100% |
| $NAV_f$ | 2279% | 2107% | 1236% | 1706% | 1533% |
| Return (Ann) | 17,43% | 15,97% | 12,98% | 14,77% | 14,20% |
| Vol (Ann) | 23,02% | 23,07% | 22,89% | 22,06% | 21,99% |
| Sharpe | 0,76 | 0,69 | 0,57 | 0,67 | 0,65 |

uses a single-linkage algorithm, but other hierarchical clustering methods can also be applied. Experiments show that using a positive semi-definite neighbor of the sensitivity matrix significantly improves performance, aligning with recursive bisection weight computation principles.

## 13.6 CONCLUSION

This work advances the state-of-the-art by incorporating sensitivity dynamics information, approximated with neural networks, into portfolio optimization. Unlike factor model approaches, it uses public and listed information as drivers of asset returns, which are accessible and computationally efficient. Sensitivity information of constituents with respect to portfolio drivers adds directionality to the risk measure, enhancing diversification through return and risk dynamics. The commonality principle selects optimal portfolio drivers maintaining maximum idiosyncratic risk representation while adding systematic representation. Including sensitivity dynamics information with respect to public and listed drivers results in a less computationally expensive solution, less dependent on distributional assumptions, and improves diversification by adding directionality or dynamic behavior information of constituents. Over-performance compared to other out-of-sample methods indirectly proves superiority over risk factor methods by using smart beta factor ETFs as common drivers, projecting constituents into their sensitivity space, and optimizing with the sensitivity matrix and HSP.

Further contributions include using hierarchical clustering on the sensitivity matrix to solve the convex optimization problem by mapping risk from the embedded sensitivity space to the volatility risk measure, as the sensitivities hierarchies are preserved in both spaces. The method is termed Hierarchical Sensitivity Parity (HSP). This method improves upon the HRP method, based on correlation matrix hierarchies, by diversifying based on sensitivity matrix hierarchies. Projection hierarchies of constituents with respect to common drivers provide greater diversification than hierarchies of asset correlations, as demonstrated in experiments. It performs better in rallies and drawdowns, consistently delivering superior risk-adjusted returns due to the use of future trajectory information of risk and diversification from the space of sensitivity dynamics.

# PART Five

# Backtesting

CHAPTER 14

# Backtesting in Portfolio Management

## 14.1 INTRODUCTION

Backtesting is a fundamental process in the validation of quantitative trading strategies. It involves applying a trading strategy to historical market data to evaluate its performance. The primary goal is to estimate how well the strategy might perform in the future based on its historical behavior. The importance of backtesting in the context of portfolio management cannot be overstated, as it allows portfolio managers to understand the potential risks and returns of their strategies before deploying real capital (Bailey et al., 2014).

The concept of backtesting has evolved alongside advancements in computing power and the availability of high-frequency financial data. Initially, backtesting was a manual process, limited by the computational tools of the time. With the advent of modern computing, the scope and accuracy of backtesting have significantly improved. This chapter delves into the methodologies of backtesting, focusing on key aspects such as data preparation, performance metrics, common pitfalls, and advanced techniques.

## 14.2 DATA PREPARATION AND HANDLING

Accurate data preparation is critical for effective backtesting. Financial data can be sourced from various providers, including Bloomberg, Reuters, and Yahoo Finance. The data types typically used in backtesting include price data, volume data, and fundamental data such as earnings and dividends (Chan, 2013).

Data cleaning involves removing errors and inconsistencies in the dataset. Common preprocessing steps include handling missing values through interpolation or imputation, adjusting for stock splits and dividends, and normalizing data to ensure consistency. Ensuring that all datasets are synchronized in terms of time is crucial for accurate backtesting.

This involves aligning data from various sources and ensuring that timestamps match across all datasets.

Mathematically, if $p_t$ represents the price at time $t$, then adjusted prices $\tilde{p}_t$ after accounting for dividends $d_t$ and splits $s_t$ can be given by:

$$\tilde{p}_t = \frac{p_t + d_t}{s_t}.$$

High-frequency data (e.g., tick data) can provide more detailed insights into intraday price movements but also introduces higher noise levels and requires more sophisticated handling techniques. Conversely, daily or monthly data may smooth out noise but might miss short-term trading opportunities.

## 14.3 IMPLEMENTATION OF TRADING STRATEGIES

The trading strategy should be implemented in a systematic manner, often using algorithmic trading software. This includes defining entry and exit rules, position sizing, and risk management protocols.

Trading rules are the backbone of any trading strategy. These rules can be based on technical indicators, fundamental analysis, or a combination of both. For instance, a simple moving average crossover strategy might involve buying a stock when its short-term moving average crosses above its long-term moving average.

The moving averages can be defined as:

$$\text{SMA}_{\text{short}}(t) = \frac{1}{n_{\text{short}}} \sum_{i=0}^{n_{\text{short}}-1} p_{t-i}$$

$$\text{SMA}_{\text{long}}(t) = \frac{1}{n_{\text{long}}} \sum_{i=0}^{n_{\text{long}}-1} p_{t-i}.$$

Position sizing determines the amount of capital allocated to each trade. This can be based on fixed dollar amounts, fixed percentages of the portfolio, or more complex methods such as the Kelly criterion, which is given by:

$$f^* = \frac{bp - q}{b},$$

where $f^*$ is the fraction of the portfolio to bet, $b$ is the odds received on the bet, $p$ is the probability of winning, and $q$ is the probability of losing ($q = 1 - p$) (Efron and Tibshirani, 1994).

Risk management is a critical component of any trading strategy. Techniques include setting stop-loss orders, limiting the amount of capital at risk in any single trade, and diversifying the portfolio across different assets and markets.

## 14.4 TYPES OF BACKTESTS

There are three principal methods of conducting a backtest: walk-forward testing, resampling, and Monte Carlo simulations. Each of these methods has unique challenges and benefits (Joubert et al., 2024).

### 14.4.1 Walk-forward Backtest

The most widely used backtesting method is walk-forward testing, also referred to as historical backtesting. In this approach, the strategy is assessed against a series of subsequently observed events and asset price moves from a past period. The main benefit of the walk-forward method is that the results and performance characteristics are easy to analyze, interpret, and compare between different periods. However, one of the principal limitations is that only a single path is evaluated, which raises the risk of overfitting. The observed past performance may not be indicative of future results since the underlying relationships that the strategy aims to exploit may not be repeated.

### 14.4.2 Resampling Method

The resampling method includes techniques such as cross-validation and bootstrapping. Cross-validation involves splitting observations into groups and alternating between them for training and validation purposes. Bootstrapping entails drawing observations from the sample at random using varying logic. The advantage of these methods is the availability of multiple paths to evaluate the strategy and check its robustness. However, the observed performance across multiple past paths may not accurately represent the future.

In bootstrapping, given a time series of returns $\{r_t\}$, we generate multiple resampled series $\{r_t^*\}$ by sampling with replacement from the original data.

### 14.4.3 Monte Carlo Simulations and Generative Models

Monte Carlo simulations require an understanding of the data generation process for their construction. This method enables the generation of additional data with properties resembling those observed in the real data.

The main benefit of this method is that the observed performance is indicative of future outcomes, provided the data generation process is unchanged and correct. However, creating an accurate data generation process can be challenging.

For instance, generating price paths using Geometric Brownian Motion (GBM) can be modeled as:

$$dS_t = \mu S_t dt + \sigma S_t dW_t,$$

where $S_t$ is the asset price, $\mu$ is the drift coefficient, $\sigma$ is the volatility, and $W_t$ is a Wiener process or Brownian motion.

In the next Chapter, we suggest new tools to generate scenarios and joint probability distributions as Variational Autoencoders (VAE) and Generative Adversarial Networks (GAN).

## 14.5 PERFORMANCE METRICS

Common performance metrics used in backtesting include Return on Investment (ROI), Sharpe ratio, Maximum Drawdown, and Alpha and Beta. ROI measures the profitability of the strategy and is calculated as the percentage increase in the value of the portfolio over the backtest period. The Sharpe Ratio assesses risk-adjusted return, considering both the returns and the volatility of the portfolio (Bailey et al., 2014).

$$\text{ROI} = \frac{\text{Ending Portfolio Value} - \text{Starting Portfolio Value}}{\text{Starting Portfolio Value}}. \tag{14.1}$$

The Sharpe ratio is defined as:

$$\text{Sharpe ratio} = \frac{E\left[R_p - R_f\right]}{\sigma_p},$$

where $R_p$ is the return of the portfolio, $R_f$ is the risk-free rate, and $\sigma_p$ is the standard deviation of the portfolio's excess return.

The Maximum Drawdown evaluates the largest peak-to-trough decline during the backtest period, providing insight into the worst-case scenario for the strategy. It is calculated as:

$$\text{Max Drawdown} = \min_{t\in[0,T]} \left( \frac{\text{Portfolio Value}_t - \text{Portfolio Value}_{\text{peak}}}{\text{Portfolio Value}_{\text{peak}}} \right).$$

Alpha and Beta are metrics from the Capital Asset Pricing Model (CAPM) that assess performance relative to a benchmark, with Alpha representing the excess return and Beta indicating the sensitivity of the portfolio to market movements. They are defined as:

$$R_i - R_f = \alpha + \beta\left(R_m - R_f\right) + \epsilon_i,$$

where $R_i$ is the return of the investment, $R_f$ is the risk-free rate, $R_m$ is the return of the market, $\alpha$ is the intercept (Alpha), $\beta$ is the slope (Beta), and $\epsilon_i$ is the error term.

Another important metric is the Sortino ratio, which is similar to the Sharpe ratio but differentiates harmful volatility from total overall volatility by using the standard deviation of negative asset returns, known as downside deviation:

$$\text{Sortino ratio} = \frac{R_p - R_f}{\sigma_d},$$

where $\sigma_d$ is the downside deviation.

## 14.6 AVOIDING COMMON PITFALLS

Overfitting occurs when a model is excessively complex, capturing noise rather than the underlying data pattern. Techniques to avoid overfitting include cross-validation, out-of-sample testing, and simplifying the model (Efron and Tibshirani, 1994). Look-ahead bias happens when future data is inadvertently used in the backtest, leading to unrealistic performance results. Ensuring that only historical data available at the time of trading decisions is used is crucial. Survivorship bias arises when only active securities are included in the backtest, ignoring those that have delisted. Including historical data for all securities, including those that have failed, is necessary for an accurate assessment (Bailey et al., 2014).

Additionally, one must be aware of data-snooping bias, which occurs when a strategy is repeatedly evaluated on the same dataset. This can lead to spurious findings that are not robust in out-of-sample data. To mitigate this, researchers can use walk-forward optimization, where the strategy is optimized on a rolling basis over different time periods.

## 14.7 ADVANCED TECHNIQUES

Walk-forward analysis involves repeatedly optimizing the strategy on a training set, and then evaluating it on a subsequent testing set. This simulates the process of applying the strategy in a real-world scenario. Monte

Carlo simulation involves running the backtest many times with random variations in the data to assess the robustness of the strategy. This provides a distribution of potential outcomes rather than a single result.

Another advanced technique is bootstrap resampling, which involves generating multiple samples from the historical data with replacement. This allows for estimating the distribution of returns and assessing the variability of the strategy's performance (Efron and Tibshirani, 1994).

Machine learning techniques are also becoming increasingly popular in backtesting. Methods such as reinforcement learning can be used to develop trading strategies that adapt and improve over time based on market conditions. However, these techniques require careful validation to avoid overfitting and ensure robustness.

## 14.8 CASE STUDY: APPLYING BACKTESTING TO A REAL-WORLD STRATEGY

To illustrate the practical application of backtesting, we present a case study of a momentum-based trading strategy. Momentum strategies exploit the tendency of stocks that have performed well in the past to continue performing well in the future (Chan, 2013).

The strategy involves ranking stocks based on their past 12-month returns and forming a portfolio of the top decile of stocks. This portfolio is rebalanced monthly, and performance is tracked over a 10-year historical period.

The ranking of stocks $R_i$ can be mathematically expressed as:

$$R_i = \frac{P_t - P_{t-12}}{P_{t-12}},$$

where $P_t$ is the price at time $t$ and $P_{t-12}$ is the price 12 months earlier.

The backtest results indicate that the momentum strategy outperforms the market benchmark, with a higher average annual return and a higher Sharpe ratio. However, the strategy also exhibits significant drawdowns during market downturns, highlighting the importance of risk management.

## 14.9 IMPACT OF MARKET CONDITIONS ON BACKTEST RESULTS

Market conditions can significantly impact the performance of a trading strategy. For example, trend-following strategies may perform well in trending markets but poorly in choppy, sideways markets. Conversely, mean-reversion strategies may struggle during strong market trends.

It is important to backtest strategies across different market regimes to ensure robustness. This can be done by segmenting the historical data into bull markets, bear markets, and sideways markets and analyzing the strategy's performance in each regime.

Scenario analysis can also be used to assess how the strategy would perform under extreme market conditions, such as financial crises or periods of high volatility. This helps in understanding the potential risks and stress-evaluating the strategy.

## 14.10 INTEGRATION WITH PORTFOLIO MANAGEMENT

Backtesting is not only useful for individual trading strategies but also for portfolio management. By backtesting different strategies within a portfolio context, managers can understand how each strategy contributes to the overall portfolio performance and risk (Bailey et al., 2014).

Portfolio optimization techniques, such as mean-variance optimization and the Black-Litterman model, can be used to allocate capital among different strategies based on their expected returns and risks. The mean-variance optimization problem can be formulated as:

$$\min_{\mathbf{w}} \mathbf{w}^T \Sigma \mathbf{w} \quad \text{subject to} \quad \mathbf{w}^T \mathbf{1} = 1 \quad \text{and} \quad \mathbf{w}^T \mu \geq \mu^*,$$

where $\mathbf{w}$ is the weight vector, $\Sigma$ is the covariance matrix of returns, $\mathbf{1}$ is a vector of ones, $\mu$ is the expected return vector, and $\mu^*$ is the target return.

Backtesting these allocation models helps in validating their effectiveness in achieving the desired portfolio objectives.

Incorporating backtesting into the portfolio management process allows for dynamic rebalancing and adaptation to changing market conditions. This ensures that the portfolio remains aligned with the investor's risk tolerance and investment goals.

## 14.11 TOOLS AND SOFTWARE FOR BACKTESTING

Various tools and software are available for backtesting trading strategies. Some popular options include:

1. Zipline-Reloaded is a Pythonic algorithmic trading library built on top of "Zipline". It is designed for backtesting trading strategies in a consistent and reproducible manner. Zipline-Reloaded supports multiple asset classes and provides functionalities for event-driven backtesting, performance analysis, and live trading. This library is particularly

useful for quant traders and researchers who need a robust and flexible tool for developing and testing trading algorithms (Jansen, 2021).

2. Python libraries: Libraries such as Pandas, NumPy, and Backtrader provide powerful tools for data manipulation and backtesting. Python's flexibility and extensive ecosystem make it a popular choice for quantitative researchers (Chan, 2013).
3. MATLAB: MATLAB offers a range of toolboxes for financial analysis and backtesting. Its high-level language and built-in functions make it suitable for rapid prototyping and testing.
4. R: R provides packages like quantmod and TTR for financial data analysis and backtesting. Its statistical capabilities are particularly useful for performance analysis and risk assessment.
5. Professional software: Platforms like TradeStation, MetaTrader, and Bloomberg Terminal offer comprehensive solutions for backtesting and implementing trading strategies in live markets.

Choosing the right tool depends on factors such as the complexity of the strategy, the availability of data, and the user's programming skills. It is important to use reliable and well-documented tools to ensure the accuracy of backtest results.

## 14.12 REGULATORY CONSIDERATIONS

Backtesting and the use of algorithmic trading strategies are subject to regulatory oversight. Regulators such as the Securities and Exchange Commission (SEC) in the United States and the Financial Conduct Authority (FCA) in the UK have guidelines and rules to ensure market integrity and investor protection.

Compliance with these regulations is essential to avoid legal and financial repercussions. This includes maintaining accurate records of backtesting methodologies, assumptions, and results. Additionally, strategies must be regularly reviewed and updated to reflect changing market conditions and regulatory requirements.

Understanding the regulatory environment and its implications for backtesting and algorithmic trading is crucial for portfolio managers and quantitative researchers (Bailey et al., 2014).

## 14.13 CONCLUSION

Backtesting is an essential tool in the development and validation of trading strategies. While powerful, it must be conducted with rigor to avoid common biases and pitfalls. Advanced techniques such as walk-forward analysis and Monte Carlo simulation can enhance the robustness of backtest results, providing a more reliable assessment of a strategy's potential performance (Bailey et al., 2014).

By understanding the impact of market conditions, integrating backtesting with portfolio management, and using appropriate tools and software, portfolio managers can develop effective and resilient investment strategies. Staying informed about regulatory considerations will ensure that these strategies remain relevant and compliant in an ever-changing financial landscape.

# CHAPTER 15

# Scenario Generation

Scenario generation is a fundamental aspect of risk management and portfolio optimization, providing a framework for modeling and simulating potential future market conditions. This chapter explores various methods of scenario generation, including historical scenarios, bootstrapping scenarios, copula-based scenarios, risk factor model-based scenarios, time series model scenarios, variational autoencoders, and generative adversarial networks. Each method is discussed in detail, with mathematical formulations and relevant citations.

## 15.1 HISTORICAL SCENARIOS

Historical scenarios use past data to simulate future conditions. This approach assumes that historical patterns may repeat or provide insights into future market behavior.

Mathematically, let **X** be the matrix of historical returns where each row represents a different time period, and each column represents a different asset:

$$\mathrm{X} = \begin{bmatrix} r_{1,1} & r_{1,2} & \cdots & r_{1,n} \\ r_{2,1} & r_{2,2} & \cdots & r_{2,n} \\ \vdots & \vdots & \ddots & \vdots \\ r_{m,1} & r_{m,2} & \cdots & r_{m,n} \end{bmatrix},$$

where $r_{i,j}$ represents the return of asset $j$ at time $i$. Historical scenarios are generated by sampling rows from **X** (Tsay, 2010).

## 15.2 BOOTSTRAPPING SCENARIOS

Bootstrapping scenarios involve resampling with replacement from historical data to generate new samples. This technique preserves the distributional properties of the original data.

Given a time series of returns $\{r_t\}$, bootstrapping generates a new series $\{r_t^*\}$ by randomly sampling with replacement:

$$\{r_t^*\} = \{r_{t_1}, r_{t_2}, \ldots, r_{t_m}\},$$

where $t_i$ are randomly chosen indices from the original series (Efron and Tibshirani, 1994).

## 15.3 COPULA-BASED SCENARIOS

Copula-based scenarios separate the modeling of marginal distributions from the dependence structure between variables. Copulas allow for flexible modeling of dependencies.

Let $F_X(x)$ and $F_Y(y)$ be the marginal cumulative distribution functions (CDFs) of two random variables $X$ and $Y$. The joint CDF $H(x,y)$ can be expressed using a copula $C$ as:

$$H(x,y) = C(F_X(x), F_Y(y))$$

The copula $C$ captures the dependence structure between $X$ and $Y$ (Nelsen, 2006).

## 15.4 RISK FACTOR MODEL-BASED SCENARIOS

Risk factor models use key economic and financial variables to generate scenarios. These models assume that asset returns are driven by underlying risk factors.

Consider a linear factor model:

$$R_i = \alpha_i + \beta_{i1}F_1 + \beta_{i2}F_2 + \cdots + \beta_{ik}F_k + \epsilon_i,$$

where $R_i$ is the return of asset $i$, $F_j$ are the risk factors, $\beta_{ij}$ are the factor loadings, and $\epsilon_i$ is the idiosyncratic error term. Scenarios are generated by simulating the risk factors $\{F_j\}$ (Ross, 1976).

## 15.5 TIME SERIES MODEL SCENARIOS

Time series models such as Autoregressive Integrated Moving Average (ARIMA) and Generalized Autoregressive Conditional Heteroskedasticity (GARCH) are used to model and forecast financial time series.

An ARIMA(p, d, q) model is defined as:

$$\Delta^d y_t = \phi_1 \Delta^d y_{t-1} + \cdots + \phi_p \Delta^d y_{t-p} + \theta_1 \epsilon_{t-1} + \cdots + \theta_q \epsilon_{t-q} + \epsilon_t,$$

where $\Delta^d$ denotes differencing, $\phi_i$ are the autoregressive coefficients, $\theta_i$ are the moving average coefficients, and $\epsilon_t$ is the white noise error term.

A GARCH(1, 1) model for volatility clustering is given by:

$$\sigma_t^2 = \alpha_0 + \alpha_1 \epsilon_{t-1}^2 + \beta_1 \sigma_{t-1}^2,$$

where $\sigma_t^2$ is the conditional variance, $\alpha_0$, $\alpha_1$, and $\beta_1$ are parameters, and $\epsilon_t$ is the error term (Bollerslev, 1986).

## 15.6 VARIATIONAL AUTOENCODERS

Variational Autoencoders (VAEs) are generative models that learn the underlying distribution of data through a latent space representation.

The VAE consists of an encoder that maps input data $x$ to a latent variable $z$, and a decoder that reconstructs $x$ from $z$:

$$z \sim q_\phi(z|x) \quad \text{and} \quad x' \sim p_\theta(x|z).$$

The objective is to maximize the Evidence Lower Bound (ELBO):

$$\mathcal{L} = \mathbb{E}_{q_\phi(z|x)}\left[\log p_\theta(x|z)\right] - \mathrm{KL}\left(q_\phi(z|x) \,||\, p(z)\right),$$

where $q_\phi$ and $p_\theta$ are parameterized by neural networks, and KL denotes the Kullback-Leibler divergence (Kingma and Welling, 2014).

Noguer and Pacheco (2023) applied VAE models to financial time series, demonstrating their effectiveness in capturing the distribution of returns for SP500 and Heston Model scenarios. The encoder maps input data to a latent representation, while the decoder reconstructs the data from this representation. The VAE objective function is given by:

$$\mathcal{L}(\theta, \phi; x) = \mathbb{E}_{q_\phi(z|x)}\left[\log p_\theta(x|z)\right] - \mathrm{KL}\left(q_\phi(z|x) \,||\, p(z)\right).$$

## 15.7 GENERATIVE ADVERSARIAL NETWORKS (GANs)

Generative Adversarial Networks (GANs) consist of two neural networks: a generator and a discriminator. The generator creates synthetic data, while the discriminator evaluates its authenticity.

The generator $G$ maps a noise vector $z$ to data $x$, and the discriminator $D$ attempts to distinguish between real and synthetic data:

$$G(z) \text{ and } D(x).$$

The GAN objective is a minimax game:

$$\min_G \max_D \mathbb{E}_{x \sim p_{\text{data}}(x)} \left[logD(x)\right] + \mathbb{E}_{z \sim p_z(z)} \left[log(1 - D(G(z)))\right].$$

The generator aims to minimize this objective, while the discriminator aims to maximize it (Goodfellow et al., 2014).

Noguer and Pacheco (2023) explored the application of GANs to financial time series, highlighting their potential for generating realistic market scenarios. They noted that while GANs can produce high-quality synthetic data, care must be taken to ensure the stability and convergence of the training process.

# Appendix

## A.1 SOFTWARE AND TOOLS FOR PORTFOLIO OPTIMIZATION

This chapter provides an overview of various software resources and tools that are commonly used in portfolio management. These resources include programming languages, libraries, and platforms that facilitate the implementation and analysis of portfolio management techniques.

Several programming languages are particularly useful for portfolio management due to their robust libraries and support for mathematical and statistical operations.

Python offers a variety of packages specifically designed to assist with portfolio allocation. Below are detailed descriptions of three key packages: "PyPortfolioOpt," "Riskfolio-Lib," and "SciFolio."

1. PyPortfolioOpt
   **Description:** PyPortfolioOpt is a comprehensive library for portfolio optimization in Python. It provides tools for mean-variance optimization, the Black-Litterman model, and various risk models. The library is designed to be easy to use, yet powerful enough for advanced users. PyPortfolioOpt simplifies the process of creating optimized portfolios by providing functions for calculating expected returns, risk matrices, and efficient frontiers (Robertson, 2020).
2. Riskfolio-Lib
   **Description:** Riskfolio-Lib is a library for portfolio optimization and quantitative strategic asset allocation. It includes tools for risk parity, hierarchical risk parity, Black-Litterman allocation, and various risk measures like CVaR and EVaR. This library is especially useful for constructing portfolios that are robust to various risk factors. Riskfolio-Lib provides a wide range of functionalities to manage complex portfolio optimization problems, making it suitable for both academic research and practical applications (Cajas, 2021).
3. SciFolio
   **Description:** SciFolio is a library for advanced financial portfolio analysis and optimization. It leverages SciPy for optimization and provides tools

for robust portfolio construction, including various risk metrics and constraints. SciFolio aims to facilitate the implementation of sophisticated portfolio optimization techniques, enabling users to incorporate custom risk measures and optimization constraints into their models (Developers, 2021).

4. Zipline-Reloaded
   **Description:** Zipline-Reloaded is a Pythonic algorithmic trading library built on top of "Zipline." It is designed for back testing trading strategies in a consistent and reproducible manner. Zipline-Reloaded supports multiple asset classes and provides functionalities for event-driven back testing, performance analysis, and live trading. This library is particularly useful for quant traders and researchers who need a robust and flexible tool for developing and testing trading algorithms (Jansen, 2021).

# Bibliography


Acerbi, C. and Tasche, D. (2002a). On the coherence of expected shortfall. *Journal of Banking & Finance* 26 (7): 1487–1503.

Acerbi, C. and Tasche, D. (2002b). Spectral measures of risk: A coherent representation of subjective risk aversion. *Journal of Banking & Finance* 26 (7): 1505–1518.

Acharya, V.V. and Pedersen, L.H. (2005). Asset pricing with liquidity risk. *Journal of Financial Economics* 77 (2): 375–410.

Adler, M. and Dumas, B. (1983). International portfolio choice and corporate finance: A synthesis. *Journal of Finance* 38 (3): 925–984.

Aguilar, O. and West, M. (2000). Bayesian dynamic factor models and portfolio allocation. *Journal of Business & Economic Statistics* 18 (3): 338–357.

Ahmadi-Javid, A. (2011). Entropic value-at-risk: A new coherent risk measure. *Journal of Optimization Theory and Applications* 155: 1105–1123.

Almahdi, S. and Yang, S.Y. (2017). Adaptive portfolio asset allocation optimization with deep learning. *International Journal of Financial Studies* 5 (4): 25.

Almgren, R., Thum, C.A., Hauptmann, E. et al. (2005). Equity market impact. *Risk* 18: 57–12.

Amihud, Y. (2002). Illiquidity and stock returns: Cross-section and time-series effects. *Journal of Financial Markets* 5 (1): 31–56.

Amihud, Y. and Mendelson, H. (1986). Asset pricing and the bid-ask spread. *Journal of Financial Economics* 17 (2): 223–249.

Ang, A. (2014). *Asset Management: A Systematic Approach to Factor Investing*. Oxford: Oxford University Press.

Ang, A. (2023). Trends and cycles of style factors in the 20th and 21st centuries. *Journal of Portfolio Management* 49 (2): 33–56.

Ang, A., Chen, J., and Xing, Y. (2006). Downside risk. *Review of Financial Studies* 19 (4): 1191–1239.

Angstmann, C., Henry, B., and McGann, A. (2019). Time-fractional geometric brownian motion from continuous time random walks. *Physica A: Statistical Mechanics and its Applications* 526: 121002.

Arlot, S. and Celisse, A. (2010). A survey of cross-validation procedures for model selection. *Statistics Surveys* 4: 40–79.

Artzner, P., Delbaen, F., Eber, J.-M. et al. (1999a). Coherent measures of risk. *Mathematical Finance* 9 (3): 203–228.

Asness, C.S., Moskowitz, T.J., and Pedersen, L.H. (2013). Value and momentum everywhere. *Journal of Finance* 68 (3): 929–985.

Avellaneda, M. (2020). Hierarchical PCA and applications to portfolio management. *Revista Mexicana de Economía y Finanzas* 15 (1): 1–16.

Avramelou, L., Nousi, P., Passalis, N. et al. (2024). Deep reinforcement learning for financial trading using multi-modal features. *Expert Systems with Applications* 238: 121849.

Avramov, D. and Zhou, G. (2010). Bayesian portfolio analysis. *Annual Review of Financial Economics* 2 (1): 25–47.

Back, K. E. (2017). *Asset Pricing and Portfolio Choice Theory*. Oxford: Oxford University Press.

Bacon, C. R. (2008). *Practical Portfolio Performance Measurement and Attribution*. New Jersey: John Wiley & Sons.

Bacry, E., Mastromatteo, I., and Muzy, J.-F. (2015). Hawkes processes in finance. *Market Microstructure and Liquidity* 01 (01): 1550005.

Bäuerle, N. and Rieder, U. (2011). *Markov Decision Processes with Applications to Finance*. Berlin: Springer Science & Business Media.

Bagnara, M. (2024). Asset pricing and machine learning: A critical review. *Journal of Economic Surveys* 38 (1): 27–56.

Bailey, D.H., Borwein, J.M., de Prado, M.L. et al. (2014). Pseudo-mathematics and financial charlatanism: The effects of backtest overfitting on out-of-sample performance. *Notices of the American Mathematical Society* 61 (5): 458–471.

Balbás, A., Garrido, J., and Mayoral, S. (2009). Properties of distorsion risk measures. *Methodology and Computing in Applied Probability* 11 (3): 385–399.

Ball, R., Sadka, G., and Sadka, R. (2009). Aggregate earnings and asset prices. *Journal of Accounting Research* 47 (5): 1097–1133.

Ballestero, E. (2005). Mean-semivariance efficient frontier: A downside risk model for portfolio selection. *Applied Mathematical Finance* 12 (1): 1–15.

Banz, R. W. (1981). The relationship between return and market value of common stocks. *Journal of Financial Economics* 9 (1): 3–18.

Barberis, N. (2000). Investing for the long run when returns are predictable. *The Journal of Finance* 55 (1): 225–264.

Bardi, M. and Capuzzo-Dolcetta, I. (2009). *Optimal Control and Viscosity Solutions of Hamilton-Jacobi-Bellman Equations*. Birkhäuser Boston: Modern Birkhäuser Classics.

Barillas, F. and Shanken, J. (2018). Comparing asset pricing models. *Journal of Finance* 73 (2): 715–754.

Barras, L., Scaillet, O., and Wermers, R. (2010). False discoveries in mutual fund performance: Measuring luck in estimated alphas. *Journal of Finance* 65 (1): 179–216.

Basak, S. and Chabakauri, G. (2010). Dynamic mean-variance asset allocation. *Review of Financial Studies* 23 (8): 2970–3016.

Basel (2019). Minimum capital requirements for market risk. *Bank for International Settlements*.

Basu, S. (1977). Investment performance of common stocks in relation to their price-earnings ratios: A test of the efficient market hypothesis. *Journal of Finance* 32 (3): 663–682.

Bates, D.S. (1988). Pricing options under jump-diffusion processes. Working Paper 37–88, Wharton School Rodney L. White Center for Financial Research. Date unknown.

Bates, D.S. (2015). Jumps and stochastic volatility: Exchange rate processes implicit in deutsche mark options. *The Review of Financial Studies* 9 (1): 69–107.

Bäuerle, N. and Rieder, U. (2011). *Markov decision processes with applications to finance*. Berlin: Springer Science & Business Media.

Bellman, R. (1952). On the theory of dynamic programming. *Proceedings of the National Academy of Sciences of the United States of America* 38 (8): 716–719.

Bellman, R. (1957). *Dynamic programming*. New Jersey: Princeton University Press.

Berger, J.O. (1985). *Statistical decision theory and Bayesian analysis*. Berlin: Springer Science & Business Media.

Bernard, J.M. and Smith, A.F.M. (2000). *Bayesian Theory*. New Jersey: Wiley.

Bernouilli, D. (1954). Exposition of a new theory on the measurement of risk. *Econometrica* 22 (1): 23–36.

Bershova, N. and Rakhlin, D. (2013). The non-linear market impact of large trades: Evidence from buy-side order flow. *Quantitative Finance* 13 (11): 1759–1778.

Bertsekas, D. (2012a). *Dynamic Programming and Optimal Control: Volume I*. Athena Scientific optimization and computation series. Belmont, Massachusetts: Athena Scientific.

Bertsekas, D. (2012b). *Dynamic Programming and Optimal Control: Volume II. Approximate Dynamic Programming*. Athena Scientific optimization and computation series. Belmont, Massachusetts: Athena Scientific.

Bertsekas, D. (2019). *Reinforcement Learning and Optimal Control*. Athena Scientific optimization and computation series. Belmont, Massachusetts: Athena Scientific.

Bertsekas, D. P. and Tsitsiklis, J.N. (1996). *Neuro-dynamic Programming*. Belmont, Massachusetts: Athena Scientific.

Bertsimas, D. and Lo, A.W. (1998). Optimal control of execution costs. *Journal of Financial Markets* 1 (1): 1–50.

Bielecki, T.R. and Pliska, S.R. (1999). Risk-sensitive dynamic asset management. *Applied Mathematics and Optimization* 39 (3): 337–360.

Bielecki, T.R. and Pliska, S.R. (2005). Risk sensitive portfolio optimization. *Journal of Applied Mathematics and Stochastic Analysis* 2005 (3): 255–283.

Bielecki, T.R., Pliska, S.R., and Sherris, M. (2005). Risk sensitive asset management with transaction costs. *Finance and Stochastics* 9 (1): 59–82.

Bishop, C. and Bishop, H. (2023). *Deep Learning: Foundations and Concepts*. New York: Springer International Publishing.

Björk, T., Murgoci, A., and Zhou, X.Y. (2014). Mean-variance portfolio optimization with state-dependent risk aversion. *Mathematical Finance* 24 (1).

Black, F. (1972). Capital market equilibrium with restricted borrowing. *Journal of Business* 45 (3): 444–455.

Black, F. (1989). Universal hedging: How to optimize currency risk and reward in international equity portfolios. *Financial Analysts Journal* 45 (4): 16–22.

Black, F. (1993). Beta and return. *Journal of Portfolio Management* 20 (1): 8–18.

Black, F., Jensen, M., and Scholes, M.S. (1972). The capital asset pricing model: Some empirical findings. In: *Studies in the Theory of Capital Markets* (ed. M. Jensen), 79–124. Westport: Praeger Publishers.

Black, F. and Litterman, R. (1990). *Asset Allocation: Combining Investor Views with Market Equilibrium*. New York: Goldman Sachs & Co.

Black, F. and Litterman, R. (1991a). Asset allocation: Combining investor views with market equilibrium. *Journal of Fixed Income* 1: 7–18.

Black, F. and Litterman, R. (1991b). *Global Asset Allocation with Equities, Bonds and Currencies*. New York: Goldman Sachs & Co.

Black, F. and Litterman, R. (1992a). Global portfolio optimization. *Financial Analysts Journal* 48 (5): 28–43.

Blume, M.E. and Friend, I. (1973). A new look at the capital asset pricing model. *Journal of Finance* 28 (1): 19–33.

Bollerslev, T. (1986). Generalized autoregressive conditional heteroskedasticity. *Journal of Econometrics* 31 (3): 307–327.

Bouchaud, J.-P. (2010). Price impact. In: *Encyclopedia of Quantitative Finance*. New Jersey: Wiley.

Bouchaud, J.-P., Gefen, Y., Potters, M. et al. (2004). Fluctuations and response in financial markets: The subtle nature of 'random' price changes. *Quantitative Finance* 4 (2): 176–190.

Boutyour, Y. and Idrissi, A. (2023). *Deep Reinforcement Learning in Financial Markets Context: Review and Open Challenges*. Cham: Springer Nature Switzerland.

Boyd, S., Busseti, E., Diamond, S. et al. (2017). Multi-period trading via convex optimization. *Foundations and Trends® in Optimization* 3 (1): 1–76.

Boyd, S. and Vandenberghe, L. (2004). *Convex Optimization*. Cambridge University Press.

Brandt, M.W. and Santa-Clara, P. (2006). Dynamic portfolio selection by augmenting the asset space. *The Journal of Finance* 61 (5): 2187–2217.

Breiman, L. (2001). Random forests. *Machine Learning* 45: 5–32.

Brennan, M. J. and Subrahmanyam, A. (1996). Market microstructure and asset pricing: On the compensation for illiquidity in stock returns. *Journal of Financial Economics* 41 (3): 441–464.

Brochu, E., Cora, V.M., and De Freitas, N. (2010). A tutorial on bayesian optimization of expensive cost functions, with application to active user modeling and hierarchical reinforcement learning. *arXiv preprint arXiv: 1012.2599*.

Brodie, J., Daubechies, I., De Mol, C. et al. (2009). Sparse and stable markowitz portfolios. *Applied Mathematics* 106 (30): 12267–12272.

Bryzgalova, S., Pelger, M., and Zhu, J. (2019). Forest through the trees: Building cross-sections of stock returns. *SSRN*.

Bühler, H., Gonon, L., Teichmann, J. et al. (2019). Deep hedging. *Quantitative Finance* 19 (8): 1271–1291.

Cajas, D. (2021). Riskfolio-lib: Portfolio optimization and quantitative strategic asset allocation in python. https://github.com/dcajasn/Riskfolio-Lib.

Cajas, D. (2023a). A graph theory approach to portfolio optimization. *SSRN Electronic Journal* https://ssrn.com/abstract=4602019.

Cajas, D. (2023b). A graph theory approach to portfolio optimization part II. *SSRN Electronic Journal* https://ssrn.com/abstract=4667426.

Campbell, J.Y., Chacko, G., Rodriguez, J. et al. (2004). Strategic asset allocation in a continuous-time var model. *Journal of Economic Dynamics and Control* 28 (11): 2195–2214.

Campbell, J.Y., Grossman, S.J., and Wang, J. (1993). Trading volume and serial correlation in stock returns. *The Quarterly Journal of Economics* 108 (4): 905–939.

Carhart, M.M. (1997). On persistence in mutual fund performance. *Journal of Finance* 52 (1): 57–82.

Cavalcante, R.C., Brasileiro, R.C., Souza, V.L. et al. (2016). Computational intelligence and financial markets: A survey and future directions. *Expert Systems With Applications* 55: 194–211.

Cazalet, Z. and Roncalli, T. (2014). Facts and fantasies about factor investing. *SSRN*.

Chamberlain, G. and Rothschild, M. (1983). Arbitrage, factor structure and mean-variance analysis on large asset markets. *Econometrica* 51 (5): 1281–1304.

Chan, E. (2013). *Algorithmic Trading: Winning Strategies and Their Rationale*. New Jersey: John Wiley & Sons.

Chan, K., fu Chen, N., and Hsieh, D.A. (1985). An exploratory investigation of the firm size effect. *Journal of Financial Economics* 14 (3): 451–471.

Chan, K.C. and Chen, N.-F. (1991). Structural and return characteristics of small and large firms. *Journal of Finance* 46 (4): 1467–1484.

Chan, K.C., Jegadeesh, N., and Lakonishok, J. (1996). Momentum strategies. *Journal of Finance* 51 (5): 1681–1713.

Chan, L.K.C., Karceski, J., and Lakonishok, J. (1998). The risk and return from factors. *Journal of Financial and Quantitative Analysis* 33 (2): 159–188.

Chaves, D.B., Hsu, J.C., Li, F. et al. (2011). Risk parity portfolio vs. other asset allocation heuristic portfolios. *Journal of Investing* 20 (1): 108–118.

Chaves, D.B., Hsu, J.C., Li, F. et al. (2012). Efficient algorithms for computing risk parity portfolio weights. *Journal of Investing* 21 (3): 150–163.

Chen, L., Da, Z., and Schaumburg, E. (2015). Implementing Black-Litterman using an equivalent formula and equity analyst target prices. *Journal of Investing* 24 (1): 34–47.

Chen, N.-F. (1991). Financial investment opportunities and the macroeconomy. *Journal of Finance* 46 (2): 529–554.

Chen, N.-F., Roll, R., and Ross, S.A. (1986). Economic forces and the stock market. *Journal of Business* 59 (3): 383–403.

Chen, P., Lezmi, E., Roncalli, T. (2019). A note on portfolio optimization with quadratic transaction costs. *SSRN*.

Chinco, A., Clark-Joseph, A.D., and Ye, M. (2019). Sparse signals in the cross-section of returns. *Journal of Finance* 74 (1): 449–492.

Chordia, T., Roll, R., and Subrahmanyam, A. (2000). Commonality in liquidity. *Journal of Financial Economics* 56 (1): 3–28.

Clarke, R., De Silva, H., and Thorley, S. (2006). The fundamental law of active portfolio management. *Journal of Investment Management* 4 (3): 54–72.

Cochrane, J.H. (2011). Presidential address: Discount rates. *Journal of Finance* 66 (4): 1047–1108.

Congdon, P. (2010). *Applied Bayesian Hierarchical Methods*. Oxfordshire: Taylor & Francis.

Connor, G. (1995). The three types of factor models: A comparison of their explanatory power. *Financial Analysts Journal* 51 (3): 42–46.

Connor, G., Goldberg, L.R., and Korajczyk, R.A. (2010). *Portfolio Risk Analysis*. Princeton: Princeton University Press.

Connor, G. and Korajczyk, R.A. (1986). Performance measurement with the arbitrage pricing theory: A new framework for analysis. *Journal of Financial Economics* 15 (3): 373–394.

Connor, G. and Korajczyk, R.A. (1987). Estimating pervasive economic factors with missing observations. *SSRN*.

Connor, G. and Korajczyk, R.A. (1991). The attributes, behavior and performance of US mutual funds. *Review of Quantitative Finance and Accounting* 1: 5–26.

Constantinides, G. and Malliaris, A. (1995). Portfolio theory (Chapter 1). In: *Handbooks in Operations Research and Management Science* (eds. R. Jarrow, V. Macsimovik, and W. Ziemba), 1–30. Amsterdam: Elsevier Science.

Cont, R. and Kan, Y.H. (2013). Dynamic hedging of portfolio credit derivatives. *SIAM Journal on Financial Mathematics* 2 (1): 112–140.

Coqueret, G. and Guida, T. (2023). *Machine Learning for Factor Investing: Python Version*. Boca Raton: Chapman & Hall/CRC.

Crandall, M.G., Ishii, H., and Lions, P.-L. (1992). User's guide to viscosity solutions of second order partial differential equations. *Bulletin of the American Mathematical Society* 27 (1): 1–67.

Cvitanić, J. and Karatzas, I. (1992). Convex duality in constrained portfolio optimization. *The Annals of Applied Probability* 2 (4): 767–818.

Cybenko, G. (1989). Approximation by superpositions of a sigmoidal function. *Mathematics of control, signals and systems* 2 (4): 303–314.

Dai, M., Xu, Z.Q., and Zhou, X.Y. (2010). Continuous-time markowitz's model with transaction costs. *SIAM Journal on Financial Mathematics* 1 (1): 96–125.

Daniel, K., Jagannathan, R., and Kim, S. (2012). Tail risk in momentum strategy returns. *NBER* 18169.

Davis, J.L., Fama, E.F., and French, K.R. (2000). Characteristics, covariances and average returns: 1929 to 1997. *Journal of Finance* 55 (1): 389–406.

Davis, M.H. and Norman, A.R. (1990a). Portfolio selection with transaction costs. *Mathematics of operations research* 15 (4): 676–713.

De Moor, L., Dhaene, G., and Sercu, P. (2015). On comparing zero-alpha tests across multifactor asset pricing models. *Journal of Banking & Finance* 61: S235–S240.

DeMiguel, V., Martín-Utrera, A., Nogales, F.J. et al. (2020). A transaction-cost perspective on the multitude of firm characteristics. *Review of Financial Studies* 33 (5): 2180–2222.

Deng, G., Dulaney, T., McCann, C. et al. (2013). Robust portfolio optimization with value-at-risk-adjusted sharpe ratios. *Journal of Asset Management* 14: 293–305.

Denneberg, D. (1990). Premium calculation: Why standard deviation should be replaced by absolute deviation. *ASTIN Bulletin* 20 (2): 181–190.

Developers, S. (2021). Scifolio: Advanced financial portfolio analysis and optimization. https://github.com/scifolio/scifolio.

Ding, R. and Uryasev, S. (2022). Drawdown beta and portfolio optimization. *Quantitative Finance* 22 (7): 1265–1276.

Ding, Z. and Martin, R.D. (2017). The fundamental law of active management: Redux. *Journal of Empirical Finance* 43: 91–114.

Dixon, M., Halperin, I., and Bilokon, P. (2020). *Machine Learning in Finance: From Theory to Practice*. New York: Springer International Publishing.

Dixon, M.F. and Halperin, I. (2020). G-learner and girl: Goal based wealth management with reinforcement learning. *arXiv preprint arXiv: 2002.10990.*

Dixon, M.F. and Klabjan, D. (2020). Bayesian optimization for financial investment and trading. *Journal of Risk* 22 (5): 1–23.

Dowd, K., Cotter, J., and Sorwar, G. (2008). Spectral risk measures: Properties and limitations. *Journal of Financial Services Research* 34: 61–75.

Drew, M.E., Naughton, T., and Veeraraghavan, M. (2003). Firm size, book-to-market equity and security returns: Evidence from the shanghai stock exchange. *Australian Journal of Management* 28 (2): 119–139.

Duvenaud, D. (2014). Automatic model construction with gaussian processes. *PhD thesis*, University of Cambridge, Cambridge.

Dybvig, P.H. and Pezzo, L. (2020). Mean-variance portfolio rebalancing with transaction costs. *SSRN*.

Dybvig, P.H. and Ross, S. A. (1985). Yes, the APT is testable. *Journal of Finance* 40 (4): 1173–1188.

Efron, B. and Tibshirani, R.J. (1994). *An Introduction to the Bootstrap*. New York: CRC Press.

Einicke, G.A. (2014). Iterative frequency-weighted filtering and smoothing procedures. *IEEE Signal Processing Letters* 21 (12): 1467–1470.

Elie, R. and Touzi, N. (2008). A risk-sensitive stochastic control approach for hedge funds. *Mathematics and Financial Economics* 2 (1): 1–25.

Engle, R. (2002). Dynamic conditional correlation: A simple class of multivariate generalized autoregressive conditional heteroskedasticity models. *Journal of Business & Economic Statistics* 20 (3): 339–350.

Evans, L.C. (2010). Partial differential equations. American mathematical society, *Providence, R.I.*

Fabozzi, F.J., Kolm, P.N., Pachamanova, D.A. et al. (2007). *Robust Portfolio Optimization and Management*. New Jersey: Wiley Finance.

Fama, E.F. (1965a). The behavior of stock-market prices. *Journal of Business* 38 (1): 34–105.

Fama, E.F. (1965b). Portfolio analysis in a stable paretian market. *Management Science* 11 (3): 404–419.

Fama, E.F. (1981). Stock returns, real activity, inflation and money. *American Economic Review* 71 (4): 545–565.

Fama, E.F. (1996). Multifactor portfolio efficiency and multifactor asset pricing. *Journal of Financial and Quantitative Analysis* 31 (4): 441–465.

Fama, E.F. and French, K.R. (1989). Business conditions and expected returns on stocks and bonds. *Journal of Financial Economics* 25 (1): 23–49.

Fama, E.F. and French, K.R. (1992). The cross-section of expected stock returns. *Journal of Finance* 47 (2): 427–465.

Fama, E.F. and French, K. R. (1993). Common risk factors in the returns of stocks and bonds. *Journal of Financial Economics* 33: 3–56.

Fama, E.F. and French, K.R. (1998). Value versus growth: The international evidence. *Journal of Finance* 53 (6): 1975–1999.

Fama, E.F. and French, K.R. (2010). Luck versus skill in the cross-section of mutual fund returns. *Journal of Finance* 65 (5): 1915–1947.

Fama, E.F. and French, K.R. (2012). Size, value and momentum in international stock returns. *Journal of Financial Economics* 105: 457–472.

Fama, E.F. and French, K.R. (2015). A five-factor asset pricing model. *Journal of Financial Economics* 116 (1): 1–22.

Fama, E.F. and MacBeth, J.D. (1973). Risk, return and equilibrium: Empirical tests. *Journal of Political Economy* 81 (3): 607–636.

Farmer, J.D., Gerig, A., Lillo, F. et al. (2013). How efficiency shapes market impact. *Quantitative Finance* 13 (11): 1743–1758.

Feng, G., He, J., Polson, N.G. et al. (2023). Deep learning in characteristics-sorted factor models. *Journal of Financial and Quantitative Analysis* 1–36.

Feng, M., Wächter, A., and Staum, J. (2015). Practical algorithms for value-at-risk portfolio optimization problems. *Quantitative Finance Letters* 3 (1): 1–9.

Fernández, A. and Gómez, S. (2007). Portfolio selection using neural networks. *Computers & Operations Research* 34 (4): 1177–1191.

Fischer, T.G. (2018). Reinforcement learning in financial markets - a survey. FAU Discussion Papers in Economics 12/2018 Friedrich-Alexander University Erlangen-Nuremberg, Institute for Economics.

Fisher, G.S., Maymin, P.Z., and Maymin, Z.G. (2015). Risk parity optimality. *Journal of Portfolio Management* 41 (2): 42–56.

Fisher, I. (1906). *The Nature of Capital and Income*. New York: Macmillan.

Flannery, M.J. and Protopapadakis, A.A. (2002). Macroeconomic factors do influence aggregate stock returns. *Review of Financial Studies* 15 (3): 751–782.

Fleming, W.H. and McEneaney, W.M. (1995). Risk-sensitive optimal control and differential games. *Stochastic Theory and Adaptive Control* 185–197.

Fleming, W.H. and Sheu, S.-J. (2006). Risk-sensitive portfolio optimization with full and partial information. *The Annals of Applied Probability* 16 (3): 1523–1547.

Fleming, W.H. and Soner, H.M. (2006). *Controlled Markov Processes and Viscosity Solutions, volume 25 of Stochastic Modelling and Applied Probability*, 2e. New York: Springer Science & Business Media.

Fong, K.Y.L., Holden, C.W., and Trzcinka, C.A. (2017). What are the best liquidity proxies for global research? *Review of Finance* 21 (4): 1355–1401.

Frankfurter, G. M. and Seagle, H.E.P.J.P. (1976). Performance of the sharpe portfolio selection model: A comparison. *Journal of Financial and Quantitative Analysis* 11 (2): 195–204.

Frazier, P.I. (2018). A tutorial on bayesian optimization.

Furman, E., Wang, R., and Zitikis, R. (2017). Gini-type measures of risk and variability: Gini shortfall, capital allocations and heavy-tailed risks. *Journal of Banking & Finance* 83: 70–84.

Föllmer, H. and Schied, A. (2016). *Stochastic Finance: An Introduction in Discrete Time*. Berlin: De Gruyter.

García-Galicia, M., Carsteanu, A.A., and Clempner, J.B. (2019). Continuous-time reinforcement learning approach for portfolio management with time penalization. *Expert Systems with Applications* 129: 27–36.

Garnett, R. (2023). *Bayesian Optimization*. Cambridge: Cambridge University Press.

Gatheral, J. (2010). No-dynamic-arbitrage and market impact. *Quantitative Finance* 10 (7): 749–759.

Gatheral, J., Jaisson, T., and Rosenbaum, M. (2018). Volatility is rough: Quatitative finance. *Quantitative Finance* 18 (6): 933–949.

Gelman, A., Carlin, J.B., Stern, H.S. et al. (2013). *Bayesian Data Analysis*, 3e. Boca Raton: Chapman and Hall/CRC.

Gelman, A. and Hill, J. (2006). *Data Analysis using Regression and Multilevel/hierarchical Models*. Cambridge: Cambridge university press.

Giglio, S., Kelly, B., and Xiu, D. (2022). Factor models, machine learning and asset pricing. *Annual Review of Financial Economics* 14: 337–368.

González, A. and Rubio, G. (2011). Portfolio choice and the effects of liquidity. *SERIEs* 2: 53–74.

Goodfellow, I., Bengio, Y., and Courville, A. (2016). *Deep Learning*. Massachusetts: MIT Press.

Goodfellow, I., Pouget-Abadie, J., and Mirza, M. (2014). Generative adversarial nets. In: *Advances in Neural Information Processing Systems* 27.

Goodwin, T.H. (1998). The information ratio. *Financial Analysts Journal* 54 (4): 34–43.

Gopal, A. (2024). Neuralfactors: A novel factor learning approach to generative modeling of equities. *arXiv*.

Green, J., Hand, J.R.M., and Zhang, X.F. (2017). The characteristics that provide independent information about average U.S. monthly stock returns. *Review of Financial Studies* 30 (12): 4389–4436.

Green, R.C. and Hollifield, B. (1992). When will mean-variance efficient portfolios be well diversified? *Journal of Finance* 5 (47): 1785–1809.

Grinold, R.C. (1989). The fundamental law of active management. *Journal of Portfolio Management* 15 (3): 30–38.

Grinold, R.C. (2006). A dynamic model of portfolio management. *Journal of Investing Management* 4 (2): 5–22.

Grinold, R.C. and Kahn, R.N. (2000). *Active Portfolio Management: A Quantitative Approach for Producing Superior Returns and Controlling Risk*. New York: McGraw-Hill.

Gu, S., Kelly, B., and Xiu, D. (2020). Empirical asset pricing via machine learning. *Review of Financial Studies* 33 (5): 2223–2273.

Guasoni, P. and Weber, M. (2017). Dynamic trading volume. *Mathematical Finance* 27 (2): 313–349.

Guermat, C. (2014). Yes, the CAPM is testable. *Journal of Banking & Finance* 46: 31–42.

Gârleanu, N. and Pedersen, L.H. (2013). Dynamic trading with predictable returns and transaction costs. *Journal of Finance* 68 (6): 2309–2340.

Halperin, I. (2024). Quantum economics and finance. *Quantum Economics and Finance* 1 (1): 51–73. Article reuse guidelines: sagepub.com/journals-permissions.

Han, J., Jentzen, A., and E, W. (2018). Solving high-dimensional partial differential equations using deep learning. *Proceedings of the National Academy of Sciences* 115 (34): 8505–8510.

Harvey, C. R., Liu, Y., and Zhu, H. (2016). . . . and the cross-section of expected returns. *Review of Financial Studies* 29 (1): 5–68.

Hasbrouck, J. and Seppi, D. J. (2001). Common factors in prices, order flows and liquidity. *Journal of Financial Economics* 59 (3): 383–411.

Hasselt, H. (2010). Double q-learning. *Advances in neural information processing systems* 23.

Hastie, T., Tibshirani, R., and Friedman, J. (2009). *The Elements of Statistical Learning*. Berlin: Springer.

Haugh, M., Iyengar, G., and Song, I. (2014). A generalized risk budgeting approach to portfolio construction. *Journal of Computational Finance* 21 (2): 29–60.

He, G. and Litterman, R. (1999). *The Intuition behind Black-Litterman Model Portfolios*. New York: Goldman Sachs & Co.

Heaton, J., Polson, N., and Witte, J. (2017). Deep learning for finance: Deep portfolios. *Applied Stochastic Models in Business and Industry* 33 (1): 3–12.

Hendricks, D., Patel, J., and Zeckhauser, R. (1993). Hot hands in mutual funds: Short-run persistence of relative performance 1974–1988. *Journal of Finance* 48 (1): 93–130.

Hens, T., Mayer, J., and Xia, Y. (2018). Deep reinforcement learning in financial markets. *Swiss Finance Institute Research Paper.* 20–54.

Heston, S.L. (1993). A closed-form solution for options with stochastic volatility with applications to bond and currency options. *The Review of Financial Studies* 6 (2): 327–343.

Hicks, J. (1935). A suggestion for simplifying the theory of money. *Economica* 2 (5): 1–19.

Hicks, J. (1939). *Value and Capital: An Inquiry Into Some Fundamental Principles of Economic Theory*. Oxford: Clarendon Press.

Higham, N.J. (1988). Computing a nearest symmetric positive semidefinite matrix. *Linear Algebra and its Applications* 103: 103–118.

Hoang, D. and Wiegratz, K. (2023). Machine learning methods in finance: Recent applications and prospects. *European Financial Management* 29 (5): 1657–1701.

Hornik, K. (1991). Approximation capabilities of multilayer feedforward networks. *Neural networks* 4 (2): 251–257.

Horváth, B., Muguruza, A., and Tomas, M. (2021). Deep learning volatility: A deep neural network perspective on pricing and calibration in (rough) volatility models. *Quantitative Finance* 21 (1): 11–27.

Howard, R.A. (1960). *Dynamic Programming and Markov Processes.* Massachusetts: MIT press.

Howard, R.A. and Matheson, J.E. (1972). Risk-sensitive markov decision processes. *Management science* 18 (7): 356–369.

Huberman, G. and Halka, D. (2001). Systematic liquidity. *Journal of Financial Research* 24 (2): 161–178.

Huberman, G. and Stanzl, W. (2004). Price manipulation and quasi-arbitrage. *Econometrica* 72 (4): 1247–1275.

Huge, B. and Savine, A. (2020). Differential machine learning.

Hurst, B., Johnson, B.W., and Ooi, Y.H. (2010). Understanding risk parity: So, you think you're diversified. *AQR Capital Management.*

Ibrahim, S.N.I., Misiran, M., and Laham, M.F. (2021). Geometric fractional brownian motion model for commodity market simulation. *Alexandria Engineering Journal* 60 (1): 955–962.

Idzorek, T.M. (2004). A step-by-step guide to the black-litterman model. *Zephyr Associates Inc.*

Ingersoll, J.E. (1984). Some results in the theory of arbitrage pricing. *Journal of Finance* 39 (4): 1021–1039.

Ingersoll, J.E. (1987). *Theory of Financial Decision Making.* Maryland: Rowman & Littlefield Publishers.

Iyengar, G. and Kang, W. (2005). A fast and simple algorithm for computing the investment frontier. *Management Science* 51 (11): 1683–1691.

Iyengar, G. and Liang, A. (2005). Robust dynamic asset allocation with model misspecification. *Mathematics of Operations Research* 30 (4): 839–856.

Jacquier, A. and Kondratyev, O. (2022). *Quantum Machine Learning and Optimisation in Finance: On the Road to Quantum Advantage.* Birmingham: Packt Publishing Ltd.

Jagannathan, R. and McGrattan, E.R. (1995). The capm debate. *Federal Reserve Bank of Minneapolis Quarterly Review* 19 (4): 2–17.

Jaillet, P., Lamberton, D., and Lapeyre, B. (1990). Variational inequalities and the pricing of american options. *Acta Applicandae Mathematica* 21 (3): 263–289.

Jaisson, T. (2015). Market impact as anticipation of the order flow imbalance. *Quantitative Finance* 15 (7): 1123–1135.

Jansen, S. (2021). Zipline-reloaded: A pythonic algorithmic trading library. https://github.com/stefan-jansen/zipline-reloaded.

Jegadeesh, N. and Titman, S. (1993). Returns to buying winners and selling losers: Implications for stock market efficiency. *Journal of Finance* 48 (1): 65–91.

Jensen, G.R., Johnson, R.R., and Mercer, J.M. (1997). New evidence on size and price-to-book effects in stock returns. *Financial Analysts Journal* 53 (6): 34–42.

Jensen, M.C. (1972). Capital markets: Theory and evidence. *Bell Journal of Economics and Management Science* 3: 357–398.

Jensen, M.C. and Benington, G.A. (1970). Random walks and technical theories: Some additional evidence. *Journal of Finance* 25 (2): 469–482.

Jiang, W. (2020). Stock price prediction based on deep learning and attention mechanism. *IEEE Access* 8: 177205–177214.

Jiang, W. and Xu, J. (2017). Continuous-time mean-variance portfolio selection: A reinforcement learning framework. *arXiv preprint arXiv: 1703.10065.*

Jiang, Y., Olmo, J., and Atwi, M. (2024). Deep reinforcement learning for portfolio selection. *Global Finance Journal* 62: 101016.

Jiang, Z., Xu, D., and Liang, J. (2017). A deep reinforcement learning framework for the financial portfolio management problem. *arXiv preprint arXiv: 1706.10059.*

Jobson, J. D. and Korkie, B. (1980). Estimation for markowitz efficient portfolios. *Journal of the American Statistical Association* 75 (371): 544–554.

Johnson, R.A. and Wichern, D.W. (2007). *Applied Multivariate Statistical Analysis.* London: Pearson.

Jolliffe, I.T. (2002). *Principal Component Analysis*. Berlin: Springer.

Jorion, P. (1986). Bayes-stein estimation for portfolio analysis. *Journal of Financial and Quantitative Analysis* 21 (3): 279–292.

Joubert, J., Sestovic, D., and Barziy, I. (2024). The three types of backtests. *SSRN.*

Jusselin, P. and Rosenbaum, M. (2020). No-arbitrage implies power-law market impact and rough volatility. *Mathematical Finance* 30 (4): 1309–1336.

Kaae, C.E. and Karppinen, J.A. (2022). Hierarchical risk parity - a hierarchical clustering-based portfolio optimization. Master's thesis, Copenhagen Business School.

Kaelbling, L.P., Littman, M.L., and Cassandra, A.R. (1998). Planning and acting in partially observable stochastic domains. *Artificial intelligence* 101 (1–2): 99–134.

Kakade, S.M. (2002). A natural policy gradient. *Advances in Neural Information Processing Systems* 14.

Kalita, D. and Lyakhov, P. (2022). Moving object detection based on a combination of kalman filter and median filtering. *Big Data and Cognitive Computing* 6 (4): 142.

Kalman, R.E. (1960). A new approach to linear filtering and prediction problems. *Journal of Basic Engineering* 82 (1): 35–45.

Kariya, T. and Kurata, H. (2004). *Generalized Least Squares.* New Jersey: Wiley.

Kaya, H. and Lee, W. (2012). Demystifying risk parity. *SSRN.*

Keim, D.B. and Stambaugh, R.F. (1986). Predicting returns in the stock and bond markets. *Journal of Financial Economics* 17 (2): 357–390.

Kelly, B.T., Pruitt, S., and Su, Y. (2019). Characteristics are covariances: A unified model of risk and return. *Journal of Financial Economics* 134 (3): 501–524.

Kim, S., Shephard, N., and Chib, S. (1998). Stochastic volatility: Likelihood inference and comparison with arch models. *The review of economic studies* 65 (3): 361–393.

Kingma, D.P. and Welling, M. (2014). Auto-encoding variational bayes. In: *Proceedings of the International Conference on Learning Representations (ICLR)*.

Kocijan, J. (2009). Gaussian process models for systems identification, forecasting and control. *IEEE Control Systems Magazine* 29 (4): 108–109.

Kolm, P.N. and Ritter, G. (2019). Modern perspectives on reinforcement learning in finance, *Modern Perspectives on Reinforcement Learning in Finance* 1–12.

Kolm, P. N., Ritter, G., and Simonian, J. (2014a). Black-Litterman and beyond: The Bayesian paradigm in investment management. *Journal of Portfolio Management* 47 (5): 91–113.

Kolm, P.N., Tütünkü, R., and Fabozzi, F.J. (2014b). 60 years of portfolio optimization. *European Journal of Operational Research* 234: 356–371.

Kothari, S.P., Shanken, J., and Sloan, R. G. (1995). Another look at the cross-section of expected stock returns. *Journal of Finance* 50 (1): 185–224.

Kraus, A. and Litzenberger, R.H. (1976). Skewness preference and the valuation of risk assets. *The Journal of Finance* 31 (4): 1085–1100.

Krishnamurthy, V. (2016). *Partially Observed Markov Decision Processes*. Partially Observed Markov Decision Processes: From Filtering to Controlled Sensing. Cambridge: Cambridge University Press.

Krokhmal, P., Palmquist, J., and Uryasev, S. (2001). Portfolio optimization with conditional value-at-risk objective and constraints. *Journal of Risk* 4 (2): 43–68.

Krzemienowski, A. and Szymczyk, S. (2016). Portfolio optimization with a copula-based extension of conditional value-at-risk. *Annals of Operations Research* 237: 219–236.

Kurpiel, A., bullet, L., and Iv, F. (1999). Option hedging with stochastic volatility. *SSRN*.

Kushner, H. and Dupuis, P.G. (2013). *Numerical Methods for Stochastic Control Problems in Continuous Time*. Berlin: Springer Science & Business Media.

Kusuoka, S. (2001). On law invariant coherent risk measures, In: *Advances in Mathematical Economics*, (eds. S. Kusuoka and T. Maruyama), 83–95. Japan: Springer.

Kyle, A.S. (1985). Continuous auctions and insider trading. *Econometrica* 53 (6): 1315–1336.

Lai, T.L., Xing, H., and Chen, Z. (2011). Mean–variance portfolio optimization when means and covariances are unknown. *Annals of Applied Statistics* 5 (2A): 798–823.

Laloux, L., Cizeau, P., Bouchaud, J.-P. et al. (1999). Noise dressing of financial correlation matrices. *Physical Review Letters* 83 (7): 1467–1470.

Ledoit, O. and Wolf, M. (2003). Improved estimation of the covariance matrix of stock returns with an application to portfolio selection. *Journal of Empirical Finance* 10 (5): 603–621.

Ledoit, O. and Wolf, M. (2004). A well-conditioned estimator for large-dimensional covariance matrices. *Journal of Multivariate Analysis* 88 (2): 365–411.

Levy, R.A. (1967). Relative strength as a criterion for investment selection. *Journal of Finance* 22 (4): 595–610.

Lewellen, J. (2015). Momentum and Autocorrelation in Stock Returns. *The Review of Financial Studies* 15 (2): 533–564.

Liberzon, D. (2011). *Calculus of Variations and Optimal Control Theory: A Concise Introduction*. New Jersey: Princeton University Press.

Lintner, J. (1965). The valuation of risk assets and the selection of risky investments in stock portfolios and capital budgets. *Review of Economics and Statistics* 47 (1): 13–37.

Liu, F. and Wang, R. (2021). A theory for measures of tail risk. *Mathematics of Operations Research* 46 (3): 1109–1128.

Liu, R., Muhle-Karbe, J., and Weber, M.H. (2017). Rebalancing with linear and quadratic costs. *SIAM Journal on Control and Optimization* 55 (6): 3533–3563.

Lohre, H., Neugebauer, U., and Zimmer, C. (2012). Diversified risk parity strategies for equity portfolio selection. *Journal of Investing* 21 (3): 111–128.

Lohre, H., Opfer, H., and Orszag, G. (2014). Diversifying risk parity. *Journal of Risk* 16 (5): 53–79.

Lora-Millan, J.S., Hidalgo, A.F., and Rocon, E. (2021). An IMUs-based extended Kalman filter to estimate gait lower limb sagittal kinematics for the control of wearable robotic devices. *IEEE Access* 9: 144540–144554.

Lu, Z., Pu, H., and Wang, F. (2017). The expressive power of neural networks: A view from the width. *Advances in Neural Information Processing Systems* 30.

Luenberger, D. G. (1997). *Investment Science*. Oxford: Oxford University Press.

Lwin, K.T., Qu, R., and McCarthy, B.L. (2017). Mean-var portfolio optimization: A nonparametric approach. *European Journal of Operational Research* 260 (2): 751–766.

López de Prado, M. (2016a). Advances in financial machine learning. *The Journal of Financial Data Science* 1 (1): 64–74.

López de Prado, M. (2016b). Building diversified portfolios that outperform out of sample. *Journal of Portfolio Management* 42 (4): 59–69.

López de Prado, M. (2018). *Advances in Financial Machine Learning*. New Jersey: Wiley.

Magill, M.J. and Constantinides, G.M. (1976). Portfolio selection with transactions costs. *Journal of Economic Theory* 13 (2): 245–263.

Maillard, S., Roncalli, T., and Teïletche, J. (2010). The properties of equally weighted risk contribution portfolios. *Journal of Portfolio Management* 36 (4): 60–70.

Mandelbrot, B. (1963). The variation of certain speculative prices. *Journal of Business* 36: 394–419.

Mankert, C. and Seiler, M.J. (2011). Mathematical derivations and practical implications for the use of the Black-Litterman model. *Journal of Real Estate Portfolio Management* 17 (2): 139–159.

Mantegna, R.N. (1999). Hierarchical structure in financial markets. *The European Physical Journal B* 11 (1): 193–197.

Mantegna, R.N. and Stanley, H.E. (2000). *An Introduction to Econophysics: Correlation and Complexity in Finance*. Cambridge: Cambridge University Press.

Markowitz, H. (1952). Portfolio selection. *Journal of Finance* 7 (1): 77–91.

Markowitz, H. (1959). *Portfolio Selection: Efficient Diversification of Investments*. Connecticut: Yale University Press.

Markowitz, H. (1991). Foundations of portfolio theory. *Journal of Finance* 46 (2): 469–477.

Markowitz, H. (1999). The early history of portfolio theory: 1600–1960. *Financial Analysts Journal* 55 (4): 5–16.

Markowitz, H., Tod, P., Xu, G. et al. (1993). Computation of mean-semivariance efficient sets by the critical line algorithm. *Annals of Operations Research* 45: 307–317.

Marschak, J. (1938). Money and the theory of assets. *Econometrica* 6 (4): 311–325.

McNeill, A.J., Frey, R., and Embrechts, P. (2005). *Quantitative Risk Management: Concepts, Techniques and Tools*. New Jersey: Princeton University Press.

Mei, X., DeMiguel, V., and Nogales, F.J. (2016). Multiperiod portfolio optimization with multiple risky assets and general transaction costs. *Journal of Banking & Finance* 69: 108–120.

Meng, T.L. and Khushi, M. (2019). Reinforcement learning in financial markets. *Data* 4 (3): 110.

Merton, R.C. (1969a). Lifetime portfolio selection under uncertainty: The continuous-time case. *The Review of Economics and Statistics* 51 (3): 247–257.

Merton, R.C. (1971). Optimum consumption and portfolio rules in a continuous-time model. *Journal of economic theory* 3 (4): 373–413.

Merton, R.C. (1972). An analytic derivation of the efficient portfolio frontier. *Journal of Financial and Quantitative Analysis* 7 (4): 1851–1872.

Merton, R.C. (1973). An intertemporal capital asset pricing model. *Econometrica* 41 (5): 867–887.

Merton, R.C. (1980). On estimating the expected return on the market: An exploratory investigation. *Journal of Financial Economics* 8 (4): 323–361.

Meucci, A. (2005). *Risk and Asset Allocation*. Berlin: Springer-Verlag.

Meucci, A. (2008). Fully flexible views: Theory and practice. *Risk* 21 (10): 97–102.

Meucci, A. (2009). Managing diversification. *Risk* 22 (5): 74–79.

Meucci, A. (2010). Black-Litterman approach. In: *Encyclopedia of Quantitative Finance* (ed. R. Cont). New York: Wiley.

Michaud, R.O. (1998). *Efficient Asset Management: A Practical Guide to Stock Portfolio Optimization and Asset Allocation*. Oxford: Oxford University Press.

Misiran, M., Lu, Z., Teo, K.L. et al. (2012). Estimating dynamic geometric fractional brownian motion and its application to long-memory option pricing. *Dynamic Systems and Applications* 21 (1): 49.

Mnih, V., Kavukcuoglu, K., Silver, D. et al. (2013). Playing atari with deep reinforcement learning. *CoRR* abs/1312.5602.

Mnih, V., Kavukcuoglu, K., Silver, D. et al. (2015). Human-level control through deep reinforcement learning. *nature* 518 (7540): 529–533.

Moallemi, C.C. and Sağlam, M. (2013). Dynamic portfolio choice with linear rebalancing rules. *Journal of Financial and Quantitative Analysis* 48 (1): 1–31.

Moody, J. and Saffell, M. (2001). Learning to trade via direct reinforcement. *IEEE transactions on neural Networks* 12 (4): 875–889.

Moreau, L., Muhle-Karbe, J., and Soner, H.M. (2017). Trading wiht small price impact. *Mathematical Finance* 27 (2).

Moro, E., Vicente, J., Moyano, L.G. et al. (2009). Market impact and trading profile of hidden orders in stock markets. *Physical Review E* 80 (6).

Mossin, J. (1966). Equilibrium in a capital asset market. *Econometrica* 34 (4): 768–783.

Murphy, K.P. (2023). *Probabilistic Machine Learning: Advanced Topics*. Massachusetts: MIT Press.

Nazareth, N. and Ramana Reddy, Y.V. (2023). Financial applications of machine learning: A literature review. *Expert Systems With Applications* 219: 119640.

Nelsen, R.B. (2006). *An Introduction to Copulas*. Berlin: Springer.

Neuberg, L.G. (2003). Causality: Models, reasoning and inference, by Judea Pearl, cambridge university press 2000. *Econometric Theory* 19 (4): 675–685.

Ng, D.T. (2004). The international CAPM when expected returns are time-varying. *Journal of International Money and Finance* 23 (2): 189–230.

Noguer, M. and Pacheco, D. (2023). Generative models for time series in finance. Technical report, Artificial Intelligence in Finance Institute. Available at https://ssrn.com/abstract=4343967.

Noguer, M. and Zoonekynd, V. (2022). Equity machine factor models. *SSRN*.

Noguer i Alonso, M. and Antolin Camarena, J. (2023). Physics-informed neural networks (PINNs) in finance. Available at SSRN.

Øksendal, B. (2014). *Stochastic Differential Equations: An Introduction with Applications,* 6e. Hochschultext / Universitext. New York: Springer.

Padakandla, S., K.J.P, and Bhatnagar, S. (2019). Reinforcement learning in non-stationary environments. *arXiv preprint arXiv: 1905.03970.*

Pan, J., Zhang, Z., and Zhou, X. (2018). Optimal dynamic mean-variance asset-liability management under the heston model. *Advances in Difference Equations* 2018: 1–16.

Papadimitriou, C.H. and Tsitsiklis, J.N. (1987). The complexity of markov decision processes. *Mathematics of Operations Research* 12 (3): 441–450.

Pástor, Ł. and Stambaugh, R.F. (2000). Comparing asset pricing models: an investment perspective. *Journal of Financial Economics* 56 (3): 335–381.

Pástor, Ł. and Stambaugh, R.F. (2003). Liquidity risk and expected stock returns. *Journal of Political Economy* 111 (3): 642–685.

Peng, X.B., Kumar, A., Zhang, G. et al. (2019). Advantage-weighted regression: Simple and scalable off-policy reinforcement learning. *CoRR*, abs/1910.00177.

Peskir, G. and Shiryaev, A. (2006). *Optimal Stopping and Free-Boundary Problems*. Berlin: Springer Science & Business Media.

Petters, A.O. and Dong, X. (2016). *An Introduction to Mathematical Finance with Applications: Undertanding and Building Financial Intuition*. New York: Springer.

Pflug, G.C. (2000). Some remarks on the value-at-risk and the conditional value-at-risk. In: *Probabilistic Constrained Optimization: Methodology and Applications* (ed. S. Uryasev). New York: Kluwer Academic Publishers.

Pham, H. (2009). *Continuous-time Stochastic Control and Optimization with Financial Applications*, vol. 61. Berlin: Springer Science & Business Media.

Piotroski, J.D. (2000). Value investing: The use of historical financial statement information to separate winners from losers. *Journal of Accounting Research* 38: 1–41.

Piri, F., Salahi, M., and Mehrdoust, F. (2014). Robust mean-conditional value at risk portfolio optimization. *International Journal of Economic Sciences* 3 (1): 2–11.

Pizarroso, J., Portela, J., and Muñoz, A. (2021). Neuralsens: Sensitivity analysis of neural networks.

Pogue, G.A. (1970). An extension of the markowitz portfolio selection model to include variable transactions' costs, short sales, leverage policies and taxes. *Journal of Finance* 25 (5): 1005–1027.

Polson, N.G. and Tew, B.V. (2000). Bayesian portfolio selection: An empirical analysis of the s&p 500 index 1970–1996. *Journal of Business & Economic Statistics* 18 (2): 164–173.

Powell, W. (2011). *Approximate Dynamic Programming: Solving the Curses of Dimensionality.* Wiley Series in Probability and Statistics. New York: Wiley.

Powell, W. (2022). *Reinforcement Learning and Stochastic Optimization: A Unified Framework for Sequential Decisions.* New York: Wiley.

Pozzi, F., Matteo, T.D., and Aste, T. (2013). Spread of risk across financial markets: Better to invest in the peripheries. *Scientific Reports* 3: 1665.

Prigent, J.-L. (2007). *Portfolio Optimization and Performance Analysis.* Boca Raton: Chapman & Hall/CRC.

Prince, S. (2023). *Understanding Deep Learning.* Massachusetts: MIT Press.

Puterman, M. (2009). *Markov Decision Processes: Discrete Stochastic Dynamic Programming.* Wiley Series in Probability and Statistics. New York: Wiley.

Qian, E. (2011). Risk parity and diversification. *Journal of Investing* 20 (1): 119–127.

Qian, E.E. (2005). Risk parity portfolios: Efficient portfolios through true diversification. *PanAgora Asset Management.*

Qian, E.E. (2006). On the financial interpretation of risk contribution: Risk budget do add up. *Journal of Investing Management* 4 (4): 41–51.

Qian, E.E., Hua, R.H., and Sorensen, E.H. (2007). *Quantitative Equity Portfolio Management: Modern Techniques and Applications.* Boca Raton: Chapman & Hall/CRC.

Rachev, S.T., Hsu, J.S.J., Bagasheva, B.S. et al. (2008). *Bayesian Methods in Finance,* 1e. Hoboken, NJ:Wiley.

Raffinot, T. (2018a). Hierarchical clustering-based asset allocation. *Journal of Portfolio Management* 44 (2): 89–99.

Raffinot, T. (2018b). The hierarchical equal risk contribution portfolio. *SSRN.*

Raissi, M., Perdikaris, P., and Karniadakis, G. (2019). Physics-informed neural networks: A deep learning framework for solving forward and inverse problems involving nonlinear partial differential equations. *Journal of Computational Physics* 378: 686–707.

Rao, A. and Jelvis, T. (2022). *Foundations of Reinforcement Learning with Applications in Finance*. Chapman & Hall/CRC Mathematics and Artificial Intelligence Series. Boca Raton: CRC Press.

Rapach, D.E. and Zhou, G. (2020). Time-series and cross-sectional stock return forecasting: New machine learning methods. In: *Machine Learning for Asset Management: New Developments and Financial Applications*. (ed. E. Jurczenko), New York: ISTE & Wiley.

Rasmussen, C. and Williams, C. (2005). *Gaussian Processes for Machine Learning*. Adaptive Computation and Machine Learning series. Massachusetts: MIT Press.

Reichenbach, H. (1956). *The Direction of Time*. New York: Dover Publications.

Reinganum, M.R. (1981). Misspecification of capital asset pricing: Empirical anomalies based on earnings' yields and market values. *Journal of Financial Economics* 9 (1): 19–46.

Reisman, H. (1988). A general approach to the arbitrage pricing theory (apt). *Econometrica* 56 (2): 473–476.

Reisman, H. (1992). Intertemporal arbitrage pricing theory. *Review of Financial Studies* 5 (1): 105–122.

Richardson, H. R. (1989). A minimum variance result in continuous trading portfolio optimization. *Management Science* 35 (9): 1045–1055.

Riedel, F. (2003). Dynamic coherent risk measures. *Stochastic Processes and their Applications* 112 (2): 185–200.

Robert, C.P. (2007). *The Bayesian Choice: From Decision-Theoretic Foundations to Computational Implementation*, vol. 2. New York: Springer.

Roberts, S., Osborne, M., Ebden, M. et al. (2013). Gaussian processes for time-series modelling. *Philosophical Transactions of the Royal Society A: Mathematical, Physical and Engineering Sciences* 371 (1984): 20110550.

Robertson, T. (2020). Pyportfolioopt: Financial portfolio optimisation in python. https://github.com/robertson/pyportfolioopt.

Rockafellar, R.T. and Uryasev, S. (2000). Optimization of conditional value-at-risk. *Journal of Risk* 2: 21–42.

Rockafellar, R.T. and Uryasev, S. (2002). Conditional value-at-risk for general loss distributions. *Journal of Banking & Finance* 26: 1443–1471.

Rodriguez Dominguez, A. (2023). Portfolio optimization based on neural networks sensitivities from assets dynamics respect common drivers. *Machine Learning with Applications* 11: 100447.

Rogers, L. and Singh, S. (2010). The cost of illiquidity and its effects on hedging. *Mathematical Finance* 20 (4).

Roll, R. (1977). A critique of the asset pricing theory's tests part i: On the past and potential testability of the theory. *Journal of Financial Economics* 4 (2): 129–176.

Roll, R. and Ross, S.A. (1980). An empirical investigation of the arbitrage pricing theory. *Journal of Finance* 35 (5): 1073–1103.

Roncalli, T. (2020). *Handbook of Financial Risk Management*. Boca Raton: Chapman & Hall/CRC.

Roncalli, T. and Weisang, G. (2016). Risk parity portfolios with risk factors. *Quantitative Finance* 16 (3): 377–388.

Rosenberg, G., Haghnegahdar, P., Goddard, P. et al. (2016). Solving the optimal trading trajectory problem using a quantum annealer. *IEEE Journal of Selected Topics in Signal Processing* 10 (6): 1053–1060.

Ross, S.A. (1976). The arbitrage theory of capital asset pricing. *Journal of Economic Theory* 13 (3): 341–360.

Ross, S.A. (1977). The current status of the capital asset pricing model (capm). *Journal of Finance* 33 (3): 885–901.

Rostek, S. and Schöbel, R. (2013). A note on the use of fractional brownian motion for financial modeling. *Economic Modelling* 30: 30–35.

Rouwenhorst, K.G. (1998). International momentum strategies. *Journal of Finance* 53 (1): 267–284.

Roy, A.D. (1952). Safety first and the holding of assets. *Econometrica* 20 (3): 431–449.

Rubinstein, M. (2002). Markowitz's "portfolio selection": A fifty years retrospective. *Journal of Finance* 57 (3): 1041–1045.

Sood, S., Papasotiriou, K., Vaiciulis M. et al. (2023). Deep reinforcement learning for optimal portfolio allocation: A comparative study with mean-variance optimization. *Association for the Advancement of Artificial Intelligence.*

San Roque, A. M. (1996). *Aplicación de técnicas de redes neuronales artificiales al diagnóstico de procesos industriales. PhD thesis,* Universidad Pontificia Comillas.

Särkkä, S. and Solin, A. (2019). *Applied Stochastic Differential Equations*. Institute of Mathematical Statistics Textbooks. Cambridge: Cambridge University Press.

Satchell, S. and Scowcroft, A. (2000). A demystificatiion of the black-litterman model: Managing quantitative and traditional portfolio construction. *Journal of Asset Management* 1 (2): 138–150.

Schulman, J., Wolski, F., Dhariwal, P. et al. (2017). Proximal policy optimization algorithms. *arXiv preprint arXiv: 1707.06347.*

Schuss, Z. (2009). *Theory and Applications of Stochastic Processes: An Analytical Approach* Applied Mathematical Sciences: New York: Springer.

Sezer, O.B., Gudelek, M.U., and Ozbayoglu, A. M. (2020). Financial time series forecasting with deep learning: A systematic literature review: 2005–2019. *Applied Soft Computing* 90: 106181.

Shahriari, B., Swersky, K., Wang, Z. et al. (2016). Taking the human out of the loop: A review of bayesian optimization. *Proceedings of the IEEE* 104 (1): 148–175.

Shanken, J. (1982). The arbitrage pricing theory: Is it testable? *Journal of Finance* 37 (5): 1129–1140.

Sharpe, W. F. (1964). Capital asset prices: A theory of market equilibrium under conditions of risk. *Journal of Finance* 19 (3): 425–442.

Shen, Y., Tobia, M.J., Sommer, T. et al. (2014). Risk-sensitive reinforcement learning. *Neural computation* 26 (7): 1298–1328.

Shreve, S.E. and Soner, H.M. (1994a). Optimal investment and consumption with transaction costs. *The Annals of Applied Probability* 4 (3): 609–692.

Silver, D., Lever, G., Heess, N. et al. (2014). Deterministic policy gradient algorithms. In: *International conference on machine learning* Pmlr, 387–395.

Skaf, J. and Boyd, S. (2009). Multi-period portfolio optimization with constraints and transaction costs. *Working paper*.

Soize, C. (2017). *Uncertainty Quantification: An Accelerated Course with Advanced Applications in Computational Engineering*. Interdisciplinary Applied Mathematics. New York: Springer International Publishing.

Solnik, B.H. (1974). An equilibrium model of the international capital market. *Journal of Economic Theory* 8 (4): 500–524.

Solnik, B.H. (1983). International arbitrage pricing theory. *Journal of Finance* 38 (2): 449–457.

Sorensen, E.H., Miller, K.L., and Ooi, C.K. (2000). The decision tree approach to stock selection. *Journal of Portfolio Management* 27 (1): 42–52.

Sotomayor, L.R. and Cadenillas, A. (2009). A partially observed markov decision process for dynamic asset allocation. *Stochastic Analysis and Applications* 27 (6): 1101–1126.

Spaan, M.T. (2012). A concise introduction to models and methods for automated planning. *AI Communications* 25 (4): 331–351.

Stefanovits, D. (2010). Equal contributions to risk and portfolio construction. *Master's thesis* ETH Zurich.

Sullivan, T. (2015). *Introduction to Uncertainty Quantification*. Texts in Applied Mathematics. New York: Springer International Publishing.

Sutiene, K., Schwendner, P., Sipos, C. et al. (2024). Enhancing portfolio management using artificial intelligence: Literature review. *Frontiers in Artificial Intelligence* 7: 1371502.

Sutton, R. and Barto, A. (2018). *Reinforcement Learning, second edition: An Introduction Adaptive Computation and Machine Learning series*. Massachusetts: MIT Press.

Sutton, R.S., McAllester, D.A., Singh, S.P. et al. (2000). Policy gradient methods for reinforcement learning with function approximation. *Advances in Neural Information Processing Systems* 12.

Särkkä, S. and Svensson, L. (2023). *Bayesian Filtering and Smoothing, 2e*. Cambridge: Cambridge University Press.

Tan, Z., Yan, Z., and Zhu, G. et al. (2019). Stock selection with random forest: An exploitation of excess return in the chinese stock market. *Heliyon* 5: e02310.

Tibshirani, R. (1996). Regression shrinkage and selection via the lasso. *Journal of the Royal Statistical Society: Series B (Methodological)* 58 (1): 267–288.

Tola, V., Lillo, F., Gallegati, M. et al. (2008). Cluster analysis for portfolio optimization. *Journal of Economics Dynamics and Control* 32 (1): 235–258.

Tóth, B., Lempérière, Y., Deremble, C. et al. (2011). Anomalous price impact and the critical nature of liquidity in financial markets. *Physical Review X* 1: 021006.

Touzi, N. (2012). *Optimal Stochastic Control, Stochastic Target Problems and Backward SDE* vol. 29. New york: Springer Science & Business Media.

Tsay, R.S. (2010). *Analysis of Financial Time Series*. New York: Wiley.

Tsitsiklis, J.N. and Van Roy, B. (1997). An analysis of temporal-difference learning with function approximation. *IEEE transactions on automatic control* 42 (5): 674–690.

Uryasev, S. (2000). Conditional value-at-risk: Optimization algorithms and applications. *Financial Engineering News* 14.

Uspensky, J.V. (1937). *Introduction to Mathematical Probability*. New York: McGraw-Hill.

Vasicek, O. (1977). An equilibrium characterization of the term structure. *Journal of Financial Economics* 5 (2): 177–188.

Vaswani, A., Shazeer, N., Parmar, N. et al. et al. (2017). Attention is all you need. In: *Advances in Neural Information Processing Systems* (eds. I. Guyon, U.V. Luxburg, S. Bengio, H. Wallach, R. Fergus, S. Vishwanathan and R. Garnett). vol. 30. New York: Curran Associates, Inc.

Venturelli, D., Mandrà, S., Knysh, S. et al. (2015). Quantum optimization of fully connected spin glasses. *Physical Review X* 5 (3): 031040.

Wang, H. and Zhou, X.Y. (2019). Continuous-time mean-variance portfolio selection: A reinforcement learning framework.

Wang, S., Huang, W., and Zhang, Z. (2021). Deep reinforcement learning for portfolio management: A survey. *arXiv preprint arXiv: 2107.06881*.

Webster, K.T. (2023). *Handbook on Price Impact Modeling*. Boca Raton: Chapman & Hall/CRC.

Wey, M.A. (2023). A derivation of the Black-Litterman formula and its symmetry property. *Economic Letters* 231. 111303.

Wiese, M., Knobloch, R., Korn, R. et al. (2020). Deep hedging: learning to simulate equity option markets. *Quantitative Finance* 20 (8): 1325–1340.

Williams, C.K. and Rasmussen, C.E. (1996). Gaussian processes for regression. 514–520.

Williams, J.B. (1938). *The Theory of Investment Value*. Amsterdam: North Holland Publisher.

Wu, B. and Li, L. (2024). Reinforcement learning for continuous-time mean-variance portfolio selection in a regime-switching market. *Journal of Economic Dynamics and Control* 158: 104787.

Wu, Y., Hernández-Lobato, J.M., and Ghahramani, Z. (2019). Quantitative stock selection strategies based on financial time series forecasting using gaussian processes. *Expert Systems with Applications* 122: 270–281.

Yong, J. and Zhou, X.Y. (1999). *Stochastic controls: Hamiltonian systems and HJB equations volume 43 of Applications of Mathematics*. New York: Springer Science & Business Media.

Zhang, A., Lipton, Z., Li, M. et al. (2023). *Dive into Deep Learning*. Cambridge: Cambridge University Press.

Zhang, Z., Zohren, S., and Roberts, S. (2020). Deep reinforcement learning for trading—a critical survey. *arXiv preprint arXiv: 2010.06196*.

Zhao, S., Lu, Q., Han, L. et al. (2015). A mean-cvar-skewness portfolio optimization model based on asymmetric laplace distribution. *Annals of Operations Research* 226: 727–739.

Zhou, X.Y. and Li, D. (2000a). Continuous-time mean-variance portfolio selection: A stochastic lq framework. *Applied Mathematics and Optimization* 42 (1): 19–33.

Zhou, X.Y. and Yin, G. (2003a). Markowitz's mean-variance portfolio selection with regime switching: A continuous-time model. *SIAM Journal on Control and Optimization* 42 (4): 1466–1482.

Zou, H. and Hastie, T. (2005). Regularization and Variable Selection Via the Elastic Net. *Journal of the Royal Statistical Society Series B: Statistical Methodology* 67 (2): 301–320.

# Index

## E



## F



## G

## N



## O

## R

## U



## V



## W



## X-Y-Z